THE TRUE COST OF
CONFLICT

THE TRUE COST OF
CONFLICT

Edited by
Michael Cranna

Project Director
Paul Eavis

Authors
Nils Bhinda, Angela Burke, Gordon Macdonald,
Ian Robinson, Nicholas Shalita, David Shave,
Shaun Vincent and Gregory Quinn

THE NEW PRESS · NEW YORK

95 96 97 98   9 8 7 6 5 4 3 2 1

ISBN 1-56584-268-5
Library of Congress Catalog Card Number 94-73945

First published in 1994 by Earthscan Publications Limited, 120 Pentonville Road, London N 9JN
Published in the United States by The New Press, New York
Distributed by W. W. Norton & Company, Inc., New York, NY 10110

Established in 1990 as a major alternative to the large, commercial publishing houses, The New Press is the first full-scale nonprofit American book publisher outside of the university presses. The press is operated editorially in the public interest, rather than for private gain; it is committed to publishing in innovative ways works of educational, cultural, and community value that, despite their intellectual merits, might not normally be "commercially" viable. The New Press's editorial offices are located at the City University of New York.

Production management by Kim Waymer

Printed in the United States of America

CONTENTS

LIST OF ILLUSTRATIONS

THE EAST TIMOR CONFLICT

THE IRAQ CONFLICT

THE KASHMIR CONFLICT

THE MOZAMBIQUE CONFLICT

THE PERU CONFLICT

THE SUDAN CONFLICT

THE FORMER YUGOSLAVIA CONFLICT

ACRONYMS AND ABBREVIATIONS

ACDA	Arms Control and Disarmament Agency
ACFOA	Australian Council for Overseas Aid
ALP	Australian Labour Party
ANC	African National Congress
APODETI	Timorese Democratic Association
APRODEV	Association of World Council of Churches related to Development Organization in Europe
ASDT	Social Democrat Association of Timor
AURI	Indonesian airforce
BAe	British Aerospace
BAKIN	Indonesian intelligence service
BJP	Bharatiya Janata Party (Indian Hindu fundamentalist political party)
bn	billion
BPHRG	British Parliamentary Human Rights Group
BSF	Kashmiri paramilitary group
CAAT	Campaign Against Arms Trade
CAFOD	Catholic Association for Overseas Development
CIA	(US) Central Intelligence Agency
CIIR	Catholic Institute for International Relations
CMEA	Council for Mutual Economic Assistance
CNDDHH	Cordinadora Nacional de Derechos Humanos (Peru)
CNRM	National Council of Maubere Resistance (East Timor)
COMECOM	Council for Mutual Economic Assistance
CORAH	Upper Huallaga Valley Coca Reduction Programme (Peru)
CRPF	Kashmiri paramilitary group
DEA	(US)Drug Enforcement Agency
DM	Deutschmark
DTI	(UK) Department of Trade and Industry
DUP	Democratic Unionist Party (Sudan)
EBRD	European Bank for Reconstruction and Development
EC	European Commission
ECHO	EC Humanitarian Office
ECOSOC	Economic and Social Council
ECTF	EC Task Force
ECU	European currency unit
EIU	Economist Intelligence Unit
EPRDF	Ethiopian People's Revolutionary Democratic Front
ERP	(World Bank) economic restructuring programme
EU	European Union
FDI	foreign direct investment
FEPOMUVES	Popular Federation of Women of Villa El Salvador (Peru)
FIDH	Federation Internationale des Ligues des Droites de l'Homme
FRETILIN	Revolutionary Front for the Independence of East Timor
FRG	Federal Republic of Germany

G7	Group of Seven countries (US, UK, Italy, Japan, Germany, France, Canada)
GATT	General Agreement on Tariffs and Trade
GDP	gross domestic product (please explain what 'real' GDP is)
GNP	gross national product
GPIE	Office for Foreign Investment Promotion (Mozambique)
HDZ	Croat Democratic Union
HOS	Croat Defence Forces
HVO	Croatian Defence Council
ICRC	International Committee of the Red Cross
ID	Iraqi dinars
IFAD	International fund for Agricultural Development
IISS	International Institute for Strategic Studies
IMF	International Monetary Fund
IMF	International Monetary Fund
IMR	Infant mortality rate
INIDEN	Investigacion de la Defensa Nacional (Peru)
IPIS	International Peace Information Service
IPJET	International Panel of Jurists on East Timor
IR	Iranian rials
IUCN	International Union for the Conservation of Nature and Natural Resources
JKLF	Jammu and Kashmir Liberation Front
JNA	Yugoslav National Army
KCHR	Kashmir Council for Human Rights
km	kilometres
LDC	less developed country
LIC	low intensity conflict
LRA	Lord's Resistance Army (Uganda)
LSE	London School of Economics
m	million
MEA	Mutual Economic Assistance
MEED	Middle East Economic Digest
MEES	Middle East Economic Survey
MMR	maternal mortality rate
MOD	(UK) Ministry of Defence
MRTA	Movimiento Revolucionario Tupac Amaru (Peru)
mw	megawatt
na	not applicable
NAFTA	North American Free Trade Agreement
NAO	National Audit Office
NATO	North Atlantic Treaty Organization
NCEC	Northern California Ecumenical Council
NEFA	North East Frontier Administration (of Kashmir, before 1987)
NGDO	non-governmental development organization
NGO	non-governmental organization
NIF	National Islamic Front (Sudan)
NOVIB	Netherlands Organization for International Development
ODA	Overseas Development Agency
ODA	Overseas Development Aid
ODI	Overseas Development Institute
OECD	Organization for Economic Cooperation and Development

ONUMOZ	UN Operation in Mozambique
OPEC	Organization of Petroleum-Exporting Countries
PDF	Popular Defence Force (Sudan)
PKI	Indonesian communist party
PLO	Palestinian Liberation Organization
PSA	Public Safety Act (Kashmir)
PSG	Peru Support Group
Pu	plutonium
R CRORE	Kashmiri currency
R	(South African) rand
RENAMO	Resistencia Nacional Mocambicana (Mozambican national resistance)
RIIA	Royal Institute for International Affairs
Rp	Indonesian currency
SADC	South African Development Community
SADCC	Southern African Development Coordination Conference
SDA	Party of Democratic Action (Bosnia-Herzegovina)
SENDERO	Sendero Luminoso (Shining Path) - Peruvian terrorist group
SIPRI	Stockholm International Peace Research Organization
SNI	National Association of Industries (Peru)
SOAS	School of Oriental and African Studies (London)
SPLA	Sudan Peoples' Liberation Army
sq	square
TADA	Terrorist and Disruptive Activities Act (Kashmir)
TAPOL	Indonesia human rights campaign
UAE	United Arab Emirates
UDT	Timorese Democratic Union
UN	United Nations
UNDP	UN Development Programme
UNESCO	United Nations Educational, Scientific and Cultural Organization
UNHCR	United Nations High Commission for Refugees
UNICEF	UN International Children's Emergency Fund
UNIDO	UN Industrial Development Organization
UNITA	National Union for the Liberation of Angola
UNPA	UN Protected Area
UNPROFOR	UN Protection Force (in former Yugoslavia)
UNSCOM	The United Nations mission to destroy Iraqi weapons of mass destruction
USAID	United States Agency for International Development
USIP	United States Institute of Peace
WHO	World Health Organization
WOLA	Washington Office for Latin America
YuD	Yugoslav dinar
Z$	Zimbabwean dollar
ZNA	Zimbabwean National Army

ACKNOWLEDGEMENTS

The publication of this book has been made possible only by the generous contributions from many individuals and organizations .

It is the result of a two-year project, developed and led by Saferworld in cooperation with an international Task Force, consisting of Council For A Liveable World, Human Rights Watch, the Netherlands Organization for International Development Cooperation (NOVIB), Oxfam and World Vision International. Saferworld is especially grateful to the Joseph Rowntree Charitable Trust, Ploughshares Fund, Northern Foods, NOVIB and World Vision International for their financial support of the project.

This project would not have been possible without the ideas and hard work of a number of people connected to Saferworld, including Inger Buxton, Peter Davies, Maria Dimitropoulou, Sue Maskell, Fiona Pickup, Hilary Pinder, Struan Stevenson, Dr Raj Thamotheram, Hugh Venables and Ian Woodmansey.

The editor would like to thank those individuals who provided detailed comment on drafts of the book. These include Dr Mahmud Ali, Malcolm Chalmers (Department of Peace Studies, University of Bradford), Tessa Cubitt (University of Portsmouth), Professor Graham Chapman (School of Oriental and African Studies), Dr Mark Duffield (Centre for Urban and Regional Studies, University of Birmingham), Professor Reg Green (Institute of Development Studies, University of Sussex), Wolfgang Mallman, Dr Siraj Shah (Kashmir Council for Human Rights), Professor Ron Smith (Birkbeck College, University of London), Susie Symes (The Royal Institute of International Affairs), Dr John Taylor (South Bank University), Mark Turpin, Roger Williamson (Centre for Defence Studies, King's College) and Dr Anthony Zwi (London School of Hygiene and Tropical Medicine).

Many individuals have contributed valuable advice, time and data to the project. Saferworld would especially like to thank Beyan Alaraji (Inter-Faith International), Neven Andelic, Robert Archer (Christian Aid), Rosalind Bain, Martin Bax (Aprodev), Ian Beard, Carmel Budiarjo (TAPOL), Tim Caswell, Narnita Chadha, Margaret Clark (Africa-Europe Faith & Justice Network), Ben Cohen (Action for Bosnia), Dr Tom Daffern (University of London), Anna Gomez (The Portugese Embassy), Sarah Graham Brown (Gulf Information Project), Ernst Gulcher (IPIS), Dr Sahib Al Hakim (Organisation of Human Rights in Iraq), Dr Reinhard Hermle (Misereor), Jonathan Humphries (British Coalition for East Timor), Ian Lee Doucet (Medical Education Trust), James Mackie (NGDO-EC Liaison Committee), Joanne Macrae (London School of Tropical Medicine), Dr Subrata Mitra (University of Hull), Pieter van Rossem (Pax Christi International), Kumar Rupesinghe (International Alert), Dr Khadiga Safwat (the Middle Eastern & African Research Centre of Wales), Frank Schwalba-Hoth (World Watch Institute), Iain Scobbie (University of Dundee), Catherine Scott (Catholic Institute of International Relations), Susan Scott-Parker, Shelly Shackleton, Mehtab Shah (Institute of Commonwealth Studies), Börje Sjöqvist (Swedish Red Cross), Sarah Smith, Irene van Staveren (Oikos), Simon Stocker (Eurostep), Mohammed Sulamein (Institute for African Alternatives), Martin Summers (CAFOD), Dr Alex Vines (Africa Watch), Brian Wood (Amnesty International), Dr Peter Woodward (Reading University), David Wright (Save the Children) and Dr Steve Wright (Omega Foundation).

Saferworld would also like to thank the many other organizations who have contributed information to this project: Amnesty International, Africa Rights, Catholic Institute of International Relations, Ethiopian Trade and Promotional Council, The Foreign and Commonwealth Office, Latin American Bureau, Latin American Infor-mation Centre, Overseas Development Institute, Pakistan High Commission, Physicians for Human Rights, Quaker Council for European Affairs, Refugee Council, Save the Children, Sudan Human Rights Organisation, UNHCR, UNICEF and United Nations Information Office.

Naturally, the responsibility for the content of the book lies with the authors and the editor.

FOREWORD

by The Rt Hon Lord Judd of Portsea

If an anthropological expedition from another galaxy arrived on earth it would surely be impossible for them to give a rational explanation of human behaviour. How would they explain why we spend 250 times more on arms than we do on peacekeeping? What would they say about the 22 million people killed in wars since 1945? About the fact that 84 per cent of those killed were civilians - compared to 50 per cent of casualties in the Second World War? About the 24 million people forced to flee and become displaced people within their own countries, and the 18 million who have become refugees abroad, all as a result of conflict?

The intergalactic explorers would quickly abandon our planet to its own devices and look for more promising signs of civilization elsewhere.

It is an extraordinary fact that so much of the work done to raise the quality of life of our fellow human beings is frustrated and negated by conflict. Every major famine in recent years has taken place in a war zone. In my six years as Director of Oxfam our priority was, as it is now, long term development. But over 50 per cent of Oxfam's work was in areas of conflict. In Africa 70 per cent of our work was war-related, and remains so today. In the 1990s all the relief and development agencies are grappling with humanitarian suffering and death, in what Oxfam has called 'a decade of disasters'. They are disasters, in the main, not caused by natural phenomena but by conflict. Instead of promoting independence and develop-ment, the agencies are having to deal with the collapse of civil society and economic destruction.

So it is high time we took a fresh look at conflict. We particularly need a greater awareness of the cost of conflict. The true costs are often diffuse or unknown, and they are certainly taken to be secondary to the apparent economic benefits to Western countries of the arms trade. But a broader evaluation of the costs that result from the arms trade shows this easy assumption to be false.

Nowhere is this clearer than in Somalia. The cost to the United States of Operation Restore Hope – one aspect of which involved rounding up all the weapons sold to Somalia – roughly equalled the value of the arms sold to the Siad Barre regime during the 1980s.

The True Cost of Conflict offers a timely and much needed fresh look at how we evaluate the costs and benefits of conflict. The research team at Saferworld and their international partners deserve thanks and congratulations for the way they have set the evidence before us. The evidence should challenge policy makers and those who advise our governments to look again at the priorities they put on preventive diplomacy and peacekeeping compared to what they spend on arms and the arms trade.

Anyone who is concerned about the threat facing our world from the spread of conflict will welcome this book. I wholeheartedly commend it.

ABOUT SAFERWORLD

Saferworld is an independent foreign affairs think-tank and public education group. It is committed to alerting governments of the need for new approaches to dealing with armed conflicts around the world. Saferworld's special strength is its capacity to identify key issues on which movement is possible, and to harness the diverse contributions of a wide range of people, from political leaders to concerned members of the public, in order to inspire creative solutions. Enquiries about publications or membership are welcome at:

Saferworld
82 Colston Street
Bristol BS1 5BB
United Kingdom
Phone 0272 276435 Fax 0272 253305

INTRODUCTION

Five years after the collapse of the Soviet Union and the end of the Cold War there are more regional conflicts and civil wars than at any time this century. There is hardly a region of the planet that is today free from destructive conflict and most of the 42 million displaced people in the world today are victims of wars and fighting. Some 22 million people have been killed in conflicts since 1945. The hope for a reduction in conflict is far from being realised.

The True Cost of Conflict is an attempt to calculate the price of conflict to the human race. This ambitious project was begun in early 1993 when Saferworld set up an international enquiry into the true cost of conflict. The idea was to examine this cost, not only in terms of the deaths and casualties directly inflicted on the participants in conflict and their victims, but also the economic cost to the countries involved as well as to their trading and investment partners. The enquiry also examined the social, developmental, environmental and strategic costs of conflict. And it attempted to isolate and assess the benefits, mainly economic and strategic, that are perceived to derive from conflict.

A key motive for this book is to encourage people to look at conflict in new ways and to widen public discussion of the subject. By laying bare the true costs and benefits of conflict in a way not done before, the book aims to bring new insights to the debate on global security. Also, by identifying the economic costs of these conflicts to the Western world, it aims to alert Western voters to the consequences of their governments' current approaches to conflict prevention and management, as well as to their policies on arms exports. If it can be demonstrated that conflicts fail an economic cost-benefit test, then perhaps a new set of arguments and concerns will become relevant to the debate.

If it could be shown that wars in 'far away places of which we know little' (as Chamberlain remarked of Czechoslovakia) actually have costs for Western nations and their citizens, as well as for the direct victims seen every night on television, then a new dimension of economic self-interest might be added to the public's concern about conflict. Policy makers and politicians would perhaps have more reason to reappraise their policies. The interests of their own constituents would be at stake. *The True Cost of Conflict* sets out to present the voting public with the facts.

Of course, the study of conflict is not new. There have been many studies of individual conflicts: what their causes have been, how they have been conducted or how they might be ended. This is the first attempt, Saferworld believes, to evaluate their costs and benefits.

The book consists of seven studies of individual conflicts. The conflicts selected are: the Gulf War, Indonesia's invasion of East Timor, the civil wars in Mozambique and Sudan, Peru's guerrilla war, Kashmir's independence struggle and the war in ex-Yugoslavia.

They have been chosen to represent the different kinds of conflict that occur, from wars between nations to guerrilla campaigns. The countries they occur in represent the world's major regions. Some involve only local combatants while others have prompted the outside world to become directly involved. Some have international strategic significance, others excite moral concern among the international community, while one or two scarcely attract attention beyond their borders.

The choice of countries featured, whether as a focus of the conflict, or as neighbouring countries drawn into it, or whether as representative of the international community, is illustrative only. Clearly, other conflicts could have been studied, or other neighbouring countries included.

Methodology – A Cost-benefit Analysis

Each study follows a similar pattern. A brief introduction sets the conflict in context and defines the period of the conflict being studied. This is important because some of the conflicts – such as the Gulf war – are episodes in a longer history of wars in a particular region. However, there is no attempt to analyse the causes of each conflict because that has been well done elsewhere and is beyond the intention of the book.

Next the costs incurred by the country where the conflict has taken place are analysed, quantitatively and qualitatively, under a number of headings. The costs to *development* are examined, with particular reference to health and education. The costs to the *economy* and *infrastructure* are assessed, using conventional measures of production, debt, inflation, and so on. A section headed 'Civil and political rights' deals with the obvious human costs of conflict, the deaths, abuses, detentions and other indignities. Where relevant data are available, an attempt is made to assess the *environmental* costs and the impact of *refugees.*

The study also looks at certain neighbouring countries involved in the conflict to examine the costs they have incurred. It then assesses the impact of the conflict on the economies of the Western industrialised nations.

Where possible, each study also attempts to assess the *benefits* which have accrued from the conflict, whether to the country where it takes place, to its neighbours, or to countries in the wider economic community. This is to allow a comparison to be made between the apparent benefits of the conflict and the costs. Such a comparison should allow foreign policy making to be viewed with greater clarity, and permit short-term expediency to be weighed against long-term disadvantage.

Finally, and speculatively, each study asks the question: what might the economic benefits to the country in conflict and to the international community have been *if the conflict had not occurred?* This is answered by examining a neighbouring country at a similar state of development before the conflict, and which has itself been free of conflict during the period under study. Evidently this approach raises major questions about the comparability of different countries, but it is intended to be illustrative rather than conclusive.

Each study presents a combination of quantitative data for the sake of comparability, and qualitative information in the form of eyewitness accounts, case studies and the like, to give a feel for the impact of conflict on the lives of those it touches.

Is a Reduction in Conflict Possible?

Having presented the facts about costs and benefits, with the aim of spurring policy makers into action, the final section of the book sketches some policy options; alternative ways in which governments of the international community could deal with conflict more effectively. Saferworld believes there are practical actions the international community can take now to reduce the likelihood of conflict and to tackle it when it breaks out.

For example, there is a case for democratic nations, while they still have influence and authority in world affairs, agreeing on common principles for arms exports and formulating and agreeing effective criteria for international involvement in conflict areas. The proposals presented are not intended to be exhaustive; they are indications of the policy initiatives which are open to the international community in dealing with conflict.

Limitations and Assumptions

The True Cost of Conflict is a highly ambitious attempt to identify the price of war: as far as is known, the first of its kind. The motive for doing so is to strengthen the hand of those who are working to make conflict more manageable and less likely.

It is not, however, a polemic. The researchers have tried to be independent and academically rigorous in the presentation of information, as far as the availability of data and the structure of the book allow. Inevitably, and rightly, the book will be judged on its academic merits, and it is important to lodge a number of caveats and assumptions.

Plainly, conflict is not the only cause of impoverishment, destruction, disease and other ills suffered by mankind. Many other factors, from droughts and natural disasters to man-made economic calamities are involved. *The True Cost of Conflict* tries to demonstrate what the impact of conflict has been over and above these other factors, and how it has sometimes exacerbated them.

It has been difficult to find contemporary data about some of the conflicts. This is particularly so for the intra-state conflicts, like those in Kashmir and Sudan, where regions rather than nations are involved, and regional statistics are unavailable. It is particularly difficult for the conflicts which are still raging, such as in former Yugoslavia. Thus it has not been feasible to include all the costs that ideally should have been included.

It is also difficult to attribute costs to a specific period of a conflict when, as in Kashmir again, fighting has been going on at different levels of intensity for a long time.

The studies are clearly speculative, some would say dubious, when they deal with the *benefits* of conflict, and particularly when making the attempt to imagine what would have happened if the conflict had not occurred. Yet it was felt crucial to try

and present each study, in part, as a cost-benefit exercise. This, after all, is the recognised mode of assessing whether a commercial project or a public enterprise is worth undertaking. If government attention can be directed to the real costs and benefits of conflict then issues such as allowing arms exporters free access to the world's trouble spots might be seen in a different light.

Also crucial to the exercise is the inclusion of Western nations and the costs and benefits they experience from the conflicts. In this case both costs and benefits tend to be remote, sometimes long-term and certainly difficult to pin down. A typical cost could be the loss of future investment or trading opportunities. A benefit could be the securing of a sea route threatened by an aspiring independence movement.

It is still largely the international community which has the power and influence to make conflict less likely. So it is central to the thesis of the book that these Western costs and benefits should be included.

The Collaborative Process

The production of this book has not simply been a conventional research project. From the start Saferworld has been keen to take on board the views of human rights organizations, environmental groups and development specialists, as well as academics and international relations experts. Collaboration with other groups was a key part of the process that has led to the book. Altogether, some 85 organizations, from many countries, have joined in the study. A task force of six international organizations was formed to take the project forward: Oxfam, NOVIB, Human Rights Watch, World Vision International, Council for a Liveable World, and Amnesty International.

The project began with three workshops held in Brussels in the spring of 1993, focusing on developmental, human rights and environmental aspects of conflict. These workshops were important in setting priorities and directions for the project in a lively and immediate way.

Later, Saferworld used the same technique in starting to research particular conflicts. So a workshop on Kashmir, for example, brought together people who had been directly affected by the conflict – Kashmiris who had lost relatives in the fighting, as well as Indians and Pakistanis – and also academics specializing in the region. Many of the people who attended these workshops subsequently became an important resource of information and advice to the researchers who worked on the individual country studies.

It is entirely appropriate that such a wide range of organizations and experts should have been involved in developing the thinking behind this project. If there is to be a reduction in the destructive cycle of conflict on our planet then new ideas about how to deal with it are needed. New ideas require new insights and fresh ways of looking at old problems. The aim of *The True Cost of Conflict* is to offer a fresh look and new insights into the ancient problem of war and conflict, and to raise questions about the old assumptions of *realpolitik* in the conduct of foreign policy.

1

THE EAST TIMOR CONFLICT
(1975–   )

Ian Robinson

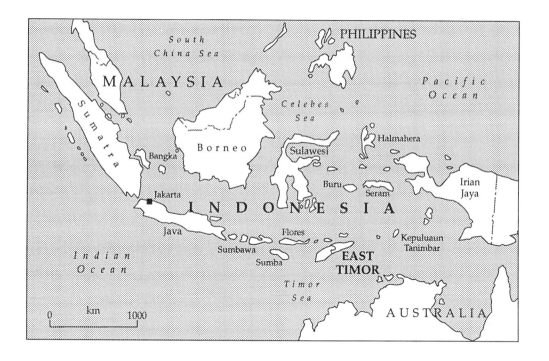

Area (000sq km)	14,874
Population (000)	555
Human Development Index	na
Population density (per sq km)	37
Capital	Dili

KEY IMPACTS OF THE CONFLICT

ON EAST TIMOR

- Amnesty International and Americas Watch, put the cost of the Indonesian occupation at 210,000 deaths out of a population in 1975 of 650,000
- There is one police officer, soldier or informant for every ten native Timorese
- Infant mortality is 160 per 1000, the second highest in the world
- After the invasion in 7 December 1975, the Indonesians had killed nearly all the Timorese teachers who had begun to build up an education system.
- 400 schools were lost in the invasion
- In 1990, only 0.15 per cent of the working population of East Timor had been to University, and of these 25 per cent were unemployed
- East Timor has the poorest schooling and achievement record of the whole of Indonesia
- Children have great difficulty in following the lessons; because of their malnutrition they cannot concentrate for long.
- Agricultural output fell after the invasion from 42,800 tonnes in 1973 to 12,800 tonnes in 1976
- Since the invasion 'there has been not a single US dollar of foreign investment in East Timor'
- Areas would be saturation-bombed to prepare for military advance, with forested areas being bombed to defoliate, and sprayed with chemicals to destroy crops and livestock
- Forest fires were started deliberately to clear areas

ON INDONESIA

- The Indonesian army sustained some 20,000 casualties
- Social development expenditure has increased from US$3.6 million in 1976/77 to US$55.3 million in 1981/82 and US$83 million in 1982/83
- For much of the 1980s East Timor received the highest per capita budget allowance in Indonesia
- The Catholic Institute for International Relations (CIIR) estimates that the conflict costs Indonesia US$1 million per day.

ON AUSTRALIA

- Australia has had to bear the costs of up to 5000 East Timorese refugees
- Its constant support for the Indonesian regime has inflicted some political damage

ON THE WEST

- Excepting recent events in Somalia, the invasion of East Timor is one of two major historical incidents that have seriously undermined the authority and reputation of the United Nations

INTRODUCTION

Geography

The island of Timor is situated at the most easterly tip of the Indonesian archipelago, 500 kilometres north of Australia, and covers approximately 32,000 square kilometres, an area slightly larger than Belgium. The climate is dry and hot with a short rainy season between November and February. The vegetation of the poor soils consists mainly of savannah and the remains of former rich sandalwood forests.

East Timor comprises the territories of the former colony of Portuguese Timor, including the eastern half of Timor island, the Oe-Cusse enclave, Atauro island and the islet of Jaco. Its total area measures 14,874 square kilometres, an area slightly larger than Kuwait, and is more mountainous than the western half of the island.

People

The population of East Timor was formed by Malay, Melanesian and Polynesian settlers. When the first Portuguese missionaries reached East Timor around 1515, animist religion dominated. With the permanent settlement of Portuguese Dominican friars in the late sixteenth century, the culture and religion of the colony developed in a direction quite different from the rest of the Indonesian archipelago.

This long history of Portuguese Roman Catholic influence distinguishes East Timor from all the surrounding island communities, the majority of which are Islamic. By 1970, 30 per cent of East Timorese were Catholic, with two-thirds animist and only 0.04 per cent considering themselves Muslim – compared with 87 per cent Muslim in Indonesia.[1] By 1992 more than 80 per cent of East Timorese considered themselves Catholic, mainly due to the fact that the Indonesian authorities forbid the animist faith.

The two main languages in East Timor are Tetum, considered the lingua franca, and Portuguese. However, it is thought that around 40 per cent of the population understand neither of these languages and speak one of at least 15 other languages found in the territory.[2] Since the invasion in 1975, Bahasa Indonesia (the language of Indonesia) has been imposed on the population and is compulsory in government schools.

The Conflict

The Portuguese first settled in 1566 but disputed control with the Dutch for the next three centuries. In 1913, East and West Timor were separated in an agreement between the two colonial powers. The Dutch colony (West Timor), together with the rest of the Dutch East Indies, became independent in 1949 under the name of Indonesia.

The Portuguese continued their rule of East Timor until the fall of the Lisbon-backed Caetano regime in 1974, after which a process of decolonisation began, culminating in the repatriation of 80 per cent of the Portuguese administrative staff. Political parties were allowed for the first time, with two main parties soon emerging. By the end of May, three main political parties had been formed. The smallest, the Timorese Democratic Association (APODETI) supported union with Indonesia. The Indonesian intelligence service BAKIN encouraged the creation of the APODETI party, but it failed to gain more than 5 per cent support for its integrationist policies. The Timorese Democratic Union (UDT), the most influential party at first, supported federation with Portugal and the integration of Timor in a commonwealth of Portuguese-speaking countries. Finally the Social Democratic Association of Timor (ASDT), later to become the Revolutionary Front for the Independence of East Timor (Fretilin), advanced more radical ideas, wanting the right to independence through progressive autonomy, self-reliance and strict economic controls.

Elections were held in July of 1975, and Fretilin, as a result of its successful health, education and agricultural programmes,

3

obtained 55 per cent of the vote. The UDT promptly staged a coup with Indonesian backing, but were defeated in September 1975, and retreated to the neighbouring Indonesian province of West Timor. Fretilin's reforms continued; delegations visiting in mid-October from the Australian Labour Party (ALP) and the Australian Council For Overseas Aid (ACFOA) commented favourably, highlighting the popular support for these programmes.[3] The Fretilin commissions, run collectively by army personnel, central committee members and professional advisers in areas such as agriculture, education and nursery provision, became the organisational core of reconstruction in the regions. By the end of October 1975 trading networks and food distribution had been reorganized and by 15 November the first coffee crop was exported.

With the failure of the coup, the Indonesian forces mounted increasingly aggressive border raids from West Timor throughout October, attacking the border towns of Batugade and Balibo, killing several Western journalists in the process. Reporting these engagements as a resurgence of the civil war, Indonesia invaded East Timor on 7 December 1975, in order to 'reinstate law and order'. Later that same month, the UN Security Council called on Indonesia to withdraw.

Since the invasion, there have been 18 years of human rights abuses and bloodshed under the Suharto regime, which is still in power today. Throughout this period the Indonesian forces have fought a guerrilla war with Fretilin forces, exacting massive costs on both sides. Indonesia has also ignored ten UN resolutions to withdraw military personnel from East Timor, and is currently under little pressure to do so. While the UN Security Council and General Assembly have repeatedly called for Indonesian forces to withdraw to allow an act of self-determination to occur, Indonesia has steadfastly refused to do so. The international community and Australia have taken no direct action against Indonesia.

The following pages illustrate the costs and benefits of the conflict to the main countries involved, since the Indonesian invasion of 1975. Attention is focused on: Indonesia, as chief antagonist; Australia, as a country that has been involved with East Timor since the Second World War; and any Western countries that have links with East Timor and/or Indonesia. Also examined are the potential benefits that might have been available to the East Timorese and Western nations had no invasion taken place and the process of decolonisation been allowed to continue.

EAST TIMOR

THE COSTS

Introduction

Prior to the invasion, and having just emerged from civil war, East Timor was a country wracked with problems. Many of its people were illiterate and health standards were poor. The economy was overwhelmingly agrarian and subsistence based, with much of the population living in small villages. However, with the dismantling of colonial rule and the formation of Fretilin and its accompanying agenda of social improvement, East Timor appeared to be about to enter a new phase of its history, characterized by social improvement and controlled development. The subsequent invasion and military occupation crushed these aspirations, and has seriously affected the social and economic development of the people.

Development

Health

The health of the people of Timor cannot be divorced from the political context of the country.[4]

4

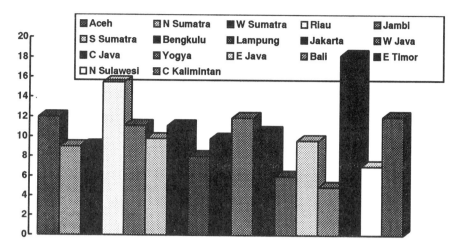

Sources: Government of Indonesia and UNICEF, *Situation Analysis of Children and Women in Indonesia*, Jakarta, December 1988.

Figure 1.1: Child malnutrition in Indonesia and East Timor:(percentage of children under 5) 1988

It is thought that up to 90 per cent of the population has been resettled with only 20 per cent of villages now occupying ancestral sites.[5] The new villages were built to ease the control of the population by the military and were to be the foundation for the Indonesian military's attempt to restructure Timorese society. Often these villages or camps were built in lowland areas infected with malaria, with poor water supplies and a much hotter climate. However, the population was forbidden to leave the camps. Indonesia's Foreign Minister acknowledged that conditions of starvation on the island of Timor were possibly worse than those experienced by Biafra and Cambodia.[6]

Foreign aid was channelled to the Indonesian Red Cross, but never reached the new camps, generally being diverted by the Indonesian military for its own use, or for use in other provinces. These camps were to have a devastating impact on the health of the Timorese.

By May 1979, the United States Agency for International Development (USAID) estimated that there were 300,000 East Timorese living in such camps. Only land within 1500 metres of the camps could be farmed, sometimes restricted to within 300 metres.

The main problem in the camps is famine. The places where people are allowed to go are very restricted, whether they are growing or harvesting crops. Most families can only have 100–200 square metres of ground ...clearly insufficient to feed a family... They have to fall back on collecting wild fruit, roots and leaves, these also in insufficient quantities because the army forbids them to go far from the camps.[7]

David Delaprez, head of the International Committee of the Red Cross (ICRC) relief operations in 1979 stated the situation was as bad as Biafra and potentially as serious as Kampuchea. One third of the 60,000 people under the ICRC programme need medical care.'[8] He went on to say: 'It was hardly surprising that foreign delegations which visited East Timor in the years after the villages were set up commented on the seeming irrationality of an agricultural sector which managed to combine population concentration, unworked fields and food shortages in its domestic economy.'[9]

5

Common diseases

Two fundamental health problems continue to plague East Timor; malnourishment and lack of hygiene. The conflict has led to many deaths from malnutrition and curable diseases such as tuberculosis, endemic malaria, pneumonia, parasitic skin infections and anaemia. This has been due in great part to forced relocation to less suitable sites and a lack of medical supplies and expertise. Infant mortality is 160 per 1000, the second highest in the world.[10] In comparison, infant mortality in Indonesia in 1992 was 68 per 1000.[11]

While the Indonesian government purports to having tackled with success the range of diseases affecting the population of East Timor, in reality the Timorese population are often too suspicious of the Indonesian doctors to take the drugs prescribed by them. Instead of using these services, they prefer to attend the weekly outdoor clinics and surgeries run by the local church health workers, where even superficial check-ups are impossible.

Education

After the invasion of 1975, 'the Indonesians had killed nearly all the Timorese teachers who had begun to build up an education system.'[12] Others had already fled over the border to West Timor with the UDT surrender or to the hills.[13] The shortage meant the Indonesian government had to bring in 410 new teachers from the islands of Java and Sulawesi.[14] In contrast to the church-run schools, government-run schools in East Timor have systematically introduced Indonesian values through the exclusive use of the Indonesian language and 'Pancasila', the militaristic ideology of the Indonesian Government.[15]

The government's *East Timor Develops* publication states that, since 1975, 400 primary schools have been built and they have an attendance of 98,850 pupils and 2446 teachers. However, before the invasion there were 463 Portuguese schools that supplied sufficient coverage for the population.[16] This implies that at least 400 schools have been lost since the invasion. In 1973 these schools achieved a literacy rate of only 7 per cent. By 1989, after 14 years of Indonesian occupation, literacy had risen to only 8 per cent despite the number of schools having grown to 708.[17]

This lack of progress is reflected in East Timor's primary school attendance rates of only 52.88 per cent for 1985, compared with an Indonesian national average of 95.88 per cent.[18] It can also be seen that the class sizes in East Timor are much higher than the rest of Indonesia: 36.9 pupils per class in East Timor compared with an Indonesian average of 30.44 per class.[19]

Figure 1.2 shows that East Timor has the poorest schooling and achievement record of the whole of Indonesia, a finding backed up by the national examination results. This is not surprising, considering schoolchildren are being taught in Bahasa Indonesia rather than Tetum. Other factors, such as the highest student/teacher ratio in the country and the second highest class size (after highly overcrowded Jakarta), have compounded the problems of East Timorese schoolchildren. The poor quality of the schooling is reflected in East Timor having the poorest primary school attendance, most parents preferring instead to send their children to the Catholic church-run schools.[20]

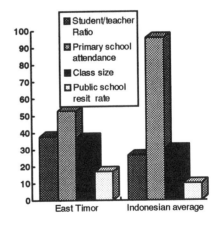

Source: USAID, op cit

Figure 1.2: Primary school performance 1985 (%)

Schools run by the church are...better than those run by the government. They...offer a broad-based education. Government schools, on the contrary, seem to be a sham. Pupils do not have books but learn by rote...Pupils have to learn Bahasa Indonesia nowadays. In a village school in Venilale...I did not see a single book...I was told repeatedly that children have great difficulty in following the lessons; because of their malnutrition they cannot concentrate for long.[21]

One report to the US Senate estimated that due to this, half a generation of Timorese children had been rendered 'mentally retarded.'[22]

Despite Indonesian attempts to provide some form of education for the East Timorese, the nature of the occupation is always likely to ensure its failure. After 16 years of occupation, the majority of the demonstrators killed at Santa Cruz in 1991 (see 'civil and political rights' section below) were the second generation of Timorese since the invasion, the same people that the Indonesian government had hoped to socialise as an indigenous support base for East Timor's incorporation into Indonesia through their education policy.[23]

Civil and Political Rights

The promising start to the future development of an independent East Timor ended with Indonesia's invasion. This was accompanied by mass murder, massive human rights abuses and a systematic attempt to dismantle the East Timorese way of life. According to US political scientist J. William Liddle, 60,000 men, women and children (10 per cent of the population) were killed in the first two months of the war as the result of fighting or war related deprivations.[24] Timor's Indonesian appointed Governor, Lopez da Cruz, in February 1976 stated that 60,000 Timorese had been killed in the three months following the invasion.[25]

Civilians as targets

Frustrated by their inability to make any headway militarily, Indonesian troops stepped up their terrorisation of the local population. Villages were destroyed and their surviving populations moved into strategic camps. Atrocities became widespread as did the use of chemical weapons. In mid-May, 67 boys were shot in Suai. In early August in the area around Zumlai, six villages were burnt and hundreds of their inhabitants executed; and so it continued. Even the newly appointed governor, former APODETI member Arnaldo Araujo, wrote to Suharto condemning the widespread killing.[26]

The 1974 Portuguese census recorded the population as 688,771. In October 1978 the Indonesian military census recorded 329,271, or a drop of 359,500. Reports already mentioned indicate that at least 100,000 had been killed in the preceding three years, which left 259,000 unaccounted for. Of this number, an unknown amount are living in the mountains, and the rest will have been killed: 'I don't think there is any case in post World War Two history where such a decline of population has occurred in these circumstances. Its incredible. Worse than Cambodia or Ethiopia.'[27]

Destruction of villages and their inhabitants

A Timorese gave an account of an incident at Lamaknan, a location in Indonesian Timor near the border. This informant said that in June last year he had been in this area where Fretilin troops were active. The Indonesians set fire to the dwellings of the East Timorese refugees who were camped there. When the refugees protested the Indonesians turned their guns on them. According to this informant, who said he was a witness to the episode, the troops shot, he thought, 2000 of the Timorese, some on their knees, others with their hands raised. The victims he said, included women and children.[28]

By 1992, new estimates of the genocide were emerging. Two independent human rights organisations, Amnesty International and Americas Watch, put the cost of the Indonesian occupation at 210,000 deaths out of a population in 1975 of 650,000.[29]

In Bangkok on November 20 1993, the Co-chairman of the Special Representative Council of Maubere Resistance, Jose

Ramos-Horta, said it was difficult to estimate the casualties after 1981 as the killing had become less widespread but the occupying troops had resorted to greater use of torture.[30]

Encirclement and annihilation

Attacks against Fretilin escalated from September 1977 onwards, coinciding with the campaign of Encirclement and Annihilation. 'After September [1978] the war intensified. Military aircraft were in action all day long. Hundreds of human beings die daily, their bodies left as food for the vultures. If bullets don't kill us, we die from epidemic disease; villages are being completely destroyed.'[31] Much of the population fled to the mountainous central area of East Timor, but following intensive bombing in 1977 and 1978 people were unable to grow food. Famine compounded the effects of injury, disease and displacement.[32] In 1978 and 1979 thousands of Timorese left the mountains, communities were split up and moved to 'strategic villages'. Survivors of the bombing and chemical attacks during the 1977 encirclement campaign described how maggots would emerge a day or two after a bombing raid and destroy crops, or how large numbers of people would become ill with diarrhoea and vomiting after drinking polluted water, in Zumalai, Matabea and many other places.[33]

The number of political prisoners held in East Timor is unknown, but estimated to be high. Known to be held at present are 120, with reports saying the number is far higher.[34] Hundreds of others have 'disappeared' and remain unaccounted for, most assumed to be dead.[35]

Military tactics for dealing with political dissent were shockingly portrayed by film footage of the Santa Cruz massacre on 12 November 1991. Two weeks after the killing of 18-year-old Sebastiao Gomes Rangel in the church of St Antonio de Motael, a memorial mass and procession to his grave was held. Thousands attended. Once in the cemetery, Indonesian soldiers arrived and opened fire on the unarmed crowd.[36] Several Western journalists were in the cemetery and witnessed the massacre, one catching it on video. Almost all those who attended the funeral were beaten. The wounded were shot or bayoneted. A recent investigation des-cribed how the wounded were fed death pills, crushed with rocks, or crushed beneath the wheels of army lorries.[37]

The international outcry over this event led to the Indonesians holding a Commission of Inquiry. But, as Michael Leifer, lecturer in South East Asian Affairs at the London School of Economics, stated at the time: 'All the people chosen [on the Commission] are servants of the Indonesian government'.[38] The Commission found that it was only possible to confirm 19 deaths and 91 injured. Jose Ramos-Horta in Geneva on 3 September 1992 stated that new data put the total dead at 273, with 376 wounded and 256 disappeared. Half the victims were under 21 years and the majority under 30 years of age.[39]

Amnesty International summed up the situation in East Timor recently, saying:

> *The human rights situation there has not improved since the Santa Cruz massacre of 12 November 1991...while there has been no single incident on a comparable scale in the past year, the overall pattern of human rights violations - encompassing short-term detention, torture and ill-treatment of suspected political opponents, intermittent political killings and 'disappearances', long-term political imprisonment after unfair trials and the intimidation of relatives and human rights workers – has continued unabated.*[40]

The Economy

East Timor has always been an agricultural society, with coffee being its major export. Food crops however, constitute the largest component of its agriculture. East Timor has not industrialized and has no manufacturing base. At present, mining is still small scale and run solely to provide the construction industry with sand and stone (see Figure 1.3)

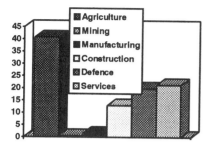

Source: Pendapatan Regional Propinsi-Propinsi di Indonesia Menurut Lapangan Usasha, Biro Pusat Statistik, 1990 and Buletin Ringkas BPS, Biro Pusat Statistik, 1992

Figure 1.3: East Timor; percentage of GDP by sector, 1983–89

Throughout the 1950s and 1960s, the UN applied pressure on Portugal to encourage decolonization, but with little effect. The newly educated Timorese elite realized that possibilities for national development existed after the colony's expansion of export crops had improved infrastructure. With the discovery of offshore oil and gas deposits at the end of the 1960s, East Timor's potential looked considerable. These oil reserves on the seabed between East Timor and Australia are calculated to contain 5 billion barrels of oil along with 50 billion cubic feet of natural gas, making it one of the 25 largest oilfields in the world.

Before the Indonesian invasion, Fretilin had managed to rebuild trading and food distribution networks, destroyed after the repatriation to Portugal of 80 per cent of the administrative staff and the short civil war.[41] Health, childcare, agricultural projects and the production of natural medicines were also organized, as East Timor increased its self-sufficiency.[42] In fact, under Portuguese rule, 50 per cent of the province's budget was provided by the local economy, but this had fallen to just 7 per cent in 1986.[43]

Agriculture

The provincial government of Timor's own statistics show that in the four years after the invasion more than 85 per cent of East

Timor's livestock was destroyed.[44] Invading forces plundered much of East Timor's natural resources, particularly its livestock.[45] The drop in bullocks and cows and the loss of tractors from looting, has meant that in only a few places have peasants been able to start tilling their land again. By 1989, the total animal population was still only 1,033,500, or 76.5 per cent of 1976 levels (Figure 1.4).[46]

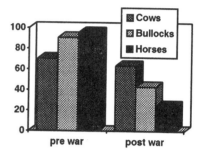

Source: Drew and Aditjondro

Figure 1.4: Livestock population in East Timor 1976–1989 (thousands)

Agricultural output also fell after the invasion from 42,800 tonnes in 1973 to 12,800 tonnes in 1976 (less than 30 per cent of pre-invasion levels) with rice output falling from 25,600 tonnes to 8100 tonnes (32 per cent of 1973 levels). (See Figure 1.5) After the Indonesian invasion, agricultural output dropped and the livestock

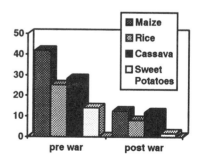

Source: Unity and Diversity; Hal Hill (ed); Buletin Ringkas BPS, June 1992

Figure 1.5: Effect of the invasion on main crop harvests (thousands of tonnes)

population was decimated. 'In the early years after integration...not only was the agricultural potential of the island put back by a decade but the human resource potential was also cut, with an alienation of the remaining workforce (who had not necessarily been hostile before) as a by-product.'[47]

In 1990, only 224,642 hectares of East Timor's 751,820 hectares of potential agricultural land was being utilized with only 69,326 hectares of this being cultivated and 17,249 hectares being irrigated.[48] Much of this under-utilization has been caused by the loss of cows, bullocks and tractors as well as the population's right to free movement.[49]

While Indonesia has encouraged the growth of plantations in East Timor, the military holds a monopoly over exports such as coffee and sandalwood oil, the importation of alcohol and the construction and public works industries. The Indonesian company PT Batara Indra Group dominates almost the entire economy of East Timor, and is owned by the three officers who commanded Operation Seroja – the invasion of East Timor in 1975. In this way, much of the capital generated by exports goes to the Indonesians rather than the indigenous population. This means that any resources developed in the future are unlikely to filter back to benefit the people of the island.

Agriculture in East Timor has been hit further by the encouragement of transmigration, with the migrants from other islands of Indonesia taking over rice fields that had formerly belonged to native Timorese, often without any compensation being paid and rather than being developed from unused land as in other provinces.[50] East Timorese have been forced off their land in the border regions with West Timor where most of the useful land has been taken for coffee plantations. This means conflict over land can only intensify in the future with the projected increase in government-sponsored and spontaneous migrants from West Timor.

Investment

The war in East Timor has effectively blocked any private investment in the province, despite the fact that there is great potential, particularly in raw materials. Since the invasion 'there has been not a single US dollar of foreign investment in East Timor'.[51] In contrast, Indonesian provinces have received an estimated US$20.6 billion between 1967 and 1992. Similarly Timorese investment during the same period totalled only US$110.1 million, an insignificant 0.1 per cent of total investment.[52]

Unemployment

With East Timor having an overwhelmingly agricultural society, most of the population is economically active and working. Problems have occurred, however, with better qualified East Timorese looking for high quality employment. The Indonesian government does not trust the Timorese population sufficiently to allow them to work in its administration in great numbers. In 1990, only 0.15 per cent of the working population of East Timor had been to university, and of these 25 per cent were unemployed. In contrast, the Indonesian average was 0.8 per cent having attended university, with only 9.6 per cent of graduates unemployed.[53]

Environment

The effect of occupation on the environment has been widespread. Apart from the destruction of villages and indigenous housing with the strategy of forced relocation during the second half of 1976,[54] there have also been reports that chemical and biological weapons have been used.

Angkasa (the Indonesian army daily report) stated that intensive bombing by AURI (the Indonesian air force) had been very effective 'because the planes were able to carry out raids as low as 100–200 metres, unloading their napalm bombs that so terrified the guerrillas'.[55]

Two sources...interviewed in East Timor, told me, without my even asking them, about a type of bomb that generated enough heat to melt the windows and glassware in the convent and that burnt human flesh. If this is so, it is likely that...defoliants such as agent orange which was used in Vietnam were also used in East Timor.[56]

Taylor[57] describes how areas would be saturation-bombed to prepare for military advance, with forested areas being bombed to defoliate, and sprayed with chemicals to destroy crops and livestock, thereby poisoning land and water. Other accounts tell of how forest fires were started deliberately to clear areas, making it more difficult for Fretilin to move freely.

Gabriel Defert, author of *Timor-Est, le Genocide Oublie*, stated in 1993:

Currently certain army units have as a main mission, to clean up the Timorese vegetation [in which].. a small group of armed men can escape patrols. More or less everywhere fires are lit in bushes and thickets, which has disastrous consequences on the ecology of the island. The East Timorese climate is extremely dry and the vegetation fragile. So after each deliberately lit fire, the only things which will grow up again will be Imperata Cylindrica, very high, dense and cutting grass, as impenetrable as [it is] noxious. [58]

Another major source of environmental degradation are the large monopolies controlled by General Benny Murdani and two of his colleagues. Their PT Batara Indra Group and its four subsidiaries have violated various articles of the Indonesian Land Reform Laws and appear to ignore the provisions of the Law on the Environment with its Presidential Decree on Environmental Impact Assessment. In this way, the effects of marble quarrying, coffee planting, civil engineering and sandalwood forest exploitation cannot be assessed or controlled.

Finally, Indonesia has granted international companies the right to explore for oil and gas in the Timor Gap, when by international law they had no right to do so. If the development is not managed properly, the populations on the south coast of East Timor may once again be displaced in the near future as the area becomes industrialized or polluted.

CONCLUSION

The destruction of East Timor's identity pre-1975 appears almost total. The people remain traumatized, alienated and un-healthy by Indonesian standards, and unconvinced by the considerable investment Jakarta has injected. The Indonesian regime's determination to use maximum violence at the smallest hint of disquiet, will ensure the alienation of much of the population, and thus a sympathetic support base for Fretilin. While East Timor has shown some improvement in its economic development, it is unclear the extent to which the indigenous population is benefiting. Moreover, it is questionable as to whether future development of resources such as minerals and oil will ever benefit the population. Finally, with a only a tiny percentage of the population reaching tertiary education, and a quarter of these never finding employment, the future indeed appears grim for the indigenous population of East Timor.

INDONESIA

THE COSTS

Introduction

With communist advances in Indo-China in the 1950s to 1970s worrying the United States and its European allies, Indonesia's anti-communist government and strategic position in South-east Asia seemed to be one of the most important boundaries to communist advances in the region. The fall of the Caetano government in 1974 and the subsequent commencement of decolonization of Portuguese Timor during 1974 and 1975 led the Indonesian government to annex the territory in order to prevent it posing a security threat to its eastern islands. It was tacitly encouraged in this task by Australia and the West, acting to safeguard their economic and strategic interests in the region.

The high costs of this invasion and the subsequent attempt to integrate East Timor as Indonesia's 27th province have impacted not just on East Timor, but also on Indonesia.

Human Cost

With the large numbers of troops and the heavy engagements with Fretilin, especially in the early years of the conflict, high casualties were inflicted on the Indonesian military. An example of this heavy fighting in 1976 was the taking of the town of Suai. It lay only 3 kilometres from the sea, but took 3000 troops four months to capture.[59] 'In spite of vastly superior resources, after 3 months the Indonesian armed forces only controlled coastal and border regions and areas accessible from the limited road network. It is believed that the Indonesian army sustained very high losses at this stage of the campaign; as many as 20,000 men according to some military analysts'.[60]

Since the invasion, the Indonesian military has maintained a massive troop presence in East Timor. At first, the view of Indonesia's military generals was that the resistance would be dealt with swiftly and the territory incorporated into the Indonesian Republic with relative ease. However, the movement for independence continues

to the present, even after Indonesia's massive troop deployment and expenditures.

Since starting with over 40,000 troops in Timor as a whole in 1975, the number has fluctuated. At all times however, there has been a minimum of 10,000 to 15,000 troops.[61] While no specific cost data relating to the occupation are available, Table 1.1 illustrates the considerable size of the continuing military operation. One can infer from this that the cost of the occupation since the invasion almost 20 years ago must be enormous.

The Economy

While the invasion of East Timor has not encouraged economic growth, it has cost the Indonesian government and its population considerably. 'The extent of the armed forces expenditure on East Timor has forced the government to reduce the share of the state budget allocated to education and health.'[62]

The Catholic Institute for International Relations (CIIR) estimates that the conflict costs Indonesia US$1 million per day. Jose Ramos-Horta estimated the cost at US$100 million per month,[63] while others have estimated more conservatively that US$5 billion since 1975 has been spent.[64] 'The cost to the Indonesians has been massive. This is not just due to administration or the cost of the transmigration programme, but also

Table 1.1: Indonesian troop numbers in East Timor 1975–1993

Invasion Operasi	10,000 Kopassandha (elite paratroopers)
Invasion Seroja	extra paratroopers
Invasion	extra 15,000 troops
Apr 1976	total of 32,000 troops in East Timor
End of 1976	40,000 troops
Operasi Persatuan Feb 1984	14,000–20,000 troops and an additional 22,000 troops
Operation Extinction	extra 27,000 troops
New offensive	30,000 troops and an additional 5000 troops
Oct 1989	21,000 troops
Mar 1990 offensive	40,000 troops and an additional 2–3000 + 6000 East Timorese and additional conscripts and 2 helicopter squadrons
Aug/Sep1992	26 battalions (19,500 troops)and an additional 20 battalions (15,000 troops)

Sources: Taylor, op cit, Coalition for East Timor, op cit, Fretilin Report in *TAPOL Bulletin* no 87, June 1988, Jose Ramos Horta, *Jane's Defence Weekly* 18/7/92, International Panel of Jurists on East Timor (IPJET)

due to policing, in a country where there is one policeman, soldier or informant for every ten native Timorese.'[65]

Added to the military cost of the invasion must be the cost of administration and routine expenditure on the East Timorese economy. Up to 80 per cent of its administration had been repatriated to Portugal by the time of the invasion. This loss had to be replaced and the costs of East Timor's budget had to be provided by the Indonesians. While 50 per cent of the budget had been provided by the East Timorese during Portuguese rule, by 1986 this had fallen to only 7 per cent, leaving the rest to be covered by the Indonesian government.[66]

Data from the Indonesian government publication *East Timor Today* shows how the budget for routine expenditure grew after the invasion (Figure 1.6).

Since 1980 the Indonesians have diversified their strategy in East Timor. Ongoing military offensives have been accompanied by a range of development initiatives directed at both consolidating integration and winning the hearts and minds of the East Timorese.

Social development expenditure has increased from US$ 3.6 million in 1976–77 to US$55.3 million in 1981/82 and US$83 million in 1982–83.[67] Much of the emphasis

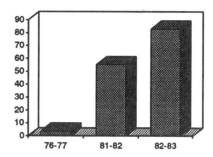

Source: Asia Partnership for Human Development Newsletter No 22 July–Aug 1983

Figure 1.7: Social development expenditure in East Timor 1976–83 (US$m)

of this development has been on the 'Indonisation' of the Timorese, especially the young, through education. This appears largely to have failed, as can be seen by the fact that almost all the population remains Catholic, and many parents refuse to allow their children to attend Indonesian schools.

The government has tried to help the East Timorese economy by targeting areas in need of help and issuing government business incentive, or 'Inpres', grants. By 1986, this meant East Timor received a larger per capita grant than any of the Indonesian provinces, US$19.[68] Further, grants such as the Sectoral Development Fund Grant and the Routine Expenditure Grant were also issued. In 1976 these totalled Rp 2.86 billion (US$1.43 million). By 1986 they had grown to Rp 74.77 billion (US$37.4 million). For much of the 1980s, East Timor received a higher per capita budget allowance than any Indonesian province.[69] (see Figure 1.8.)

In 1990, the University of Gadja Madah in Jogyakarta, Java, published a report on East Timor, commissioned by the Bank of Indonesia and the provincial government of East Timor. The report was commissioned at least partly because of the government's concern that its funds and grants were having no discernible developmental effect. The report confirmed that the East Timorese were deeply alienated from Indonesian rule, due in the main to the

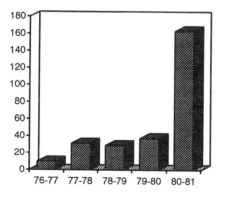

Source: Government of Indonesia *East Timor Today*, Jakarta, 1984

Figure 1.6: Indonesian expenditure in East Timor (US$m)

prevalence of abuse, violence and corruption and the exclusion from meaningful political and economic participation. It goes on to state that 'The failure of the colonial system must not be repeated by bringing in new colonists and a new model of colonialism',[70] and proceeds to recommend 13 political, social and economic measures to rectify the existing problems in East Timor. These measures included the reduction of the power of the military and central government, and the vesting of fuller authority in the civilian governor; a larger role for the church and educated youth; an end to economic monopolies and the resettlement programme, and a greater role for East Timorese in the economy. As recently as 1992, the Campaign Against Arms Trade (CAAT) stated that 100,000 citizens from provinces of Indonesia, mainly Java, had been settled in East Timor, a figure backed by the Northern California Ecumenical Council (NCEC) who describe it as an attempt by the Indonesian government to dilute the Timorese population.

THE BENEFITS

Security

Having destroyed one of the largest communist parties in the world (PKI, the Indonesian communist party) in the

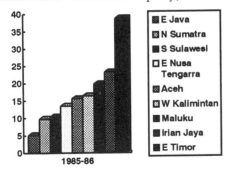

Source: Hill, op cit

Figure 1.8: East Timor and selection of provinces: per capita 'Inpres' grants 1985–86 (thousands of Rp)

process of achieving power, General Suharto's regime was perceived by the West as one of the most secure boundaries to communist advances in South-east Asia. Because of its function as a highly militarized anti-communist bulwark, Indonesia found the West willing to provide considerable amounts of some of its most sophisticated arms (see The West section).

Indonesia's fear of a communist bridgehead, coupled with its fear of a model for independence to its other islands, prompted it to initially encourage the formation of a political party in East Timor to oppose the UDT and ASDT who were both anti-integrationist. When this failed, it attempted to take control by launching a military coup, which again achieved nothing. When this also failed, it resorted to invasion.

While the communist advance in South-east Asia no longer seems to threaten, an independent East Timor is still seen by the current regime in Indonesia as a threat to its survival. While a powerful military state, Indonesia's arms purchases are principally for the purpose of controlling internal dissent. In this way, while strategic factors have become less dominant since integration, East Timor's integration is still seen as essential. Any successful independent state on the edge of its archipelago would, in Indonesia's view, still have the ability to become an example to the independence movements in other trouble spots within Indonesia, such as Aceh and Irian Jaya. The repressive nature of army action in quelling disturbances in these areas illustrates the trepidation with which Jakarta views the potential implications of internal unrest.

Economic Factors

As a result of its role as a powerful anti-communist ally in South-east Asia, Indonesia has become a major recipient of western aid and investment. Figures from the recent past demonstrate this, as illustrated in Figures 1.9, 1.10 and 1.11.

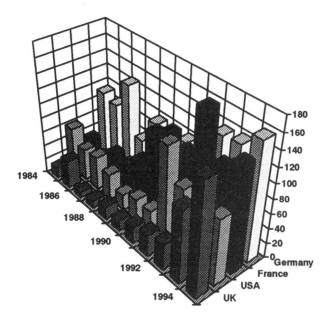

Source: Organisation for Economic Cooperation and Development (OECD) *Geographical distribution of financial flows to developing countries*, Paris, 1992, and *TAPOL, Bulletin* no 123, London, June 1994.

Figure 1.9: Principal Western aid donors to Indonesia 1984–94 (US$m)

Continued investment in the island and, more especially, in the Timor Gap oil and gas field, also encourages the Indonesian government to persevere in its policy of annexation. As mentioned, the oil and gas field is possibly one of the 25 largest in the world. Forty-five exploratory wells have been planned up to 1998 with contracts involving 55 international oil companies. At present oil is being produced from at least four of the wells.

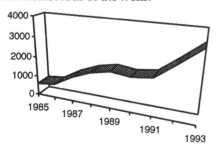

Source: World Bank, *World Development Report*, Oxford University Press 1993

Figure 1.10: Total Western aid to Indonesia 1985–93 (US$m)

Western investment has played a significant part in Indonesia's economic development. This is examined in detail in the section below on the West.

Military monopolies

PT Denok Hernandes International, owned by the Indonesian military, holds a monopoly of production and distribution over many of East Timor's export crops. While no figures are available on the extent of its profits, it can be assumed they are considerable, given its practice of paying deflated prices to the crop-growers and then making a considerable margin on the sale price on the international market. For example, in 1987, PT Denok paid local cultivators Rp1250 per kilo, and sold it in Singapore for Rp5000 per kilo; a 200 per cent mark up.[71] More recently, PT Denok has moved into controlling distribution of staple foods and household goods through another subsidiary, Toko Marina.[72]

As mentioned in the East Timor section, PT Bandara Indra Group, another military-owned monopoly, is involved in the

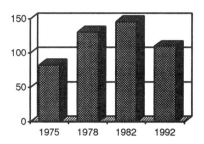

Source: Franke, op cit

*Figure 1.11: US military aid to Indonesia 1975–92
(US$m)*

exploitation of East Timor's mineral resources. Other Indonesian military monopolies profiting from activities in East Timor are: Bakrie Brothers (owned by Suharto's half-brother and son), Murdani, PT Astakona, PT Nusa Bhakti (owned by Suharto's wife) and PT Lianbau (owned by Suharto's son-in-law).[73]

PT Astakona receives substantial subsidies from East Timor's budget, as controller of farming supplies to East Timor's rural sector. In fact, with the exception of the 'traditional textiles' industry, which makes up less than 1 per cent to East Timor's GDP, Indonesian companies comprehensively dominate every other aspect of East Timor's GDP output. In this way, a considerable proportion of the aid given by Indonesia through public channels is swallowed up by subsidies, grants and incentives to Indonesian-owned monopolies.

CONCLUSION

The Indonesian government has incurred heavy costs in annexing East Timor. Despite massive investment of billions of dollars, both in terms of financial and military commitments, the population remain disenfranchized, poor and unhealthy. East Timor is more heavily subsidised than any of Indonesia's provinces, and while enormous profits have accrued to Indonesia's ruling elite through the activities of military monopolies, little concrete benefit has accrued to Indonesia as a whole.

Moreover, the bitterness of the East Timorese toward Indonesia appears as strong as ever, as demonstrated by the popularity of the sporadic protests, and Fretilin's continued popularity. However, Indonesia stands to gain from the exploitation of the Timorese oilfields, though it is still too early to calculate the returns these will produce.

Strategically, Indonesia has also benefited from the conflict. Its fervent anti-communist stance, illustrated by its determination to destroy Fretilin, which it perceived as rigidly communist and therefore a direct threat, and destruction of the PKI, its control of the major sea routes between the Indian and Pacific Oceans and the deep water Ombai-Wettar straits (discussed in subsequent sections), guaranteed it favourable relations with the US. Continued good relations between the US and Indonesia were seen as essential to the American South-east Asia strategy and provided Indonesia with political support, foreign investment and military aid.

AUSTRALIA

THE COSTS

Introduction

In December 1941, Australian commandos invaded the neutral Portuguese colony of East Timor in an attempt to prevent the Japanese building airfields from which they could launch their planned invasion of northern Australia. In a classic guerrilla campaign, the Australians disrupted a numerically superior Japanese force. However their presence in East Timor had the effect of drawing the occupying Japanese forces to communities they might otherwise have spared. The action resulted in the death of 40,000 East Timorese and 40 Australians.

As a result of its close proximity and the events of the war, there has been much interest in the East Timor conflict in Australia. It is the only Western country where the press has covered the topic regularly since the Portuguese coup of April 1974. The Australian government has had a fuller, more accurate knowledge of the East Timor situation than any other industrial nation with the result that, to some extent, other governments and other members of the UN have tended to look to Australia for guidance.

Diplomatic Costs and Refuges

Australia has suffered little direct consequence of the Indonesian invasion of East Timor. Its support for the Indonesian regime may have inflicted some international political damage. It has also had to bear the costs of up to 5000 East Timorese refugees, the largest East Timorese population outside Timor. It also has made a grant of A$250,000 in relief assistance for East Timor, implying the recognition of Indonesian sovereignty and effectively undercutting attempts by international organisations, such as the International Red Cross, to gain access to the territory.

THE BENEFITS

The Economy

Perhaps the biggest benefit to Australia has been the discovered economic potential of the disputed seabed between Australia and East Timor. As mentioned in the Indonesia 'Benefits' section, the seabed has massive potential for oil and natural gas production. In December 1991, the Australian government signed the Timor Gap Treaty with Indonesia, which approved a zone of cooperation and the confirmation of 11 oil production contracts. The Timor Gap Treaty ignores the dispute concerning Indonesia's sovereignty over East Timor and has led to the Portuguese government taking Australia to the International Court of Justice for violating international law and to defend the rights of the East Timorese. The case is still pending.

To date 11 companies (Australian, American and British, amongst others) have signed contracts for exploration of agreed zones in the Timor Sea.

CONCLUSION

Australia has, with the exception of some international political fallout, largely escaped any major economic or political damage as a result of the invasion of East Timor. While there have been some costs associated with the care of thousands of Timorese refugees, these are far outweighed by the potential returns from the oilfields to be developed in the Timor Sea.

THE WEST

THE COSTS

Introduction

Indonesia's strategic position and anti-communist stance along with its wealth of natural resources and its flexible labour market, ensured that the governments in Washington, London and Canberra have accommodated the Indonesian position in the face of international criticism.

Diplomatic Costs

Diplomatically the British and US governments have found it impossible to support Indonesia's case at the UN and have instead chosen to abstain so as to 'avoid taking sides against the Indonesian government' and thus jeopardize their economic interests in the archipelago. Britain abstained on the first UN resolution condemning the invasion, supported two others widely acknowledged to be weakly worded and watered down, and abstained on all subsequent ones.[74] As Daniel P Moynihan, former US Ambassador to the UN, states in his memoirs: 'the US wished things to turn out as they did, and worked to bring this about. The Department of State desired that the UN prove utterly ineffective in whatever measures it undertook.

This task was given to me and I carried it forward with no inconsiderable success'.[75]

Excepting recent events in Rwanda, ex-Yugoslavia and Somalia, the invasion of East Timor is one of two major historical incidents that have seriously undermined the authority and reputation of the UN. As with the Israeli invasion of the West Bank and Gaza strip, and the subsequent passing of UN resolutions demanding their immediate withdrawal, the invasion of East Timor, the subsequent passing of Security Council Resolution 384, and the resulting lack of interest in enforcing the terms of that same resolution, demonstrated that the UN, when appropriate, could be used simply as a vehicle for the protection of western interests. As Lord Judd stated: 'the government's willingness to sell arms has been translated into a consistent series of abstentions in the UN on resolutions condemning the Indonesian government. Perhaps even more sinister is the fact that this is almost certainly what lay behind the repeated, cynical manoeuvres by the British government to frustrate humanitarian initiatives by the EC under the leadership of the Portuguese during their presidency of the community.'[76]

Economic Assistance

The US government supplied the Indonesian military with the weapons needed at crucial times in the Timor campaign. Successive US governments, especially under Carter and Reagan (1976–88), created a favourable climate for Indonesian requests for arms. This resulted in an increase in military assistance, from US$83 million in 1975 to US$131 million in 1978 and US$146 million in 1982 (Figure 1.11). The US gave US$93 million worth of economic aid to Indonesia in 1992.[77]

THE BENEFITS

Security

The US position on East Timor is a reflection of its foreign policy toward South-east Asia following the end of World War II.

South-east Asia was seen as both strategically and economically important. With Indonesia being one of the largest countries in the area, good relations were essential in the Cold War era. Consistent support for the Suharto regime has been forthcoming since his rise to power in 1965. This diplomatic, political and military support has continued throughout the duration of the East Timor conflict.

In April 1975, the Cambodian regime of Lon Nol, who had come to power with American support, was overthrown. Phnom Penh was taken by Khmer troops and Pol Pot came into power. At the same time the Vietnamese communists took control of Saigon. These communist adv-ances in Indo-China, where the US had had deep political and military involve-ment, left the United States, Europe, Australia and Japan seriously concerned. US officials believed at this time that the war in Indo-China threatened their control of South-east Asia.

Indonesia, and more significantly East Timor, had great significance in US global strategy. Lying north of the island of East Timor are the Ombai-Wetar Straits, a series of extremely deep channels allowing the undetected travel of US nuclear armed submarines between the Pacific and Indian Oceans. If this route had been denied the United States, a minimum of eight days would have been added to an undetected journey between the two oceans.[78] In this period, when US officials believed that war in Indo-China threatened their strategic control of South-east Asia, continued friendly relations with Indonesia were extremely important. With an independent East Timor, there was a possibility that the US would have to negotiate with the new administration to allow passage through the straits, especially if the new Law of the Sea proposals then under discussion at the UN excluded underwater transit rights.

Documents released show that President Ford had intelligence evaluations on his desk indicating that the US could have played a role in avoiding bloodshed and war in East Timor as President Suharto was worried over US reaction to Indonesian invasion as late as 20 August 1975.[79] However the strategic importance of

Indonesia and East Timor overrode any moral issues involved.

The Economy

Arms sales

In 1975, US State Department Legal Adviser, George H. Aldrich, estimated that US arms accounted for 90 per cent of those used in the invasion. As one high-ranking Indonesian General replied when asked if US weapons were being used during the invasion of East Timor: 'Of course there were US weapons used. These are the only weapons that we have.'[80]

After the invasion American arms companies increased their sales to Indonesia. Military sales exceeded US$1000 million between 1982 and 1984. These weapons were used in the 1983–84 offensive against Fretilin. Equipment purchased included 12 F-16s, costing US$337 million in 1986.

The war in East Timor has meant continued arms sales to Indonesia. Arms used in East Timor and acknowledged by the US State Department and UK Ministry of Defence include:

- 12 F-16 Fighters
- 16 OV-10 counter-insurgency aircraft
- 45 V-150 armoured cars
- Bell UH-1 helicopters
- Bell S-61 helicopters
- 3 C-130 transport aircraft
- Patrol craft

Also included are various infantry weapons such as M-16 rifles, machine guns, mortars, recoilless rifles, ammunition and extensive communications and support equipment.[81] (See Figure 1.12.)

In April 1978, British Aerospace (BAe) announced an export order to Indonesia for 8 Hawk jet trainer aircraft worth US$300 million and agreed to supply a further 12 by 1990. Dr Peter Carey of Oxford University, commented in 1992 that 'it is well known that these aircraft are readily adaptable for ground attack and counter insurgency operations...some of these have been seen at

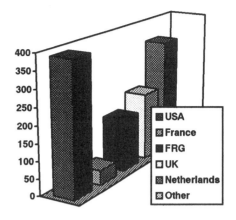

Source: Stockholm International Peace Research Institute (SIPRI) SIPRI arms transfer database, Stockholm, 1993.

Figure 1.12: Western arms sales to Indonesia; total for five year period 1988–92 (US$m)

Baucau airfield in East Timor where they have been used against the resistance'.[82] More recently, BAe was awarded a US$750 million contract for the sale of 24 Hawks, including US$300 million of accessories, with the possibility of a purchase of up to 96 aircraft possible, pending discussion between Indonesia, BAe and Rolls-Royce.[83] These contracts put the UK top of the list of main arms suppliers to Indonesia with over US$1250 million worth of agreed arms sales between 1986 and 1993.[84]

As well as these large arms deals there have been numerous other smaller deals ranging from three contracts worth over US$300 million in 1984, 1985 and 1986 for Rapier Air Defence Systems, to the sale of Parachute Equipment by Irvin GB Ltd, British Leyland armoured reconnaissance vehicles and land rovers.

Private investment

The West realized the gains that could be reaped from Indonesia's favourable political climate and saw an opportunity to benefit from its vast untapped natural resources, flexible labour market and large market potential. A liberalization of trade and investment regulations resulted in a dramatic growth of foreign investment over the last decade from only 37 projects in 1981

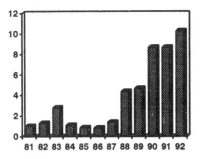

Source: Bank of Indonesia, *Report for the Financial Year 1992–93*, Jakarta, 1993

Figure 1.13: Foreign investment in Indonesia (excluding oil, gas and banking) 1981–92 (US$m)

to over 8750 in 1991 (Figure 1.13).

Since Suharto came to power in 1965, the international community has invested more than US$67 billion, including US$2.71 billion from the United States, US$9.29 billion from Europe, US$1.29 billion from Australia,[85] US$2.54 billion from Great Britain and US$13.068 billion from Japan. [86]

Similarly, G7 exports to Indonesia are considerable (Figure 1.14).

CONCLUSION

Without question, there have been considerable benefits to the international community in allowing the invasion and occupation of East Timor. Any risk of an independent East Timor triggering similar revolts in other parts of Indonesia were averted, and Indonesia remained the West's strongest bulwark against communism in South-east Asia. In addition, hundreds of millions of dollars of arms sales were secured by Western companies with the Indonesian regime, on top of the huge increases in investment that have occurred since Suharto came to power in 1967.

Against these benefits must be weighed the effect the passing of Resolution 384 and the refusal by the Security Council to enforce its conditions has had on the reputation of the UN. While the current state of the UN's reputation cannot be entirely attributed to the events surrounding the invasion of East Timor, without doubt they had some effect in demonstrating the impotence of the UN when it is confronted with a breach of international law on the one hand, and the interests of the Western powerbrokers on the other.

IF THE CONFLICT HAD NOT OCCURRED

Introduction

In this section, the aim is to show how East Timor might have developed if the invasion had not occurred, and how the international community might have benefited from this. Of the many countries in the region, Fiji is one of the most similar to East Timor. It gained its independence in 1970, five years before East Timor and after nearly a hundred years as a British colony. The two countries are almost the same size, both are islands (83 per cent of Fiji's population live on the two largest of its 100 inhabited islands) and both have similar-sized populations. While Fiji lies slightly further south, they have similar climates, suitable for plantation agriculture, and similar terrain; a mountainous interior with agriculture concentrated on the more fertile flat lands near the coast.

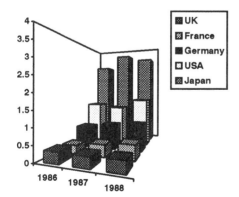

Source: International Monetary Fund (IMF), *Direction of Trade Statistics Yearbook*, 1989

Figure 1.14: Principal G7 exports to Indonesia 1986–88 (US$m)

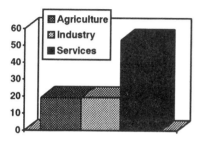

Source: Cole and Hughes, op cit

Figure 1.15: Fiji – percentage of GDP by sector, 1986

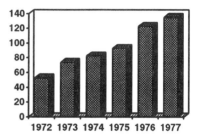

Source: Fiji 8th Development Plan: *Policies and Programmes for Social and Economic Development*, 1980

Figure 1.16: Fiji – foreign capital inflows (US$m) as % of investment 1972–77

East Timor

Fiji had a more developed manufacturing and service base at the time of independence than East Timor. However, while the manufacturing base was seen as unlikely to grow, in recent years the situation has changed enough on the island to encourage more manufacturing sector growth, due mainly to the increase in educated labour.

Fiji's economy at independence in 1970 was composed mainly of services, followed by agriculture and then industry. It can be seen from Figure 1.15 that by 1986, services had still a larger proportion of GDP, while industry had become equal to agriculture. Having managed to diversify its industrial base, and thus develop its export potential, exports rose from US$41.5 million in 1970 to nearly US$261 million in 1987.[87]

East Timor's position just south of the Nusa Tenggarra group of islands which include Flores, Komodo, Lombok and Bali, means it is ideally suited to tourism. However, since 1975 there has been no tourism and very few visitors allowed on the island. Tourism in Fiji brings in high revenues totalling US$123.6 million in 1989.[88]

Fiji has also received foreign investment, especially after independence, when development of its tourist infrastructure was underway (Figure 1.16). There has been no US foreign investment in East Timor since 1975.

At the same time, however, income levels in Fiji have risen only a little in real terms; 0.6 per cent per annum between 1976 and 1986,[89] bringing the per capita income to US$1650 in 1989.[90] It can be seen that while Fiji's development has not been startling by any account, it has allowed the income level of the population to increase to one where it is reasonably affluent by South Pacific standards.

The West

It would be inaccurate simply to juxtapose the development of foreign investment patterns of Fiji, or, for that matter, other provinces of Indonesia with East Timor, in order to present a possible parallel scenario. East Timor is, by all these regions' standards, highly undeveloped. Nevertheless, extrapolations are possible, and may be useful.

East Timor's potential vis-à-vis Western investment lies in four principal areas; mining, oil exploration in the Timor Sea, infrastructural development and tourism. As discussed earlier, the oil industry in the Timor Sea is in the process of being developed, principally because the exploration is based in the Timor Sea, safe from Fretilin's guns.

Because of Fretilin, mainland mining has not been developed by Western companies, and remains a source of considerable potential wealth. It is believed from past geological surveys and explorations for manganese, marble, copper, gold, silver, iron, oil, natural gas and coal that the province's mineral potential is quite

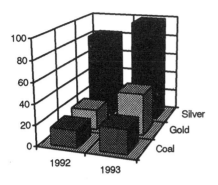

Source: Government of Indonesia, *Indonesia Handbook*, Jakarta, 1994

Figure 1.17: Coal, gold, silver production in Indonesia, 1992–93 (kg)

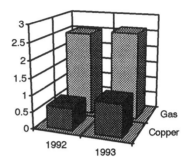

Source: Government of Indonesia, 1994, op cit

Figure 1.18: Copper and gas production in Indonesia, 1992–93 (kg)

substantial.[91] However, investment groups organized by Kadin, the Indonesian Chamber of Commerce and Industry, have so far been shunned by foreign investors because of the ongoing conflict.

An examination of the production of these minerals across Indonesia as a whole reveals some quite marked increases. (See Figures 1.17, 1.18 and Table 1.2.)

These, if extrapolated to East Timor, illustrate a significant potential for development.

Table 1.2: Percentage increase in production of minerals in Indonesia, 1992–93

Mineral	Increase
Natural gas	4.3
Coal	40
Copper	46.6
Gold	105.1
Silver	19.8

Source: Government of Indonesia, op cit 1994

Conclusion

There is undoubtedly considerable development potential in East Timor. Currently, attention is focused on the potential for oil exploration in the Timor Sea. The unstable security situation and the high profile the East Timor conflict has had in the Western media recently, have been a powerful deterrent to Western companies. Should this conflict be resolved, not only would the people of East Timor benefit from an improvement in living standards but the economic potential contained within their nation, assuming equitable distribution, would ensure considerably higher incomes.

REFERENCES

1 Barbedo de Magalhaes, Antonio *East Timor: An International Responsibility*, President's Office, Oporto University, Portugal, February 1992.
2 Mubyarto, Prof et al *East Timor: The Impact Of Integration—An Indonesian Anthropological Study* Gadjah Mada University, Joygakarta, 1990.
3 Taylor, John G, *Indonesia's Forgotten War: The Hidden History of East Timor* Zed Books, London, 1991.
4 Burgel, Dr Helga, 'East Timor' in *Medicine and War* Vol 9 No 2 April–June 1993.
5 Coalition for East Timor, *The Basic Facts*, London, 1993.
6 *Journal of Contemporary Asia*, Vol 11, No 1, 1981
7 US Agency for International Development (USAID) 'East Timor–Indonesia–Displaced Persons', Situation Report No 1, 9 October 1979.
8 Taylor, 1991, op cit.
9 Ibid.
10 *New Internationalist*, No 253.
11 United Nations Development Programme (UNDP) *Human Development Report 1993*, Oxford University Press, Oxford, 1993.
12 Burgel, 1993, op cit.
13 Taylor, 1991, op cit.
14 East Timor Provincial Government, Dili *East Timor Develops*, 1984.
15 Taylor, 1991, op cit.
16 Ibid.
17 Ibid.
18 USAID 'Indonesia - Education and Human Resources', Sector Review Vol I and II, Government of Indonesia, Dept of Educational Research, Jakarta, 1987. Tables 5.8, 5.10, 5.13, 5.17.
19 Ibid.
20 Ibid.
21 Burgel, 1993, op cit.
22 Siddel, Scott 'The United States and Genocide in East Timor' *Journal of Contemporary Asia* Vol 11 No 1, 1981.
23 Taylor, J in *Timor Link* No 23, May 1992.
24 Liddle, J William, 'Pemilu–Pemilu Orde Baru: Pasang Surut Kekusaan Politik 1992, Jakarta' in Aditjondro, George *From Memo to Tutuala: A Kaleidoscope of Environmental Problems in East Timor*, 1993, Satia Wacana Christian University, Salatiga, Central Java.
25 CIIR Comment, *East Timor–An International Responsibility*, April 1992.
26 Taylor, 1991, op cit.
27 *The Guardian* 12 February 1994
28 Taylor, 1991, op cit.
29 UN Document A/47/435 11 September 1992.
30 Reuters press release 20 November 1993.

31 Priests testimony quoted by John Pilger in *The Guardian* 12 February 1994.
32 Coalition for East Timor, op cit.
33 Taylor, 1991, op cit.
34 'Division of Information and Human Rights Education, Geneva', in *TAPOL Bulletin* No 113, October 1992.
35 'The Suppression of Dissent,' Amnesty International Report, 1992.
36 Magalhaes, 1992, op cit.
37 *The Sunday Times* 13 February 1994.
38 'Peace is Possible in East Timor' East Timor - Santa Cruz, 1992.
39 *TAPOL Bulletin*, No 113, October 1992.
40 Amnesty International 'Indonesia East Timor – A New Order? Human Rights in 1992', 13 September 1992
41 Taylor, 1991, op cit.
42 Ibid.
43 Soestaro, M, Hadi 'East Timor: Questions of Economic Viability' in *Unity and Diversity: Regional Development in Indonesia* (Ed. Hal Hill), Singapore 1989.
44 Drew, Jonathan, 'The Economic Development of East Timor since Integration with Indonesia in 1976.' MA Dissertation, School of Oriental and African Studies (SOAS), 1993.
45 Aditjondro, 1993, op cit.
46 Drew, 1993, op cit.
47 Ibid.
48 Soestaro, 1989, op cit.
49 Aditjondro, 1993, op cit.
50 Ibid.
51 Drew, 1993, op cit.
52 Ibid.
53 Ibid.
54 Taylor, 1991, op cit.
55 Angkasa, January 1993
56 Aditjondro, 1993, op cit.
57 Taylor, 1991, op cit.
58 Defert, Gabriel ; *Timor-Est, le Genocide Oublie*, Paris, 1993
59 Taylor, 1991, op cit.
60 CIIR Comment, op cit. The National Council of Maubere Resistance (CNRM) also put the number of Indonesian casualties at 20,000 between the years 1975 and 1980. Inacio Moura, a Timorese exile who left East Timor in December 1987 after working in the provincial Government for several years, estimated that over 15,000 troops had been lost by Indonesia since 1975.
61 TAPOL Bulletin No 87 June, 1988.
62 Aditjondro, 1993, op cit.
63 *Jane's Defence Weekly*, 18 July 1992.

64 Drew, 1993, op cit.
65 Stahl, Max *The Observer Magazine* 'Procession of Death'23/2/92.
66 Drew, 1991, op cit.
67 Asia Partnership for Human Development – *Newsletter* No 22 July/Aug 1983.
68 Drew, 1993, op cit.
69 CIIR Comment, 1992, op cit.
70 Mubyarto, 1990, op cit.
71 Taylor, 1991, op cit.
72 Ibid.
73 Ibid.
74 Curtis, Mark, The West, Indonesia and East Timor (revised text) Coalition for East Timor, London, November 1993.
75 Retboll, Torben; 'The East Timor Conflict and Western Response' *Bulletin of Concerned Asian Scholars* Vol 19 No 1, 1987.
76 *TAPOL Bulletin* No 112, August 1992.
77 Sidell 1981, op cit, and Franke, Richard, W 'East Timor:The Responsibility of the United States,' *Bulletin of Concerned Asian Scholars*, Vol 15 No 2, 1983.
78 Taylor, 1991, op cit.
79 Franke, 1983, op cit.
80 Siddel, 1981, op cit.
81 Curtis, 1993, op cit.
82 Ibid.
83 *The Financial Times* 11 June 1993
84 Stockholm International Peace Research Institute 1986–90 (US$522 million plus US$750 million Hawk deal in 1993).
85 Bank of Indonesia – *Report of the Financial Year 1992/93.*
86 Bank of Indonesia, 1992–3, op cit and TAPOL Indonesia Backgrounder 1992.
87 Bank of Indonesia, 1992–3, op cit.
88 Fiji Bureau of Statistics Current Economic Statistics January 1990.
89 Kasper, W, Bennet, J & Blandy R, *Fiji: Opportunity from Adversity?* Centre for Independent Studies, London, 1988.
90 *World Bank Development Report 1991.*
91 Soesastro, 1989, op cit.

2

THE IRAQ CONFLICT
(1990–)

Gregory Quinn

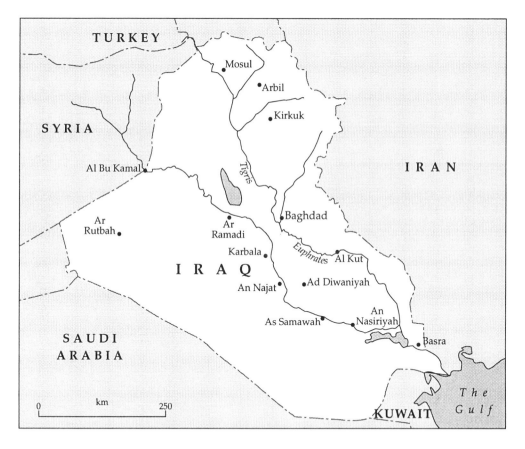

Area (000sq km)	435
Population (m)	19.6
Human Development Index	0.59
Population density (per sq km)	45
Capital	Baghdad

KEY IMPACTS OF THE CONFLICT

ON IRAQ

- At least 56,000 Iraqi soldiers and 3000 civilians were killed. Some estimates range up to 115,000 and 3500 respectively.
- Some 40 tonnes of depleted uranium remain with a potentially harmful effect for 500,000 people. The major problem lies with the long-term effects of this uranium if it gets into the food chain or water table.
- 50,000 people could have a reduced life expectancy due to smoke pollution from the sabotaged oil wells.
- Prior to sanctions the inflation rate stood at a level of 45 per cent. Between August 1990 and January 1991 sanctions caused food prices to jump by 1000 per cent.
- GDP decreased from US$66 billion in 1989 to an incredible US$245 million in 1991.
- The cost of reconstruction is estimated at between US$100–200 billion.
- Infant mortality increased by 100 per cent between 1990 and 1992.
- Forty per cent of schools have been destroyed.
- Approximately 600 bombs, rockets and artillery shells fired daily failed to explode. Between 1.6 and 1.8 million pieces of unexploded ammunition are alleged still to lie in Iraq.

ON KUWAIT

- In Kuwait City, 200 buildings including hotels, parliament, the National Museum, libraries, the Emir's Palace, hospitals, and government offices were set on fire by the Iraqis as they fled.
- In the first five months of occupation, 10,000 Kuwaitis are believed to have been detained, whilst extrajudicial killings may have totalled over 1000.
- A French team clearing 6 kilometres of beach in Kuwait City found 15,000 mines, but as it estimated that it would miss 2 per cent of all mines 300 may be left in the sand.
- An overall figure of between US$50 to 100 billion has been put forward as an estimate for reconstruction costs in Kuwait following the invasion and occupation.
- The Iraqi invasion led to the systematic rape of Kuwaiti women by the invading forces. Hopes that the Muslim army of one Arab country would not mistreat the women of another Arab country were quickly dashed.
- The United States Corps of Engineers estimated that an area of Kuwait equal in size to that of Northern Ireland was covered by oil.
- Kuwait paid US$22 billion to the allies for the war effort.
- Kuwaiti GDP fell from US$24.25 billion in 1989 to US$11.2 billion in 1991 as a result of the war, before rising to US$21.74 billion in 1992.

ON SAUDI ARABIA

- Official Saudi Government estimates say that an oil slick which covered an area of Saudi coast from Abu Ali island to the town of Al-Khadji – a distance of approximately 560 kilometres – contained between 0.5 and 2.5 million barrels of oil The size of the slick can be compared with the Exxon Valdez incident in Prince William Sound, Alaska, in 1989 when 0.25 million barrels of oil went into the sea. Estimates have said that the Saudi coastline will take at least a decade to recover.

- Saudi Arabia must be concerned about the possibility of indigenous or Iran-sponsored Islamic fundamentalism gaining a foothold in Iraq, given the increasingly vulnerable state of the current regime. If this were to be the case, this would pose a direct threat to Saudi Arabia.
- It has been estimated that total Saudi costs associated with the conflict (including such issues as aid payments and contributions to Allied forces) have been not less than US$62 billion.
- In 1991 the Saudis borrowed a total of US$8.5 billion on the international markets – an unprecedented situation. This total included US$7 billion for the Saudi Government and US$1.5 billion for the state-owned oil company.

ON THE WEST

- 148 US soldiers were killed in action and 458 were wounded. Additionally, approximately 55 US aircraft were lost during the war. Forty-seven British servicemen and women were killed during the conflict and 540 injured. In total the RAF lost 7 Tornadoes in training and combat. Two French soldiers were killed.
- The British involvement in the conflict coalition is estimated to have cost US$2.17 billion
- Western companies supplied the necessary equipment for Iraq to build its chemical and missile facilities. Consequently, when the coalition armies faced Iraqi forces after the invasion of Kuwait, they often found themselves confronted by their own technology and equipment.
- The British Overseas Development Agency (ODA) has spent approximately US$100 million on aid to Iraqi civilians between the period April 1991 and June 1994.

INTRODUCTION

Geography

Iraq is mostly marsh and mountain, but areas of fertile land lie between the Tigris and Euphrates rivers. Situated at the top of the Persian Gulf, it shares a long border with Iran, with whom it fought an eight-year war between 1980 and 1988. Until the invasion of Kuwait in 1990 Iraq's major export was oil.

The People

The population is split mainly into three ethnic groups–Shia Muslim, Sunni Muslim, and Kurd. The Shia are the largest single group and mostly inhabit the south of the country; the Sunni are the next largest, followed by the Kurds, who since the end of the war in Kuwait have controlled an autonomous area in the north of the country. Other small minorities include Turcomans, and other Christians.

The Conflict

Iraq and Kuwait had long disputed the ownership of oilfields on the Iraq-Kuwait border and islands in the northern Gulf. Verbal threats continued throughout 1990 and increased in ferocity in July when Iraq accused Kuwait of stealing US$2.4 billion worth of Iraqi oil. Increasingly bellicose, and mistaking US signals as representing ambivalence to a possible invasion of Kuwait, Iraq launched a full-scale assault on its neighbour on 2 August 1990. The US led in the formation of an alliance of Western and Arab countries to defend Saudi Arabia initially, ('Desert Shield'), and then to begin an attack on Iraqi forces to drive them from Kuwait ('Desert Storm'). The air attacks began on 17 January 1991 and the 100-hour ground war began on 24 February 1991. Iraqi forces were routed.

Scope of the Study

This study defines the conflict as events from the invasion of Kuwait on 2 August 1990, the expulsion of Iraqi forces from Kuwait on 28 February 1991, and the consequences of the Kurdish and Shia uprisings. We have chosen to look only at Iraq, Kuwait, Saudi Arabia, the United States, the United Kingdom and France, as these are the countries most directly affected by, or involved in, the 1990–91 conflict. Whilst acknowledging that the effects were more widespread, we hope that the countries chosen serve to illustrate the wide-ranging costs and consequences of the War.

The costs of the conflict have been most obvious in Iraq and Kuwait and hence we concentrate on this issue when looking at these two countries. However, we also look at the benefits of the conflict to the remaining countries.

IRAQ

THE COSTS

Introduction

In the 30 years before the 1990–91 conflict, Iraq had moved from an impoverished, Third World country, to an urban society where healthcare was good, industry was developed, and infrastructure was modern and efficient. This change had been financed by oil revenues which had steadily increased. The 1980–88 war with Iran caused economic difficulties, with res-ources switched from civilian to military projects, but had less of a direct effect on the population. Whilst not doubting there was suffering imposed by the Iran–Iraq war, this conflict has had a far more devastating effect on the standard of living of the Iraqi population.

Development

The war has caused an immediate downgrading of Iraq's development position. Martti Ahtisaari on a mission to Iraq for the UN Secretary-General in March 1991 spoke of Iraq having been bombed back 'to a pre-industrial age'.

Health

Iraqi healthcare standards had been increasing before the 1990–91 conflict. The war and its consequences, however, put a strain on the healthcare system with which it could not cope. Its position was not helped by increased malnutrition and a lack of energy or fresh water supplies due to the Allied bombing of power stations. (see 'Infrastructure' section).

By 1990 more than 90 per cent of the population lived within 5 kilometres of a hospital and infant mortality had fallen from 62 per 1000 in 1985 to 22 per 1000 at the start of 1990.[1] Figures such as these were nearly comparable with those of highly developed Western countries, and the belief was that if investment in healthcare continued, the health of the Iraqi population would further improve. The war had a severe effect on these steadily improving figures. Infant mortality rose from 22 per 1000 in 1990 to 92 per 1000 in 1991.[2] Between 1991 and early 1992 a total of 170,000 under-fives died. This represents a 100 per cent increase in the under-five mortality rate in Iraq.[3] (See Figure 2.1)

The incidence of common, preventable

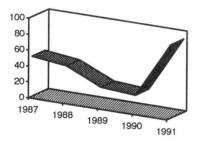

Source: UNICEF 1992, op cit

Figure 2.1: Infant mortality – Iraq (per 1000)

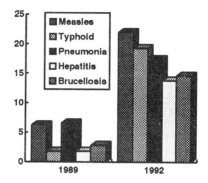

Source: Letter to UN Secretary-General from Ramsey Clark, ex-US Attorney General, 18 February 1993.

Figure 2.2: Incidence of disease – Iraq (number of cases in thousands)

diseases increased dramatically after the war. Malnutrition caused by high food prices and shortages led to an increase in the number of cases of kwashiorkor from 485 in 1990 to 13,744 in 1992, a 2800 per cent increase. The number of cases of another malnutrition disease, marasmus, rose from 5193 in 1990 to 111,477 in 1992, a 2100 per cent increase.

The destruction of water purification facilities and sanctions which prevented water purification chemicals being imported into the country, along with the destruction of sewers and increased incidence of raw, untreated sewage flowing into rivers and streets led to increases in sanitation related diseases: hepatitis cases increased from 1816 in 1989 to 13,776 in 1992, a 700 per cent rise. The cessation of the vaccination programme in January 1991, one of the most developed in countries of Iraq's status, led to the number of measles cases increasing from 6229 in 1989 to 21,823 in 1992, a 300 per cent rise.[4] (See Figure 2.2.)

Many families have become reliant on government-supplied rations, which in 1990 provided approximately 50 per cent of the minimum daily calorie requirement, and in 1991 provided approximately 60 per cent of the minimum recommended World Health Organization daily calorie intake.[5] Despite this, there has been a dramatic drop in the calorie supply. (See Figure 2.3.)

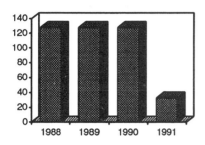

Source: UNICEF, 1992, op cit

Figure 2.3: Calorie supply – Iraq (% of minimum daily calorie requirements)

Despite the fact that sanctions were not meant to apply to medicines or medical equipment, very small amounts of medicine have been imported into the country, and hospitals lack basic spare parts to operate medical equipment. It has been estimated that only one-thirtieth of Iraq's normal drug requirements are allowed to enter the country due to sanctions, and that six months after the end of the war less than half of the medical equipment was operable.

Education

The education system also suffered greatly from the war. By 1992 the war and subsequent Kurdish and Shia uprisings had destroyed approximately 5500 educational institutions, 40 per cent of the total.[6] The completion of 1350 schools was halted by the Ministry of Education due to civil uprisings and sanctions.[7]

Economic hardship has also caused a fivefold increase in the primary school drop-out rate, from a pre-war figure of 3 per cent to 15 per cent in 1992.[8] What effect this increased drop-out rate will have on the future is not hard to understand. Fewer people will have the skills necessary to push Iraq's position in the UN Development Programme (UNDP) development index higher. An increasingly ill-educated population will further hamper future Iraqi attempts to regain its pre-war position.

Civil and Political Rights

The numbers of Iraqi casualties caused by Allied attacks have been a great source of discussion. Some sources cite 70,000–115,000 military and 3000 civilian deaths as a direct result of the war.[9] Others estimate approximately 56,000 military and 3,500 civilian deaths as a direct result of the war.[10] Indirect civilian deaths caused by the civil uprisings and infrastructural damage have been put at between 100,000–150,000 to the end of 1991.[11]

After the war, encouraged by statements by then American President George Bush, the Kurds in the north and the Shia in the south rose up against the regime of Saddam Hussein. The rebellion was brutally crushed. Torture, repression, and mass extrajudicial killings occurred in the Kurdish area and civilians fleeing to Turkey and Iran were also bombarded by Iraqi forces. Refugees interviewed by Amnesty International talked of civilians being executed, used as 'human shields', and crushed by tanks.[12] Saddam is also using drought and hunger to crush the rebellions.

By any means possible

West of the River Tigris, dams and embankments have been constructed to block water from entering the marshlands of southern Iraq. Lush marshlands, dating back thousands of years, have been converted into vast expanses of dry cracked mud. Fish and wildlife have died, as have livestock, thereby leaving no livelihood for the marsh people. Severe hunger and thirst lead to debilitating illnesses and death. Dried ground allows Saddam's forces to advance, shell settlements and burn down or bulldoze entire villages. Debilitation of the people makes it harder for them to flee to safety. Every single person escaping from the Marshes has immediate relatives who have been killed or who have disappeared. Of the approximately 500,000 residents of the marshlands at the end of the conflict, only a few scattered handfuls remain.

The people of Iraq are desperate for food. Local production of rice, wheat and oats, as well as fruits from orchards, would help in the fight against hunger. Instead, while Saddam berates the world community for supposedly not allowing enough food into Iraq, and alleging all along that his draining of the marshes is purely to reclaim land for agricultural purposes, he is deliberately destroying important farm-lands, either by drying them up or by flooding them. Agricultural lands west of the Tigris, such as al-Majar, al-Salman, al-'Adl, al-Maimouna, have been made useless by the drying of the region. More recently, farmlands east of the Tigris, such as al-Kahla' and al-Msharrah, have been inundated by as much as 2.5 metres of water.[13]

Evidence suggests that there is a concerted policy to destroy the Marsh Arabs. A videotape of the Iraqi Prime Minister made in 1991, in which he instructs the army to wipe out three specific Marsh Arab tribes has been widely broadcast. The policy of wiping out the Marsh Arabs had been in existence since before the war as the Iraqi documents from 1989 published by the UN Special Rapporteur in February 1993 show.[14]

The northern Kurds who are still resident in Iraq have suffered due to the international sanctions on Iraq, and due to an economic blockade of their region by Iraqi troops after their withdrawal from the region in September/October 1991. This blockade was tightened in early 1992 and the Iraqi Army is alleged to have used a deliberate policy of harassment to clear the villages along this de facto border of 200,000 inhabitants.

The Economy

When the Allies began their air attacks on Iraq in January 1991 one of their main targets was Iraqi oil-refining and oil-producing, infrastructure.

The imposition of sanctions in August 1990 which prevented the sale of Iraqi oil coupled with the destruction caused by the Allied air attacks depleted Iraqi GDP to an incredible US$245m in 1992 from a peak of US$66.2 billion in 1989 (assuming the more accurate black market rate of exchange of US$1=ID35 and not the official rate of US$1=ID0.31). (See Figure 2.4.)

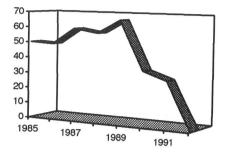

Source: EIU Country Report: *Iraq*, Fourth Quarter, 1993

Figure 2.4: GDP – Iraq (US$bn)

This dramatic decrease in GDP has obviously greatly affected the population. GDP per capita has collapsed from a peak of US$3,578 in 1989 to US$13 (assuming black market exchange rate) in 1992.[15] The government therefore lacks funds to invest in infrastructure and services destroyed during the Allied air and ground attacks. Sanctions, and continued Iraqi refusal to accept UN conditions for the sale of oil, ensure that the government receives little income. The only sales of oil have been unofficial and have been the product of illicit sales across the Iraq-Jordan border, in contravention of UN sanctions. These sales are estimated to have netted Iraq US$2 billion between March 1991 and March 1992.[16]

The Allied destruction of many of Iraq's manufacturing capabilities has caused much suffering and a large increase in the number of unemployed. The unemployed totals have also risen due to the demobilization of many Iraqi soldiers. In 1990 the International Institute for Strategic Studies said that Iraq had an army of approximately 1 million; in 1992 it said that the army totalled 383,000.[17]

The economic position of ordinary Iraqis has not been helped by rampant inflation since the end of the war. Prior to sanctions the inflation rate stood at a level of 45 per cent.[18] Between August 1990, and January 1991 sanctions caused food prices to jump by 1000 per cent[19] and in 1991, inflation stood at 1546 per cent, a state of hyperinflation.[20]

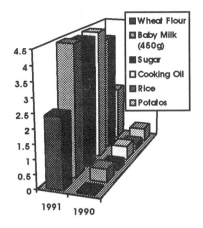

4.5
4
3.5
3
2.5
2
1.5
1
0.5
0

■ Wheat Flour
■ Baby Milk (450g)
■ Sugar
□ Cooking Oil
■ Rice
■ Potatos

1991   1990

Source: Dréze and Gaidar, op cit

Figure 2.5: Food prices – Iraq (ID per kg)

Compensation claims against Iraq (mostly by Kuwaitis and immigrant workers affected by the invasion of Kuwait) were estimated to reach US$100 billion in 1991 according to one UN official. This would mean that Iraq would have to pay compensation for 20 years after it resumed oil sales.[21] By May 1994 it was estimated that an initial compensation payment of US$2.7 billion had been made from Iraq's frozen foreign assets. If Iraq were made to repay all this compensation then the future development prospects for it are bleak.

Infrastructure

Infrastructure was, after Iraqi armed forces, the most important target for Allied attack. One hundred and thirty-four bridges were destroyed in Baghdad and south-east Iraq in a concerted effort to prevent the movement of troops and war equipment. Once the war ended, this destruction seriously affected the ability of the Iraqi people to move around the country, and prevented the movement of civilian goods and material.[22]

Estimates have been made that the total cost of reconstruction in Iraq is somewhere between US$100 billion and US$200 billion.[23] The July 1991 UN Mission of Prince Sadruddin Aga Khan reported that

Iraq needed approximately US$22 billion over one year to restore its civilian economy and provide services. US$6.85 billion over one year was estimated to be needed to provide greatly reduced services such as: two-fifths of the pre-war per capita level of clean drinking water and sewage treatment; imports for health services; food imports to bring the supply per capita to that recommended by the World Food Programme for disaster stricken populations; resources to restore one half of the pre-war power generation capacity; and the repair of some oil facilities.[24]

Immediately after the end of the war, oil refining, which had been repeatedly targeted by the Allies, was at 3 per cent of its pre-war level.[25] The Iraqi power generation system was also heavily targeted.[26] Immediately after the end of the war power generation stood at 4 per cent of its pre-war level. The severe shortage of power caused many problems for the population. Heating could not be guaranteed in the winter, nor could any sort of cooling system (equally important) in the summer. More seriously, hospitals were unable to sterilize instruments or operate vital equipment. Water purification plants were unable to operate, which led to contaminated water being used for all tasks from washing to cooking. Irrigation of crops was hampered due to the lack of electricity for water pumps and subsequently the next harvest suffered, increasing further the food shortages.[27]

The sewage disposal system was also damaged by Allied bombing. In south Iraq in August 1991 it was estimated that 30 per cent of hospital water sources were faecally contaminated, which led to increased disease in those facilities designed to prevent them.[28] In other parts of Baghdad and the south the destruction of sewers and lack of power for sewage treatment centres led to raw sewage being discharged into rivers which would be used by the population for daily chores.[29] From Baghdad alone it was estimated that approximately 70 million litres of untreated water were being pumped into the Tigris every hour.[30]

The destruction of power plants which supplied water purification plants has led to a sharp decrease in the amount of potable water available to the population. In 1992 it has been reported that 50 per cent of the water supply was polluted and therefore unfit to drink.[31]

The Environment

The war had an enormous effect on the Iraqi environment. Tonnes of munitions lie unexploded on the battlefield and are still injuring innocent civilians. According to one report approximately 600 bombs, rockets and artillery shells fired daily will have failed to explode.[32] An overall total of between 1.6m and 1.8 million unexploded submunitions are alleged still to lie in the area, according to William Arkin of Greenpeace.[33] A clearance operation has taken place in Kuwait, but it is not known if this has happened in Iraq. There have been reports from Iraq of many injuries caused by unexploded ordnance and mines. Iraqi Kurdistan is also believed to contain approximately 9 million mines left over from the Iran–Iraq war and the mining of the Turkish border during the conflict.[34]

An additional hazard is alleged to exist from depleted uranium weapons which were used to destroy Iraqi armour, and which now lie in what was the battle area. A secret UK Atomic Energy Authority report is cited as saying that 40 tonnes of depleted uranium remain in Iraq and Kuwait with a potentially harmful effect for 500,000 people.[35] The major problem lies with the long-term effects of this uranium if it gets into the food chain or water table.[36]

The Iraqi army, in destroying approximately 742 Kuwaiti oil wells, could have begun a chain of events which will lead to much suffering amongst the region's population. The effects of the gases released from the fires must be huge. Carcinogenic gases were estimated to be tens of times above the recognized World Health Organisation (WHO) safety limits nine months after the end of the war. One Harvard doctor has estimated that 50,000 people in Iraq and Kuwait would have a

reduced life expectancy due to the gases, whilst another has said that mortality in Kuwait and south Iraq could increase by 10 per cent because of the oil smoke pollution alone. Mystery wasting diseases are affecting children in south Iraq and no adequate explanation has been given as to their cause.[37]

The draining of the marshes by the Iraqi Government has been condemned as 'ecocide'. As well as the humanitarian aspects of this action, many species of wildlife found only in the marshes will be destroyed by the draining process. By May 1993, of the 20,000 square kilometres of the marshes, over 7500 had already been drained. This draining has been due to the construction of a myriad of canals which intercept the rivers which used to fill the marshes.[38]

CONCLUSION

The above catalogues the misery which the people of Iraq currently suffer. The healthcare system, the power system, the sanitation system, are close to collapse. The aid programmes continue only because of funding from non-governmental and humanitarian organizations. With an economy which has been devastated so absolutely, the population can expect to bear the burden of the Gulf war for many decades to come. Long-term problems can also be seen with the decline in numbers in education which will lead to a less skilled workforce, and the effects of environmental damage caused by both Allied and Iraqi actions during the war.

KUWAIT

THE COSTS

Introduction

The invading Iraqi forces encountered little resistance from an ill-prepared and ill-equipped Kuwaiti army. Any Kuwaiti army resistance was soon overcome by the sheer weight of Iraqi numbers.

The Iraqi occupation was marked by abuse of the population, destruction of buildings, and the looting of any items considered valuable. When Iraqi vehicles were attacked on the road to Basra at the end of the ground war, they were found to contain any items which could be transported.

An overall figure of between US$50 and US$100 billion has been put forward as an estimate for reconstruction costs in Kuwait following the invasion and occupation. Iraqi destruction was so widespread and indiscriminate that it is difficult to put an exact figure on reconstruction costs.[39]

Civil and Political Rights

There is no doubt that serious Iraqi abuses occurred during its occupation, and Amnesty International documents cases of torture, extrajudicial killings, and illegal arrests carried out by the Iraqi regime. Whilst figures were difficult to obtain, 10,000 Kuwaitis are believed to have been detained in the first five months of occupation, whilst extrajudicial killings may have totalled over 1000.[40] In the first days of the invasion military personnel, other Arabs, Iraqi exiles, and Westerners were rounded up by the Iraqis and some were sent to Iraq. Kuwaiti resistance activity led to widespread arrests, torture, and summary executions.[41]

In 1993 the Kuwaiti government handed a list of 610 missing Kuwaitis who are believed to be held in Iraq to the Iraqi government who deny having any knowledge of such hostages.[42] A report by the International Committee for Solidarity with Kuwaitis Missing and Held Prisoner of War says that 627 Kuwaitis are still held in Iraq.[43] After Martii Ahtisaari, the UN Undersecretary General for Administration and Management visited Kuwait at the end of March 1991 he accused Iraq of making 'a deliberate attempt to extinguish Kuwait'.

Abuses of Kuwaitis by Iraqi occupation forces

There were three officers in the interrogation room when I went in. One asked the questions, another took notes and the third stood by the door, holding a gun. I was asked for my nationality card. Then the officer asked me, 'Are you happy with the situation [ie. the situation in Kuwait] in which you find yourselves?' I replied: 'Yes, we are fine'. The officer then said, 'We are here to help you in the uprising'. When I replied that there had been no uprising, the officer standing by the door hit me on the head with his rifle. I was immediately taken to another room where I was subjected to torture for about one hour. They applied electricity to my fingers and genitals, and I was beaten with sticks. My friend whom I had seen earlier was brought into the room. One of the officers said 'Execute them', but another officer replied, 'No, only one of them'. So they shot my friend there and then, in front of me. They shot me in my left leg. I received no treatment for the wound until my release five days later.[44]

The Iraqi invasion led to the systematic rape of Kuwaiti women by the invading forces. Hopes that the Muslim army of one Arab country would not mistreat the women of another Arab country were quickly dashed. It is estimated that 1,000 Kuwaiti women were raped in Iraqi detention centres which were also used for torture. Kuwaiti doctors estimated that approximately 300 pregnancies occurred because of these rapes. The belief is that the actual number of rapes was much higher but that many have gone unreported due to family shame and the perceived stigma of rape which would affect a woman's future marriage prospects. Many women fled to Egypt or the Philippines for abortions. Rape has been kept silent, leading to few court cases. Families are against publicizing a crime which they see as having brought shame on to their families.[45]

The non-Kuwaiti population was vital to the economic success of Kuwait.

Palestinians, Jordanians and others did many of the menial jobs which Kuwaitis refused to do. In 1985 out of a total population of 1.697 million, 1.016 million (59.9 per cent) were non-Kuwaiti and only 0.681m (40.1 per cent) were classed as Kuwaiti.[46]

Abuses of Jordanians/Palestinians and others by Kuwaitis after the liberation

Palestinian Usama Suhail Hussain 'disappeared' for nearly one month following his arrest at the end of February 1991. His relatives then located him at the Juveniles Prison (Sijn al-Ahdath), but they were not allowed to see him and he remained in incommunicado detention until July 1991, after he had been tried and sentenced by the martial law court in June 1991 for working during the occupation at the Iraqi-run newspaper 'al-Nida'. He was sentenced to death but this was later commuted to life imprisonment. He is said to have been tortured with electric shocks, beaten repeatedly and burned with cigarettes, and is alleged to have been threatened with further ill-treatment if he mentioned the torture during his trial. He is currently being held at Kuwait Central Prison.

Palestinian Iyad 'Aqrabawi, 13 years old 'disappeared' after his arrest along with three young men at Sabhan petrol station at the beginning of March 1991. Armed Kuwaiti civilians were said to have controlled the petrol stations at the time. On about 10 March 1991 he was found dead in the street in al-Khaldiyya, showing signs of having been beaten. His identity card was found on his body. He had been shot through the head.

Palestinian student Muhammad Shawkat Yusuf was arrested on 19 May 1991 by armed Kuwaiti civilians and subsequently taken to al-Nugra police station, where he may have been killed. According to reports, his body was taken from the police station to al-Sabah Hospital mortuary on 23 May 1991. His body was discovered on 25 May 1991 in a rubbish dump in al-Jabiriyya. His eyes had been gouged out and there was a bullet hole in his cheek.[48]

After liberation many Kuwaitis believed that the Palestinians and many other foreign workers had collaborated with the

Iraqis and had to be punished. The Palestinians were singled out for mistreatment by the Kuwaiti authorities and many were convicted at trials which Amnesty International has said were unfair partly due to the fact that many defendants were not allowed access to lawyers or family.[47]

In February 1994 Amnesty reports suggested that 120 people were still being held in prison in Kuwait serving sentences for collaboration after unfair trials. Reports of torture being used by the Kuwaiti authorities continued to appear despite claims by the Kuwaiti Crown Prince in May 1991 that he would move to rid the Kuwaiti police force of 'bad elements'.[49]

The Economy

The effect of the war on the Kuwaiti economy is readily demonstrated. Kuwaiti GDP fell from US$24.25 billion in 1989 to US$11.2 billion in 1991 as a result of the war, before rising to US$21.74 billion in 1992 (Figures 2.6 and 2.7). This recovery was mainly due to a massive international operation to repair the damaged oil wells, plus a Kuwaiti push to increase oil production, despite possible damage to reserves.[50]

Iraq attempted to sabotage 810 of Kuwait's 1080 oilwells. Of these 742 were set on fire, damaging 5 per cent beyond repair and burning an estimated 3 per cent of oil reserves.[51] The cost to the Kuwaiti

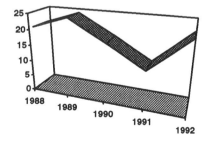

Source: EIU Reports 1993, op cit

Figure 2.6: GDP – Kuwait ($bn)

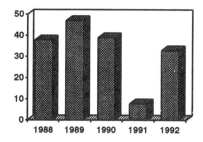

Source: EIU Reports, 1990, 1993, op cit

Figure 2.7: Exports – Kuwait (% GDP)

government of capping these wells and repairing other oil facilities came to US$1.5 billion.[52] Kuwaiti oil production fell from a peak figure of 2.04 million barrels per day in 1990 to an estimated 0.19 million barrels in 1991, before recovering to 1.05 million barrels per day in 1992.[53]

Kuwait paid US$22 billion to the Allies for the war effort.[54] Of this figure the biggest amount went to the United States (US$13.5 billion) whilst the United Kingdom received an estimated US$660 million in cash from the Kuwaiti government.[55] Between 1990 and 1993, Kuwait purchased US$3.8 billion worth of military equipment from the United States.[56] This represents a 72.6 per cent increase in the 1986–89 period.[57]

These large amounts, a desire not to liquidate all overseas assets, and the massive reconstruction needs led Kuwait to borrow on the international credit market for the first time in its history in October 1991. A loan of US$5.5 billion was negotiated to be repaid over a five-year period beginning in 1995.[58]

Infrastructure

The Iraqi occupation caused major infrastructural damage. Soldiers plundered, looted, burned and destroyed many buildings, mainly in Kuwait City. Two hundred buildings in Kuwait City, including hotels, parliament, the National Museum, libraries, the airport, the Emir's Palace, hospitals, and government offices were set on fire as the Iraqis fled.[59] Medical,

oil, and power facilities were among the main targets for Iraqi destruction. (See Table 2.1).

Table 2.1: Assessment of major damage to Kuwait's infrastructure

Infrastructure	Cost (US$bn)
Oil industry	5
Electrical system	1
Ports, airport and national airline	2
Road transport fleet (public and private)	5
Telecommunications network	1
Radio, TV and press services	0.5
Housing sector	2.5
Hotels	0.5
Wholesale and retail establishments	1
Other urban infrastructure (eg government buildings, recreation centres)	0.5
TOTAL	19

Source: Report to the UN Secretary-General by a United Nations Mission led by Mr Abdulrahim A Farah, assessing the scope and nature of damage inflicted on Kuwait's infrastructure during the Iraqi occupation (S/22535)

The Environment

The Kuwaiti environment was subjected to extensive damage due to both Allied and Iraqi actions. Most damage occurred as a consequence of the Iraqi destruction of over 700 oilwells, but Allied bombings also released oil into the Gulf and greatly affected the desert landscape, especially in Saudi Arabia.[60]

The health effects of the oil fires have been much debated. The main problems have arisen from the fact that no coordinated examination of the situation which occurred after the war, and no valid data from before the war, existed with which to make comparisons. The high concen-trations of carcinogenic substances in the air are bound to have had some effect on the population's health but no firm conclusions can be reached. The general consensus is that the oil smoke pollution will have caused long-term effects not yet apparent.[61]

The smoke produced by the oilwell fires led to the largest single loss of Allied life on 21 March 1991 when more than 90 Senegalese soldiers were killed as their plane crashed in these smoke clouds.[62]

The extinguishing of the oil fires did not end the pollution caused by this Iraqi sabotage. Whilst smoke pollution ceased, the uncapped oilwells continued to gush oil onto the desert landscape. Those sent in to cap the wells were unable to keep up with those who extinguished the fires. Huge lakes of oil formed in the desert. The World Conservation Monitoring Centre in Cambridge even suggested that burning wells ultimately caused less pollution damage than unburning gushers.[63] In November 1991 the United States Corps of Engineers estimated that an area of Kuwait equal in size to that of Northern Ireland was covered by oil.[64] Although the Kuwaiti government has now cleared up most of this oil, the fact that it lay on the desert surface will prove to be a danger in the future. It will have covered vegetation, preventing growth; and animals, especially cattle, will have ingested oil, leading to a health risk to anyone eating the meat.[65] Most importantly, it will probably have leached into the ground water, contaminating it with dangerous compounds.[66] What contamination of the water and food supply has occurred as a result of these oil lakes is unknown as no studies have been conducted into the possible long-term effects.

In the early stages of the recovery operation in Kuwait, minefields hampered the activities of those seeking to extinguish the oil fires; at later stages, however, the oil lakes were a dangerous distraction for those who sought to clear Iraqi mines and defuse munitions. The oil has flooded ammunition bunkers and covered minefields, making a dangerous job even more difficult.[67] Mine clearance operations have managed to clear most of Kuwait City, but no operation can be 100 per cent successful and some mines have been missed. A French team clearing four miles of beach in Kuwait City found 15,000 mines, but as it estimated that it would miss 2 per cent of all mines, 300 were left in the beach, resulting in it not being reopened by the end of 1991.[68] By the middle of November 1991 175 square kilometres of land were claimed to have been cleared of more than 20,000 unexploded devices.[69]

A low estimate put the number of mines in Kuwait at 500,000; higher estimates say Iraq planted millions. A British Royal Engineers major said in 1991 that he believed the clear-up operation would take twenty years, not two as the Kuwaiti Government said.[70] Up to January 1992 1000 people are believed to have been injured by mines which still remain in Kuwait City; additionally, live shells and munitions still constitute a danger to many, especially children.[71]

CONCLUSION

The situation in Kuwait is now returning to what it was pre-war, with oil providing the Kuwaiti wealth. The physical damage has been, or is being, repaired. The people have, however, been greatly affected by the invasion psychologically, given the brutal nature of the Iraqi occupation, in which the civilian population were often deliberately and actively targeted. The government's financial situation has worsened due to the need to borrow for reconstruction, to finance arms purchases, and to pay the Allies. The fall in the price of oil has further hit revenues from Kuwait's most important export. However, overseas investments are huge and most Kuwaitis are still supported by government subsidies on basic foodstuffs and commodities.

SAUDI ARABIA

THE COSTS

Introduction

Saudi Arabia was the staging post for Allied operations in the conflict. American forces were originally sent there in the days after the Iraqi invasion of Kuwait to defend the kingdom from any possible Iraqi attack. Saudi Arabia formed the main base for air operations against Iraqi forces from 17 January 1991, and for ground operations during the 100-hour war from 24 February 1991. Before the Iraqi invasion of Kuwait the Saudis attempted to mediate in the dispute between Kuwait and Iraq, but without success.

The Economy

The financial cost of the war has proven to be a burden on the Saudi economy. Imm-ediately after the war began the Saudi government pledged US$13.5 billion to the United States to cover the costs of the war.[72] Saudi government estimates show that in 1990 the kingdom made extra payments of US$20 billion due to the war, and in 1991 extra payments of US$35 billion. These figures included aid to front-line states and increased military expenditure.[73] One other source has said that the Saudi government paid not less than US$62 billion in total in costs for the war,[74] whilst another has said that spending associated with the Gulf crisis equalled US$49.7 billion.[75]

The large amounts paid affected the fiscal situation of the kingdom. Despite the fact that the Saudis increased oil output to cover the loss of Iraqi supplies, the costs involved in fighting the war far exceeded the increased income from oil sales.[76] The figures for Saudi GDP are deceptive as they show a rise from US$81.2 billion in 1989 to US$110.97 billion in 1992.[77]

However, the increase in costs caused by the war and the increased arms sales offset increases in GDP. Oil sale profits were US$15 billion higher than pre-crisis expect-ations, but the crisis imposed unexpected costs far exceeding this figure.[78] This led to an unprecedented situation in 1991 when the Saudis borrowed a total of US$8.5 billion; US$7 billion of this was for the Saudi government, whilst the remaining US$1.5 billion was for the state-owned oil company, Aramco.[79] In 1992 the deficit amounted to 9.2 per cent of GDP, twice the comparable figure for the United States.[80]

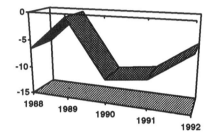

Source: EIU Reports, 1993, op cit

Figure 2.9: Trade deficit – Saudi Arabia ($USb)

The Saudis spent approximately US$14.5 billion on defence and rearmament in 1992.[81] Since the conflict, the value of arms sales agreements between Saudi Arabia and the US has risen dramatically, from US$4.1 billion between 1986–89 to US$30.4 billion between 1990 and 1993.[82] In the five years from 1993 the Saudis are expected to spend over US$20 billion on

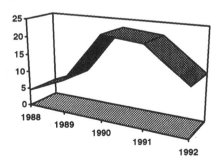

Source: EIU Reports, 1993, op cit

Figure 2.8: GDP growth rate – Saudi Arabia (%)

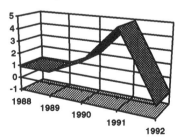

Source: EIU Reports, 1993, op cit

Figure 2.10: Inflation rate – Saudi Arabia (%)

imported weapons.[83] Since the end of the 1990–91 conflict the Saudis have ordered US$25 billion worth of American weapons alone.[84] The country's financial difficulties are leading to calls to cut back on this expenditure or reschedule the payments.[85]

The Environment

The main costs to the Saudi environment were caused by the oil slick that travelled down the Gulf from Kuwait and by the Allied presence in the desert. In addition it can be assumed that smoke from the burning oilwells in Kuwait has had an effect on the population of Saudi Arabia.

Official Saudi government estimates say that the slick contained between 0.5 million and 2.5 million barrels of oil.[86] The size of the slick can be shown by the fact that the Exxon Valdez incident in Prince William Sound, Alaska, in 1989 put 0.25 million barrels of oil into the sea. The slick covered an area of Saudi coast from Abu Ali island to the town of Al-Khafji, a distance of approximately 560 kilometres.[87]

The long-term effects of the oil slick have been disputed. Most opinions suggest that the bulk of oil was washed ashore as a thick mousse which covered flat areas up 100 metres inland.[88] Saltmarshes and mangrove swamps which are sheltered and provide valuable feeding grounds for many species of marine life were greatly affected due to the fact that they tend to trap the oil.[89] Estimates have said that these areas will take at least a decade to recover from the effects of the oil.[90]

The Saudi government spent most effort during the war on protecting desalination plants and industrial areas from the effects of the oil slicks. This left many beaches and animal habitats exposed, and consequently they suffered much damage.[91] Total bird mortality has been estimated at 15,000–30,000, mostly caused by smothering.

Finally, the Allied presence led to large amounts of rubbish, sewage and toxic materials being produced. Estimates put the total amount of sewage at 205–245 million litres. All this rubbish, sewage, etc. was buried in sand pits. In the long-term it is not inconceivable that some of these materials will leak into the desert soil and eventually contaminate the water table.[92]

Refugees

The immediate aftermath of the invasion led to increased tension between Yemen and Saudi Arabia over the latter's perception that Yemen was supporting Iraq. This led to the expulsion and harassment of many Yemenis, who were encouraged to leave the country. By the end of 1990 800,000 Yemenis had fled Saudi Arabia back to Yemen.[93] This large number of returnees led to a 7 per cent increase in the population of Yemen, and a 6 per cent decrease in the population of Saudi Arabia.[94] Despite the fact that most of the Yemeni community was self-contained, the loss of such a large proportion of the population in Saudi Arabia caused a decrease in domestic demand for goods and services, and an increase in the demand for foreign (particularly Asian and Egyptian) labour to make up for the lost workforce.[95]

By late 1993 approximately 23,000 Iraqi refugees remained in Saudi Arabia.[96]

Political Costs

Since the end of the conflict the Saudi government has come under pressure to improve democracy and accountability in the country, not least from the numbers of intellectuals returning from foreign education. Critics see the present system as one where over 3000 members of the Royal family are free to act as they wish. Discontent with the regime has increased as the country's economic situation has worsened. As the economic situation remains fragile due to the low oil price of US$13 a barrel and the extravagant expenditure on armaments, the Saudi government may be forced to reassess the unwritten agreement between it and the population of 'no representation equals no taxation'.[97] Such a reassessment could undermine the unquestioned right of the King to continue in control.

By late 1993 King Fahd, responding to public and international pressure, began to institute a narrow set of political reforms. A structure of regional government was established which included the creation of regional councils. King Fahd's choices for the members of these councils have been praised and suggestions have been made that the councils will have more power than originally assumed.[98] A Consultative Council (*majlis*) was appointed in August 1993, finally coming into operation in January 1994. Questions asked about this new system included whether or not it would become an institutionalized pro-government lobby, or if it would promote public debate. The King is known to favour the former option.[99]

Strategic Costs

Despite obvious relief at seeing the demise of Saddam's army as an effective fighting force and thus the possible threat of invasion averted, Saudi Arabia is left with a number of considerable strategic concerns. Firstly, Saddam Hussein remains in power, and as the sanctions bite, is believed to be becoming increasingly desperate. Given their unequivocal support for the war against Hussein, coupled with their geographic proximity, it would not be surprising if the Saudis felt concerned about the possibility of a move against them by Saddam, whose military capability is being rebuilt. Moreover, given Iraq's highly unstable state, Saudi Arabia must be concerned about the possibility of indigenous or Iran-sponsored Islamic fundamentalism gaining a foothold. If this were to be the case, it would pose a direct threat to Saudi Arabia, and would be of enormous concern to the West. Thus, Saudi Arabia still has a potentially dangerous neighbour. It is perhaps unsurprising that they are currently involved in massive purchases of arms.

THE BENEFITS

Saudi actions in the conflict led to it consolidating its position as a strong regional leader, as well as showing that strong Arab countries do not pose a threat to Western interests. Despite having to rely on the West for military protection, it was the fact that the Saudis were so closely involved in the planning and operation of the war which ensured that other Arab states remained in the coalition. The perception has been that the Saudis have long been the West's closest ally in the Arab world. The US has continued to supply weapons to the Saudis throughout the 1980s despite Israeli condemnation, and when the Americans sought financial and political support for the recent Arab-Israeli peace process they turned to the Saudis for this support.

The Saudi role in the war, and the importance the West placed in it as a regional power, ensured that there would be little Western governmental pressure for political reform.

Finally, the Saudis gained economically from increasing oil production to make up for that lost with the withdrawal of Iraqi supplies. Saudi oil production increased from 5.16m barrels per day in 1989 to 8.41m barrels per day.[100] In 1990 the kingdom received increased oil profits due to the war, which totalled US$15 billion.[101] In 1992 Saudi Arabia produced 3.25m barrels of oil per day more than it had done in 1989; this indicates an extra daily oil income of US$65 million (assuming an oil price of US$20 per barrel in 1992). The kingdom acknowledges that when Iraq returns it will have to cut its oil quota, but it is unwilling to do so until then. The belief is that if it refuses to cut its quota until Iraq returns to the market it will be able to cut from a higher position and thus end up with a larger quota than it originally had before the invasion of Kuwait.

CONCLUSION

The Saudis were essential to the prosecution of the war. Saddam tried to bring about the collapse of the coalition by linking his fight against the West with the Palestinian problem, and by attacking Israel with Scuds in an attempt to provoke retaliation. Without the continued support of the Saudis the Allies would have been unable to hold the coalition forces together during this Iraqi pressure.

With the invasion of Kuwait Saudi Arabia had little option but to defend itself by calling for support from its Western allies. However, as has been shown, the defence of Saudi Arabia was extremely costly. Financially the country is facing great difficulties; as these economic difficulties continue so pressure for increased political freedom will continue. government spending will have to be cut back, to ensure that the budget deficits do not become crippling. Whether or not state subsidies and lack of taxes can continue indefinitely is open to debate.

THE WEST

THE COSTS

Introduction

This section looks at the cost of conflict to the US, UK and France as these were the three countries which formed the basis of the Allied forces which fought against Iraq. In addition they have been the countries which have benefited most since the end of the war.

In the decade before the Iraqi invasion of Kuwait, the United States and the countries of NATO had supported Iraq in its war against fundamentalist Iran. When the Iran–Iraq war ended in 1988 this support continued as the United States wished to ensure that there would be a bulwark keeping Iran in check. Such Western support for Iraq continued until

Iraq invaded Kuwait in August 1990.

The American contribution to the Allied effort in the conflict was the largest of any nation. An American commanded the Allied effort and decisions concerning the conduct of the war remained in American hands.

The US, UK and France had all been involved in the arming of the Iraqi army and the supply of equipment to allow Iraqi development and production of chemical and nuclear weapons, and missiles, especially in the late 1980s. For example in the period 1985–92 the major Western European countries exported arms worth approximately US$4.1 billion to the Iraqi government.[102] Whilst the Soviets were also a major arms supplier in the 1980s, suffice it to say that the Iraqi military machine would not have been as well armed as it was but for the considerable assistance given by Western countries in terms of equipment and training.

The Economy

The United States

The US Budget Director, Richard Darman, estimated in 1991 that the military operation in Kuwait cost the US US$61 billion. As foreign pledges totalled approximately US$54 billion, the actual cost to the US was approximately US$7 billion.[103] Some of this cost would be absorbed in the existing budget.[104] Some estimates say that the war only cost the US US$45 billion, and that as it received US$53 billion in contributions it made a profit of US$8 billion. The US$61 billion figure was said by Congress to be too high as it was based on an assumption that all destroyed equipment would be replaced, which would not necessarily be the case.[105] The difference in figures from different sources only serves to show how difficult monetary assessment of military activities is.

In the first four months of 1991 the US provided assistance to refugees and displaced persons worth US$53m. America took an active role in 'Operation Provide

Hope' to aid the Kurds in Turkey and northern Iraq. Up to 16 April 1991, 8600 US forces had been committed to this cause. The US had dropped 1197 tons of aid from military planes.[106] From October 1991 to September 1992 (fiscal year 1992) the United States admitted 3442 refugees. From October 1992 to September 1993 (fiscal year 1993) the United States admitted 4600 Iraqi refugees.[107]

Prior to the war the United States had been Iraq's largest export market, whilst American companies had a large share of the Iraqi market.

In 1988 16 per cent of Iraq's exports went to the US (US$1.77 billion worth); in 1989 this had risen to 19.2 per cent (US$2.8 billion); and in 1990 (prior to the invasion) 28.5 per cent (US$2.71 billion) of Iraqi exports went to the US. Over 90 per cent of Iraqi exports to the US were of petroleum and petroleum products. The value of this trade to Iraq was substantial in the late 1980s. In 1989 Iraq exported approximately US$211 million worth of petroleum and products each month to the United States. In 1990 (prior to the invasion) US$269 million worth of petroleum and products were exported to the United States by Iraq.[108]

The United States also had a large share of the Iraqi import market. In 1988 12 per cent (US$858 million worth) of Iraqi imports came from the United States; in 1989 this had risen to 12.5 per cent (US$960 million), but it fell to 10.7 per cent (US$546 million) in 1990 (prior to the invasion).[109] These figures show that the United States had a trade deficit with Iraq; it imported more than it exported. However, the value of the Iraqi market should not be underestimated and some American companies are probably suffering from the effects of losing this market. However, these losses have been offset overall by the fact that American companies have won many new contracts in Saudi Arabia and Kuwait.

The United Kingdom

The British involvement in the conflict coalition is estimated to have cost US$3.96 billion. Of this total the UK received US$3.07 billion in foreign pledges, leaving a net military cost of US$890m. However, in addition to this military cost, US$1.28 billion had to be paid to British companies under the Export Credits Guarantee Department insurance scheme which underwrote British contracts in Iraq. Between 1983 and 1990 the British government provided a total of US$1.8 billion worth of credit guarantees to UK companies exporting to Iraq. Of this total between US$300 million and US$375 million was set aside for the sale of defence related equipment. Most of these credit guarantees have not been recovered, leaving the government to reimburse the suppliers.[110] Therefore the total cost of the war to the UK was US$2.17 billion.[111]

The British Overseas Development Agency has spent approximately US$100 million on aid to Iraqi civilians between the period April 1991 and June 1994.[112]

Prior to the invasion of Kuwait the UK had been one of Iraq's main sources of imports. In 1988 8 per cent (US$572 million worth) of Iraqi imports came from the UK, in 1989 this figure had remained steady in percentage terms at 7.9 per cent, but had risen in value to US$607 million. In the first six months of 1990 Iraqi imports from the UK totalled 8.4 per cent (US$428 million).[113]

The loss of the Iraqi market has therefore had an effect on some British companies. Smaller British companies have been most affected, whilst larger ones have taken short-term costs whilst readjusting to new markets. For some small companies such as Partex (a firm which exported automotive spares to Iraq) the Iraqi market was the only one it had. The closure of this market no doubt put many companies into financial difficulty, at a time when recession was beginning and the chances of finding new markets was slim.

The United Nations

In 1991 the UNHCR relief programme in Iraq was allocated US$74.9 million, in 1992 it was allocated US$22.7 million.[114] By January 1994 UNICEF had received

US$32.3 million to cover its activities in Iraq, but this was only 38 per cent of the US$85 million it had appealed for.[115] Thus, despite the fact that the war finished three years ago, and that Western contributions to the relief effort are tailing off, we can see that millions of dollars have had to be spent on refugees from Iraq, as well as those civilians in Iraq who are suffering as a direct result of it.

Despite the efforts of the UN, criticisms of its aid programme in Iraq have been wide and varied. Various NGOs have spoken about how they believe that what aid has been given is insufficient to answer all the needs of the population, but one of the main criticisms of the UN programme has been that it has been organized in conjunction with the Iraqi government and under its supervision. Ahmed Chalabi of the Iraqi National Congress claimed in August 1993 that the UN operation succeeded in putting US$250 million into Iraqi government coffers in 1992, making it a significant proportion of national income. This came about due to the fact that all relief assistance is exchanged at the official government rate of ID1 = US$3.1, when the black market (and more realistic) rate in 1992 was ID30 = US$1. In addition the UN has worked through Iraqi companies nominated by the Iraqis, leading to an estimated US$10m in profit for the Iraqi government.[116]

The United Nations mission to destroy Iraqi weapons of mass destruction (UNSCOM), is expected to produce figures for the cost of the operation in December 1994. However, the scope of this operation is bound to make these costs substantial. According to the UK Foreign Office there have been 84 inspection missions to May 1994, with several more due in coming months.[117] These inspection missions have destroyed 30,000 warheads, 350,000 litres of chemical agents, and 1.5 million litres of raw materials at the Muthanna industrial complex alone. In the field of munitions, nearly 13,000 155-millimetre shells, and 70,000 122-millimetre rockets filled with approximately 300 tonnes of mustard gas and nerve agents have been destroyed.[118]

Such operations, along with the long-term monitoring regime to ensure Iraq does not restart production of such weapons of mass destruction, are bound to cost large sums. It is unfortunate that figures will not be available until after the publication of this study.

Human and Equipment Costs

The United States, United Kingdom and France

Along with masses of equipment and material, 541,000 American soldiers were deployed. Of these soldiers, 148 were killed in action and 458 were wounded. Additionally, approximately 55 US aircraft were lost during the war.[119]

Forty-seven British servicemen were killed during the conflict; this included nine deaths which had been caused by 'friendly fire'. In addition 540 British soldiers were injured.[120] In total the RAF lost 7 Tornadoes in training and combat.[121]

Two French soldiers were killed during the course of the war.

Soon after the end of the conflict some US and UK veterans became sick with an unknown disease. This was later named 'Desert Storm Syndrome' and had a multitude of symptoms ranging from chronic fatigue to collapse of the immune system. The condition affects up to 7000 US veterans.[122] An external paper from the Medical Educational Trust has proposed several possible causes for 'Desert Storm Syndrome'. These include post-traumatic stress disorder, sandfly infections, vaccinations used in anticipation of Iraqi chemical and biological attack (some vaccinations had not been approved by US Federal Drug administration), exposure to the effects of oil smoke or oil spills, contaminated water, effects of sprays used to control flies and mosquitoes, depleted uranium exposure, or even actual exposure to Iraqi chemical or biological attack.[123]

Desert Storm Syndrome

Sylvia Grein, 300 Combat Support Battalion, US Army describes her experiences: 'I was in the psychiatric ward for five and a half months. There they did a medical board ... I repeatedly asked them to look at other things that were wrong with me, and they continued to claim this was a psychological disorder and that's all there was ... I finally went on to the Indiana University Hospital in Indianapolis and a doctor there found that my immune system was broken down. I had no immune system and he requested that the military doctors then do a liver biopsy. They refused. I was verbally chastised for going outside the military system. I was told I could and may lose my military medical benefits if I continued to seek help outside of the military system ...'

Long Term Costs

In the past Iraq was seen as a valuable buffer against the fundamentalism of Iran. In the 1980s the Bush administration and the Thatcher government continued to tacitly approve the sale of dual-use equipment to the Iraqis after the war with Iran had finished.

The invasion of Kuwait and the subsequent American-led coalition which defeated the Iraqis left the US and UK in an awkward position. Iraq, the counterbalance to Iran, was now the enemy. There were fears that the Iranians would now be free to spread their fundamentalism across the Middle East. Both governments were in a difficult position with regard to Saddam Hussein and Iraq. They did not want to see Iraq split into factions and seemed to prefer to allow Saddam Hussein to continue in control as long as he did not become so powerful that he believed he could successfully invade a neighbouring country.[124]

There can be no doubt that many in the US and UK now believe that a defeated Iraq could lead to a resurgent Iran. The Western nations, and in particular the US, now seek to conduct a policy of 'dual containment' of both Iraq and Iran. The belief is that both will remain hostile to the West for the foreseeable future, and that there should be moves to isolate them further in an attempt to weaken them. Economic restrictions are seen as the best weapon to achieve this. This is a particular departure for the US who, in the past, sought to build up one of these nations in order to balance the other's military and political influence, a so-called attempt at regional 'balance-of-power'.[125] It is important not to ignore the potential longer-term effects of such a policy of 'dual containment'. Whilst the West is united in its stand against Iraq there seems to be less agreement over whether or not Iran should continue to be isolated. Many European companies are keen to reinstate trade relations with what had been a profitable area of business. Whilst the Americans are vehemently opposed to such actions, European support for increased trade could undermine relations between the major Western powers. Additionally, a policy of isolating Iran and Iraq could increase extremism and extremist actions by agents acting for both Iran and Iraq.

Aside from Iraq and Iran there is another issue which could prove a challenge to the Western governments, namely, that of the Kurds. The Kurdish issue is one of the most intractable in the region, and continued Western support for the Kurds could have implications for Western relations with Turkey which is fighting its own war against Kurdish separatists in south-east Turkey. According to Amnesty International and *Jane's Defence Weekly*, it was Turkish actions against the Kurdish population (coupled with fears that German arms were being used in such actions), that led the German government to stop arms exports to Turkey in November 1991.[126] This policy was, however, quietly reversed in June 1992.

The Kurdish issue may now have less relevance to the Western governments since in the past year Western media attention has moved onto other areas such as Bosnia. Whilst continuing humanitarian aid to the Kurds, the American administration and the British Foreign Office have continually said that they will not recognize an independent Kurdish state, mainly for fear of angering Turkey, which has a pivotal role as a Western ally in the region.[127]

However, the Kurdish issue is one which could become increasingly important in the future. If Saddam Hussein continues to grow in confidence he may seek to crush the Kurds who are one of the main opponents to his rule. If he does move against them what will the West do? Will it be ready to go to war to protect the Kurds? The Gulf conflict may have solved some short-term problems, such as a powerful Iraq, but surely it has only served to throw up new challenging strategic questions which the West has yet to answer satisfactorily.

THE BENEFITS

The United States

Strategic considerations

The war ensured that the United States became the protector of the two most important oil states in the Gulf–Saudi Arabia and Kuwait. A ten-year US–Kuwait defence pact signed after the end of the war allowed US forces to train in the region as well as stockpile arms and supplies there. Access to airfields and ports was also negotiated. The Pentagon announced a plan to spend US$350 million upgrading two Kuwaiti airfields.[128] The war, therefore, led to the US gaining vital military bases and rights in the economically vital Gulf region.

Despite the fact that the United States had evidence of Iraqi construction of weapons of mass destruction and had allowed this to continue, the war did ensure that these weapons would be destroyed. Once the existence of such weapons had become known to the public, the US supported moves for their destruction.

Pressure from some Arab states, along with a realization that the best way to secure US interests in the Middle East was Arab-Israeli peace, led to the US pushing for a Middle East peace conference in October 1991. Whilst peace would ease the suffering of the people of the region as the Americans proclaimed, such a peace would also be of great benefit to the US. With Arabs and Israelis living in peace there would be less chance of an attack on US interests or vital oil supplies in the region.[129]

The Middle East peace process is still continuing at the present time. Recognition of the Palestine Liberation Organisation (PLO) by Israel and vice-versa was the first step in a process which has led to the formation of an autonomous Palestinian area in Jericho and the Gaza Strip. There has been condemnation from extremists on both sides of the divide in Israel over this area, and it still remains to be seen how successful it will be.

The economy

The US was also the main benefactor of the increased arms purchases made by the Middle Eastern countries in the aftermath of the war. A February 1992 Arms Control Association report estimated that American arms sales to the region since the invasion of Kuwait totalled US$19 billion.. Weapons including heavy artillery, tanks, aircraft and helicopters had been sold to eight countries: Bahrain, Egypt, Israel, Kuwait, Morocco, Oman, Saudi Arabia and the United Arab Emirates (UAE).

Even this large figure has been seen as an underestimation of actual US arms sales to the region. The Congressional Research Service (CRS) estimated that between 1990 and 1993, the US had secured arms transfer deals worth US$39.4 billion to the Middle East since the Iraqi invasion of Kuwait. Saudi Arabia alone had placed orders for US$30.4 billion.[130] Other large purchase orders had been received from Kuwait and Israel. The Bush administration even predicted that in 1992 US arms sales would be worth US$35 billion, most of this going to the Middle East.[131] In 1993, the US dominated the international arms export market, accounting for 72.6 per cent of all arms transfer agreements, with the Middle East the principal recipient, purchasing 68 per cent of all its arms from the US.[132]

Private American companies received large orders for their weaponry. Fourteen Patriot missile batteries and 758 missiles were bought by Saudi Arabia in January 1992; this added to six batteries which had been sold in late 1990. The total cost was approximately US$4.3 billion. Sikorsky sold helicopters to Saudi Arabia at a cost of US$121 million.[133] General Dynamics sold 236 M1A2 Main Battle Tanks to Kuwait, on top of an order of 465 M1A2 tanks from Saudi Arabia in 1989 and 1990 which were due to be delivered in 1993.[134] McDonnell Douglas received an order from Saudi Arabia for 72 F-15 fighters in 1992 which was worth hundreds of millions of dollars, as well as a repair contract for F-15s already in the Saudi airforce worth US$5.2 million, and an upgrade contract for Saudi F-15s worth US$48 million.[135]

American companies also had the largest role in the post-war reconstruction of Kuwait. The Bechtel Corporation managed the programme to control the Kuwait oil fires, a contract that was estimated to be worth approximately 12 per cent of the total programme cost of US$1.8 billion or US$216 million.[136] Two of the four contractors chosen by Bechtel to carry out onshore repairs to oil-gathering facilities were American, Foster Wheeler and Fluor Daniel. The sole contractor chosen to restore offshore structures was also American, McDermott International.[137] Bechtel had 1000 employees and 9000 subcontractors involved in reconstruction work in Kuwait.[138]

The American government benefited from large pledges to cover the cost of their war effort. Over US$54.5 billion were received by the US (see Table 2.2).

The United Kingdom

The economy

The British government received pledges to cover the cost of fighting the war from many different countries (see Table 2.3).

US companies were the main bene-factors of the military and civil contracts to rebuild and rearm Kuwait and Saudi

Table 2.2: Major Allied financial commitments to the US (US$m)

Country	First payment	Second payment	TOTAL
Saudi Arabia	3339	13,500	16,839
Kuwait	2506	13,500	16,006
UAE	1000	3,000	4000
Japan	1740	9000	10,740
Germany	1072	5500	6572
Korea	80	305	385
Other	3	17	20
TOTAL	9740	44,822	54,562

Source: Freedman and Karsh; *The Gulf Conflict 1990-91; Diplomacy and War in the New World Order*, Faber & Faber, London 1993.

Arabia. This US dominance led to much ill-feeling in other countries who believed that the American administration had pressurized Kuwait and Saudi Arabia to award contracts to American companies. Denials of this by both Kuwaiti and US sources did not reassure British companies, especially after 1992 when Kuwait cancelled a contract for 236 Challenger 2 tanks from Vickers in favour of the American M1A2 tank.

Whilst the US became the dominant force in protecting the region, Kuwait also looked to the UK for future protection. On 11 February 1992 a UK–Kuwait Defence Pact was signed which, like the September

Table 2.3: Major Allied financial commitments to the UK

Country	Payment (US$m)
Kuwait	990
S. Arabia	873
UAE	417
Germany	411
Japan	288
Korea	27
Other	220
TOTAL	3226

Source: Freedman & Karsh, 1993, op cit; and NAO, 'Ministry of Defence: The Costs and Receipts Arising from the Gulf Conflict', HMSO, 2 December 1992. Note: An exchange rate of £1 = US$1.5 has been used when converting figures

1991 US–Kuwait Defence Pact, covered the sale of equipment, training, and joint exercises. Between 1990 and 1993, the UK received US$4.6 billion from arms export deliveries to the Middle East. The Middle East accounted for 94 per cent of all UK arms transfer agreements for the same period.[139]

In the nine months after the end of the war UK companies had won over US$720m worth of civil orders in the Gulf. This amounted to approximately 20 per cent of all contracts, and was second only to the US. The amount of reconstruction work needed in Kuwait was less than originally expected. However, some valuable contracts were awarded to British companies, for example, British Petroleum received a contract from the Kuwaiti state oil company to share know-how and research programmes which would help Kuwait reinstate its production capacity, manage its reserves of oil, and conduct accurate war damage assessments.[140]

British trade officials have made the point that UK exports to Kuwait are now reaching levels seen before the war. In 1992 approximately US$393m worth of goods were exported to Kuwait, compared with approximately US$267 million in 1991. They also said that although most contracts in Kuwait were being carried out by US companies, they were being administered using British personnel or the British offices of those companies.[141] As the work was being done by UK citizens and through British subsidiaries of US companies it can be claimed that the UK has benefited through increased revenues for British workers, and a steady supply of work for Britons working for American subsidiaries.

France

The economy

France was by far one of the largest suppliers of military equipment to Iraq prior to the conflict, and indeed had been since the Arab–Israeli war of June 1967. Weapons sold included: Mirage fighters;

various types of missiles including Exocets; armoured vehicles; helicopters; and even tanks.[142] The French had also been the main force behind the construction of the Osirak nuclear reactor near Baghdad, had provided initial supplies of uranium, and had trained upwards of 200 Iraqi technicians and scientists.[143]

Between 1992 and 1993, France agreed arms deals and orders to the Middle East worth US$4.3 billion.[144]

CONCLUSION

The war has seemed to have benefited the American, British and French governments in the short-term. Although the war incurred large military costs, these have been mostly offset by payments from other countries, such as Kuwait, Japan, Saudi Arabia and Germany. American influence in a region vital for the supply of oil has increased more than that of any other country. The West has also benefited from arms exports and civil contracts. However, looking beyond the short term, we can see that problems may arise in the future. Problems which will be far from easy to solve.

The West's attitude of selling weapons to a regime that they believed they could control backfired dangerously in 1990. This should provide a lesson in reality for these arms suppliers. The war should show that it is impossible to control an autocratic figure who is prone to instigating conflict and who has acted with little regard to others, let alone as a method to protect important strategic interests in the long term.

From an economic viewpoint the value of selling arms to countries as a way of gaining revenue has also been questioned. Professor Ron Smith of Birkbeck College, London, has suggested that the competitiveness of the arms market and excess supply indicates that profits can only be made with government subsidization (eg, by financing research and development and helping marketing) of such sales. Such subsidies, it is argued, could outweigh any profits received from arms sales, making an overall negative return to the country.[145]

Having encouraged the growth of military power of Iraq under Saddam, the Western countries are now in a difficult position with regard to what they should do with him. If Saddam is overthrown, who will replace him? Is there a valid replacement? Would the downfall of Saddam lead to the spread of fundamentalism and extremism from Iran? These are all questions which the G7 countries and their Middle Eastern allies must now seriously consider.

Related to this is the issue of the future of the Kurds in Iraq. At present the West seems content to allow the situation to continue as it is. However, as Saddam Hussein continues to grow in strength, the West will be faced with the possibility of an Iraqi attack against the Kurds and will be forced to decide whether or not it will intervene directly to protect them.

Finally, the Middle East peace conference, and subsequent discussion, provided initial optimism for an end to the dispute between Israel and the PLO. Expectations of a quick peace were always over-optimistic. At the present time, chances of a comprehensive peace are slim, but at least discussions are still continuing. Whether the positive results will have any lasting effect is difficult at this stage to determine.

IF THE CONFLICT HAD NOT OCCURRED

Introduction

By its very nature, speculating on the potential benefits of conflict not occurring using cross-sectional analysis is difficult. It is difficult to measure what would have happened, and it is difficult to find countries of similar standing with which to make comparisons. The countries chosen are all from the Middle East and were chosen on the grounds that they had similar economies and patterns of development, in addition to their cultures being similar.

However, we have been careful to take into account the effect the war with Iraq had on oil prices, which benefited the other OPEC countries. To represent these benefits as benefits that might have accrued to Iraq had the war not occurred would obviously be erroneous.

Iraq

Without the war, the Iraqi standard of living would probably have continued to rise. Despite massive spending on military equipment in the three decades prior to the conflict, Iraq had moved from an impoverished Third World country to an urban society where healthcare was good, industry was developed, and infrastructure was modern and efficient. This development had been financed by oil revenues which had increased over these 30 years. By the start of 1990, infant mortality had fallen to 22 per 1000, nearly comparable with that of highly developed Western countries.[146]

Despite the fact that the oil price after, and prior to, the war was stagnating (a major cause of the Iraqi–Kuwait dispute), GDP in other countries in the region has continued to rise albeit at reduced rates after the war (Figure 2.11)

The economic situation in Iran is difficult to judge, due to the fact that there

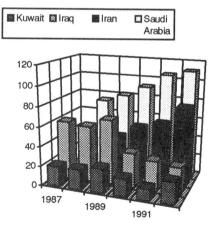

Source: EIU Reports, 1993, op cit
Note: Iran figures are derived from the 1992 exchange rate (pre-float) of US$1: 65.5IR.

Figure 2.11: Comparative GDPs (US$bn)

was no floating exchange rate until 1993. Official figures prior to this date greatly overvalued the Iranian rial, ensuring that GDP figures cannot be accurately obtained. However, actual GDP growth can be measured, and is seen to have risen from 3.5 per cent in 1989 to 9.9 per cent in 1990 and 7.1 per cent in 1991, and then dipped to 4.5 per cent in 1992.[147] Despite this dip, an estimated growth rate of 4.5 per cent is impressive in times of global recession, when Western countries are reporting expected growth rates of less than 1 per cent. Iranian exports, having risen from US$13.08 billion worth in 1989, have remained steady at around the US$18–$19 billion mark in 1990, 1991, and 1992.

As standards of living would have increased without the war, we can assume that the Iraqi population would have increased their incomes and consumption (although reservations must be expressed about the continued military expenditure and the potential effect this could have had on government expenditure on the population, given the falling oil price). We can also assume that a smaller percentage of the population would have been affected by poverty and unemployment as the job market would have expanded with the economy.

The West

If no conflict had occurred then the Western nations would not have been forced to expend large amounts of effort and resources on a costly military campaign. Even though these direct costs have been largely paid by other nations, indirect costs of the war such as aid, and continuing the operation to protect the Kurds in Northern Iraq, would not have occurred without the conflict. The lack of an expensive aid programme such as that in operation in Iraq would have helped the Western countries in a period of recession such as that just encountered.

From an economic standpoint, without the war, Iraq could have continued to be an important market for Western goods and services, and a market which would have

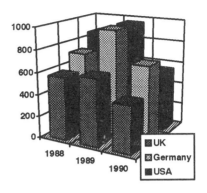

Source: EIU, Reports, 1990, 1992 & 1994, op cit

Figure 2.12: Iraqi imports from G7 (US$m)

expanded as the standard of living increased (See Figure 2.12).

Iraq's most important import was wheat. Approximately 2 million tonnes of wheat were imported by Iraq each year from 1985. In 1989 the United States exported agricultural products to Iraq worth US$791 million; this figure was due to increase to US$900 million in 1990 but the trade embargo imposed by the UN in the aftermath of the invasion of Kuwait stopped this. This trade was obviously of great value to the United States, and its loss has been felt by the American farmers. It can be safely assumed that if the war had not occurred this cereal trade would have continued greatly benefiting American farmers.[148]

Iraq also imported large amounts of other products from Western countries. In the period January–April 1990 the United Kingdom exported approximately US$9.5 million worth of chemicals to Iraq each month, in addition to US$26 million of machinery per month, and US$5 million worth of scientific equipment. The United Kingdom was the second largest supplier to Iraq after the United States. West Germany and France followed.[149] (See Figure 2.13) It is apparent, therefore, that the main exporters to Iraq, and those which make the most from the Iraqi market, turn out to be the countries Iraq ended up fighting in 1991.[150]

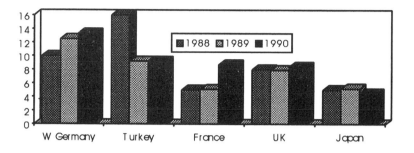

Source: EIU Reports 1990, 1991 & 1994, op cit
Note: 1990 figure is for a unified Germany and not just West Germany.

Figure 2.13: Countries of origin of Iraqi imports (%)

The Iraqi market was therefore a valuable one for Western countries, and one that had been producing increasing revenues in the period before the war. Compared with some other countries the values of sales to Iraq may not have been huge, but in times of recession any market is valuable.

Imports to Iran rose from US$13.45 billion in 1989 to US$25.44 billion in 1992. In 1992, of the Western countries, Germany had the largest percentage of exports to Iran, totalling 24.2 per cent (US$6.16 billion), the United Kingdom had 4.8 per cent (US$1.22 billion), and the United States had 3.6 per cent (US$916 million).[151] Iran is approximately four times the size of Iraq, and has three times the population, so direct comparisons are not accurate. However, we can surmise that if the market in a pariah state like Iran is so valuable, and has increased to such an extent, then the value of the Iraqi market would have increased dramatically as it was considered a friend of the West. Western exports to Iraq would therefore have been worth an increasing amount had the war not occurred.

Conclusion

As mentioned previously, potential benefits of war not occurring are difficult to measure. However, given the level of Western sales to Iraq prior to the war, along with the increased demand that a better standard of living would have led to, we can assume that the West would have increased the volume of exports to (and therefore revenue from exports to) Iraq if the war had not happened. Having looked at Western trade with Iran and found that it has increased since the end of the conflict, we can safely assume that trade with Iraq would have increased similarly. We can only speculate, but, given the volume of trade before the war, and the amount of trade the West has done with other countries in the region since the end of the war, a valuable market has been lost in Iraq.

However, we must take into account that the West has received large orders for military equipment from countries in the region, especially Kuwait and Saudi Arabia, but we can say that these sales will lead only to short-term profits. If Iraq had continued to be an important economic market then profits for the West in the long-term may well have exceeded those gained from short-term arms sales.

REFERENCES

1 UNICEF, 'Women and Children in Iraq: A Situation Report', December 1992; and A Ascherio, et al, 'Effect of the Gulf War on Infant and Child Mortality in Iraq', *New England Journal of Medicine*, 24 September 1992.

2 Ibid.

3 Harvard Study Team Report, 22 May 1991; and A Ascherio, et al 24 September 1992, op cit.

4 Ascherio, A, 24 September 1992, op cit; General Ramsey Clark, Letter to UN secretary-general Boutros Boutros Ghali, 18 February 1993; International Study Team: 1991; UNICEF Situation Report: 1992; Harvard Study Team Report, 22 May 1991; and Doucet, I L & Haines, A, 'Continuing Health Costs of the Gulf War', *Medical Educational Trust*, Update, November 1993.

5 UNICEF, Situation Report, 1992, op cit.

6 UNESCO, 'Iraq: Education and the Embargo', UNESCO Sources, No 49, July/August 1993.

7 UNICEF, 'Women and Children in Iraq: A Situation Report', December 1992; and Nimri Aziz, B, 'Where Students Struggle to Survive', *The Guardian*, December 1992.

8 *Gulf Newsletter: 1992*; Gulf Information Project, 'Gulf Information Pack', Refugee Council, January 1994; and UNICEF, 'Iraq 1994: The Crisis Continues', UNICEF Report, February 1994.

9 Doucet, & Haines, 1993, op cit.

10 Daponte, B O, 'A Case Study in Estimating Casualties from War and its Aftermath: the 1991 Persian Gulf War', *PSR Quarterly*, Vol 3, June 1993.

11 Daponte, and Doucet, & Haines 1993, op cit.

12 Amnesty International, 'Iraq: The Need for Further United Nations Action to Protect Human Rights', MDE 14 June 1991, July 1991.

13 Iraqi Civilian Aid, 'Fresh Water – Newest Weapon of Mass Destruction in Iraq', Press Release, 24 February 1994.

14 Gulf Information Project, 'Gulf Information Pack', Refugee Council, January 1994; and Viewpoint '93 guide produced to compliment Viewpoint '93 programme, 'Saddam's Killing Fields', which was produced by Rebecca Dobbs, written and presented by Michael Wood, and broadcast in October 1993.

15 Economist Intelligence Unit, Country Report: *Iraq 1992–1993*.

16 Ibid.

17 Economist Intelligence Unit, 'Country Profile: *Iraq 1991–92, 1992–93*.

18 Economist Intelligence Unit, Country Profile: *Iraq 1990–91*.

19 Hoskins, E, 'The Truth Behind Economic Sanctions', Report of the Gulf Peace Team, May 1991.

20 Drèze, J, & Gaidar, H, 'Hunger and Poverty in Iraq, 1991', *Development Economics Research Programme Discussion Paper* No 32, (London: LSE, 1991).

21 *MEED*, 10 July 1992.

22 Jansen, G, 'Proud and Defiant', *Middle East International*, 15 May 1992, p 8; and Reuters Report, 'Iraq Claims Rapid Progress', *Toronto Star*, 12 January 1992.

23 Doucet & Haines, 1993, op cit.

24 Refugee Council, 1994, op cit; and Prince Sadruddin Aga Khan, 'UN Special Report on Humanitarian Needs in Iraq', 15 July 1991.

25 Jansen, 1992, op cit, and Reuters 1992, op cit.

26 In 1990 the power stations provided a peak load of 5,162 MW with some spare capacity. International Study Team Survey Report, October 1991.

27 Doucet, & Haines, 1993, op cit; Refugee Council, January 1994, op cit.

28 Ibid.

29 UNICEF, December 1992, op cit; and Harvard Study Team Report, May 1991, op cit.

30 *Middle East Economic Digest*, 6 March 1992.

31 Jansen, May 1992, op cit.

32 Ringle, K, 'After the Battles, Defusing the Debris', *The Washington Post*, 1 March 1991.

33 Doucet, & Haines, 1993, op cit.

34 Refugee Council, January 1994, op cit.

35 Doucet, I L, 'Desert Storm Syndrome, Sick Soldiers and Dead Children?', *Medical Educational Trust* Background Paper No 14, November 1993; and Cohen, N & Wilkie, D, 'Gulf Teams Not Told of Risk From Uranium', *The Independent on Sunday*, 10 November 1991. However, documents obtained under Freedom of Information requests in the United States suggest that 300 tonnes of depleted uranium could lie in Iraq and Kuwait from 1m depleted uranium rounds which were fired by Allied forces.

36 Iraqi children are also reported to have been seen playing with, and keeping, discarded depleted uranium shells. There is no evidence to suggest that these shells have had any effect on Iraqi children or other civilians or soldiers but there has been no attempt to monitor the long-term problems caused by these shells.

37 Approximately 20,000 tonnes of sulphur

dioxide, 250 tonnes of carbon monoxide, 500 tonnes of nitrogen monoxide and 1,500 tonnes of sulphur particles went into the atmosphere from the fires every day. (Kerber: 1992). A separate report from the World Meteorological Organisation said that in May 1991 over 40,000 tonnes of sulphur dioxide (more than the daily emissions of the UK, France and Germany together), and 500,000 tonnes of carbon dioxide and other pollutants were released by the fires daily. Soot was deposited around the region, and found as far away as the Himalayas and Hawaii. (McCloskey: 1991; and Gulf Information Pack: 1994).

38 Tickell: 1993; and Viewpoint '93 guide: 1993, op cit; and Gulf Information Pack: 1994.
39 Doucet and Haines, November 1993, op cit.
40 Amnesty International, 'Iraq/Occupied Kuwait: Human Rights Violations Since 2 August', MDE 14/16/90, December 1990.
41 Fisk, R, 'Something Evil Has Visited Kuwait City', *The Independent*, 28 February 1991; and Refugee Council, January 1994, op cit.
42 Refugee Council, January 1994, op cit.
43 Richards, C, 'Campaign to Free Kuwaitis', *The Independent*, 22 July 1993.
44 Amnesty International, December 1990, op cit.
45 Based on Evans, K, 'Kuwait's Rape Children Offer Bitter Reminder', *The Guardian*, 29 July 1993.
46 Economist Intelligence Unit, Country Profile: *Kuwait*, 1990–1.
47 Ibid.
48 From Amnesty International, 'Kuwait: Cases of 'Disappearance', Incommunicado Detention, Torture and Extrajudicial Execution under Martial Law', AI Index: MDE 17/02/92, October 1992.
49 Ibid and Richards, C, 'Kuwaitis still committing rights abuses', *The Independent*, 24 February 1994.
50 Economist Intelligence Unit, Country Report: *Kuwait*, fourth quarter 1993.
51 Economist Intelligence Unit, Country Profile: *Kuwait*, 1990–91.
52 Hardy, R, *After the Storm: Internal Stability of the Gulf States*, RIIA, 1992.
53 Economist Intelligence Unit, Country Report: *Kuwait* fourth quarter 1993.
54 MEED, 27 December 1991, op cit; and Hardy, 1992.
55 National Audit Office, 'Ministry of Defence: The Costs and Receipts Arising From the Gulf Conflict', HMSO, 2 December 1992.
56 Sadowski, Y M, *Scuds or Butter? The Political Economy of Arms Control in the Middle East* Washington: Brookings Institution, 1993.
57 Grimmett, R F, 'Conventional Arms Transfers to the Third World, 1989–93', CRS Report for Congress USA, July 1994.
58 Economist Intelligence Unit, Country Profile: *Kuwait*, 1991–2; and Hardy, 1991, op cit.
59 Christian Wolmar, 'Kuwait Liberated', *The Independent*, 27 February 1991; and Fisk, February 1991, op cit.
60 Refugee Council, January 1994, op cit.
61 Ibid and Kerber, L G A T, 'The Global Alliance 1992 Report', *Global Alliance*, 25 May 1992; Pain, S 'Is Kuwait's Foul Air Fit to Breathe?' *New Scientist*, 26 October 1991; Doucet, & Haines, 1993, op cit; and Greenpeace International, 'The Environmental Legacy of the Gulf War', 1992.
62 Letter from Dr Wolfgang Mallman, 6 July 1994.
63 Pearce, F and Pain, S 'Oil From Kuwaiti Wells Still Pouring Into the Desert', *New Scientist*, 9 November 1991.
64 Ibid and Greenpeace International, 1992, op cit.
65 Greenpeace International, 1992, op cit.
66 Jasem Al-Besharah of the Kuwait Institute for Scientific Research has put this theory of the danger to the water supply forward in Pearce, & Pain, November 1991, op cit.
67 Pearce, & Pain, November 1991, op cit.
68 Brown, P, 'Defusing the Unexploded Legacy of War in Kuwait', *The Guardian*, 16 September 1991.
69 *MEED*, 22 November 1991.
70 Brown, September 1991, op cit.
71 Refugee Council, January 1994, op cit.
72 Economist Intelligence Unit, Country Report: *Saudi Arabia* first quarter 1991.
73 Economist Intelligence Unit, Country Report: *Saudi Arabia* first quarter 1991.
74 Hardy, 1992, op cit.
75 *MEES*: 6 January 1992.
76 Economist Intelligence Unit, Country Report: *Saudi Arabia* first quarter 1991.
77 Economist Intelligence Unit, Country Report: *Saudi Arabia*, fourth quarter 1993.
78 ODI, 'Economic Crisis in the Arab World', *ODI Briefing Paper*, March 1992.
79 Sadowski, 1993, op cit.
80 Hirst, D, 'Heads in the Sand', *The Guardian*, 14 August 1993; and Gerth, J, 'War Costs and High Living Erode the "Saudi Dream"', *The International Herald Tribune*, 23 August 1993.
81 *MEES*, 'Arab Military Expenditure Well Ahead of World Levels, New Study Shows', 16 August 1993.
82 Kemp, P, 'No Dividend From the New World Order', *MEED*, 6 November 1992 and Grimmett, 1994, op cit.
83 Economist Intelligence Unit, Country Report: *Saudi Arabia*, fourth quarter 1993.
84 The Economist, 'Saudi Arabia: Pressured Reform', 15 January 1994.
85 Ibid.
86 The oil slick from Iraq and Kuwait stopped moving south after it hit Abu Ali island in Saudi Arabia. In the immediate aftermath of the war aerial and satellite photographs of the slick were rarely seen and experts from France, America, and the UK who had toured the Gulf were discouraged from talking about the slick's effects
87 McCloskey, C, 'Legacy of Oil War', *UNEP–UK News*, Summer 1991.
88 One source suggests that the features of the Gulf could in themselves help prevent damage. These would include the high salinity of the water which would cause the oil to float and

therefore evaporate coupled with a high bacteria count which would help to digest the organic oil. Additionally, wave action would help dilute the oil, and any oil which reached the beaches could be easily scooped up as most of the beaches and mudflats are flat and not rocky which had hampered the cleanup in Prince William Sound.

89 McCloskey, 'Legacy of Oil War', UNEP–UK News, 1991; and Greenpeace International, 1992, op cit.

90 Ibid.

91 Ibid; Refugee Council, 1994, op cit; and Greenpeace International, 1992, op cit.

92 McCloskey, 1991, op cit; Kerber, May 1992, op cit; and Greenpeace International, 1992, op cit.

93 Refugee Council, January 1994, op cit; Van Hear, N 'Migrant Workers in the Gulf', *Minority Rights Group, Update*, 1992; Edge, S 'Migrants Come Home to Roost', MEED, 4 October 1991; and Doucet, & Haines, 1993, op cit.

94 Edge, 1991, op cit.

95 Van Hear, 1992, op cit.

96 Refugee Council, 1994, op cit.

97 Matthews, R, & Nicholson, M, 'Desert Kingdom's Flight of Fancy', *Financial Times*, 18 February 1994; Colvin, M, 'Saudi Defector Hides from Royal Wrath', *The Sunday Times*, 3 July 1994; and *The Economist*, 'Saudi Arabia: Pressured Reform', 15 January 1994.

98 *The Economist*, 15 January 1994, op cit.

99 Economist Intelligence Unit, Country Report: *Saudi Arabia*, 1993; and Matthews & Nicholson, 18 February 1994, op cit.

100 Economist Intelligence Unit, Country Report: *Saudi Arabia*, fourth quarter 1993.

101 ODI, March 1992, op cit.

102 Grimmett, R F, 'Conventional Arms Transfers to the Third World', *Congressional Research Service*, Library of Congress, 19 July 1993.

103 However, this US$61 billion figure has been disputed by the American General Accounting Office, which has said that this figure is too high and takes into account defence expenditure which would have occurred even if the war had not happened.

104 Riddell, P, 'Arab Countries Still Owe $7bn for Gulf War Costs', *The Financial Times*, 2 August 1991.

105 Willett, S, 'The Economic Implications' in Gow, J, (ed), *Iraq, The Gulf Conflict and the World Community* London: Brassey's, 1993.

106 AID Fact Sheet, 'Iraq: Displaced Persons and Refugees', 18 April 1991.

107 *Gulf Newsletter*, Refugee Council, Oct/Nov 1993.

108 Economist Intelligence Unit, Country Report: *Iraq* first quarter 1990, 1991 & 1994.

109 Economist Intelligence Unit, Country Report: *Iraq* first quarter 1990, 1991 & 1994.

110 O'Neill, S, '£250m Loans Supported Defence Deals', *The Daily Telegraph*, 18 November 1992; and Hencke, D, & Norton-Taylor, R, 'Taxpayers Meet Bill for Baghdad Forces', *The Guardian*, 17 November 1992. An exchange rate of £1:$1.5 has been used when converting figures.

111 Details from White, D, 'Gulf War Bill Expected to Top £1.4bn', *The Financial Times*, 2 December 1992; and NAO, 'Ministry of Defence: The Costs and Receipts Arising from the Gulf Conflict', HMSO, 2 December 1992. An exchange rate of £1:$1.5 has been used when converting figures.

112 ODA, 'Britain to Help Rehabilitate Villages in Kurdish Areas in Northern Iraq', Press Release 53/94, 17 June 1994.

113 Economist Intelligence Unit, Country Report: *Iraq* first quarter 1990, 1991 and 1994.

114 UNHCR Report: 1993, op cit.

115 UNICEF, 'Iraq 1994: The Crisis Continues', UNICEF Report, February 1994.

116 Vallely, P, 'How He Is Getting His Cash', *The Daily Telegraph*, 25 August 1993.

117 Foreign and Commonwealth Office, Security and Arms Control, No. 5, June 1994.

118 Ibid.

119 Friedman, N, *Desert Victory: The War for Kuwait Annapolis*, US Naval Institute, 1991.

120 Doucet & Haines, 1993, op cit.

121 Friedman, 1991, op cit.

122 *The Independent*, 'Gulf Veterans Claim for 'Desert Storm Syndrome', 1 March 1994.

123 Doucet, I, 'Desert Storm Syndrome, Sick Soldiers and Dead Children?', *Medical Educational Trust, Background Paper* No 14, November 1993.

124 This desire to see Iraq united and acting as a buffer against Iran is one other explanation for why the Allies did not wish to follow the Iraqi army further north into Iraq to destroy it and depose ; and also explains why Allied forces did not prevent the crushing of the rebellions in north and south Iraq in March/April 1991. The official reason given for not following the Iraqi troops was that the UN mandate did not allow this.

125 Smith, R J, & Williams, D, 'US Wants to Isolate Both Iran and Iraq', *The International Herald Tribune*, 24 May 1993; and Rosenthal, A M, 'Keep Iraq and Iran Contained', *The International Herald Tribune*, 23 June 1993.

126 'Stoltenberg Resigns', *Jane's Defence Weekly*, 11 April 1992.

127 To encourage the Kurds to return to Iraqi Kurdistan, the West implemented a 'safe haven' policy shortly after the failure of the March 1991 uprisings. The 'safe haven' included an Allied military presence in the Dohuk governate until September 1991 as well as an air exclusion zone north of the 36th parallel. Unfortunately this did not cover all of Iraqi Kurdistan but did encourage most Kurds who had fled to Turkey to return. A second air exclusion zone which prevented Iraqi air flights was implemented over the Marshes, south of the 32nd parallel on 27 August 1992. On one occasion at least, Allied planes flying in this air exclusion zone have fired on, and destroyed Iraqi fighters. No Security Council Resolutions were sought to back the air exclusion zones, or 'safe haven', but the initiators (France, UK and US) appealed under Resolution 688 which

demands Iraq cease repression of its people, but does not contain a mandate for military action. This did not however, prevent the shooting down of Iraqi fighters.

128 Gulf Information Project, *Gulf Newsletter*, No 1, November 1991.

129 Economist Intelligence Unit, Country Report: *USA* third quarter 1991.

130 Grimmett, 1994, op cit.

131 Kemp, November 1992, op cit.

132 Grimmett, 1994, op cit.

133 Economist Intelligence Unit, Country Report: *Saudi Arabia* first quarter 1992.

134 *MEED*, 'Battle for the Gulf Tank Market', 6 November 1992.

135 The war led to a large rearmament programme in Saudi Arabia. The United States has become central to Saudi defence policy and remains the main supplier of arms. However, there has been some movement to increased supplies from European NATO countries as problems arise in the US Congress over supplying arms to the Saudis. Most of the Congressional pressure against arms sales has come about due to pressure from the pro-Israel lobby which does not wish to see an Arab neighbour well-armed with sophisticated equipment. Despite Congressional restrictions however, the US arms industry has sold large amounts of equipment to the Saudis.

136 Johanthan Crusoe, 'The Capping of the Oil Wells', *MEED*, 22 November 1991.

137 Ibid.

138 Cohen, & Wilkie, November 1991, op cit.

139 Grimmett, 1994, op cit.

140 Donovan, P, 'BP to Help Rebuild Kuwait's Oilfields', *The Guardian*, 28 July 1992.

141 Evans, K, 'Business Brisk, But Bonanza Hopes Dashed', *The Guardian*, 25 February 1993.

142 Alhakim, S and Alhakim, A, 'A List of Military Equipment and Armaments Supplied to The Iraqi Armed Forces Prior to the 1991 Gulf War', Organisation of Human Rights in Iraq, June 1993; and Sampson, A, *The Arms Bazaar in the Nineties: From Krupp to Saddam* (Revised Edition) London: Coronet Books, 1991.

143 Darwish, A, & Alexander, G, *Unholy Babylon: The Secret History of Saddam's War* London: Victor Gollanz, 1991.

144 Grimmett, 1994, op cit.

145 Smith, R, 'How Will Limitations Affect the Overall Economies of Exporter Nations, and How Could Any Negative effects be Minimised?', in *Nine Questions on International Arms Exports Control*, Saferworld/Oxford Research Group, October 1992.

146 UNICEF, December 1992, op cit.

147 Economist Intelligence Unit, Country Report: *Iran* first quarter: 1994.

148 Economist Intelligence Unit, Iraq: Country Profile: *Iraq* 1991–92.

149 In 1987 West Germany's main exports to Iraq were chemicals (US$3.7m per month), metal manufactures (US$3.4m per month), and machinery (US$14.6m per month). France's main exports in 1988 were chemicals (US$2.9m per month) and machinery (US$16.9m per month).

150 Economist Intelligence Unit, Country Report: *Iraq* third quarter 1990.

151 Economist Intelligence Unit, Country Report: *Iran* first quarter 1994.

3

THE KASHMIR CONFLICT (1990–   )

Nils Bhinda

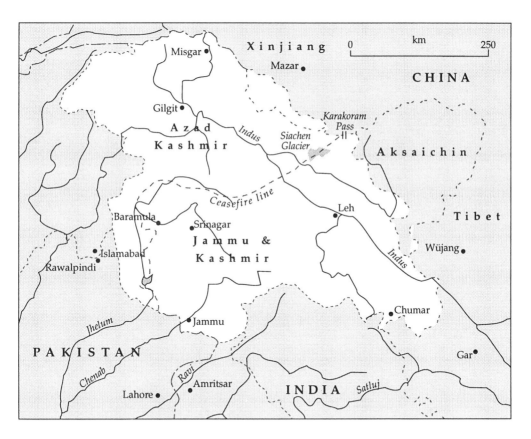

Area (000sq km)	*219*
Population (m)	*12*
Human Development Index	*na*
Population density (per sq km)	*50*
Capital	*Srinagar*

KEY IMPACTS OF THE CONFLICT

ON KASHMIR

- Since 1990 it has been estimated that between 12,000 and 25,000 have died in Kashmir. A total of 1306 people died and hundreds were injured or abducted in the first seven months of 1994.
- Approximately 2200 cases of gunshot wounds were treated in one Srinagar hospital between January 1992 and October 1992.
- Two-hundred schools have been burned to the ground.
- Infant mortality in Kashmir is put at 1 in 5 mainly due to common diseases caused by impure water.
- By 1991, 3000 businesses and shops had been destroyed by the Indian army.
- Kashmir's tourist industry has been severely affected by the conflict. In 1988 722,000 people visited Kashmir, in 1992 only 10,400.
- Indian legislation has meant that since 1990 thousands of people have been detained without trial in Kashmir.
- At least 15,000 to 20,000 Kashmiri detainees are experiencing a subhuman existence in jails throughout India.
- By 1993 approximately 150,000 Kashmiri Hindus were in refugee camps in the plains.

ON INDIA

- In 1992, India spent $193 million on Kashmir.
- Both India and Pakistan have threatened to use nuclear weapons against each other in conflagrations resulting from the Kashmir conflict.
- Based in Kashmir are 400,000 Indian security personnel. Between 1990 and 1993, 560 were killed.
- In the period 1988–92 India spent over $12 billion on imports of conventional arms, more than that spent by Saudi Arabia or Iraq in the same period.
- In 1992, the US Congress voted to cut $24 million of its foreign aid to Kashmir to express disapproval at humans rights abuses in Kashmir.

ON PAKISTAN

- Between 1978 and 1991 Pakistan's defence budget increased sevenfold. The defence budget for 1992–93 at $3 billion marks an 8 per cent increase on the previous year. Defence accounted for almost 40 per cent of government spending.
- Given debt service payments of $3.5 billion, the above expenditure on defence meant that little over $0.1 billion was left for development purposes.
- Pakistan purchased some US$5.4 billion worth of conventional weapons between 1988 and 1992.

ON CHINA

- instability in Kashmir, which is no longer confined just to the Valley, may spill over into the unstable Muslim-populated province of Xinjiang, in China itself.
- The conflict threatens important Chinese trade routes (road links through Aksaichin, and the Karakoram Highway).

ON THE WEST

- The continuing presence of nuclear weapons in both India and Pakistan is a major concern for the West which believes that the potential for nuclear war in the region is high.
- Fears have been expressed of nuclear proliferation as Pakistan, with aid reduced, seeks to maintain revenues.

INTRODUCTION

Geography

Kashmir's total area is 218,780 square kilometres. In a central Asian position it shares borders with India to the south, Pakistan to the West, Afghanistan to the north-west, China to the north and east, and Tibet to the east.

The People

Kashmir accommodates a spread of three religious groups plus tiny other minorities. The Valley of Kashmir is predominantly Muslim, whereas Hindus are concentrated in Jammu, and the capital Srinagar. Likewise, Sikhs live in Jammu and Srinagar. Buddhists concentrate largely in Ladakh.[1]

The Conflict

The state of Jammu and Kashmir came into being in the nineteenth century after an agreement between Gulab Singh (who was declared Maharaja of Jammu and Kashmir in the Treaty of Amritsar in 1846) and the British.

With Indian independence on 15 August 1947 and the creation of Pakistan, the princely states (ie those not directly ruled by the British, but nevertheless indirectly influenced by British rule) were left to decide their status. Acting on the hesitation of the Maharaja, tribal raiders spilled over the border from Pakistan.[2] With the tacit acquiescence of the Pakistan government and arms from the Pakistan army, they sought to force the Maharaja's hand in Pakistan's favour.

Fearing for his position, the Maharaja turned to India for support in October 1947. Prime Minister Nehru sent the army on the condition Jammu and Kashmir (hereafter referred to as 'Kashmir') acceded to India. What followed is still a subject of intense debate and controversy. According to some, the Instrument of Accession was signed on 26 October. Others argue the instrument was never signed.[3] The Accession in any case was scheduled to last for only six months, after which time a plebiscite would be held enabling the Kashmiri people to decide their own future. This plebiscite has yet to be held. Whatever the true course of events, tens of thousands of Indian soldiers were flown into Kashmir. Within days, the rebels were forced back, and eventually established a provisional government of Azad ('free') Kashmir in the parts they still held.

India and Pakistan have fought three wars, in all which Kashmir has been an integral part, and in two of them, the principal cause. Since 1984, tensions have centred on the Siachen Glacier in Kashmir, with regular skirmishes between the Indian and Pakistan armies.

The first Indo-Pakistan war

In January 1948 India lodged a formal complaint to the UN that insurgents were using Pakistani territory as a base for their operations, and were being supplied and trained by Pakistan. Both sides refused to accept all the UN's terms under which the plebiscite would be held and in May Pakistani troops entered Kashmir for the first time. In January 1949 a ceasefire was agreed by both sides.[4] During the 1950s and 1960s, Kashmir became increasingly integrated into the Indian Union. Similarly, the ties between Pakistan and Azad Kashmir had grown stronger.

The second Indo-Pakistan war

In 1965, armed infiltrators invaded Indian-administered Kashmir from Azad Kashmir, seeking to inspire revolt. India responded by invading Pakistan and by placing troops in Azad Kashmir. A ceasefire was declared at the command of the UN a month later. The two sides agreed their differences should be settled peacefully, and armed forces were withdrawn to their pre-1965 positions.

The third Indo-Pakistan War (1971) and the Simla Agreement (1972)

Following civil war in East Pakistan, which separated to become Bangladesh, India and Pakistan both crossed the ceasefire line in Kashmir, claiming new territory. The 1972 Simla Agreement saw Prime Minister Indira Gandhi of India and President Zulfiqar Ali Bhutto of Pakistan agree with the UN a new line of control based on the ceasefire line of the 1971 war (a slight variation of the 1949 ceasefire line). India has since argued for the withdrawal of the UN presence, as all UN resolutions had been superseded at Simla. Pakistan disagree, however, claiming they did not accept the ceasefire line as a border, and have reserved the right to return to the UN should bilateral talks fail. Pakistan's diplomatic strategy has featured attempts to 'internationalize' the issue, encouraging the UN to resume its engagement.

The Siachen Glacier

During the 1980s, conflict has centred on the Siachen Glacier, an area close to the ceasefire line within Kashmir, so inhospitable no borderline was drawn for it. In 1984 India moved in its troops, allegedly to preempt Pakistan. Pakistan did likewise, and skirmishes have been common. This is an important by-product of the instability caused over Kashmir. Attempts to make the Glacier a demilitarized zone have failed.

In 1962 India also fought a war with China in Kashmir, which it lost. The outcome of tensions with China since the 1950s has been the Chinese occupation of the eastern part of Kashmir, Aksaichin. China's stake in Kashmir reflects the importance of Aksaichin as a trade route through China and the insecurity China perceives at its borders with Kashmir. In particular, it fears instability in Kashmir could exacerbate the problems it faces from Islamic fundamentalists in its own province of Xinjiang.

The contemporary official Indian position on the accession has altered, from the Indian government's position stated by Prime Minister Nehru in 1947. Nehru declared he had no desire to interfere in the affairs of Kashmir once the invasion had been repelled, and law and order restored. On 28 November 1947 he stated: 'The fate of Kashmir is ultimately to be decided by the people. The pledge we have given, and the Maharaja supported, is not only to the people of Kashmir, but to the world. We will not and cannot back out of it.'

The Indian government now regards Kashmir as an integral part of India. S B Chavan, Indian Home Minister, stated this year, 'We will never allow Jammu and Kashmir to be either merged or become independent. Barring that, some details, some adjustments here and there can be thought of.'[5]

Guerilla groups

The diversity of opinion in Kashmir has led to frustration being channelled through dozens of guerrilla groups. Their activities have increased since 1989. The two main groups are the Jammu and Kashmir Liberation Front (JKLF), and the Hezbol Mujaheddin.

The JKLF assert their interest in a united, independent and secular Kashmir. The Hezbol Mujaheddin are an Islamic fundamentalist group, promoting an Islamic state, and unity with Pakistan. Each group has its own agenda on Kashmir, and relations with their neighbours. What they have in common are calls for UN intervention, and the respect of UN resolutions. 'Moreover, in the light of repression from the late 1980s by a largely non-Muslim Indian army, elements of the largely Muslim Kashmiri population have appealed to Hindu Kashmiris to stay.

Scope of the Study

For the purposes of this study Kashmir will be studied 'geographically' in terms of its three separately administered parts. The subject of this report is Indian-administered Kashmir, which includes the Valley of Kashmir, Jammu and Ladakh. The second region, Azad Kashmir, comprises the 'Federally Administered Northern Areas' officially under the direct administration of Pakistan since 1982,[7] and a narrow stretch of territory to the south-West. The third region (looked at in the China section), is Aksaichin in the east, under the direct administration of China.

While tensions have been evident since 1948, this study focuses on the conflict in Indian-administered Kashmir since 1989, when tensions escalated between the Indian army and parts of the Kashmiri population (some sections of which are supported by Pakistan). It assesses the costs of the conflict to the Kashmiri people, in addition to the costs and benefits of the conflict to India and Pakistan. Because China continues to play a significant role in the region, the study examines the role it has played in the conflict. Finally, an assessment is made of the impact of the conflict on those Western governments and the former USSR, which have been the major source of support for both India and Pakistan.

KASHMIR

THE COSTS

Introduction

Given press censorship and the state of affairs in Indian-administered Kashmir at present, accurate measures of the costs of conflict are difficult to obtain. Due to the collapse of central administration in Indian Kashmir, there is no central means of data collection. Available data, since 1990 in particular, are based on informed estimates. Since 1990, information tends to be qualitative. As the conflict is ongoing, there has been no opportunity for retrospective quantitative analysis of the conflict period. However, it can be said that unrest in Indian-administered Kashmir since 1989 has claimed many lives, and has wrought destruction to economy and society.

Development

Health

Community health has been crippled through the actions of both the Indian security forces and the militants. There has been a marked increase in psychiatric disorders, attributed to the traumas of security force repression. Immunization, nutrition, maternal and child health programmes have ceased in rural areas due to lack of staff, curfews, crack-downs, and difficult transport. Before the conflict, for example, rural immunizations were carried out under the nationwide 'Door-to-Door' programme. In 1989–90, doctors reported around 60 per cent of Kashmir's children were successfully immunized, and the drop-out rate was very low. Since the conflict escalated in 1990, however, the programme has had to be suspended, as workers have been unable to visit rural areas.[8] The normal immunization rate in the Srinagar area has markedly declined since 1990. Many professionals, including medical personnel, have fled Kashmir. Murders of suspected informants have included health personnel.[9]

Threats to health personnel
Methodical threats, attacks and harassment through detention of doctors and medical staff are frequent. Several have been killed on duty, and others have been tortured.[10] This has led to the attrition of health care professionals, and staff and supply shortages. Most district hospitals and primary care centres are not functioning for these reasons. This has put greater pressure on the hospitals in Srinagar, which are already overburdened, and short of staff and supplies. The attrition rate (1990–92) is put at 30 percent for doctors, and 80 per cent for nurses, compounded by a 30 per cent decrease in the number of medical school graduates in the state.

Overcrowding in Srinagar's hospitals

Overcrowding is severe in Srinagar's hospitals. The 700-bed Medical College has received over 1000 patients from May 1992 to October 1992. One of its four operating theatres was used for 2276 cases of gunshot wounds, from January 1992 to October 1992. Sixty-six cases of acute renal failure after torture have also been reported here (1989–93). The department of surgery lost 60 per cent of its staff in 1990, and remains 30 per cent understaffed. There are around 10 nurses during the day, and 5 at night for the whole hospital, whereas before 1990, there were 50 for each shift. Ambulance services ceased to function early in 1992, as drivers have been assaulted and killed by security forces in the course of their duties. Injuries not related to the conflict go unattended, and consequences can be fatal.[11]

Sewage remains untreated as it was before 1990, flowing openly on roads in inner cities. Srinagar has no domestic fresh water supply, in spite of its location in the midst of mountains, lakes and rivers. The high rate of infant mortality, placed at 1 in 5 by the Department of Epidemiology, Kashmir, is due to common diseases such as gastro-enteritis which result from impure water. Other related illnesses are hepatitis, polio-myelitis, cholera and typhoid. Of all illnesses, 40 per cent can be attributed to polluted water.[12]

Education

The education system in parts of Indian-administered Kashmir has collapsed. Parents fear for the lives of their children on the journey to and from school.[13] Amnesty also reports attacks on teachers by the police force. Two hundred schools have been burned down.[14] Order, continuity, organization and administration have broken down at the University of Srinagar, as well as at most of Indian Kashmir's schools and colleges. Security forces frequently conduct searches on campus. As with the medical institutions above, attendance by both students and staff is poor, with classes cancelled in protest

against the actions of the security forces, and calls to boycott by the militant organizations.

The literacy rate was 27 per cent in 1981 in Indian-administered Kashmir.[15] The serious disruptions to the education system since 1990 are likely to have negatively affected this already low figure. By contrast India's adult literacy rate in 1990 was 48.2 per cent, and Pakistan's was 34.8 per cent.[16] Taking literacy to be an important measure of human development, this comparison is highly revealing of Kashmir's under-development as a whole, relative to both India and Pakistan.

Civil and Political Rights

Law and order

Since the insurgency began in late 1989, government services, administration, and the criminal justice system have all collapsed.[17] Kashmir has no democratic institutions. Direct rule from Delhi has been imposed. The rule of law has been suspended, to be replaced with emergency legislation that allows the security forces unfettered activity. Judges' orders are ignored on the grounds the courts are 'tainted'.[18] The rights to free assembly, freedom to worship, freedom of speech, and other basic human rights have been frequently violated, according to the British Parliamentary Human Rights Group (BPHRG).[19]

The Indian government has placed overall command of security operations in the valley in the hands of the army,[20] with local police disarmed. However, organization is poor as there is little coordination between the various elements of the paramilitary (the Border Security Force and Central Reserve Police Force) and the army. Poor leadership, lack of accountability, and an over-zealous desire to achieve results has contributed in part to the perpetration of brutal excesses.[21]

Several thousand have been detained without trial since 1990 under the Public Safety Act (PSA) and the Terrorist and Disruptive Activities Act (TADA). The

Table 3.1:Number of Deaths

Source	Period	Total Deaths
Shah	1990-93	19,593
Moore et al	1990-93	12-22,000
Indian Officials	1990-93	6200
Militant Groups	By 1992	25,000

Sources: Shah, S, 'The Kashmir Conflict', Kashmir Council for Human Rights and Kashmir Watch, London, 1994; Moore, M and Anderson, J, 'Kashmir's Brutal and Unpublicised War', *Voice of Kashmir*, Vol 4, No 3, December 1993; Amnesty International "India: 'An Unnatural Fate': 'Disappearances' and Impunity in the Indian States of Jammu and Kashmir and Punjab", AI Index: ASA 20/42/93, London: International Secretariat, and Gopsill, T and Struk, J, 'Human Rights Violations in Kashmir', British Parliamentary Human Rights Group, 1992

wording of TADA is so general as to have led to the arrests of even peaceful dissenters. To date, no one arrested under TADA has ever been convicted. Unofficial estimates place the number of detainees under these and similar laws as high as 20,000.[22] As a consequence of the collapse of the judiciary, lawyers have been unable to pursue simple open-shut cases. An important example is the arrest and indefinite detention of minors, sometimes as young as 12 years. Numbers of such detainees are now so great, authorities have been forced to permit teachers to conduct examinations in the cells.[23]

Data on human rights abuses by militant groups are considerably harder to come by, and where they exist are in far less detail than the equivalent information gathered on the Indian security forces. This does not mean however that militant abuses do not occur, but highlights the need for more information on this aspect of the conflict.

The cost in human life

It is impossible to obtain precise figures, either for the total number of people who have died in the last few years in Kashmir, or for those victims who have died during their detention by the Indian security forces. Figures provided by serious sources do not agree,[24]

Given these acknowledged limitations, the figures in Table 3.1 are intended to illustrate the nature, if not the degree, of suffering. It is widely acknowledged by the American State Department and other sources mentioned in the table that civilians suffer the greatest number of casualties.

Attacks by all sides against those who have spoken out against abuses

Disturbingly, human rights activists, doctors and others who have spoken out against abuses by both militants and Indian forces have themselves become targets. In December 1992 HR Wanchoo, a civil liberties activist and retired trade unionist, was killed by unknown assassins. In February 1993 evidence strongly suggests Dr Farooq Ashai (Professor of Orthopaedics and documentor of cases of torture and indiscriminate shootings) was murdered by Indian security forces outside his home. In March 1993, Dr AA Guru, Professor of Cardiology and member of the JKLF, was kidnapped and assassinated by unknown gunmen. In December 1993 Professor Awani (Head of the Department of Political Sciences, Srinagar) was murdered by unidentified gunmen. In most instances there is not enough evidence to link the perpetrators to the crime. However, the nature of the murders, and the identity of the victims, provides us with a clear motive, of silencing outspoken critics of the parties involved in the conflict.[25]

The International Committee of the Red Cross (ICRC) has been forbidden by the Indian government to operate in Kashmir (Amnesty, and Drs Petersen and Vedel of Physicians for Human Rights, Denmark.)[26] More broadly, human rights groups in general, including Amnesty, have been prohibited from entering Kashmir by the Indian authorities.[27] Their absence to date is consistent with the official Indian line that 'the Kashmir issue' is an internal problem, and therefore does not justify the interference of outside groups.

Curfews

Dusk to dawn curfews have been imposed by the Indian security forces since conflict flared in 1990. This is intended to suppress militant activity. Curfew hours are from 1900 to 0500 hours.[28] From April 6 to April 23 1990, the entire valley remained under continuous 24 hour curfew.[29] It has served to intimidate the population as a whole. This may be deliberate punishment, as the army often suspects civilians of sheltering militant activists.

Torture and physical abuse

Most of those arrested by the security forces are tortured.[30] Torture is used to coerce detainees to reveal information about suspected militants, or to confess to militant activity.[31] Amnesty International, the Kashmir Council for Human Rights, the Medical Educational Trust and the BPHRG all agree that such tortures do occur: severe beatings, suspension by the feet or hands for prolonged periods (leading to gangrene, and possible amputation), burning, stretching the legs apart, sexual molestation, rubbing chilli powder into the eyes and rectum, enucleation of eyes and forced consumption of liquid while the penis is tied with thread, until the bladder ruptures.

Militant organizations have also committed abuses, including assassination, kidnapping and torture. Journalists have been targeted, as have the security forces and suspected informers. Incidents of rape at the hands of militants are not uncommon.[32] Often, incidents arise in which no group will take responsibility. Further, militants have reportedly used hospitals as sanctuaries. This endangers the lives and security of civilians. By compromising the neutrality of medical personnel (guaranteed under international law) it endangers their lives and security also.[33]

Disappearances

Disappearances are also common, with Amnesty listing 128 examples between January 1990 and September 1993.[34] Paramilitary groups (the Border Security Forces and Central Reserve Police Force) are largely responsible for unacknowledged detentions and disappearances.[35]

Most of the disappeared have been young men suspected of links with one of the many armed secessionist groups. Arrests tend to be arbitrary, based on religion (ie Muslim), sex, age, and place of residence if close to an area of militant activity. Records of arrests are not kept. They may be fabricated retrospectively when necessary to respond to habeas corpus.

Conditions and treatment of detainees in prison

At least 15,000 to 20,000 Kashmiri detainees are experiencing 'a subhuman existence' in jails throughout India, according to a J & K Bar Association report (3/93). Detention is commonly without charge or trial. Those who speak out against their conditions are subject to tear-gassing and beatings with lathi (bamboo sticks). The Kot Balwal jail near Jammu is described as typical. Over 1600 prisoners are held in a 650-capacity prison, in ten poorly ventilated and unhygienic barracks; malnutrition is widespread, and the food unhealthy; skin disorders, malaria, chronic diarrhoea, mental strain and psychiatric disorders are common.[36]

Freedom of the press

India's media are generally freer than Pakistan's. However on the subject of Kashmir both India and Pakistan have connived to keep Kashmir out of the media spotlight. At the start of insurgency in January 1990, India adopted strict and effective censorship over Kashmir. Thirty foreign journalists were expelled. The only permitted reports are those of Indian correspondents after official press briefings. Three local Urdu papers were closed in April 1990. Journalists and editors have been kidnapped, harassed and beaten, and their offices destroyed by security forces.[37] Murder and kidnap have been conducted by militants and paramilitary alike:[38] violence against the press is a means of intimidation adopted by both sides, to silence voices of dissent.

The Economy

Indian-administered Kashmir has depended on a narrow range of income-earning activities; tourism and cottage industries such as handicrafts are the backbone of the state's economy. Carpets, papier maché, shawls, wood-carving and embroidery generate employment, and around 115,243 persons work in 26,332 formally registered units. Such small-scale activity yields substantial foreign exchange: over Rs154 billion (US$4.9 billion) in 1992.39

Handicrafts are also acknowledged by the Indian government to be of significant importance to the Indian economy as a whole. According to the 1981 Census, 'The Valley of Kashmir has been known in the country and abroad as a prominent production centre of traditional handicrafts. The artistic beauty of Kashmiri handicraft products enjoys a world-wide reputation, and contributes as much to the promotion of tourism to Kashmir as to the strengthening of the general economy of the state'.40

Since much work in this sector is performed in homes, the curfew has not affected production too severely.41 Moreover, as the production processes utilize hand-operated tools and looms, output does not rely on an erratic supply of electricity. However, sales and distribution will have been hit. Daily wage earners have been severely affected, as people are too afraid to go out under conditions of arbitrary arrest, curfew, crack-down, and poor transport. Three thousand businesses and shops had been destroyed by 1991 by the army.42 Dr Siraj Shah of the Kashmir Council for Human Rights (KCHR) estimates that around 15 per cent of Muslims from the Kashmir Valley have migrated in search of work. There are an increased number of Kashmiri businesses in Delhi, but villagers tend to stay put due to lack of resources, skills, and education.

Kashmir's tourist industry has been shattered since the conflict worsened in late 1989. In 1988, 722,000 people visited Kashmir, injecting $200m into the local economy. In 1992, 10,400 visited. Most of the state's hotels have been commandeered by the security forces. The decline in tourism has had knock-on effects on the rest of the economy. Incomes derived from tourists by taxi drivers, bus companies and the handicrafts trade have declined accordingly. The many thousand houseboat owners have left in large numbers, with the owners joining militant groups, or seeking other forms of activity.43

About 80 per cent of the state's population is dependent on agriculture for work. Paddy, wheat and maize are the major crops.44 Before Indian intervention, Kashmir was self-sufficient in foodgrain and livestock. Shortages have been registered since 1953 and food and livestock prices have rocketed due to excessive demand. A system of rationing has been introduced, where supplies are subsidized, though quality is allegedly poor.45

The conflict has also dealt a severe blow to Kashmir's ability to become involved in potentially lucrative large-scale industries such as hydro-electric power generation or agro-food processing. Various factors prevent Kashmir from competing for these business opportunities. These relate directly or indirectly to the conflict. Firstly, the conflict itself hinders the establishment of new ventures. In the case of Britain for example, Kashmir is perceived as a 'no go

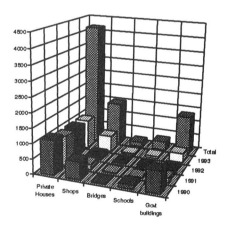

Source: United Kashmir (UK) May/June, 1994

Figure 3.1: Destruction of Property – Kashmir

area',[46] with the British High Commission advising people not to visit. Any business visits seeking out new ventures would thus be ruled out. Even if visits were possible, instability and insecurity in the region, heightened by the kidnapping of two British tourists in June 1994, is a major hurdle to investment.

There are other factors that deter investment, apart from the conflict, but these factors are made worse by the conflict. The poor state of Kashmir's infrastructure, poor roads and rail networks, make transport costs expensive, and increase journey times. With poor links to ports, this is disastrous for trade in perishable agricultural produce.

Infrastructure

Since accession to India, there has been negligible industrial development. Dr Shah of the KCHR attributes this partly to 'the appointment of a succession of corrupt Kashmiri rulers appointed by New Delhi, serving themselves rather than Kashmir'.[47] Since the conflict escalated in 1989 state administration has collapsed in the face of centralized Indian military rule. While infrastructure and public works were fairly poor to begin with, they have deteriorated further as a consequence of the conflict. Another source confirms this, describing 'total disarray' in the civil administration, and its stalling effect on schools, dispensaries, electricity and water departments.[48] Without order there is no maintenance or investment, and services decline. Without civil administration, there can be no return to 'normalcy'.

All towns and 89 per cent of villages in Indian-administered Kashmir had been electrified by 1986.[49] The Statistical Outline of India 1988–89 asserts this had risen to 92 per cent of villages by 1987–88; that is, 5976 villages electrified in total, compared with a figure of 383 for 1965–66. Supply was erratic, however, and with the deterioration of the conflict it has become increasingly so. In winter in Srinagar, blackouts lasting for weeks are not uncommon.[50]

Roads tend to be of a poor quality, with the relative exception of the national highway linking Kashmir with Delhi. Local roads tend to be mud, or partially surfaced.[51] Thus they are vulnerable to the vagaries of weather. Maintenance has suffered with the collapse of state administration since 1990. One-hundred and fifty bridges have been destroyed in the conflict.[52]

The postal service does not function due to curfews, censorship and the dangers staff face in delivery. Before the conflict there were 746 bank branches. Shah asserts these have all closed, save for the Jammu and Kashmir State Bank.[53]

The Environment

Massive troop deployments along the ceasefire line since the First Indo-Pakistan War in 1947, have taken their toll on the forest reserves. Ancient forests have been denuded by the Indian army, for the construction of roads, bridges, checkpoints and residential barracks. With the current standing army in the Kashmir Valley numbering between 300,000 and 600,000, pressure on timber resources for firewood, fuel and cooking is greater at the present stage of the conflict than ever before. In addition, timber has been transported to India for use in railways and construction. Alleged corruption among Kashmiri officials (appointed from New Delhi) has led to ruthless exploitation of forest lands, occasionally sold to timber smugglers.[54]

Extensive deforestation has also taken its toll on the local economy. Communities who once earned their living from the manufacture of the Kashmiri *kangri* (a partially woven pot used as a source of heat during winter) have found their raw materials (in particular the branches of highly pliable trees called kani) have dried up. Small communities depended upon these resources for their survival.[55] Attempts at reforestation under the state forestry department have failed. A World Bank–funded social forestry project worth Rs25 billion (US$775 million) collapsed. This is attributed to a lack of commitment, and corruption on the part of the state forest department.[56]

The loss of natural habitat is also affecting wildlife. Threatened species include the snow leopard, the flying squirrel, the long-tailed Himalayan marmot, the Himalayan black bear, the lynx, the shapu, the blue sheep, the big-horned sheep, and the urian. Many species of deer are also under threat of extinction.

Refugees

By 1993, almost all 150,000 Kashmiri Hindus were in refugee camps in the plains. This brought to an end the centuries of peaceful coexistence between them and the Muslim majority. Between the start of 1990, when the conflict escalated, and September 1990, 48,894 migrant Hindu families had registered in Jammu. In addition, 10,000 Sikhs and other minorities have registered. In Azad Kashmir, 29,000 Muslim migrants have registered.[57] According to FIDH 8304 refugees from Indian-administered Kashmir have been registered in Azad Kashmir between March 1990 and March 1993. Over the same period, it is believed an estimated 1000 families (4000 to 5000 individuals) who are not registered have been sheltered by relatives.[58]

Health care and education provision in refugee camps is limited. There is usually one primary school per camp, and teachers are often refugees themselves. A shortage of materials, comfort, and educational policy, combined with a lack of basic amenities, hamper educational development among children. Medical facilities are basic, and doctors and medicines scarce.

Accommodation is limited to one tent per family. One space serves for cooking, living and sleeping. There is inadequate protection from the variable climate. Heavy rains lead to ground deterioration, weakening the foundations for the camps. Infrastructure is also basic. Water and electricity, supplied by the authorities, is limited. Also, sanitation is poor with one crude toilet for every 20 persons.

FIDH also identifies a group of 'quasi-refugees', also known as 'line of control affectees'. The line of control refers to the border between Indian-administered Kashmir and Azad Kashmir. They estimate around 4875 families (amounting to around 24,375 individuals) have been displaced, believed temporarily, from their settlements and villages on the Azad side.[59]

CONCLUSION

The above demonstrates the precarious situation in Indian-administered Kashmir. The Kashmiri economy and population have endured much suffering as a result of the conflict. Physical repression, and the understandable unwillingness of foreign businesses to invest in Kashmir, have damaged whatever industries Kashmir had, and prevented the growth of new ones. Civilians have suffered the majority of casualties and are often subjected to physical abuse from all sides. Development efforts in Kashmir have stopped, with a consequent drop in the standard of living and levels of education. The continued presence of the Indian army and militant activity ensures that Kashmir remains unstable and underdeveloped. The collapse of the education system ensures that in the future there will be a shortage of skilled individuals. The conflict will continue to destroy Indian-administered Kashmir's second most important source of revenue, tourism. As long as the conflict continues the situation cannot improve.

INDIA

THE COSTS

Introduction

The importance of Kashmir to India is shown in the following quote from retired Indian Foreign Secretary J N Dixit: 'Kashmir in my assessment is the core issue affecting the geopolitical equations in the subcontinent and the stability and security of India'.[60] Yet, since January 1990, calls for a breakaway from India, whether for self-determination, or for accession to Pakistan, have grown in their intensity and their demonstration through violence. Denied the electoral option, opposition has been channelled through militant organizations, and all sides have responded to atrocities with further atrocities. The situation poses a serious challenge to India as a secular state, that strongly rejects the principle of a nation established solely on religious identities. India and Pakistan have fought three wars (two over Kashmir). Relations are at a low ebb again over Kashmir, reflected in skirmishes since 1984 on the Siachen Glacier, and a protracted diplomatic stalemate.

Human Costs

Between 1990 and 1993 Indian officials say that 560 members of the Indian security forces were killed during the conflict in Kashmir, with 1558 injured in 1992 alone.[61] A report in Le Monde on 15 June 1994 said that to date a combined total of 1000 Indian and Pakistani soldiers had died or disappeared, with 3000 wounded as a result of the conflict on the Siachen Glacier alone.[62]

The Economy

India is a vast country with pressing security needs, both internally (Kashmir and Punjab) and externally (Pakistan and China). As such, the military amounts to a huge drain on national resources. In 1990, India spent some Rs 176.84 billion ($10.1 billion) on the military, amounting to 3.3 per cent of GDP.[63] Between 1989 and 1991, India's rate of economic growth declined by 40 per cent, its level of debt increased by over 20 per cent, but defence expenditure kept pace with inflation, and is estimated to be about 13 per cent of 1994's total budget.[64] It is important to remember, however, that the Kashmiri conflict is just one justification for India's high military expenditure. However, operations in Kashmir have proven to be a considerable strain on India's resources. In 1993, six army divisions were operating in Kashmir with a strength of 130,000. In addition, there are an almost equal number of paramilitaries, comprising the Border Security Force, the Central Reserve Policy Force and the Indo-Tibetan Border Police Force. Given this presence, there is almost one soldier for every ten Kashmiris.[65] Lord Avebury estimates the presence of 400,000 army personnel in Kashmir.[66] (This represents just under half, or 44 per cent, of total Indian army strength.)

Since the establishment of India's Department of Atomic Energy in 1954, up to 1991, India spent US$2.3 billion on its nuclear weapons programme. Much of this amount went on purchasing or building reactors (from which it has extracted and reprocessed plutonium for use in warheads) and their associated infrastructure[67] (see Table 3.2)

Table 3.2: India's nuclear infrastructure

Facility	Pu output pa[68]	IAEA safeguards
Madras I	60kg/12 weapons	None
Madras II	60kg/12 weapons	None
Dhruva	25kg/5 weapons	None
Cirus	9kg/1 weapon	Peaceful

Source: Carnegie Task Force on Non-proliferation and South Asian Security.

India's nuclear programme

India is a de facto nuclear power. Since conducting its peaceful nuclear explosion in 1974 India has expanded significantly its nuclear potential and may possess an undeclared stockpile of nuclear devices. It has been estimated that India could theoretically have produced more than 200 nuclear devices by the end of 1992.

India's most likely means of delivering an atomic bomb would be by aircraft, specifically via Jaguar or MiG-27 ground attack aircraft (supplied by UK/France and the former Soviet Union respectively) and the MiG-23/MiG-29 and Mirage 2000 fighter-interceptors (supplied by the former Soviet Union and France respectively).

India is also actively pursuing the development of missile systems, as follows:

Table 3.3: India's missile systems

Short-range missile under development

Type	Payload	Max range
Rohini	400kg	130km
Prithvi SS-350	500kg	350km

Short-range missile in service

Type	Payload	Max range
Prithvi SS-150	1000kg	150km
Prithvi SS-250	500kg	250km

Intermediate-range missile in development

Type	Payload	Max range
Agni	1000kg	2500km
ASLV variant (SLV)	500kg	4000km

Source: *Jane's Defence Weekly*, London, 30 April 1994

State security-related expenditure on the Kashmir conflict by the end of 1992 was evaluated by the Kashmir Times as follows. US$13 million was paid to migrant workers, and in cash relief each year. Employees received US$21 million in salaries. US$9 million was paid in relief compensation to victims, with each victim receiving US$1400. In 1991/92 the state government had to borrow US$150 million from the Jammu and Kashmir Bank.[69] High state expenditure is set to continue. In May 1994 Indian officials stated their intention to spend US$48 million (1.5 billion rupees) on Kashmir each year, 'in the hope of weening people away from secessionist rebellion'.[70]

The scale of security expenditure on Kashmir has drawn criticism from within the Indian authorities. Salman Kurshid, India's Minister of State for External Affairs, stated 'it's an absurd figure we're spending for absolutely no reason what-soever' on troop deployments in the Valley, and along the Indo-Pakistan border.[71]

Figure 3.2 shows that, given total world imports of conventional weapons of

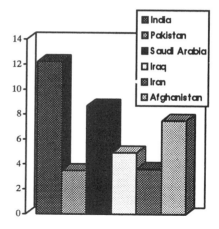

Source: SIPRI, *1993 Yearbook*.

Figure 3.2: Value of purchases of conventional weapons by regional countries 1988–92 ($bn)

US$151 billion between 1988 and 1992, India's share amounted to a staggering 8.1 per cent of this figure. Of the total for less developed countries (LDCs), India's share was around 14 per cent. As a per centage of national imports in 1990, conventional arms constituted 14.8 per cent, compared with a developing country average of 3.1 per cent.[72] This fell to 12 per cent in 1991 in the dying days of the Cold War. However, the decline was proportionately less than the fall in the LDC average of 2 per cent.[73]

As James Woolsey, the CIA Director, has said: 'Neither India nor Pakistan seems to scrimp on resources for their expensive military programmes, despite their economic conditions and widespread poverty among their citizens'.[74]

In addition to security expenditures and security issues, India faces a non-compliant population in the Valley of Kashmir, in response largely to India's actions there. For example, since insur-gency began, no Kashmiri has paid either direct or indirect tax, nor electricity or water bills, by militant diktat.[75]

Political Costs

Domestic political costs

The imposition of martial law in Kashmir has led many global human rights groups and political commentators to conclude the Indian administration has become akin to that of a conquering power, punishing militants and civilians alike. Indeed, large parts of the Kashmiri population, particularly in the Valley, have turned against the Indians. Popular sympathies in Indian-administered Kashmir now lie with those endorsing a separation from India. Some push for a secular and united Kashmiri state, while others endorse unity with the Islamic state of Pakistan.

Further problems arise from the threatened spread of the conflict. Up until now it has largely been concentrated in the predominantly Muslim-populated Kashmir Valley. It now appears that the conflict is spreading from the Valley to Doda, Jammu and Udhampur. Foreign mercenaries have based themselves in Doda, where mountains and forests provide excellent concealment to guerrilla armies. Indian intelligence estimates 800 mercenaries to be operating in the Valley itself in mid-1994, and suspect Pakistan will send another 5000 before the winter snows clear. Pakistan's frequent attacks on Indian human rights violations in Kashmir provide moral, political and diplomatic support to the militants.

The instability created by the Indian government's policies in Kashmir is also believed to be jeopardising the possibility of fair or credible elections. If elections are held in the future, it is believed that they would almost certainly be boycotted by the militant groups, and 'by today's mood [the boycott] will be heeded, leading to farcical voting per centages'.[76] The Hurriyat, the only party with a political platform in Kashmir, might stay out, leaving only the Indian Congress (I) and National Conference to contest. As the Congress (I) Party rules India it is unlikely that it would do well in Indian-administered Kashmir. The National Conference would also fare badly after its 1987 alliance with Rajiv Ghandi's Congress (I) Party (which came to power in rigged elections), and the fact that the Conference leader, Farooq Abdullah, is despised because he is associated with central Indian authority.

International political costs

Statements from human rights groups and political commentators are finding receptive ears in the West. Since the last meeting of the Human Rights Commission in Geneva, there has been increasing pressure for the ICRC to visit Kashmir. Indeed a visit may be scheduled very soon.[77] Three European ambassadors have already visited Kashmir, and 15 more were due in early 1994. These new pressures on India reflect Pakistan's success at internationalizing the Kashmir issue. This has been Pakistan's aim since they complied with an approach that excluded the international community, in the wake of their defeat in the 1971 war.

India risks the disfavour of the international community, and the impact that will have on aid. To date, however, the response has been little more than token. In 1992 the US House of Representatives voted to cut US$24 million off its foreign aid bill to India, to express disapproval at alleged human rights abuses by India in Kashmir and Punjab. This was part of a US$1.4 billion package in development aid.[78] More significantly, India faces the threat of economic sanctions from the powerful Organization of Islamic Countries, which met in Pakistan during the summer of 1993.[79]

Given the increased concern the US has shown over the Kashmir issue, and India's recent concession to allow representatives from certain human rights groups into Kashmir,[80] it is clear the human rights issue is gaining prominence. The question then becomes whether the West will use the economic stick against India, and if so how powerfully it will be wielded.

Refugees

In addition to those registered in Jammu (see Kashmir section) 11,438 Hindus had registered in Delhi, and 2701 Hindu families in various parts of India, by 1990, in response to the insurgency.[81]

Strategic Costs

India-Pakistan relations have 'never been this bad, [There may be a] cataclysm around the corner if the situation does not improve'. [India and Pakistan] are at a 'prolonged crisis stage.'[82]

Given the nature of the Kashmir conflict and Pakistan's involvement, the conflict has important knock-on effects for India's overall security programme. Kashmir symbolizes the major flashpoint between India and Pakistan and has already been the cause of two wars in the recent past. So long as there is no mutually favourable settlement over Kashmir, Indo-Pakistan relations are likely to remain perilously poor in general. This is reinforced by lucrative political mileage for leaders who adopt a tough and uncompromising stance on the issue. The existence in both Pakistan and India of ballistic missile programmes provides evidence that both sides will have the capability to use nuclear weapons if they so desire.

Nuclear strikes have been threatened twice in the last ten years. In 1984 (two years before Pakistan was acknowledged to have nuclear capacity) the CIA is alleged to have tipped off Pakistan about India's intentions to strike Kahuta, where Pakistan built its nuclear bomb. This led Pakistan to threaten India with the destruction of all its nuclear plants, and the consequent poisoning of all major cities with nuclear fallout. President Ghulam Ishaq Khan of Pakistan asserted his belief India would have attacked in 1984, had not Mrs Gandhi died.

The second incident occurred in early 1990, when Pakistan threatened India with first use of nuclear weapons if tension continued to escalate in Kashmir. In response, rumours spread of an impending Indian strike on Kahuta.[83]

The effectiveness of Pakistan's threat is openly questioned by the Director of the Institute for Defence Studies and Analyses in India, who states most major cities and nuclear installations lie outside the maximum range of Pakistani fighter-bombers. Thus the only way to compensate would be with sea-based air-to-air refuelling. This would however require the aid of a third party, and only the US and Saudi Arabia have refuelling tankers in the region.[84] However, since many of India's nuclear installations are located in coastal areas, for example near Bombay and Madras, they are vulnerable to naval attack, with moderately short-range missiles launched from submarines. Thus, in spite of the fact some sites (such as Nagpur and Hyderabad) cannot be reached, Pakistan would still be able to inflict severe damage. Accordingly, this is a serious concern for India.[85]

THE BENEFITS

Strategic Benefits

The majority of the population in India and all the major political parties there perceive that India's security is dependent on India retaining control of Indian-administered Kashmir. To the extent to which the current conflict prevents the creation of an independent Kashmir, the conflict will be perceived as beneficial to India. This has been the situation since Indian independence as shown in Nehru's telegram to British Prime Minister Clement Attlee on 25 October 1947, which summed up the geopolitical aspect as follows: 'Kashmir's northern frontiers...run in common with those of three countries, Afghanistan, the USSR and China. Security of Kashmir, which must depend upon its internal tranquillity and existence of stable government, is vital to security of India.'[86]

Such concerns continue, with attention focused on Pakistan's border. Retired Indian Foreign Secretary J N Dixit states, 'Any erosion of Indian jurisdiction'[over Kashmir accordingly] 'diminishes India's strategic defence capacity'.[87] Whether the conflict in Kashmir enhances India's security is open to question.

Domestic Concerns

Perhaps most important of all, however, is the preservation of India's territorial integrity. India comprises a number of states, united since independence on secular lines, based on a multiplicity of identities and associations. The religious makeup of Kashmir exemplifies the secular principles upon which India was founded, and India is keen to ensure that this situation continues.

Given its professed secular nature then, India's success can be judged on the success of the integration of its various communities. If, in the case of Kashmir, certain elements feel they would like to separate from the Union (whether to join with the Islamic state of Pakistan, or to pursue self-determination) this is perceived by the Indian authorities as a challenge to the principles underlying India's existence, and thus to India itself. There is the fear separation by one state will have knock-on effects: other states may be encouraged by successful secession elsewhere, to express their dissatisfaction with central rule in a similar way.

This fear is very real, and is frequently expressed in official statements, especially on the subject of Kashmir. Such officials consider the accession of Kashmir to India to be final. S B Chavan of the Indian government recently stated 'We will never allow Jammu and Kashmir to be either merged or become independent. Barring that, some details, some adjustments here and there can be thought of'.[88] J N Dixit argues that questioning the legality of the accession of Kashmir to India, in addition to separatist tendencies within Kashmir on the basis of religion, 'is a prescription for the disintegration of the Indian Union'.[89] On this basis, many view the conflict in Kashmir as being beneficial to all Indians as it shows a desire on the part of the Indian government to uphold the Union.

Furthermore, lucrative political mileage can be gained by leaders who are tough and uncompromising on the issue of Kashmir. Under unstable political conditions in both India and Pakistan, rulers have taken a strong stance against each other with respect to Kashmir. For example, V P Singh, Indian Prime Minister in the early 1990s and leader of the unstable coalition that removed Rajiv Gandhi from power, used the Kashmir issue to strengthen the position of his minority government. He stated India would not concede Kashmir to Pakistan without a war, and that, 'They will have to pay a very high price and we have the capacity to inflict heavy losses'. In part, this aggressive stance was intended to appease the Hindu fundamentalist Bharatiya Janata Party (BJP); the BJP were crucial to the survival of Singh's coalition, and pressured him 'to match words with actions'.[90] Accordingly, Singh called for India 'to prepare psychologically for war'.[91]

Economic Benefits

The conflict could be said to benefit certain sectors of the Indian economy, especially that of the defence industrial sector. The arms and nuclear industries receive a great deal of investment as a result of high defence expenditure. As well as providing jobs, investment in the military industry enables India to advance technologically and to earn valuable foreign exchange through military sales.

CONCLUSION

It would seem that the costs of the conflict in Kashmir are still perceived to be a price worth paying. Kashmir has become such an important domestic political issue, Indian politicians have little room to manoeuvre. Indeed, a withdrawal from Indian-administered Kashmir could undermine the Indian Union, by setting an example to separatist forces elsewhere in the country. The costs of the conflict continue to drain national resources and cause military casualties. With legitimacy of central authority lost, order has been imposed by force. Although India has the military strength to do this, the war will be difficult to win by conventional means.

PAKISTAN

THE COSTS

Introduction

*Establishment of a durable peace and
normalisation of relations between
Pakistan and India is inextricably linked
with settlement of the Kashmir question.
So also are the prospects for co-operation
in the South Asian region.[92]*

The Pakistani government and population
see India as the major threat to the
continued survival of their nation. Against
this background, the conflict in Kashmir is
the most important security concern for
Pakistan. Benazir Bhutto of Pakistan swore
a 1000-year war to liberate Kashmir, and
appropriated US$5 million for Pakistani
rebel fighters in the Indian-administered
region.[93] In addition, the Pakistan military
has admitted to providing support and
training to the Hezbol Mujaheddin, with
training camps established in Azad
Kashmir. Strong evidence suggests military
support has also been provided, and in
August 1993 the President of Pakistan
encouraged the freedom fighters to
continue their struggle.

Pakistan is one of the world's poorest
countries, ranked 132 out of 173 in terms of
human development.[94] Its significant
defence budget means opportunities for
development are forgone.

The Economy

From a budgetary point of view, military
and strategic concerns have taken
precedence over the well-being of the
population and economy. In absolute
economic terms the costs to Pakistan of this
military competition far outweigh those to
India. Where Pakistan's defence spending-
to-GNP ratio is around twice India's, in
absolute terms its military budget is less
than a third of India's. Given massive

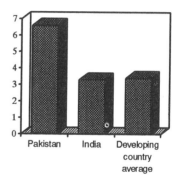

Source: United Nations Development Programme,
Human Development Report Oxford University Press,
London, 1993

*Figure 3.3: Percentage of GDP spent on military
(1990)*

budget deficits and the neglect of human
development, Pakistan appears to be
harbouring unrealizable (and at least
unsustainable) military ambitions. Figures
3.3 and 3.4 compare Pakistan's military
expenditure with that of India's and the
developing country average.

Between 1978 and 1991, Pakistan's
defence budget increased sevenfold. The
defence budget for 1992–93 at US$3 billion
(82 billion rupees) marks an 8 per cent
increase on the previous year. Given debt
service payments of US$3.5 billion (93
billion rupees), little over US$0.1 billion (3.3
million rupees) was left for development.
Defence expenditure and debt servicing
together exceeded government tax revenue,

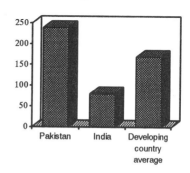

Source: UNDP, 1993, op cit

*Figure 3.4: Military expenditure as % of amount
spent on education and health combined, 1990*

71

with defence accounting for almost 40 per cent of government spending.[95] As shown in Figure 3.2, Pakistan purchased US$3.486 billion worth of conventional weapons in the period 1988–92.[96] Tables 3.4 and 3.5 detail Pakistan's nuclear infrastructure and missile delivery systems.

Pakistan's nuclear programme

'We will eat grass if necessary, to pay for it!'
(Zulfiqar Ali Bhutto).

Pakistan is generally perceived as a threshold nuclear power. Estimates as to the actual status of the Pakistani nuclear weapons programme vary from possession of most or all of the necessary components to that of a small stockpile of nuclear weapons. Pakistan's nuclear weapons programme is based upon highly enriched uranium and it has been estimated that it could have produced sufficient quantities of this material for 24 weapons by the end of 1992. Pakistan has its own natural sources of uranium which is enriched at the centrifuge enrichment plant at Kahuta.

Pakistan's most likely means of delivering an atomic device would be by aircraft, specifically via the F-16 or Mirage V supplied by the US and France respectively.

Pakistan's military ambitions have also demanded around three times as many of its people, as a percentage of total population, to enter its armed forces as India.[98]

Table 3.4: Pakistan's nuclear infrastructure

Facility	WGU[97] output	IAEA safeguards
Kahuta	21–63kg/1–4 wpns	None

Source: Carnegie Task Force on Non-proliferation and South Asian Security.

Strategic Costs

Conflict with India

India's willingness to go to war with Pakistan over Kashmir has been demonstrated twice in the past. The fervour

Table 3.5: Pakistan's missile systems

Short-range missile under development		
Type	*Payload*	*Max range*
Hatf IA	500kg	100km

Short-range missile in service		
Type	*Payload*	*Max range*
CSS-7(DF-11/M-1)	500kg	300km

Intermediate-range missile in development		
Type	*Payload*	*Max range*
Hatf III	500kg	600km

Source: *Jane's Defence Weekly*, London, 30 April 1994

with which India continues to hold on to Kashmir implies a willingness to do so again. As mentioned earlier, a full-scale Indo-Pakistan war which would include the use of nuclear weapons is not impossible. The Kashmir issue is central to Indo-Pakistan relations and hence could be the catalyst for any war. In this context, former Prime Minister Nawaz Sharif's recent confession that Pakistan does possess nuclear weapons (an unprecented move) can only stoke up the insecurity India feels.

Furthermore, India asserts that this is a fight not just over a piece of land, but a challenge to its territorial integrity, and therefore the foundations upon which it was built, and that it will therefore use all means at its disposal to defend its interests.[99] While both sides can inflict unprecedented damage on one another, it is likely, given India's military superiority and greater geographical size, that Pakistan would suffer considerably greater damage The aftermath of such a war could be damaging to Pakistan's own unity. With a debilitated central government, separatists in Sindh and Baluchistan, strongly resentful of perceived power concentration in Punjab under previous governments (i.e. those of Zia ul-Haq and Nawaz Sharif), would take advantage, reflecting the situation in 1971 when a weak Pakistani government was forced to part with its eastern wing, which became Bangladesh.

Changing international alliances

During the Soviet occupation of Afghanistan, Pakistan benefited from US military support. With the end of the Cold War, Pakistan's old allies have realigned themselves. Pakistan is no longer an important strategic ally to the USA. It was valued highly in this role during the Soviet occupation of Afghanistan, when the USA used Pakistan as a 'middle man' to pass on weapons to the Mujaheddin guerillas. In this way, Pakistan acquired US funds and weapons for its own uses. A 'considerable cut', usually estimated as at least 40 per cent, was derived by Pakistan 'from those arms destined for the Afghan resistance', with US knowledge (Lamb, C., 1991, p 268, op cit). A The old pacts (India and the USSR against Pakistan, China and the US) have ceased to be relevant and the US has sought to normalize its relations with a much larger, more powerful India.

The US's new stance is reflected in the economic and military aid freeze (of aid worth about US$750,000 per year) imposed by President Bush in October 1990, sanctions that reflect a growing impatience with Pakistan over its nuclear weapons build-up but tolerated under Reagan as the price of Pakistan's support for US operations in Afghanistan.. Although the sanctions are limited, they indicate this shift. They have proved to be a nuisance in the short term; for example, F-16 fighter jets have had to be grounded due to lack of spare parts.[100]

Political costs

Pakistan may also face isolation and condemnation from the West for its support for militants in Kashmir; Pakistan's military itself has admitted to aiding militants. Pakistan's support of the Islamic groups who favour union with Pakistan, in particular Hezbol Mujaheddin, runs serious risk of backfiring on them. For example, recent demonstrations took place following the assassination of a prominent religious leader. Over 100,000 Kashmiris took to the streets against the pro-Pakistan militants, in the belief the Hezbol Mujaheddin was responsible for the death. The protesters called not only for *azadi* (freedom), but, for the first time since the unrest started, were shouting 'Down with Hezbol Mujaheddin', and 'Death to Pakistan'.[101] While Pakistan seeks to exploit the bitterness felt against India, it is itself, along with its sympathizers in Kashmir, coming to be seen as a threat to this drive for *azadi*.

THE BENEFITS

Political Benefits

There are a number of domestic and regional benefits to Pakistan of the conflict in Kashmir. Firstly, if Indian-controlled Kashmir were to accede to Pakistan, this would reverse the humiliation of the 1971 war. Also, it may challenge Indian territorial integrity if Indian fears of a series of internal crises are realized, as other groups push for separate status (eg. Punjab). This outcome would give Pakistan a far stronger hand in the region. Of course, if Kashmir acceded to India the reverse would also be true and the foundations upon which Pakistan is based would be threatened (For more on this issue see the Indian benefits section.) Secondly, even if India were to maintain its grip on Kashmir, which is clearly possible in military terms, the Pakistani government believe a prolonged conflict would cause substantial political damage, in addition to economic and military costs, to India. As in India, there is much political mileage to be made from these issues in Pakistan, in condemning Indian actions and calling for support for Kashmiri independence.

The growing number of damning reports from organizations such as Asia Watch and Amnesty concerning the nature of India's rule over Kashmir is exploited to the full by official Pakistani statements which seriously tarnish India's image in the international community (see Sattar, ref. 92, for an example). Any cost to India, whether diplomatic, economic, or territorial, is in some way perceived as a benefit to Pakistan. Pakistan has used the issue of human rights as a lever over India whenever possible. For example, in return for direct talks with India which for the first time would discuss all aspects of Kashmir, Pakistan has agreed to withdraw a resolution it tabled at the UN General Assembly, on Indian human rights violations in Kashmir.[102]

If successful in these efforts to emphasize Indian human rights abuses, Pakistan will be able to offset the legacy of the 1972 Simla Agreement, when, after having been defeated, Pakistan was forced to accept bilateral talks with India as the basis for all future negotiations over Kashmir. This gave India strategic advantage, by superseding UN resolutions for a plebiscite, for Pakistan agreed not to table an objection to Indian rule, thus ruling out international intervention.

The Economy

The American aid freeze has served further to encourage Pakistan to attempt to achieve arms self-sufficiency. Similar to the situation in India, the investment in the

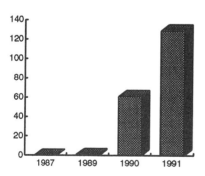

Source: SIPRI
Note: trend indicators only, measured in US$ million at constant (1990) prices.

Figure 3.5: Exports of major conventional weapons by Pakistan[104]

defence industry has served to increase jobs and technological advance. Arms self-sufficiency would be beneficial to Pakistan in that its strength would not be conditional upon the vagaries of external pacts. Self-sufficiency would thus enable Pakistan to maintain a consistently strong position against India over Kashmir.

There have also been spin-off benefits from Pakistan's military programme. Pakistan has started to export small arms, explosives and propellants to the Gulf states, earning US$45 million in 1992, and seeking to earn US$370 million by 1997.[103] According to SIPRI estimates exports of major conventional weapons by Pakistan have soared in recent years (Figure 3.5)

CONCLUSION

Pakistan is successfully conducting a diplomatic campaign to rectify any military imbalance between itself and India over Kashmir. Although this may be politically beneficial in the short-term, the strategic costs in a volatile political climate far outweigh these gains. The perceived conflict with India costs Pakistan more 'economically' than it does India, and hampers development efforts to a greater extent. However, because of the importance of Kashmir to Pakistan, both domestically and as a way to put pressure on India, it is unlikely that Pakistan will lessen such efforts in order to improve development.

Abdul Sattar, former Minister for Foreign Affairs for Pakistan, succinctly sums up the effects of the continuing Kashmir conflict: 'Continued delay in the settlement of the Kashmir question benefits none of the parties; its resolution would serve the interests of all: Kashmiris above all, but also India and Pakistan. Peace and stability would bring dividends, release resources for the acceleration of the development process, pave the way for economic cooperation and also enhance the attraction of the region with more than a billion people from other countries interested in trade and investment'.[105]

CHINA

THE COSTS

Introduction

Territorial disputes have been at the heart of animosity between China and India. In 1952, Prime Minister Nehru asserted his view that China was a threat to India. During the 1950s, tensions between the two nations grew. In 1962 they went to war, and India was decisively beaten. The outcome of this tension was China's claim to, and occupation of, Aksaichin (the eastern part of Kashmir). In the war with India, China claimed and occupied both Aksaichin, and the North East Frontier Administration (NEFA–what was to become the Indian state of Arunachal-Pradesh in 1987). On its victory, China enforced a ceasefire, and told India it would return NEFA, but under no circumstances would it part with Aksaichin. There has been no further military conflict over this region, and both Rajiv Gandhi and the present Prime Minister N Rao, have tacitly accepted the status quo.[106]

Strategic Costs

While it can be said that the present division of Kashmir suits China, there is no reason to suggest the current conflict can benefit China in any way. Rather, China fears the instability in Kashmir, which is no longer confined just to the Valley, may spill over into the unstable Muslim-populated province of Xinjiang, in China itself. Thus, while it fears an independent Kashmir would create unrest among Islamic fundamentalists in Xinjiang (on the border with Kashmir) and also threaten important Chinese trade routes (road links through Aksaichin, and the Karakoram Highway), a continued conflict could achieve the same result as separatist frustrations grow. Given that the unrest has not been successfully contained, continued conflict can in no way be in China's interest. It has already been noted that growing frustration seeks increasingly radical or fundamentalist channels to express itself. The longer the conflict continues, and the more people turn to these methods, the greater will be the threat to China's own internal security. Regional insecurity is therefore not in China's interest. It also fears the knock-on effect of the Kashmir conflict in Xinjiang (if realised) could be exploited by a foreign power. In particular, China is wary of an independent Kashmir becoming 'an American surrogate on its southern border'. In spite of its friendship with the USA, Chinese authorities suspect the Americans of already 'undermining' them in Tibet and Xinjiang, and consequently seek at all costs to avoid a scenario where Kashmir could become another base for destabilization. (Quotes taken from *Daily Telegraph*, 4 January 1994.)

THE BENEFITS

Strategic Benefits

Although China and India have not been to war over Kashmir, China has a strong interest in, and therefore an agenda on, the future of Kashmir. China does not want to see an independent Kashmiri state, hence any conflict which ensures that this does not happen is perceived as a benefit by China. China's benefits from its administration of the eastern part of Kashmir (Aksaichin) are largely strategic. Chinese involvement rests first on the perception that its border with Indian-administered Kashmir is an area of potential instability and thus danger to the Chinese mainland, and second with its belief that Aksaichin has vital strategic importance because of its comprehensive road network and the trade routes that cross it.

Until the end of the Cold War, China had unambiguously taken sides in the ongoing war of nerves between India and Pakistan. Animosity with India, which had led to war in 1962, led China to seek a strategic ally in Pakistan. 'China was the chief instrument by which Pakistan got its bomb', providing 'critical technology, design data, training, and even nuclear materials'.[107]

Further links have been established with Pakistan since 1982, with the construction of the Karakoram Highway, an all-weather motorway stretching from China into Pakistan-administered Kashmir, through the Karakoram Pass.[108] This highway provides China's access to the Indian Ocean. By creating this important trade and transport link, China has given Pakistan a reason to preserve the status quo.[109]

CONCLUSION

Since the Cold War ended, there has been a slight 'warming' of relations between India and China. It is sensible for China to seek stable relations with such a large and powerful neighbour. However, it is not in China's interests to abandon Pakistan. There are still internal security concerns, and the country needs to keep open its road links through Aksaichin, and the Karakoram Highway.

THE WEST

THE COSTS

Introduction

Western intervention in South Asia until the collapse of the Soviet Union rested on strategic concerns. Given close relations between India and the Soviet Union, it seemed natural for China and Pakistan, both having fought wars with India, to enter into cordial relations with the US. However, with the decline of the USSR, the situation is radically different. This section focuses on the US, the UK and Germany since, aside from the Soviet Union, they have been the major sources of support for both India and Pakistan.

Strategic Costs

To the extent to which the Kashmir conflict exemplifies the military confrontation between India and Pakistan, the West faces a number of strategic concerns. The largest potential cost to the West may arise from the possibility of a full-scale Indo-Pakistan war in which nuclear weapons could be used, if past threats are to be believed. The ramifications of such an action are not difficult to imagine. Moreover, responsibility for a limited nuclear war would also lie with the West (and the Soviet Union) as main suppliers of conventional weapons and nuclear technology.

The G7 have tended to tie military development in the countries they sponsor, to short-term geopolitical considerations and this exacerbates any instability already present. With regard to India and Pakistan, favour and disfavour accrue according to how much they are perceived to be geopolitically valuable at any moment in time.

At a time of increasing intra-state conflict, Kashmir could be yet another conflict that tests further the credibility of the UN, assuming the UN takes a wider interest in this war. There is also the danger that the West will become involved in a difficult peacekeeping mission between India and Pakistan.

THE BENEFITS

The Economy

Again, to the extent to which Kashmir has been a priority security concern for India and Pakistan, the West has benefited economically from the sales of military equipment and technology to both countries.

Arms sales to India and Pakistan by the West (plus China and the former USSR), have proved highly lucrative. Sales to India of major conventional weapons amounted to US$12.236 billion (1990 prices) between 1988 and 1992. For Pakistan the figure was US$3.486 billion.[110] These figures are broken down in Table 3.6

Table 3.6: *Conventional weapons sales to India and Pakistan 1988–92 (US$m)*

	India	Pakistan
USA	10	1119
USSR/Russia	9364	–
France	387	55
UK	1044	158
China	–	1935
Germany	261	–
Other Europe	1053	58
Other	117	161
Total	12,236	3486

Source: SIPRI, *Yearbook 1993.*

The figures in Table 3.6 also reflect Cold War rivalries during that period. The US and China (Pakistan's largest supplier) sold mainly, or only, to Pakistan. Similarly, the former USSR sold exclusively to India. These figures do not account for sale of the nuclear and dual-use technologies which have been crucial to both India and Pakistan.

In the post-Cold War situation and as arms transfers patterns are beginning to change, economic considerations come to the fore. Hence, in 1992, for the first time in many years, the US sold weapons to India.

German arms sales

West Germany has provided experts since 1976 to help India with guidance and navigation systems, capable of guiding satellites and warheads. It has helped India construct rocket test facilities, and simulate high altitude rocket tests. Software, computers and rocket parts have also been provided. Germany has helped India become self-sufficient in the creation of carbon composites: these can be used as heat shields for both rocket nozzles and the nose cones of ballistic missiles as they re-enter the earth's atmosphere.[111]

Western private sector involvement

Where India has not been able to import arms and technology legally, it has resorted to smuggling and dual-use technology. Private Western firms have sold crucial dual-use technology on a large scale. The German company Siemens sold technology enabling the manufacture of heavy water (the same system it sold to Libya for mixing poison gas). Software to run the system came from ICI in Britain and MTI in the US. Minicomputers for this software came from the Digital Equipment Corporation of the US, and Kellogg USA managed the whole system.

CONCLUSION

Whilst direct costs to the West of the conflict in Kashmir are small, some potential major costs may occur. Both India and Pakistan have refused to sign the Nuclear Non-proliferation Treaty for nuclear weapons and believe nuclear strength is essential to protect their respective territorial integrities. In an unstable political environment where rulers struggle to win legitimacy from their own people, taking a tough stance over Kashmir becomes a sure way of appealing to a broad section of the population in both India and Pakistan. With tensions over Kashmir at a high, the dangers of a confrontation between India and Pakistan must also be said to be high. What has to be avoided is the slow drift to war. The implications of an absolute war in South Asia, using the highly destructive military technology and know-how from the West, Russia and China, are devastating. In general, the end of the Cold War has not meant an end to the tensions between India and Pakistan. 'The removal of one source of antagonism has revealed many others' says the UNDP (see ref. 73). Reflecting this identified general trend, tensions between India and Pakistan over Kashmir have 'never been this bad': both sides are in a 'prolonged crisis stage', says Dr Raja Mohan (see ref. 82).

IF THE CONFLICT HAD NOT OCCURRED

Introduction

With stability in Kashmir comes the possibility of development through investment, and hence the potential for international and local businesses to profit. The purpose of this section is to explain how Kashmir could have developed economically, if the conflict had not occurred. It will also discuss whether the countries of the West could have benefited from a stable Kashmir.

Kashmir

India, with its vast climatic and geographical variations, has the capacity to grow almost any agricultural product. The Kashmiri climate is well suited to fruit orchards and certain vegetables, which in the past it has grown for both subsistence and cash. Agro-food processing is thus a viable industry for investment. According to the UK Department of Trade and Industry (DTI), India is not yet realizing its potential in this field. With moves to economic liberalization however, this is likely to change. A state such as Himachal Pradesh on Kashmir's southern border, with fertile soils and favourable climate,

could benefit from this. Kashmir's geography and climate are also favourable for hydro-electric power generation. Hydro-electric power generation presently does not meet India's needs (based on information from the DTI), yet there is much potential that may be exploited. The states with this potential are those in the north, and north-east of India, whose river systems flow from the Himalayas (for example, Himachal Pradesh, and the states to the east of Bangladesh).

Without conflict, Kashmir's shattered tourist industry may well have continued to grow. In 1988, 722,000 people visited Kashmir, injecting US$200m into the local economy. In 1992, only 10,400 visited. An increase in tourist numbers would have a knock-on effect on other elements of the economy such as taxi drivers, bus companies, and the handicrafts trade.

Conclusion

Potential benefits of the Kashmir conflict not occurring are difficult to measure. Potential benefits are most obvious for Kashmir, which would have gained economic growth through its tourist industry, and in industries such as power generation.

If the conflict had not occurred, there is reason to believe that Kashmir would have benefited in similar ways to other states with similar resource bases, under the recent Indian free market reforms.

REFERENCES

1 Lunn, J, 'Kashmir', House of Commons Background Paper, No 272, 11 June, 1991.
2 Ibid.
3 Lamb, A, *Birth of a Tragedy: Kashmir 1947* Hertingfordbury: Roxford Books, 1994.
4 United Nations, *The Blue Helmets: A Review of United Nations Peace-keeping* (Second Edition), United Nations Department of Public Information, 1990.
5 *India Today*, 15 March 1994.
6 Lunn, June, op cit; and Amnesty International, 'India: 'An Unnatural Fate': 'Disappearances' and Impunity in the Indian States of Jammu and Kashmir and Punjab', AI Index: ASA 20/42/93,

London: International Secretariat, December 1993.
7 Schwartzberg, J *An Historical Atlas of South Asia* (Second Impression) Oxford: Oxford University Press, 1992.
8 Asia Watch and Physicians for Human Rights, 'Rape in Kashmir: A Crime of War', May 1993.
9 Gossman, P, and Iacopino, V, 'The Crackdown in Kashmir: Torture of Detainees and Assaults on the Medical Community', Asia Watch and Physicians for Human Rights, February 1993.

10 Ibid.
11 Varadarajan, P 'Kashmir: A People terrorised: A Report on Extra-judicial Executions, Rape, Arbitrary Arrests, Disappearances and Other Violations of Basic Human Rights by the Indian Security Forces in Indian-Administered Kashmir', Paris, Federation Internationale des Ligues des Droties de l'Homme, Rapport No 167.
12 Shah, S 'Environmental Terrorism: A Policy of Economic Repression in Kashmir', Unpublished Paper, 1994a.
13 Shah, S, 'The Kashmir Conflict', Kashmir Council for Human Rights and Kashmir Watch, London, 1994b.
14 Bose, A C, 'Kashmir's Cry for Justice', 1993.
15 *India 92*, 1993 Update.
16 United Nations Development Programme, *Human Development Report 1993* London: Oxford University Press, 1993.
17 Gupta, S, 'India-Pakistan Relations: On a Short Fuse', *India Today*, 15 March 1994, and Shah, 1994, op cit.
18 Bhatia, S, 'Brutal Crackdown on Kashmir', *The Observer*, 23 May 1993.
19 Gopsill, T, and Struk, J, 'Human Rights Violations in Kashmir', British Parliamentary Human Rights Group, 1993.
20 Amnesty International, 1993, op cit.
21 Ibid.
22 Ibid Amnesty International, 1993; and Gopsill, and Struk, 1993, op cit.
23 Bhatia, 1993, op cit.
24 Jaudel, E, et al, 'Violations of Human Rights Committed by the Indian Security Forces in Jammu and Kashmir, 10 to 18 April 1993', Federation Internationale des Ligues des Droites de l'Homme, Rapport No 172, Paris, May 1993.
25 Shah, 1994, op cit; Moore, M and Anderson, J, 'Kashmir's Brutal and Unpublicised War', *Voice of Kashmir*, Vol 4, No 3, December 1993; Media Transcription Service, ref: 2337, Channel 4 News, 1 April 1993; Amnesty International 1993, op cit; Asia Watch and Physicians for Human Rights, 'Rape in Kashmir: A Crime of War', May 1993; and Shah in conversation, 17 February 1994
26 Petersen, H, and Vedel, O, 'A Mission to Kashmir: testimonies of Torture and Killing of Civilians', Physicians for Human Rights, Denmark, June 1993.
27 Bedi, R, 'Conflict in Kashmir Continues', *Jane's defence Weekly*, 3 July 1993.
28 Gopsill, and Struk, 1993, op cit.
29 Shah, 1994b, op cit.
30 Ibid.
31 Gossman, and Iacopino, 1993, op cit.
32 Amnesty International, 1993, op cit.
33 Gossman, and Iacopino, 1993, op cit.
34 Amnesty International, 1993, op cit.
35 Ibid.
36 Kashmir Watch, 15 October 1993; and Shah, 1994b, op cit.
37 Shah, 1994b, op cit.
38 Amnesty International, 1993, op cit.
39 India 92, 1993, op cit.
40 Census of India 1981, 'Handicraft Survey Report: Kangri and Willow Wicker Basketry', Part XD, Series 8: Jammu and Kashmir, 1981.
41 Interview with Dr Siraj Shah, Kashmir Council for Human Rights, 17 February 1994.
42 Asia Watch, 'Kashmir Under Siege: Human Rights in India', 1991.
43 Shah, February 1994, op cit.
44 *India 92*, 1993, op cit.
45 Shah, 1994a, op cit.
46 Unattribuatable Department of Trade and Industry source.
47 Shah, February 1994, op cit.
48 Gupta, S, 'India-Pakistan Relations: On a Short Fuse', *India Today*, 15 March 1994.
49 Indian Statistical Abstract 1989.
50 Shah, 1994a, op cit.
51 Ibid.
52 Shah, 1994b, op cit.
53 *India 92*, 1993.
54 *Mountain Valley Journal*, Kashmir, February 1993; and Shah 1994a, op cit.
55 Shah, 1994a, op cit.
56 Ibid.
57 Shah, 1994b, op cit.
58 Jaudel, E, 1993, op cit.
59 Ibid.
60 Dixit, J N, 'Kashmir: The Contemporary Geopolitical Implications for India and for Regional Stability and Security', Presentation given at The Geopolitics of the Kashmir Dispute Seminar, SOAS, 8 April 1994.
61 Amnesty International, 1993, op cit.
62 *Le Monde*, 15 June 1994.
63 United Nations Development Programme, *Human Development Report 1993* Oxford: Oxford University Press, 1993.
64 *Arms Trade News*, 'Kashmir: Weapons Fuel India-Pakistan Tension', August–September 1993.
65 Bhatia, May, 1993, op cit.
66 Avebury, E; 'Kashmir; The Principle of Self-Determination,' *Voice of Kashmir*, June 1994.
67 Burrows, W, and Windrem, R, *Critical Mass: The Dangerous Race for Superweapons in a Fragmenting World* New York: Simon and Schuster Ltd, 1994.
68 Annual plutonium output.
69 Shah, 1994b, op cit.
70 *The Guardian*, 9 May 1994.
71 Moore and Anderson, J 1993, op cit.
72 United Nations Development Programme, 1993, op cit.
73 United Nations Development Programme, *Human Development Report 1994* Oxford: Oxford University Press, 1994.
74 CIA Director, R James Woolsey, in *Arms Trade News*, 'Kashmir: Weapons Fuel India-Pakistan Tension', August–September 1993.
75 Bedi, July 1993, op cit.
76 Gupta, March 1994, op cit.
77 Ibid.
78 *Voice of Kashmir*, 'House Votes to Cut India Aid', September 1992.
79 Bedi, July 1993, op cit.

80 Gupta, March 1994, op cit.

81 Shah, 1994b, op cit.

82 Dr C Raja Mohan, Research Associate at the Institute for Defence Studies and Analyses, New Delhi, and fellow of the US Institute for Peace, in *Arms Trade News*, 'Kashmir: Weapons Fuel India-Pakistan Tension', August–September 1993.

83 Burrows and Windrem, 1994, op cit.

84 Singh, J, 'The Wars That Never Were', *India Today*, 28 February 1994.

85 Interview with Professor Graham Chapman, SOAS, 16 June 1994.

86 Lamb, 1994, op cit.

87 Dixit, April, 1994, op cit.

88 *India Today*, 15 March 1994.

89 Dixit April 1994, op cit.

90 Lamb, 1991, op cit.

91 Gupta, March 1994, op cit.

92 Sattar, A, 'Kashmir: Struggle for Freedom', 1994, Presentation given at The Geopolitics of the Kashmir Dispute Seminar, SOAS, 8 April 1994.

93 Burrows, and Windrem, 1994, op cit.

94 United Nations Development Programme, *Human Development Report 1993* Oxford: Oxford University Press, 1993).

95 Matthews, R, 'Pakistan: On the Road to Economic Reality', *Jane's Defence Weekly*, 3 July 1993.

96 SIPRI, *Yearbook 1993*.

97 WGU = Weapons grade uranium

98 United Nations Development Programme, *Human Development Report 1993* Oxford: Oxford University Press, 1993); and Sivard, R, World Military and Social Expenditures 1993 (Fifteenth Edition) (Washington: World Priorities, 1993).

99 Dixit, April 1994, op cit.

100 *The West Australian*, 20 January 1993.

101 *The Guardian*, 22 June 1994.

102 *International Herald Tribune*, 25 November 1993; and *The Daily Telegraph*, 31 December 1993.

103 *The West Australian*, 20 January 1993.

104 These figures are trend value indicators, not absolute amounts. Please consult SIPRI as to how these are constructed.

105 Sattar, April 1994, op cit.

106 Interview with Dr Mahmud Ali, Deputy Head Bengali Service, BBC World Service, 15 June 1994.

107 Burrows, and Windrem, 1994, op cit.

108 Schwartzberg, 1992, op cit.

109 Interview with Dr Mahmud Ali, Deputy Head Bengali Service, BBC World Service, 15 June 1994.

110 SIPRI, 1993, op cit.

111 Burrows, and Windrem, 1994, op cit79.

4

THE MOZAMBIQUE CONFLICT
(1980–1992)

Shaun Vincent

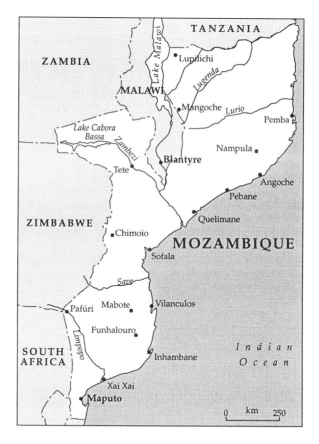

Area (000sq km)	784
Population (m)	15.6
Human Development Index	0.157
Population density (per sq km)	17
Capital	*Maputo*

KEY IMPACTS OF THE CONFLICT

ON MOZAMBIQUE

- Some 100,000 Mozambicans killed up to 1986; 95 per cent of these casualties were civilians.
- Some 10,000 to 15,000, mostly civilians, killed by landmines alone.
- Economic losses to Mozambique due to the war were US$15 billion, four times the 1988 GDP.
- By 1993 GDP/capita was less than US$100.
- By 1992 exports covered only 16 per cent of import costs.
- In 1992 aid accounted for 50 per cent of the government budget, paid for over 75 per cent of imports and accounted for more than 70 per cent of Mozambique's GDP.
- A total of US$5.9 billion of overseas aid has been despatched to Mozambique in the period 1980–91.
- The elephant population fell from between 50,000 to 65,000 in 1974 to 13,000 or less in 1990.
- There are an estimated 5.9 million illiterate adults in Mozambique today.
- In 1993 it was estimated that it would cost at least US$600 million to rehabilitate the nation's roads.
- Approximately 45 per cent of schools had been destroyed or closed by November 1987. Rehabilitating 2000 classrooms is estimated to cost at least US$4.4 million.
- By 1993 48 per cent of the total number of health posts had been destroyed.
- Over 5 million people have been displaced internally and approximately 1.7 million have been forced to flee to neighbouring countries.

ON THE SOUTH AFRICAN DEVELOPMENT COMMUNITY

- Tanzania, Zambia and Zimbabwe were attacked throughout the war, and suffered many casualties. By 1989 75 Zambians had been killed and by April 1989, 335 Zimbabweans.
- Economic costs increased as exports and imports had to be transported via South African ports which were further away than the Mozambican ports used before the war. The use of these ports is estimated to have cost SADC countries US$300 million a year by 1989.
- Refugees have caused many environmental problems in neighbouring countries, for example, in Malawi in 1989–90 Mozambican refugees stripped approximately 12 million trees to obtain building and cooking supplies; many rhinos and elephants were also slaughtered in the region's national parks.
- By 1988 the conflict had ensured that Malawi lost approximately 40 per cent of its GDP; Zimbabwe lost 25 per cent, Zambia 20 per cent and Tanzania 10 per cent.

ON SOUTH AFRICA

- South Africa's destabilization policies aimed at Mozambique and the other southern African states increased South African isolation in the early and late 1980s. By August 1985 South Africa had defaulted on repayments on US$22 billion worth of external loans.
- Throughout the 1980s total government expenditure increased by 20 per cent a year. Between 1978 and 1983 military expenditure nearly doubled.

- Small and medium size companies suffered from international isolation and the loss of regional markets.

ON THE WEST

- Total aid to Mozambique increased from US$144 million in 1981 to US$920 million in 1991, contributing to approximately 70 per cent of total Mozambican GDP. A total of US$5.9 billion of overseas aid was given to Mozambique between 1981 and 1991.

- The end of the war has ensured that aid is still needed to rebuild Mozambique. The UN mission in Mozambique requested US$560 million for operations over the period March 1993–April 1994.

- The cost of refugee programmes in countries bordering Mozambique increased by over 700 per cent between 1987–88 to US$33.5 million, and cost US$25.7 million in 1990.

- The lost potential trade with Mozambique is unquantifiable.

INTRODUCTION

Geography

Mozambique is an ex-Portuguese colony situated on the south-eastern coast of Africa. Over 90 per cent of the population are subsistence farmers producing such products as maize and cassava. It also acts as a major export route for land-locked countries in the region although this activity was severely curtailed by the civil conflict which ended in 1992.

People

The population remains loyal to tribal beliefs and traditions, and these traditions form approximately 70 per cent of the country's religion. In addition, 15 per cent of the population is classed as Christian, and 15 per cent Muslim.

The Conflict

Resistência Nacional Mocambiçana (Renamo) was founded by Portuguese special forces units who fled Mozambique for Rhodesia at independence in 1974. They moved to South Africa in 1980 where they received help from the security forces, in their stated fight against communism.

The signing of the Nkomati Accord on 16 March 1984 between South Africa and Mozambique (essentially a non-aggression treaty with both sides agreeing not to support opposing factions in each country) was a result of a military stalemate, recession in South Africa, and a deteriorating Mozambican economy. Mozambique abided by the Accord, but South Africa did not, and Renamo's activities intensified in late 1984.

The economic effects of the war led Tanzania and Zimbabwe to offer military help to Mozambique in 1985, followed by Malawi in 1986. In October 1986 the President of Mozambique, Samora Machel, was killed in an unexplained air accident. The Foreign Minister, Joaquim Chissano, seen by South Africa as more conciliatory, was installed as President.

Relations between Mozambique and South Africa improved in 1988 after talks between Chissano and President P W Botha of South Africa. When Botha was replaced by the more moderate F W De Klerk in 1989, hopes for reconciliation between the countries grew.

In 1989 the Frelimo government in Mozambique drafted a new constitution which preempted many of Renamo's demands, and this, along with declining support from South Africa for Renamo, led to talks between Renamo and Frelimo in Rome in July 1990. A peace agreement was signed in October 1992 which to date (July 1994) has been largely upheld.

This study looks at Mozambique, South Africa, the South African Development Community (SADC) states, and the western industrialized countries that have been most directly affected by, or involved in, the Mozambique conflict. The costs of the conflict have been most obvious in Mozambique and the SADC countries and hence we concentrate on this issue when looking at these countries. However, we also look at the benefits of the conflict to South Africa and the West.

The conflict in Mozambique has ensured that there is a lack of accurate quantified data. Such data which are produced by World Bank, UN and official Mozambican sources are regarded as unreliable due to the lack of government access to parts of the country during the war as well as a lack of technical wherewithal. It is therefore important to understand that such official Mozambican statistics as mentioned in this study can, at best, only provide some indication of trends in Mozambique.

The effects of conflict in context

War, colonial history, cycles of flood and drought, poor government policies, and numerous World Bank economic restructuring programmes (ERPs), resulting in massive price increases of 317 per cent for maize, 287 per cent for maize flour, and 575 per cent for rice,[1] have all interacted to create Mozambique's current difficulties. For example, the large numbers of Mozambican refugees in neighbouring countries are a result of both war and food scarcity. The severe scarcity of food can be attributed to the disruption of the rural economy by the war, poor government policies and adverse weather conditions. These factors in turn affect the health of the nation, as does the increase in food prices resulting from ERPs. Conflict has magnified all these difficulties to a point where a difficult environment in Mozambique has become an impossible one.

This study defines the conflict as events from the first South African support for Renamo in 1980, until the signing of the 1992 peace agreement, as well as subsequent political and economic events to the present time.

MOZAMBIQUE

THE COSTS

Introduction

Mozambique has been ravaged by war for the past 30 years, first in the fight for independence against Portuguese colonialists, and later in a brutal civil war carried out by the insurgent movement Renamo.

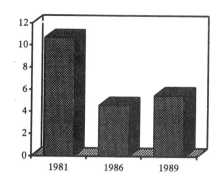

Source: Cliff and Noormahomed, 1993, op cit

Figure 4.1: Percentage of Mozambican government budget spent on health, 1981, 1986 and 1989.

This later conflict, which this study looks at, has been described as 'one of the most brutal holocausts against the human condition since World War II'.[2] The estimated cost of the war to Mozambique is colossal, it is dependent on food aid, and is amongst the poorest nations in the world. Chester Crocker, the US Under-Secretary of State for African Affairs in the late 1980s, called Mozambique one of the most 'brutalized, ravished, societies...on the face of the globe'.[3]

Development

Health

Primary health care was deemed to be a priority for the Mozambican government. Between 1975 and 1980, some 1400 health centres had opened, and a number of national preventive medicine campaigns were launched, aimed at maternal and child health care.[4]

Since 1980, drought, floods, lack of access to hard currency, falling terms of trade, rising debt service and the ravages of war have all undermined these efforts. The destruction of health facilities, dislocation of communities, lost food production and the restriction of government spending has had a serious impact on the nation's health, particularly in rural areas. For example, Renamo attacks led to many doctors fleeing rural areas. The ratio of doctors to patients declined from 1:161,000 in the early 1980s to 1:443,000 by 1985.[5]

Health facilities were a prime target for Renamo throughout the conflict, the result of which has been catastrophic, particularly in rural areas. This targeting resulted in over 2 million people (including 800,000 children) being deprived of access to health facilities by 1988, and by 1993 nearly 1000 health posts (48 per cent of the total) had been destroyed or forced to close.[6]

The pressure to limit public expenditure levels, following the Economic Restructuring Programmes in 1986, has led to the fall in expenditure per capita on health as seen below.

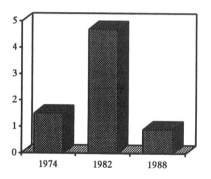

Source: Marshall, J *War, debt and structural adjustment in Mozambique: the social impact.* The North-South Institute, Canada, 1992.
Note: Marshall even suggests that the 1988 figure may be as low as $0.10 per person.

Figure 4.2: Mozambican government expenditure per capita on health care, 1974, 1982, 1988 (US$).

In Mozambique the average daily calorific intake declined steadily from 1980 to around 70 per cent of the minimum required by the end of the 1980s (Figure 4.3). By 1992 malnutrition was believed to have affected up to 50 per cent of the population, compared to only 17 per cent in 1983. Rates of chronic malnutrition in children in some rural areas may be as high as 50 per cent.[7]

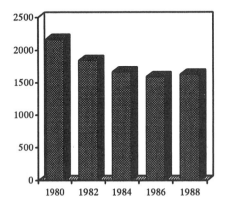

Source: World Bank, World Development Reports, Washington DC.

Figure 4.3: Daily calorie supply in Mozambique per capita.

Although there is a lack of pre-war data to compare with post-war figures, limited evidence tends to suggest that malnutrition problems have significantly increased. In Niassa province (an agriculturally rich area) malnutrition was the least common cause of death during the 1983 drought (5–8 per cent of total deaths), but by 1986 it had become the most common cause (accounting for 40 per cent of total deaths).[8] Disruption to the vaccination campaign has resulted in a dramatic increase in the severity and frequency of disease epidemics, especially amongst the displaced, and malnutrition has exacerbated the tendency to ill health.[9]

The last reliable census in 1980 gave an infant mortality rate of 16 per cent; in 1985 UNICEF estimated that this had increased to 20 per cent, and that the under-five mortality rate was between 32–37 per cent, one of the highest figures in the world. This means approximately one in three children in Mozambique will not survive beyond the age of five years.[10]

Education

The eradication of an adult illiteracy rate of between 85 per cent and 95 per cent, inherited from the Portuguese administration, has been a prime objective for the Mozambican government since independence. It has placed a high priority on education, in particular to provide a universal primary education system. Adult literacy increased to 33 per cent by 1990 (45 per cent male and 21 per cent female), and a literacy rate of 53 per cent amongst 15–19 year olds indicates that adult literacy is still improving.[11]

However, the conflict has hampered these efforts. After an initial post-independence surge, Mozambique's primary enrolment ratio has been held to less than 45 per cent because of the destruction of rural schools and the resulting lack of access for many nominally enrolled schoolchildren. This is currently the lowest primary enrolment ratio in SADC.

In 1983, 5886 schools were open, serving some 1.2 million students, but by

November 1987 over 2600 had either been destroyed or forced to close due to Renamo activities, preventing any further improvements in the education programme. Education has also suffered from forced cuts in expenditure on books and equipment. As the conflict continued, scarce resources were increasingly diverted from education to other sectors, notably defence.[12]

The UN operation in Mozambique (ONUMOZ) estimates that the cost of rehabilitating 2000 classrooms will be at least US$4.4 million. In many provinces up to 70 per cent of schools were physically destroyed by the time of the peace agreement, and an entire generation of children are uneducated. At least 10 per cent of these children have suffered from war related trauma, such as witnessing violence and suffering bereavement, which has affected their learning capabilities. There is already a lack of skilled labour and management in Mozambique;[13] the lack of an effective education system will only serve to amplify this situation.

Civil and Political Rights

Number of deaths

A conservative estimate puts the number of Mozambicans killed in the conflict to 1986 at 100,000.[14] Military casualties are probably less than 5 per cent. The majority of deaths are civilians, who have been massacred by Renamo rebels.

War injuries

A detailed study in a rural health centre over 7 months in 1989–90 reported 454 cases of war injuries, of which 379 were civilians. Of these civilian casualties, 89 per cent were children under the age of 15. Of these, 16 were under the age of five and six had been pounded with a pestle and four stabbed with a knife; hardly the types of injury associated with civilians caught in the line of fire.[15]

Renamo has brutalized the civilian population. Renamo trained children to become killers; kidnapped, starved and threatened with death, some children were forced to return to their home villages to attack their own families.

Renamo's field activities have been documented by Gersony who reports how civilians were the victims of 'purposeful shooting deaths and executions, of axing, knifing, bayoneting...and other forms of murder where no meaningful resistance or defence [was] present'.[16] He describes 'patterns of systemic rape of civilian women by Renamo combatants'. The only reward for cooperation with the rebels was the right to stay alive.

The visual impact of violence was very important, and mutilated bodies were often displayed in public to act as a deterrent. Refugee accounts of these abuses from the north, centre and south of the country were strikingly similar, suggesting that the violence was co-ordinated and systematic rather than spontaneous.[17]

The visual impact of violence

The following is an interview with a woman in the Hulene suburb of Maputo in 1992: 'Three weeks ago [mid–April 1992] some of our relatives fled from Gaza, from a village near Xai Xai called Xicote ... The Matsanga [Renamo] ordered the village elder, Nafital Panguene, to put his youngest child in the millet grinder and pound his head, so that the child did not grow into a Frelimo supporter. All villagers were made to watch this.

Landmines

Landmines have claimed between 10,000 and 15,000 mostly civilian victims.[19] In Inhambane and Gaza provinces health clinics, water wells, schools and other amenities were all mined in violation of international law. Mines have led to a large increase in the number of amputations. In Mozambique one person per 1862 is an amputee; in the United States the figure is one per 22,000 people.[20]

The danger of landmines

G Z is a twenty-year-old peasant farmer and tradesman from Zavala (Inhambane). In October 1992, G Z went into his field to cut grass. While cutting the grass his sickle hit a land mine which exploded. He was helped by friends who evacuated him by tractor to the rural hospital in Zavala. He has lost both hands and one eye and is undergoing eye surgery in Chicuque.[21]

Food as a tool of war

Famine struck Mozambique in 1983–84, 1987 and 1992, initiated by drought but fundamentally caused by war. The 1983–84 famine alone claimed approximately 100,000 lives.[22] The near total destruction of food self-sufficiency has resulted in the dependency of the rural population on imported food stuffs.

Renamo frequently ambushed international relief convoys. In 1988 alone 40 trucks were destroyed and 23 drivers and assistants killed.[23] These attacks were effective in reducing the morale of the poor and were one way in which Renamo frequently tried to persuade the rural poor to support their activities.

Both Frelimo and Renamo forces have widely attacked food production systems. Rural civilians in Zambezia province, for example, were moved to areas under government control to protect them from Renamo attacks. The abandoned fields were then destroyed to prevent rebels from obtaining food supplies at a later date. This increased the rural population's dependency on international food aid, and contributed to the 1987 famine in Zambezia. By 1990 the situation had further deteriorated in the province; adequate food supplies and health care could not be provided for the displaced population in the towns, and thousands died as a result.[24] This issue, known as a 'scorched earth policy' was widely used in the conflict by both sides.

The Economy

'For a variety of complex reasons but overwhelmingly because of the war, the economy is in ruins. Industrial output and foreign exchange earnings are minimal and internal trade and commerce have virtually come to a complete standstill. Continual raiding in rural areas has also led to greatly diminished agricultural production'.[25]

Aid dependency

Renamo has destroyed the productive capacity of Mozambique. In 1992, aid accounted for 50 per cent of the government

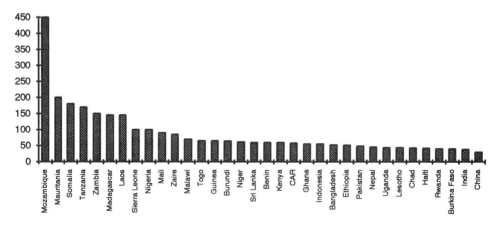

Source: *British Medical Journal*, Vol 304, 30/05/92

Figure 4.4:Total external debt as a percentage of GDP in low income economies (1989)

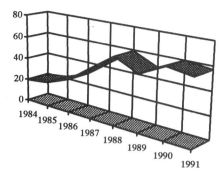

Source: World Bank, *World Development Reports*
Washington DC, 1980–1993.

*Figure 4.5: Official development assistance to
Mozambique per capita (US$).*

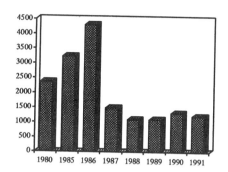

Source: World Bank, 1980–93, op cit

*Figure 4.7: Mozambican GDP for selected years
(US$m)*

budget, paid for over 75 per cent of imports
and accounted for more than 70 per cent of
the country's GDP.[26] By 1993 it had become
the most aid-dependent nation in the world
with a GDP/capita of less than US$100.[27]
(See Figures 4.4–4.7)

Estimates of the costs of conflict to the
Mozambican economy vary enormously.
Manuel Jorge Aranda da Silva, the Minister
of Commerce and National Authorizing
Officer estimated that by 1989 the country
had lost some US$4.4–6 billion, whilst a
1989 UNICEF report estimated that losses
could be in the region of US$15 billion (up
to 1988).

Agriculture

Mozambique's economy is predominantly
agriculturally based and, in times of
stability, 80–90 per cent of the working
population would be employed in agriculture. Before the conflict about 80 per cent
of exports were of agricultural origin.[30]

The conflict has prevented nearly 3
million people from farming the land, and
has been responsible for the collapse of
rural transport and marketing systems. By
1990, Mozambique had to import food
valued at US$234 million, and by 1992 only
15% of the country's food needs were
produced domestically.[31]

Recovery of the agricultural sector will

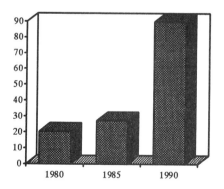

Source: World Bank, 1980–93, op cit

*Figure 4.6: Official development assistance to
Mozambique as % of GNP.*

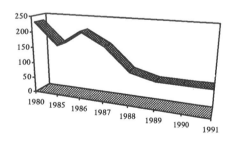

Source: World Bank, 1980–93, op cit

*Figure 4.8: Mozambican GNP/capita for selected
years (US$).*

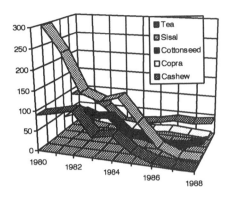

Source: Kyle, S W, 'Economic reform and armed
conflict in Mozambique' *Development*; Vol 19 No 6. 91.

*Figure 4.9: Mozambican production of selected
export crops 1980–88 (tonnes)*

be dependent on the rehabilitation of the
transport networks. In the 1993 season,
following peace and good rains, a crop
surplus was reported in many provinces.
Much of this was in danger of rotting,
however, because of the lack of transport
facilities.

Mining

Mozambique's coalmining industry has
been paralysed by the conflict. At Moatize
in Tete province, production declined from
100,000 tonnes before independence to less
than 9000 tonnes in 1986, because of
sabotage to rail lines. Mines operated at less
than 10 per cent of capacity throughout the
conflict and this alone cost the Mozambican
economy between US$9 and US$12 million
in lost exports each year.[32] In addition, the
mining company (Carbonac) only survived
due to government subsidies, another
hidden cost to the national economy.

Remittances

A large percentage of Mozambicans
worked outside the country, especially in
South Africa, and this was a valuable
source of foreign exchange for the economy.
Before independence, a peak of 118,000
Mozambican miners were employed in

South Africa, but this steadily declined
following independence. In 1986, as part of
South Africa's economic destabilization of
Mozambique, it banned recruitment of
Mozambicans and forcefully repatriated
some 60,000 others (although in January
1987, the repatriation decision was relaxed
on about 30,000 of these). This reduced
foreign exchange earnings from this source
by about 30 per cent.[33] On a micro level,
households (particularly those in southern
provinces) were heavily dependent on this
source for household income, and they
were seriously affected by the withdrawal
of these payments in the mid 1980s.

Foreign trade

The conflict, with its disruption to trade
routes and its impact on production, has
had a particularly serious effect on the
country's foreign trade. At independence
the value of exports covered around 50 per
cent of import costs, but by 1992 this had
fallen to only 16 per cent, the rest having to
be financed by donor sources.[34] The main
reason for this has been the poor performance of Mozambique's traditional exports
such as cashew nuts, cotton, sugar and tea.
By 1989 the value of exports had fallen to
around a third of what they were in 1981.[35]

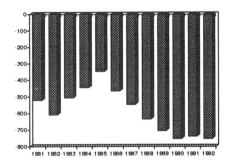

Sources: EIU 1993 op cit; Kyle, 1991
Note: 1992 figures estimated.

*Figure 4.10: Balance of Mozambique's foreign trade
1981–92 (US$m)*

Defence expenditure

Throughout the 1980s defence expenditure averaged a staggering 38 per cent of total government expenditure, one of the highest rates in the world.[36] About 70 per cent of this expenditure was on imports, which reduced the capacity to import non-war related products and diverted scarce resources from national investment programmes.[37]

Infrastructure

Transport, urban, and power infrastructure

Before independence, 80 per cent of Mozambique's foreign exchange earnings came from revenues associated with the railways and ports. In the 1960s only 20 per cent of the region's traffic went through South Africa, with the rest going through Mozambican and Angolan ports. Mozambique's railways were a vital route for imports entering southern Africa, and exports leaving it. However, Renamo attacks and poor maintenance and management have ensured that 80 per cent of the SADC's exports pass through South Africa in a reversal of the pre-conflict situation.[38]

Mozambique has three excellent ports, Maputo, Nacala and Beira, each of which is the terminus of a railway line from the interior. Of these, Beira was the least affected by the conflict. The Beira corridor is critical to the Zimbabwean economy, and up to 12,000 Zimbabwean troops protected the transport corridor during long periods of the conflict. Despite the presence of troops, the rail line was still subject to attack by Renamo, and it rarely operated at full capacity. The impact of the conflict has been far more serious for Maputo and Nacala.

Good quality roads are severely lacking in Mozambique. The main roads are ineffective for its present needs, and most run in an east-west direction (reflecting the colonial past). It is estimated that less than 10 per cent of the primary network is in

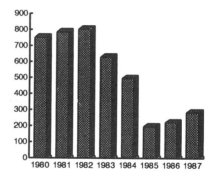

Source: The transport routes of the frontline states, Malawi and Zaire; African Section Research Department, London, October 1989

Figure 4.11: Nacala through traffic 1980–87 (000 tonnes)

good working order and less than a third is in transitable order.[39] Secondary and tertiary roads are also in poor condition and many are impassable. In 1993 the World Bank estimated that it would cost at least US$600 million to rehabilitate the nation's roads.[40] It was rarely possible to travel outside the main cities by road without a military escort, so all normal road transport ceased.

The end of the conflict has resulted in a massive increase in road traffic, over-burdening the existing network, leading to further deterioration and affecting the distribution of medicine and emergency

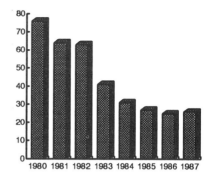

Source: African Section Research Department, 1989, op cit

Figure 4.12: Maputo through traffic 1980–87 (000 tonnes)

supplies. In 1993 the govern-ment admitted that food aid was rotting in the ports, because of lack of transport facilities to deliver it to the appropriate areas.[41] Meanwhile a mine clearance programme has already identified some 4000 kilometres of road as most urgent, but the UNHCR estimate that it will take at least seven to ten years to clear the country of mines.[42]

War, drought and famine have led to a massive increase in rural-urban migration rates, and have placed an ever-increasing strain on urban infrastructure. Between 1984 and 1988, Maputo city grew by an estimated 3.7 per cent per year, and in 1988 the Ministry of Commerce put population density in the city at an average of 6.8 persons per room.[43] Buildings and plumbing have deteriorated through neglect, creating ideal conditions for the spread of disease.

The country's natural endowments should provide it not only with a very cheap electricity supply but also a substantial surplus for export. It could sell coal and has enormous hydro-electric power potential. The export of energy has, however, been virtually halted because of the war. By 1993, energy production was not even sufficient for home demand, and Mozambique was forced to import 1500 kWh (costing US$5 million per year) from South Africa, absorbing about 10 per cent of Mozambique's total export earnings.[44]

The main problem has been the non-operation of the Cahora Bassa dam. It was built in 1974 by the Portuguese to supply South Africa with cheap electricity. Despite tripartite agreements between South Africa, Portugal and Mozambique in 1984, Mozambique has never had access to its cheap electricity. Attacks by Renamo were frequent, and by 1987 the dam was reported to be operating at only 0.5 per cent of its potential capacity.[45] The hydro-electric power installations themselves are still in a good state of repair, but the infrastructure required to deliver the power has been sabotaged by Renamo, who destroyed 60 per cent of new power lines. Total losses from these attacks up to 1988 were estimated to be at least US$130 million.[46]

The cost of repair was estimated at US$125 million (excluding the cost of removing the countless minefields surrounding the power pylons).[47]

The Environment

The war has caused the population to move to the government-controlled areas which are on the coast, along three transport corridors and in the cities. This has caused environmental problems in these regions.

Although nationally Mozambique has a sustainable wood yield which outstrips current demand by two times, deforestation has become a major problem in certain site-specific areas, in particular those surrounding urban and peri-urban zones. This has been exacerbated by the fact that 80 per cent of the country's energy consumption is currently from woodfuel.[48]

The so called 'Green Zones' surr-ounding Mozambican cities have often provided a fundamental food input into many city households but increased urbanization has led to land degradation.

Perhaps of greatest current concern is the destabilization of the coastal mangrove and coral ecosystems which act as natural barriers to erosion from the Indian Ocean. Over-exploitation of these systems has occurred due to the displaced population now living in coastal regions and using mangroves as building timber for houses and boats, and fuelwood. Over the last 25 years the area of mangrove forest has declined by some 70 per cent in Mozam-bique.[49] Coastal erosion, especially near Beira and Inhaca, could have long-term implications for the fishing industry and the 55,000 families now dependent on it.[50]

On a local scale many environmental problems have been reported, and in two recent analyses on environmental problems in Mozambique, the conflict has been noted as a critical contributor to these problems.[51]

All Mozambique's national parks are located in areas destabilized by the war and have often been abandoned by game staff, leaving them unprotected against poachers. In 1974 it was estimated that between 50,000 and 65,000 elephants were in

Mozambique but by 1990 this had fallen to around 13,350 or less.[52]

The South African Defence Forces, Renamo, Zimbabwean National Army and Frelimo have all been implicated in poaching for personal profit and to support the war. When Renamo headquarters in Gorongosa were overrun by government troops in 1985, large quantities of ivory were found.[53] Such activities will have an enormous impact on future potential export earnings from tourism.

Refugees

Statistics from ONUMOZ on refugee numbers from Mozambique are staggering. Over half the population has been affected by the conflict, over 5 million have been displaced internally, and up to 1.7 million have been forced to flee to neighbouring countries.[54] The number of displaced people in southern Africa today is greater than in any other region in the world. As Graca Machel, wife of the late President Machel, said in Zimbabwe in 1989, 'All of the front line states, all of them, are accepting the problem of Mozambican refugees as their own'.[55]

Over a million people have fled to Malawi, largely in response to the escalation of the conflict in Zambezia province. Zambezia, one of the most agriculturally rich provinces in Mozambique, was held by Renamo until 1986/87, when the Frelimo army attacked and reclaimed large areas of the province. Frelimo forces then instigated a successful scorched earth policy, making the area uninhabitable and preventing future food supplies reaching Renamo forces.[56]

Many thousands fled to South Africa where the government refused to recognize their refugee status. They were forced to live as fugitives, hidden amongst the local population to avoid arrest and deportation by the South African police. This has made counting the numbers of refugees in South Africa difficult; estimates vary from 90,000 to 250,000. The lack of refugee status meant they were unable to obtain assistance from international aid organizations such as the UNHCR, and had to rely on the generosity of the local population in the homelands. Both refugees and the local population suffered as a result.

The position of refugees

Mozambicans who found refuge in official UNHCR camps in neighbouring front line states have had many problems to contend with.

Education and training facilities were essential if the traumas of war were to be overcome, and if refugees were to be given suitable activities to become self-sufficient. In many camps the UNHCR could only provide a basic service, simply clothing and feeding the refugees

In 1990, due to the global financial crisis, the UNHCR budget was cut and many programmes or activities were delayed or cancelled.

Inevitably the cutbacks hit the most vulnerable groups, namely the young and women. Almost half of all Mozambican refugees were under the age of 15, and about three-quarters were either women or children.[57] Women in particular have suffered. Traditionally, women's work in Mozambican rural life includes the collection of firewood and water for cooking, looking after the children, washing and repairing clothes, house cleaning and the cultivation of a small garden plot, whilst men would typically build new homes, plough the fields, and take some form of off farm waged employment.

In the refugee camps, most of the work carried out by women still needed doing, but many of the men's traditional duties were absent. The distances women had to walk to collect firewood increased as population pressure took its toll on the environment, and many of the children were traumatized and difficult to control. Men, on the other hand, were rep-orted to be spending most of the day sleeping, talking and drinking, suffering from feeling a lack of purpose and reduced self-esteem.[58]

CONCLUSION

Mozambique's economic infrastructure has been virtually destroyed, and will need rebuilding almost from scratch if the country is to be able to reduce its dependence on external aid. Predominantly an agricultural economy, the rural areas have been most seriously affected. Mozambique's ability to earn foreign exchange from agriculture, its rail and ports, mining and tourism have all been seriously undermined. It is now one of the most indebted countries in the world.

The population has suffered many civil and human rights abuses while health and education standards have declined since 1980 from an already low level. Hundreds of thousands of people have died as a result of violence and war- related famine and disease. Millions have been displaced internally and over 11/2 million have been forced to flee to neighbouring countries. The long-term impact of trauma remains to be seen.

THE SADC

THE COSTS

Introduction

Zimbabwe is important to any economic grouping in southern Africa. Its independence in 1980 first opened the possibility of economic co-operation between states in the region. The Southern African Development Co-ordination Conference (SADCC) was established in Lusaka on 1 April 1980. (It later changed its name to the Southern African Development Community; SADC.) Nine states joined SADCC at its inception: Angola, Botswana, Mozambique, Tanzania, Zambia and Zim-babwe, Lesotho, Malawi and Swaziland. Namibia joined following its independence in 1990.

According to the Lusaka Declaration, the goal of SADCC was 'to liberate our economies from their dependence on the Republic of South Africa, to overcome the imposed economic fragmentation, and to coordinate our efforts toward regional and national economic development'.[59] The key to the success or failure of this goal was the

ability to rehabilitate the region's transport and communications network, particularly the ports and railways in Mozambique, Tanzania and Angola.

In early 1980 a programme was approved in which seven of the nine member states were assigned to specific tasks. The fact that Frelimo was charged with establishing a regional transport and communications commission illustrated the importance of the Mozambican infrastructure to SADCC. Mozambique's ability to provide an alternative transport route for Zambia, Zimbabwe, Malawi, Botswana and Swaziland, all of whom are landlocked, would go a long way in determining the success of SADCC's goals. By September 1980 Mozambique had already achieved much in the transport sector, and by 1981 40 of the proposed 97 SADCC transport projects were already being implemented. More than 40 per cent of the funding for these projects (70 per cent if marginal projects are excluded) was being spent in Mozambique.[60]

SADCC was therefore a threat to South African hegemony in the region. If SADCC was successful, South Africa's profits would fall and its economic leverage over the region would decline sharply. SADCC gained considerable financial support and co-operation from Europe (particularly in the transport sector). By 1986 the international community had already pledged US$1.1 billion, and a further US$1.15 billion was under discussion.[61] It is in this light that South Africa turned to its policy of destabilization.

This section illustrates some of the ways in which the conflict in Mozambique has had a profound impact upon neighbouring nations.

Civil and Political Rights

From the beginning of 1987, Renamo carried out a number of cross-border raids in Tanzania, Zambia and Zimbabwe, with the all too familiar brutality found in Mozambique.

Renamo raids against Zambia began in March 1987. At first the attacks were minor in comparison to other Renamo atrocities, but in December 1987 the first reported death of a Zambian occurred.[62] By 1989, 75 Zambians had been killed by Renamo, 41 had been injured and over 170 abducted.[63]

In 1987 Renamo began cross-border attacks in neighbouring Zimbabwe. By April 1989 it had been responsible for the deaths of 335 Zimbabwean civilians, and the abduction of a further 667.[64] Brutality was extreme. In Chipinge, a village close to the Mozambican border in the south-east of Zimbabwe, children were forced from their school dormitories. Five were killed and a further seven were mutilated.

Similar attacks on a smaller scale occurred in Tanzania. Between 1987 and April 1989, five Renamo cross-border raids were reported, in which one person was killed, 68 were abducted, and large amounts of property and food were destroyed.[65]

The Economy

Increased transport costs

The most significant economic costs which SADC nations have had to bear have been the re-routing of international trade through South Africa. In the early 1970s most of SADC's international trade went through Mozambican and Angolan ports, but by the end of the 1980s about 80 per cent of the region's trade was forced to go via South Africa. This was uneconomic for Zimbabwe, Malawi or Zambia.

The use of South African ports is estimated to have cost the SADC countries approximately US$300 million a year by 1989.[66] This represented an important source of foreign exchange loss, since increased transport costs had to be paid in US$ to South Africa.

Some of the consequences of this for two of the most affected SADC nations, Malawi and Zimbabwe, are discussed below.

Malawi
Land-locked Malawi is totally dependent upon neighbouring nations for access to

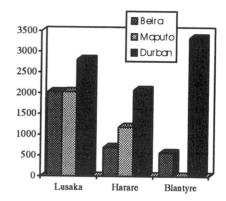

Source: The transport routes of the front line states, Malawi and Zaire. African Section Research Department, October 1989.

Figure 4.13: Railway distances to major ports (kms)

world markets. Beira in Mozambique is its nearest port. As Renamo activity increased along the corridor to Beira, the volume of Malawian trade through Mozambique declined from approximately 760,000 tonnes in 1980, to zero by 1984. Trade had to be re-routed via Durban, some 3000 kilometres further from Malawi than the nearest Mozambican port. Additional transport costs were estimated to be at least US$325 million between 1984–88, over 11 per cent of the nation's annual total export earnings.[67] This led to industrial growth falling to less than 3 per cent per annum in the 1980s, compared with 11 per cent in the 1970s.[68] This was in part due to the dependence of Malawian manufacturing industry on imported raw materials. As haulage and import costs increased, so the volume of imported raw materials declined, and processing industries suffered.

Additionally, escalating haulage costs decreased the profitability of the country's exports, and it soon became uneconomic for Malawi to export low value, high bulk, cargo. Almost 90 per cent of Malawi's total export earnings comes from the agricultural sector, in particular from tea, sugar and tobacco, typically of low value and high bulk.

The sugar industry, for example, was severely affected by this factor. Following the closure of the Beira line in October 1982, Malawi was unable to export all of its sugar, and by the end of 1983 was forced to stockpile 55,000 tonnes. This was equivalent to two-thirds of total national output, or over 60 per cent of sugar's contribution to the nation's foreign exchange earnings. By 1984 the stockpile had accumulated to 152,000 tonnes.[69]

Zimbabwe

Before the closure of the Mozambique-Rhodesia border, Beira and Maputo ports handled more than 90 per cent of Rhodesia's foreign trade. Following independence Zimbabwe intended to increase its use of these ports and by 1983, just three years after the reopening of the border, these routes handled over 50 per cent of Zimbabwe's foreign trade.[70] Not only did this reduce its dependence on South Africa, but it also made sound economic sense; shipping costs via Mozambique were approximately half of those through South Africa.[71]

The Beira–Mutare line was one of Renamo's first targets, and in 1981 (backed by South African Defence Forces commandos) it successfully destroyed the road line. The oil line via Beira was vital to the Zimbabwean economy, and by June 1982 it was reopened, releasing Zimbabwe from its dependence on South Africa for oil. This is estimated to have saved the country Z$36 million a year in oil transport costs.[72] Despite numerous attacks by Renamo, and frequent disruptions to its service (estimated to have cost US$ 6.11 million, at 1988 exchange rates), the line remained open throughout the conflict.[73] This is largely attributed to the presence of the Zimbabwean National Army (ZNA) along the Beira corridor.

By 1984 Renamo attacks on the Limpopo line effectively closed access to Maputo port from Zimbabwe. Although the Beira corridor was guarded by Zimbabwean troops, the lack of investment in Beira's port facilities meant that it could only handle a limited volume of Zimbabwe's foreign trade. The volume of Zimbabwean foreign trade via Mozam-

bique fell to little over 8 per cent by 1987 (excluding oil, petrol and lubricants). Almost all the remaining trade was forced to go through South Africa. Zimbabwe's Ministry of Transport puts the official cost of this re-routing at Z$200 million a year. By 1988 the total cost was put at Z$1.5 billion or almost US$825 million using 1988 exchange rates.[74]

In addition, a number of other indirect costs have been suffered by Zimbabwe. In particular, the destruction of Mozambican rolling stock, coupled with the increased distances to South African ports, led to a shortage of available rolling stock in Zimbabwe, the effect of which has been felt throughout the economy. In December 1988, for example, a sugar refinery was forced to close when it ran out of coal; this was due to the lack of wagons available to deliver coal from the colliery near Victoria Falls to the refinery in Harare. The lack of sugar in turn affected the breweries and other food sectors, as well as reducing government revenues and its plans to expand the sugar industry.[75]

Increased defence costs

It is clear that adverse effects of high military expenditure arising from the conflict in Mozambique have been felt by Tanzania and Zimbabwe in particular.

Tanzania

Despite its precarious economy and being one of the 25 poorest nations in the world, Tanzania made important military contributions to the Mozambican government. In June 1985 Tanzania offered training facilities for the Mozambican military which, by 1989, were estimated to have cost US$3.5 million. In 1986, Tanzania increased its commitment to Mozambique by sending a brigade of 4000 troops to Zambezia province. These troops stayed in Mozambique for two years, at an estimated cost to Tanzania of US$120 million.[76]

Zimbabwe

ZNA troops first went into Mozambique in 1982, in part to protect the vital Beira oil line, but also because of Zimbabwe's wider commitment to Mozambique. Under the terms of the 1981 Zimbabwe–Mozambique Defence Agreement, Zimbabwe stated that, 'We have concurred that an attack against Mozambique shall be regarded as an attack against Zimbabwe...'.[77]

This commitment increased in 1985 with the deployment of ZNA troops. Following the death of Mozambique's President Machel in 1986, Zimbabwe's resolve increased, President Mugabe declaring that, 'survival of Mozambique is our survival. The fall of Mozambique will certainly be our fall...All and one stand together. All and one fight together'.[78] By 1988 approximately 10,000 ZNA troops were present in Mozambique. Unofficial figures put the cost to Zimbabwe of defending trade routes in Mozambique at over US$3 million a week.[79]

Malawi and Zambia
Both incurred increased defence expenditures arising from Mozambican instability. Malawi and Zambia supplied troops and training facilities respectively.[80]

The Environment

Environmental problems in SADC nations arising from the Mozambican conflict have included the influx of Mozambican refugees, and poaching of the region's elephant and other wildlife populations, particularly in Zimbabwe and Zambia.

The major environmental problem confronting Malawi is population pressure on the land. This has been exacerbated by over one million Mozambican refugees, representing 10 per cent of Malawi's 1990 population. In some areas the number of refugees outnumbered the local population by four to one. Land and resources have been overused, leading to soil erosion and deforestation.[81] In 1989/90 alone the refugees stripped an estimated 12 million trees to obtain building and cooking supplies.[82] Deforestation has also occurred around refugee camps in Tanzania.

The war in Mozambique has also undermined efforts to conserve elephant and other endangered species in adjacent countries. Many rhinos and elephants were slaughtered in the region's national parks.[83] Most evidence supports the view that poaching was a common occurrence, and that an illegal ivory and rhino horn trade through South Africa existed. It is widely believed that the South African military and Renamo forces (and, most probably the Angolan rebel group National Union for the Liberation of Angola [UNITA] too) collaborated in a complex web of ivory and arms deals. Quite apart from the serious environmental implications of this trade, it has also severely depleted these countries of a valuable wildlife resource, upon which a high value tourist industry could have been based.[84]

Other Costs to SADC Nations

Hidden costs include falling tourist numbers, declining health and education expenditures and lost potential foreign investment: costs which are more difficult to quantify. The number of tourists to Zambia increased from 86,931 to nearly 147,000 following the independence of Zimbabwe in 1980. By 1982, with dissident action in south-western Zimbabwe and the increasing problems of war in Mozambique, the number fell to a little over 118,000, and remained at this level throughout the 1980s. Part of this fall, and the associated foreign exchange losses, can be attributed to Renamo action in Mozambique.[85]

Official SADC estimates for 1980–88 put the total cost arising from the conflict in Mozambique at at least US$60 billion. This is equivalent to two years total output for all SADC nations. Put differently, this is equal to an average of US$800 per capita per year, at a time when the average per capita income for Mozambique was less than US$200.[86] Despite the dubious reliability of statistics coming from Mozambique, any minor adjustment of these figures will not alter the fact that this is a staggering loss.

CONCLUSION

The burden imposed by the Mozambican conflict on neighbouring countries is shown in Figure 4:14.

All SADC nations have faced increased import prices, reduced export revenues, increased defence expenditure, and a reduction in the level of national investment. Some 1.7 million Mozambican refugees entering these countries have placed an enormous strain on their economies and environments. These costs have been imposed on some of the poorest countries in the world, and have seriously affected their own development programmes. The effects of this on the health and education standards of the population in such poor countries should be self-evident.

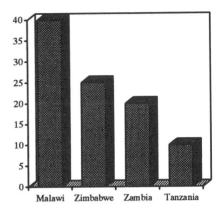

Source: UNICEF, 1989, op cit

Figure 4.14: Losses to neighbouring countries' GDP caused by conflict to 1988 (%)

SOUTH AFRICA

THE COSTS

Introduction

The conflict in Mozambique was used by South Africa as part of a regional policy of destabilization, aimed at keeping its black-ruled neighbours weak and disorganized and therefore incapable of threatening the apartheid state. Regional destabilization was itself part of a 'Total Strategy' to preserve white minority rule in South Africa.

According to Hanlon's study of apartheid power in South Africa: 'What South Africa would really like is sympathetic, non-socialist neighbours who would accept apartheid, support South Africa in world forums, and remain economically dependent on it. Since this is impossible, the main goal of the South African government is to have regional economic, military, and political hegemony. If it cannot gain its dominance by any other means, South Africa adopts the alternative objective of causing instability and chaos in unsympathetic, Marxist states'.[87]

Following the collapse of white rule in neighbouring states in the 1970s, South Africa's traditional first line of defence collapsed, leaving it prone to attack from across its borders. South Africa feared that it was facing a 'total onslaught' from international communism. Initially Mozambique and Angola were seen as the main examples of the communist thrust. Later events, including Mugabe's victory in Zimbabwe, the return to action of the African National Congress (ANC) and the opening of Eastern bloc embassies in Lesotho, appeared to vindicate the government's belief that the onslaught would occur indirectly via Soviet support for liberation movements and neighbouring governments.[88]

Whether the South African perspective of the total onslaught was realistic is questionable. If the total onslaught theory is accepted then it could be argued that destabilization prevented communists from taking control of South Africa. Although Mozambique received military and economic assistance from the Soviets, President Machel also visited Europe and the USA in 1983, to appeal for assistance and western investment in his country. The West (particularly the UK) provided Frelimo with military transport and communications equipment, as well as training facilities in Zimbabwe, which would tend to discount the total onslaught theory.

The Economy

The cost of the destabilization programme increased throughout the 1980s. Total government expenditure increased by 20 per cent a year, partly explained by the increase in defence expenditure required for the imposition of the Total Strategy. Between 1978 and 1983, military expenditure nearly doubled.[89] This was at a time when the domestic economy was experiencing the worst recession since the 1930s.

Public capital to back up government rhetoric about encouraging the formation of economic ties between Mozambique and South Africa, especially following the signing of the Nkomati Accord, was not available. When the government failed to provide money to encourage investment in Mozambique, private investors became even more sceptical of the merits of investing in a shattered country's economy. The Accord included economic concessions to South Africa's benefit which it was unable to capitalize on.[90]

In February 1983, John Barratt, Director General of the South African Institute of International Affairs, warned that the destabilization policy was discouraging the business community from investing in South Africa.[91] Domestic unrest and regional instability shook international confidence, and many international firms chose to reduce interests in South Africa. From 1976–84 an estimated R1 billion left the country, and at least the same again left in 1985 alone.[92] Fearful of the security situation, several international banks cut the length of time they were prepared to lend, eventually refusing to renew short term loans to Pretoria. By mid-1985 South African external debt totalled US$22 billion, of which US$12 billion was due in six months or less. By August 1985 the country had defaulted on its repayments.[93] The apartheid regime of the South African

government only served to reinforce many institutions' decisions to pull-out of, or restrict trade with, South Africa.

Some in the government were concerned that escalating military destabilization was tarnishing South Africa's foreign image, and that this would encourage the imposition of sanctions,[94] therefore denying the country access to overseas capital, which was desperately needed to stimulate the already depressed economy.

The cost to South African business

Small and medium-size companies were more affected by recession in the early to mid-1980s than larger conglomerates who could rely on foreign investments to ride the storm. In an effort to survive, many smaller businesses were keen to expand their operations into neighbouring countries, where considerable market potential existed. Mozambique was of particular interest because the level of private investment in the country was minimal and the potential was believed to be enormous.

Smaller businesses became increasingly disaffected with the implementation of the total strategy. Destabilization was reducing trade links between South Africa and its neighbours and increasing the resolve of SADCC.

In 1983 W B Holtes, chief executive of the South African Foreign Trade Organization, criticized the unpublicized embargo against Maputo port, which had caused South African traffic through the port to fall by 50 per cent. He declared that South Africa should fully utilize neighbouring facilities, arguing that not to do so would only encourage SADCC to build facilities to avoid using South African trade routes in the future. He believed South Africa's ability to trade with its neighbours relied on the promotion of improved two-way trade links.[95]

The euphoria with which South African businesses greeted Nkomati proved over-optimistic; it soon became clear that they would gain little from the Accord. Because of recession, very few businesses had sufficient capital available to make substantial investments in Mozambique. Most interest came from those who saw it as an undeveloped market in which they could expand their sales. What they found, however, was an economy too devastated by destabilization for it to be considered a potential market. South African policy had destroyed the very markets upon which it was hoped export-led recovery could be based. What investment interest around Maputo City remained was destroyed by Renamo attacks on several South African businessmen.

According to Hanlon's study, at the end of 1984 a clear warning as to the likely consequences of Renamo actions was given: '...if the security situation does not improve within the next six months, Nkomati will be out of the window and all these [economic] opportunities...will be lost....it is in no one's interest that the MNR [Renamo] takes over the government...With them in power and Frelimo in opposition, Mozambique will be in greater chaos than before.'[96] Renamo pressure on business targets around Maputo City continued throughout 1985–86, and South African business interests in the Mozambican economy ceased. Any American and British investment for Mozambique, which may have been channelled through Johannesburg, creating trade there, also ceased.

THE BENEFITS

The impact of military destabilization on Mozambique's economy forced the Machel government to the negotiating table in 1984 and the Nkomati Accord was signed in March that year. This pact obliged each state to respect the other's sovereignty and independence, to refrain from interfering in the other's internal affairs, and to renounce the threat or use of force against each other. It forced Mozambique to recognize South Africa's superiority, and that it was capable of instigating military destabilization at its own discretion.[97]

Mozambique kept to the Accord, and

expelled large numbers of ANC supporters from administrative bases in its territory. Although South Africa clearly ignored the Accord, Mozambique did not repudiate it, and reaffirmed it in 1985, despite increasing Renamo activity. The implications of ANC expulsions for South African security were not great as ANC activity continued in South Africa following Nkomati, and increased in scale in 1985–86. Simply preventing support for the ANC within Mozambique (and other neighbouring countries) could not stop the uprisings because the struggle was so deeply based within South Africa itself.[98] Thus any security benefits arising from the military destabilization of Mozambique can at best be described as short-term.

One industrial sector to benefit from the conflict was South Africa's defence industry. Between 1978 and 1983, military expenditure nearly doubled, and Armscor grew to become one of the 25 largest corporations in the country, producing over 75 per cent of South Africa's arms supplies.[99]

International Relations

The signing of Nkomati increased South Africa's standing in the international community. South Africa appeared to be replacing confrontation with negotiation. Its credit terms eased, and P W Botha was able to undertake an official tour of Europe in the summer of 1984. Based upon this new-found political acceptability, South Africa found some support for its declaration that it was a regional power. As Pik Botha explained, 'No problems in southern Africa can be resolved unless the legitimate interests of this regional power, South Africa, are taken into account'.[100]

Any international recognition gained from the signing of Nkomati disappeared, however, when it became clear that the Accord would not bring stability to the region, and that South Africa was not fulfilling its side of the agreement.[101] International benefits for South Africa following Nkomati were short term, and were replaced by ever-increasing isolation in the latter half of the 1980s.

Regional issues

Neighbouring states are interwoven with South Africa's economy in many ways. Although some such relationships may be mutually beneficial, most are not and provide South Africa with considerable economic leverage over the region. Destabilization was intended to ensure South Africa did not lose this control, and that it remained the region's economic focal point. By increasing the region's dependence on South Africa for employment, food, fuel and transport, it could also claim that any sanctions imposed on South Africa would hurt its neighbours as well.

Military destabilization of Mozambique helped to preserve this dependent relationship. In particular, the destruction of the country's transport infrastructure has had a significant impact, with up to 80 per cent of the region's trade going through South African ports.[102] Crucially, however, South Africa failed to break the cohesion or resolve of SADC states, and so benefits gained were less than it had hoped for. Even Mozambique, which was forced to recognize the military and economic superiority of South Africa, through the signing of Nkomati, remained an active member of SADC. SADC received considerable international aid, which helped rehabilitate the region's transport infrastructure (the UK alone provided over £50 million.)

CONCLUSION

The costs and benefits South Africa derived from the conflict in Mozambique can be attributed primarily to two interested parties amongst the ruling white elite. Any benefits which arose were mainly perceived by the military. At best these were short term, and as recent events in South Africa have shown, they failed to preserve white minority rule. The costs to South African businesses were considerable. Although business generally supported the overall objective of the Total Strategy, it could not do so at the expense of potentially profitable trade in the region. Because South Africa is a relatively high-cost producer and uncompetitive in European and North American markets, the southern Africa region is a vital export market for many of its goods. Many small and medium-sized businesses were searching for alternative markets throughout the 1980s, as the domestic economy plunged into recession and South Africa became more isolated internationally. Under these circumstances the destruction of neighbouring markets such as Mozambique, and the regional instability that resulted, was clearly an enormous cost for these businesses to pay.

THE WEST

THE COSTS

Introduction

In the following section, an assessment is made of the consequences of the Mozambican conflict to the wider international community. This approach is taken for three reasons.

Firstly, of the various impacts on the international community, perhaps the most significant is the extraordinary level of aid given to Mozambique throughout the 1980s, the majority of which was received via multilateral sources such as UNICEF and ONUMOZ. In many cases it is not practical to apportion such costs to any individual country.

Secondly, the impact on international private business interests are also considered in this section. Multinational interest in Mozambique has been limited, largely because of the poor security situation. Therefore the direct costs of the conflict to business interests have been relatively small, and are therefore considered from a general Western perspective The impact on private business has not been insignificant and one important cost has been lost investment potential (see Potential Benefits section).

Thirdly, the benefits of the conflict to the international community have also been small. Military sales to Mozambique and South Africa have not been significant, and any identifiable strategic benefits were mainly confined to the early period of the conflict. These strategic benefits were perceived mainly by the USA, and to a lesser extent the UK.

Overseas Aid

The cost of direct aid to Mozambique

In 1987 President Chissano stated: 'We salute the international community for its prompt and generous contribution, which has been fundamental in saving the lives of millions of Mozambicans'.[103] Today Mozambique is the most aid-dependent nation in the world, with overseas assistance contributing approximately 70 per cent of its total GNP, or US$57 per capita, in a country whose per capita GDP was only US$80 in 1991.[104]

A substantial quantity of this assistance

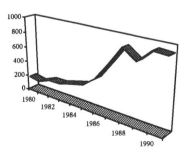

Source: World Bank,1980–1993; World Development Reports.

Figure 4.15: Total overseas aid to Mozambique (US$m)

has been in the form of emergency relief. In 1988–89 the UN appealed for a total of US$763 million.[105] In 1990–91, approximately 20 per cent of Mozambique's total external assistance was in the form of food/emergency aid.[106] In 1993, despite the end of the conflict, ONUMOZ required US$135 million for emergency relief programmes.[107] As the above graph shows, a total of US$5.9 billion of overseas aid has been despatched to Mozambique in the period 1980–91.

Overseas assistance has also been used for import financing. The war, with its disruption to trade routes and its adverse impact on production, significantly reduced Mozambique's ability to earn foreign exchange. Additionally, demands for imports to cover lost production, and the servicing of Mozambique's escalating debt, has required foreign exchange. Despite rescheduling, debt service still represents approximately 25 per cent of the country's total merchandise export value.[108] By 1992 it was estimated that the value of Mozambique's exports accounted for only 16 per cent of the nation's total imports.[109] To ensure that the debt is serviced additional finance has had to come from international donors.

The cost of refugee programmes

International donors have also supported extensive refugee programmes in Zambia, Malawi, Zimbabwe, Tanzania and Swaziland. UNHCR programmes were launched in 1986 after refugee numbers increased dramatically following an upsurge in Renamo activity. The cost of these increased by over 700 per cent during 1987–88, to US$33.5 million. In 1990 expenditure on refugee programmes totalled US$25.7 million. This is a large cost to contributors to these programmes, including Sweden, Switzerland, and the EU members.[110] Total UNHCR expenditure in the period 1987–91 was US$125.9 million. (See Figure 4.16).

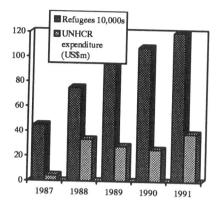

Source: UNHCR, 1991.
Note: 1991 refugee population numbers estimated.
1991 expenditure was amount requested.

Figure 4.16: UNHCR expenditure/number of refugees

The cost of the refugee repatriation programme

A major challenge facing Mozambique after the ceasefire has been the repatriation of 1.7 million external refugees, and the relocation of 5 million internally displaced people. To overcome problems of reintegration and repatriation, UNHCR drew up a regional plan in early 1993. The cost of this three-year programme, which will be borne by the international community, is estimated to be US$203 million.[111]

The cost of the transition programme

Following the October 1992 Peace Agreement, the UN announced a transition programme in which approximately 8000 military and civilian observers were to be sent to Mozambique to supervise the peace process. After several delays, by July 1993 over 6000 UN soldiers had arrived, and no non-UN troops remained in Mozambique.[112] These troops were responsible for ensuring that road, rail, and fuel links remained open during the transition process.[113] The transition programme is responsible for demobilizing Renamo and government troops, and for retraining a unified army of 30,000.[114] Funds have been provided to the main political parties to ensure that democratic elections (due to be held in October 1994) are successful. A budget totalling US$260 million has been allocated for this transition programme.[115]

The cost of peace

Following the signing of the Peace Agreement in October 1992, ONUMOZ identified two key goals for its humanitarian assistance programme in Mozambique: to encourage peacekeeping and to assist in the rehabilitation of the country. The ONUMOZ programme encompasses support for repatriation of refugees, the demobilization of armed units, emergency relief, restoration of essential services, and balance of payments and budget support. The total cost of this assistance to the donor community has been immense. For its March 1993 to April 1994 programme alone, ONUMOZ requested a total of approximately US$560 million. Some of the transition programme costs, such as demobilization, are included in this figure of US$560 million.

G7 nations have also incurred costs as a result of the rehabilitation of Mozambique's transport infrastructure. In 1988 the World Bank earmarked US$450 million for the rehabilitation of the Beira corridor, US$70 million for Maputo port, and over US$200 million for other infrastructural programmes.[116] In addition the UK has donated over £60 million in bilateral aid to SADC transport projects, of which over 50 per cent was spent in Mozambique.[117] These investments were the subject of continuing Renamo attack, and the benefits which were derived from this assistance were considerably less than they would have been in the absence of conflict.

The cost of increased aid to the SADC states

The Mozambican conflict has also affected SADC countries, especially their development efforts. Whilst acknowledg-ing that other factors have contributed to the development problems of the region, the

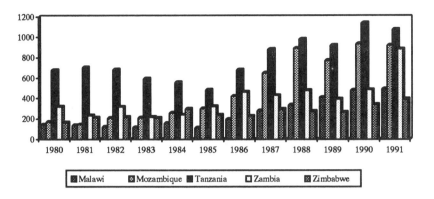

Source: World Bank, 1980–1993, op cit

Figure 4.17: Overseas Development Aid to selected SADC countries (US$m).

Mozambique conflict has had a significant impact. Although impossible to quantify the exact cost of this, it is no coincidence that those countries worst affected by the conflict (Malawi, Zimbabwe, Zambia, and Tanzania) have tended to be the ones where the quantity of aid given increased most rapidly throughout the 1980s. (See Figure 4.17)

Private Business Costs

Since independence, foreign investment in Mozambique has been negligible because of the high risk imposed by the conflict.[118] However, following the signing of the Peace Accord in 1992 there has been US$500 million of approved investment applications.[119]

'Tiny' Rowland's Lonrho (London-Rhodesia) has by far the largest foreign interests in Mozambique, with vast cotton estates valued at US$80 million. This company's experiences clearly illustrate the costs and risks imposed by the conflict on international business in Mozambique. Lonrho's assets were subject to Renamo attacks throughout the conflict, and extraordinary security measures had to be taken to protect them; for example, at Chokwe in the Limpopo Valley triple stacks

of concertina wire, watchtowers, and tanks guarded Lonrho's 2000 hectare cotton farm (see below for further details). Attacks did still occur, such as one in the early 1990s when over US$500,000 worth of chemicals and irrigation pipes were destroyed and the farm's radio operator burned to death.[120]

Protection of Lonrho's interests

In the Limpopo Valley, great triple stacks of concertina wire surrounded Lonrho's 2000 ha cotton farm at Chokwe. Watchtowers and tanks guarded the perimeter. The main buildings became fortresses. 'All our managers were used to farming with a gun on their back,' says John Hewlett, managing director in Mozambique....These battle-hardened managers were backed by a militia of 1400 men. Every morning, Hewlett recalls, tractors on the Chokwe estate would leave in convoys of five, guarded by 50 militias. The farming was planned with military precision....Routines were changed daily to foil surprise attacks. The working parties maintained constant radio contact with their headquarters during their solitary expeditions into the cotton fields...Hewlett says Lonrho's security outlays in Mozambique consumed 30 per cent of the company's operating costs—about US$1 million a year, not counting production losses due to sabotage.[121]

Clearly such actions would dissuade many potential foreign investors in Mozambique, and cost those who were already present millions of dollars. Indeed, the escalating destruction of Lonrho's interests encouraged Rowland to become actively involved in the peace process, by arranging the first meeting between President Chissano and Renamo's leader Alfonso Dhlakama in Botswana. As the *Financial Times* stated, 'There are those who believe that peace would not have returned to Mozambique had Lonrho not been involved'.[122]

Perhaps the most significant costs arising from the conflict in Mozambique have been to those who operate in the southern Africa region and who would, under normal circumstances, use Mozambique's infrastructure for access to international markets. Just as it makes no economic sense for SADC countries to use Durban as a port for international traffic, so the same is true for international businesses operating in these countries. These costs are difficult to quantify, but international businesses must have incurred additional expenses, possibly running into millions of dollars.[123]

THE BENEFITS

The benefits of the conflict to the wider international community have been small. Military sales to Mozambique and South Africa (the latter who faced a UN arms embargo from 1977 onwards) have not been significant, hence military producers have not profited financially from the war.

However some in the West, particularly the US, did perceive a strategic benefit, especially during the early period of conflict. US foreign policy in the region changed upon the election of Ronald Reagan in 1980. Anti-communism replaced human rights as the main issue, and South Africa's insistence that it was facing a total onslaught received sympathy from the US. In January 1981, South African commandos first attacked Mozambique, killing 13 ANC members in Maputo. Hanlon believes that

this raid was intended to test American opinion.[124] No objections were raised, signalling to the principal South African power organ, the State Security Council (SSC), that the American policy of 'constructive engagement' included the use of military tactics. From mid-1981 the number of South African-supported raids in the region increased.

The general sentiment was expressed by Chester Crocker, the new Under-secretary of State for African Affairs, in August 1981, when he stated that, 'We are concerned about the influence of the Soviet Union and its surrogates in Africa'.[125] These fears arose because of various interests that the West had in South Africa at the time, including Western-owned subsidiaries. Strategically, South Africa supplied many industrial and strategic minerals, for which the principle alternative supplier was the USSR. South Africa also controlled the sea route between the Atlantic and Indian oceans, through which approximately 65 per cent of Western Europe's, and 28 per cent of America's, oil imports travelled.[126]

How real the total onslaught threat was is questionable and there are a number of factors which would tend to discount this theory. The Soviets remained relatively passive in the face of increased South African aggression against Mozambique and Angola with which it had signed treaties of friendship and co-operation.[127] Secondly, in October 1983 President Machel toured Western Europe to appeal for assistance, and to stress his openness to Western private investment in Mozambique.[128] Thirdly, despite supplying Mozambique with some military assistance and cheap oil, Mozambique's application for membership of COMECOM was turned down by the Soviets. Finally, Soviet assistance was insufficient to prevent President Machel from signing the Nkomati Accord with South Africa in 1984.[129]

Such actions seriously undermined the credibility of total onslaught theorists and the strategic benefits for the West derived from South African destabilization seemed to have been lost. In the long-term the re-establishment of dialogue between the US and USSR, and President Gorbachev's emphasis on Soviet internal economic reforms rather than its foreign policy commitments, further negated any of these perceived benefits.

A further political benefit for the American government occurred when it put pressure on all states to reach a regional settlement. This was partly because of forthcoming presidential elections in November 1984. US policy towards the apartheid regime had become a political issue in the election, and if a settlement could be found it would have vindicated Reagan's policy of 'constructive engagement', boosting his chances of electoral success. Whereas the Carter administration had isolated Pretoria via sanctions, Reagan's policy encouraged dialogue and open trade between the two countries in the hope of persuading South Africa of the merits of change. In the event this was exactly what happened, with the signing of the Nkomati Accord in 1984, apparently vindicating Reagan's policy.[130]

CONCLUSION

For the West, the costs arising from the Mozambican conflict have far outweighed any perceived benefits. The cost of providing aid to Mozambique has been immense. Billions of dollars have been spent helping to ensure the basic survival of the population, yet today, following the signing of the Peace Accord, billions more are required to assist in the rebuilding of its war-torn economy. The direct costs to private business interests have not been great, but the poor security situation had an impact on those already operating in the country. In addition costs have been imposed on international business interests operating in the southern Africa region. Perhaps the most important cost this group has suffered has been the loss of any potential investment opportunities in Mozambique. (See next section.).

IF THE CONFLICT HAD NOT OCCURRED

INTRODUCTION

This section aims to investigate the potential economic benefits to Mozambique and the West, if the conflict had not occurred. By its very nature, speculating on the potential benefits of conflict not occurring using cross-sectional analysis is difficult. It is difficult to measure what would have happened, and it is difficult to find countries of similar standing with which to make comparisons. Furthermore, due to the fact that SADC countries were also greatly affected by the war, any references to such countries can only be seen as illustrative. The purpose of this section, therefore, is to identify and illustrate trends.

Mozambique

The EIU's 1993 country report states that Mozambique has a greater development potential than most other African nations, and that the country could earn valuable foreign exchange from agriculture, mining, tourism, energy and its infrastructure facilities.[131] In addition, in common with most other southern African nations, the Frelimo government has implemented extensive education and health programmes since independence. All of these potential benefits have either been severely curtailed, or lost altogether, because of the war.

Agriculture

In times of peace there is every prospect that Mozambique could feed itself using the 3000 plantations/farms left by the Portugese, which produced goods accounting for 80 per cent of exports.[132] Mozambique is divided by at least 25 rivers upon which irrigated agriculture could be developed.[133] Whilst poor government policies at independence had a severe impact on the agricultural sector, changes in the mid-1980s significantly improved producer prices, and encouraged foreign investment in areas where Mozambique had insufficient technical/managerial capacity, most notably in the plantation sector.

Infrastructure

Mozambique has the potential to earn large sums of foreign exchange from its rail and port infrastructure, providing access to world markets for neighbouring landlocked countries. Despite massive sums of money spent on rehabilitation programmes over the years, progress has been slow, and the impact not great, mainly due to repeated Renamo attacks. It is estimated that when the rail lines have been made secure, and the rehabilitation programme completed, the volume of trade through Maputo port could double, and that through Beira port increase by up to sevenfold, significantly increasing the nation's potential foreign exchange earning capacity.[134]

Tourism

Despite enormous potential, and a ready market in South Africa, the security situation has prevented the development of a tourist industry in Mozambique. In 1972 it received over 290,000 visitors, but by 1981 this had dwindled to less than 1000. In many of Mozambique's neighbouring countries the tourist industry has been an essential foreign exchange earner. In 1988, for example, Malawi received nearly 100,000 visitors, Tanzania over 150,000 and Zimbabwe 450,000. For Tanzania this earned over US$40.5 million in foreign exchange in 1988 alone.[135] One estimate calculates that Mozambique could potentially earn in excess of US$80 million from tourism in three years, equivalent to about 50 per cent of the country's total merchandise export value.[136]

Mining

Mozambique has considerable mineral resources. The most significant minerals are pegamite in Zambezia province, which are mined for columbotantalite, beryl, mica, bismuth and semi-precious stones. Mozambique also has what is probably the world's largest deposits of tantalite, which is used in the electronics industry and for the production of special steels.[137]

Despite the poor security situation, several feasibility studies were carried out by international concerns in the 1980s, which further revealed the potential for mineral exploitation in Mozambique. In 1986, Lonrho negotiated an agreement to mine gold in Manica province, where reserves are officially estimated to be 50 tonnes. In the same year a US company was given a 27-year concession to explore and mine titanium-bearing beach sand along the Zambezia coast, and in 1987 a feasibility study estimated that heavy mineral extraction from coastal sand dunes in the north-east of the country could yield US$44 million a year in revenue. Feasibility studies have been carried out on the potential for diatomite exploitation, and it is thought that significant deposits of bauxite (estimated to extend to 4 million tonnes), graphite, apatite and tin also exist in Mozambique.[138]

Other than these resources, the country's principle mineral potential is iron ore. In Tete Province, a deposit of 100 million tonnes of high-quality iron ore exists, which was mined at about 6 million tonnes annually before independence.[139]

Potentially, tantalite exploitation is Mozambique's most important mineral export, but mining of this had to be abandoned in the mid-1980s for security reasons, and by 1984 iron ore exploitation in Tete province had ceased altogether.[140] Any development rests with foreign investment.

Energy

Mozambique has an abundant energy supply, and has the potential to be a net energy exporter, selling hydroelectricity, coal and gas. The Cahora Bassa dam could earn Mozambique substantial quantities of foreign exchange through the export of hydroelectricity to South Africa.[141]

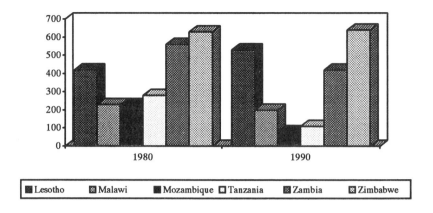

Source: World Bank, 1980–1993, op cit

Figure 4.18: GNP per capita for selected SADC countries (US$)

There are confirmed coal reserves of 6,000 million tonnes, but to date output has remained very low because of the security situation and a lack of investment in the industry.[142] Much of this investment will have to come from private international sources, which again has not been forthcoming because of the risks imposed by war.

bique appears on the bottom of the list when compared with other SADC nations. Indeed, in terms of GNP/capita indebtedness, it is one of the, if not the, poorest countries in the world (Figure 4.18, 4.19 and 4.20). In terms of overseas development assistance as a percentage of GNP, Mozambique is the most aid-dependent nation in the world.

Comparisons with other SADC nations

Despite the apparently abundant resources noted above, in almost every set of macroeconomic data available, Mozam-

The West

The potential benefits the international community could have realized in the absence of conflict in Mozambique fall into

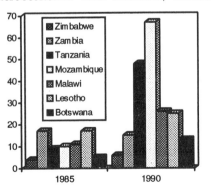

Source: World Bank, 1980–93, op cit

Figure 4.19: Total overseas development assistance as percentage of GNP for selected SADC countries.

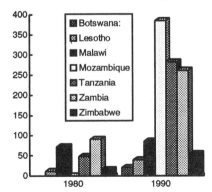

Source: World Bank, 1980–93, op cit

Figure 4.20: Total external debt as a percentage of GDP.

two main categories: the reduction in the quantity, and improved efficiency, of overseas aid; and lost private investment and trade opportunities in Mozambique's economy.

Reduced level of aid and aid efficiency

G7 nations would have saved literally millions of dollars in official overseas assistance if the conflict in Mozambique had been prevented. In terms of direct savings, there would have been no need to spend US$260 million on the UN transition programme, or the US$560 million for the ONUMOZ humanitarian assistance programme. There is also some US$30 million a year which was spent on the various refugee programmes in neighbouring countries, and the US$203 million UNHCR refugee repatriation programme. Whilst the droughts and famines which occurred in Mozambique in the 1980s may have resulted in a population exodus, it is highly unlikely that the scale would have been anything like that which was actually experienced, primarily because the severity of these famines were in large part due to the war.

In addition there are a number indirect aid savings the G7 nations would have made in the absence of conflict. Aid projects have generally been limited to urban-based and emergency programmes only, with very few concerned with issues such as long term sustainability.[143] Although emergency assistance has undoubtedly saved millions of Mozambican lives, if the war had been prevented it could have been used far more efficiently to promote sustainable economic development, thereby reducing Mozam-bique's dependency on external assistance. Furthermore, this demand on overseas assistance is likely to continue for a number of years to come, with the World Bank estimating that, by 2002, Mozambique will still require at least the same level of external aid as it receives today.[144]

Even the limited number of development projects funded by overseas sources have been seriously hampered by the conflict. As the World Bank notes, 'While investment aid has risen substantially, increased insecurity has restricted the scope of projects to mainly urban areas, with adverse impacts on the 'quality' of investment and Mozambique's absorptive capacity'.[145] Problems have also arisen from working in communities where the population is continually moving due to displacement. Coherent group structures tend to be missing, and there has been a lack of coordination between the large number of development/relief organiz-ations operating in Mozambique. This problem has been exacerbated by the non-existence of suitable baseline data from which operations can be planned.[146]

Lost private investment opportunities

In colonial times Mozambique's resources, both material and manpower, were used almost exclusively to serve the interests of other countries. Most business activities in Mozambique were managed by Portuguese expatriates, 90 per cent of whom fled the country at independence.[147] The incoming Frelimo government embarked on an ambitious nationalization programme. However the exclusion of Africans from almost all sectors of the modern economy during the colonial period created a severe shortage of suitably skilled personnel to fill the vacuum left by the departing Portuguese.

Unsurprisingly Frelimo's attempts to build a viable economy on this base proved too ambitious, and the nation's economic fortunes declined. A lack of capital for investment, and a lack of technical and management skills required to run the newly nationalized businesses were the major problems. In 1983 Frelimo instituted a number of economic reforms in an attempt to turn around the deteriorating economic situation. An important aspect of these changes, as far as G7 interests are concerned, was the change in policy towards foreign investment.

By 1984 Mozambique was encouraging

direct foreign investment in its economy, and the ERP in 1987 further enhanced this by offering a number of tax incentives to prospective investors. The Office for Foreign Investment Promotion (GPIE) was established to promote direct foreign investment in Mozambique, by providing assistance and support to prospective investors. Priority areas for investment included the export-oriented plantations, the forestry industry, the fishing industry, manufacturing industries, infrastructure, energy production, tourism and in particular the mining industry. All these sectors of the economy (and especially the mining industry) could make a significant contribution to the country's economic development, but they required capital and technical and management skills from the industrialized world, if they were to be used to their maximum advantage. The potential in these sectors was, and still is considerable, as outlined above.

One of the few private international investors who took advantage of this potential was Lonrho, whose experiences in Mozambique have been documented in the G7 costs section. Despite the formidable problems the war imposed on Lonrho's operations, its 2000-hectare irrigated farm achieved Africa's highest cotton yields in 1989, producing 20,000 tonnes. In addition Lomaco, a joint venture between Lonrho and the Mozambican government, became the biggest tomato grower in the southern hemisphere.[148]

In response to the signing of the Peace Accord in 1992, which improved business conditions and prospects of political stability, foreign investment began to flow back into the country. Within a year of the signing, approved applications for foreign investment already totalled over US$500 million, equivalent to total foreign investment in Mozambique between 1984 and 1992.[149] This would tend to suggest there is considerable interest in the Mozambican economy from overseas, and that the potential benefits from this investment would have been great if the conflict had been prevented.

Conclusion

It is extremely likely that SADC states would have benefited themselves from peace and stability in the region, thus these comparisons tend to underestimate any potential economic benefits. In addition, it is apparent that both public and private international interests stood to gain greatly if the conflict could have been avoided. Whilst it is recognized that the absence of conflict is not a sufficient condition for these benefits to be realized, and that a number of obstacles remain to be overcome in Mozambique, it is never the less a necessary condition if the various interested parties are to realize these potential benefits.

REFERENCES

1 Marshall, J 'Structural Adjustment and Social Policy in Mozambique' *Review of African Political Economy*, July 1990.

2 Minter, W The Mozambican National Resistance (Renamo) as described by ex-participants. Washington: Georgetown University, 1989.

3 Gersony, R 'Summary of Mozambican refugee Accounts of Principally Conflict-related Experience in Mozambique' Washington: Bureau for Refugee Programs, Department of State, 1988.

4 Cliff, J and Noormahomed, R 'Health as a target: Destabilisation of Mozambique'. In *Soc Sci Med 1988*, Vol 27, No 7.

5 Cliff and Noormahomed 1988, op cit; and

Economist Intelligence Unit; Country Profile,: Mozambique, 1993

6 Cliff and Noormahomed, 1988, op cit.

7 Sill, M 'A Geography of War,' *Geographical Magazine*, London, November 1992.

8 Cliff and Noormahomed, 1988, op cit.

9 Cliff and Noormahomed, 1988, op cit.

10 UNICEF, 1989; Mozambique Census, 1980, op cit.

11 UNDP, *Human Development Report 1993*.

12 Marshall, J 'War, Debt And Structural Adjustment in Mozambique: The Social Impact' The North-South Institute Canada, 1992.

13 United Nations Operation in Mozambique (ONUMOZ) 'Consolidated Humanitarian Assistance Programme for 1993–94' United

Nations Department of Humanitarian Affairs, 1993.

14 Cliff and Noormahomed, 1988, op cit.

15 Gaensly, R 1990 'Perfil Epedimiologico Dos Feridos Fe Guerra No Centro De Saude Rural Do Distrito De Massinga, Provincia De Inhambane, De Setembro De 1989 A Abril De 1990' Paper presented at the Jornadas De Saude, Quelimane, 1990. Quoted in Cliff, J and Noormahomed, 1988, op cit.

16 Gersony, 1988, op cit.

17 Ibid.

18 'Landmines in Mozambique' Human Rights Watch, Arms Project/Africa, 1992

19 'Landmines in Mozambique' Human Rights Watch, Arms Project/Africa, 1993

20 Cornish, Dr Paul, 'Controlling the Manufacture, Supply and Use of Anti-Personnel Landmines', Chatham House Discussion paper, to be published late 1994.

21 'Landmines in Mozambique', Human Rights Watch, Arms Project, 1994

22 Macrae, J and Zwi, A 'Food as an instrument of war in contemporary African famines: A review of the evidence' *Disasters*, Vol 16, No 4, 1992.

23 Hanlon, J *Mozambique: Who calls the shots?* James Currey, London 1991

24 Macrae, J, Petty, C, White, J, and Zwi, A (Eds) Conflict and international relief in contemporary African famines. Report of a meeting convened by Save the Children Fund (UK) and Health Policy Unit, London School of Hygiene and Tropical Medicine, 1992.

25 Das Gupta, A Save the Children Fund (UK) Mozambique Field Directors Report, London 1986.

26 World Bank 'Mozambique: Issues for the transition from emergency to sustainable growth' Washington DC 1993a.

27 World Bank 'World Development Report' Washington DC, 1993b

28 Glaser, T 1989 'A country report on Mozambique' *The Courier*, March–April No 114.

29 UNICEF. 1989, op cit.

30 *Africa South of the Sahara* 20th edition, Europa Publications, 1991.

31 Economist Intelligence Unit, Country Profile: Mozambique 1993–94 and Sill, M 1992 'A Geography of War' *Geographical Magazine* November 1991

32 Mozambique News Agency 'Coal exports losses amount to millions' AIM Reports, No 15 1993

33 Europa Publications, 1991, op cit.

34 Economist Intelligence Unit Country Profile: Mozambique 1993–94.

35 Glaser, 1989, op cit.

36 Johnson, P and Martin, D *Apartheid terrorism: The destabilisation report*. James Currey Ltd., London, 1989

37 Cliff, and Noormahomed, 1988, op cit.

38 Europa Publications, 1991, op cit.

39 United Nations Operation in Mozambique (ONUMOZ), 1993.

40 World Bank 1993b, op cit.

41 Africa Analysis; 05 February 1993.

42 UNHCR; Information bulletin; 12 May 1993.

43 Mayo, S, O'Keefe, P, and Sill, M *The Southern African Environment: Profile of the SADC Countries*. Earthscan, London. 1992.

44 Economist Intelligence Unit, 1993, op cit.

45 Europa Publications, 1991, op cit.

46 Cordosa, P 'War weary Mozambique needs electricity – to conserve forests', Panos Institute London, 04 November 1988.

47 SARDC, *Mozambique Chronology* 16 November 1993.

48 O'Keefe, P, Kirkby, J, and Cherrett, I 'Mozambican Environmental Problems: Myths and Realities' *Public Administration and Development*, Vol 11, 1991.

49 Sill, M 'A Geography of War' *Geographical Magazine*. November, 1992

50 Mayo, O'Keefe and Sill, 1992, op cit.

51 United Nations Environment Programme, 'Report on a Programming Mission to Mozambique' Nairobi 1988; and World Bank; 'Mozambique, Country Environmental Issues' paper, Washington DC, 1988.

52 Environmental Investigation Agency *Under Fire: Elephants in the front line*, London, 1992

53 Mozambique News Agency 1986. AIM, 10 November 1986.

54 United Nations Operation in Mozambique (ONUMOZ). 1993.

55 *Refugees*, 'Mozambican Refugees'. September 1990.

56 *Refugees*, 'Southern Africa: Conference on Refugees, Returnees and Displaced Persons.' Oslo, 22–24 October 1988, No 55, July/August 1988.

57 *Refugees*, 1988, op cit.

58 UNHCR 'The Mozambican Refugee and Returnee Programme' Report on 1990 activities and 1991 needs 1991.

59 SADCC 'Southern Africa: Toward economic liberation' a declaration by the Governments of Independent States of Southern Africa made at Lusaka on the 1 April 1980. 1980

60 Jaster, R S 'A regional security role for Africa's front line states: Experiences and prospects' Adelphi Papers No 183. The International Institute for Strategic Studies, 1983

61 Hanlon, J, *Beggar your neighbours; Apartheid power in Southern Africa*, Catholic Institute for International Relations/James Currey, London, 1986.

62 Johnson and Martin, 1989, op cit.

63 Ibid.

64 Ibid.

65 Ibid.

66 UNICEF, 1989, op cit.

67 Europa Publications, 1991, op cit.

68 Ibid.

69 Ibid.

70 Johnson and Martin, 1989, op cit.

71 Hanlon, 1986, op cit.

72 Ibid.

73 Johnson and Martin, 1989, op cit.
74 Ibid.
75 Ibid
76 Ibid.
77 Stoneman, C *Zimbabwe's Prospects: Issues of Race, Class, State and Capital in Southern Africa*, Macmillan, London, 1988.
78 Stoneman, 1988, op cit.
79 Johnson and Martin, 1989, op cit.
80 Economist Intelligence Unit. 1993, op cit and Johnson and Martin, 1989, op cit.
81 Mayo, O'Keefe and Sill, 1992, op cit.
82 *Refugees*, 1990, op cit.
83 Johnson and Martin, 1989, op cit; and Environmental Investigation Agency, 1992, op cit.
84 Johnson and Martin, 1989, op cit.
85 Ibid.
86 UNICEF, 1989, op cit.
87 Hanlon, 1986, op cit.
88 Davies, R, 'South African strategy towards Mozambique in the post-Nkomati period: A critical analysis of effects and implications' Research report No 73, Scandinavian Institute of African Studies, Uppsala. 1986
89 Hanlon, 1986, op cit.
90 Davies, 1985, op cit.
91 Hanlon, 1986, op cit.
92 Ibid.
93 Ibid.
94 Ibid.
95 Ibid.
96 Ibid.
97 Chan, S 'Exporting apartheid: Foreign policies in Southern Africa, 1978–1988' *Southern African Studies*, Macmillan Publishers Ltd, 1990
98 Hanlon, 1986, op cit.
99 Ibid.
100 Hanlon, 1986, op cit.
101 Barber, J and Barrett, J 'South Africa's foreign policy: The search for status and security 1945–1988' Cambridge studies in international relations, No 11, 1990
102 Foreign and Commonwealth Office 'Britain in Southern Africa: A Force for Peaceful Change and Development' FCO, 1989.
103 National Executive for the Emergency (CENE) and The Department for the Prevention and Combat of Natural Disasters (DPCCN) 'Rising to the Challenge: Dealing with the Emergency in Mozambique. An Inside View' CENE, Maputo, 1988.
104 World Bank, 1993b, op cit.
105 Europa Publications, 1991, op cit.
106 World Bank, 1993a, op cit.
107 United Nations Operation in Mozambique (ONUMOZ), 1993.
108 World Bank, 1993a, op cit.
109 Economist Intelligence Unit, 1993, op cit.
110 UNHCR, 1991, op cit.
111 Ibid.

112 Hanlon, J 'Fears grow over slow progress' *Mozambique Peace Process Bulletin*, Issue No 5, August, 1993
113 *Janes Defence Weekly* 'Zimbabwe makes way for UN in Mozambique' 17 April 1993.
114 United States Institute of Peace 'Special report on Mozambique' 18 May 1993, USIP, Washington DC.
115 'Mozambique: Slowly May Do It.' *The Economist*, 08 May 1993.
116 Glaser, 1989, op cit.
117 Foreign and Commonwealth Office, 1989, op cit.
118 World Bank, 1993a, op cit.
119 Ibid.
120 Crawford, L 'When Managers Carry Guns.' *The Financial Times*, London, 25 May 1994.
121 *The Financial Times*, 25 May 1994
122 Ibid.
123 Telephone conversation with Mr A Ibbott, from the UK Association of Southern Africa Business Association.
124 Hanlon, 1986, op cit.
125 Ibid.
126 Mayall, J 1988 'The South African crisis: The major external actors' In Johnson, S (Ed). 1988 *South Africa: No turning back* David Davies Memorial Institute of International Studies.
127 Guelke, A 1990 'Southern Africa and the Superpowers' In Chan, S, 1990, op cit.
128 Europa Publications, 1991, op cit.
129 Mayall, 1988, op cit.
130 Chan, 1990, op cit.
131 Economist Intelligence Unit, 1993, op cit.
132 Glaser, 1989, op cit; and Europa Publications, 1991, op cit.
133 Europa Publications, 1991, op cit.
134 Glaser, 1989, op cit.
135 Europa Publications, 1991, op cit.
136 Economist Intelligence Unit, 1993, op cit.
137 Ibid.
138 Ibid.
139 Europa Publications, 1991, op cit.
140 Ibid.
141 Ibid.
142 Economist Intelligence Unit, 1993, op cit.
143 Underwood, M, and Wyer, J 'Study of the participation by NGO's in the implementation of ODA aid policy in Mozambique' Report for the British Overseas Development Administration, 1993.
144 World Bank, 1993a, op cit.
145 Ibid.
146 Underwood and Wyer, 1993, op cit.
147 Europa Publications, 1991, op cit.
148 Crawford, 1994, op cit.
149 World Bank, 1993a, op cit, and Gonçalves, F 'Mozambique: New perspectives for economic development' *South African Political Economy Monthly* (SAPEM), February 1993.

5

THE PERU CONFLICT
(1980–   )

David Shave

Area (000sq km)	1285
Population (000)	22
Human Development Index	0.64
Population density (per sq km)	17
Capital	Lima

KEY IMPACTS OF THE CONFLICT

ON PERU

- Up to 30,000 people have died directly as a result of the war
- Peru maintained its lead for the highest number of 'disappearances' in the world for the third consecutive year in 1990.
- There are up to 5000 political prisoners. One-third may be innocent.
- Peru has been given the lowest democracy rating in Latin America, even below countries such as Guatemala and El Salvador.
- Peru has lost a quarter of a century of economic growth as a result of the war.
- Direct damage caused by Sendero Luminoso activity is estimated to have cost Peru US$22 billion.
- Infrastructural repair has cost US$9.2 billion.
- Up to 600,000 people have been displaced by the conflict. They have no official identity and are continually harassed by the army and police.
- In the conflict areas, there are approximately 25,000 people per doctor.
- Sendero Luminoso have linked up with the drug barons, which has severely militarized the war against the drug trade.
- Peru has spent more than US$200 million on arms in the last five years.
- As a direct result of Sendero attacks on electricity pylons for example, Lima lost US$6.6 million worth of earnings for every day without electricity.

ON THE UNITED STATES

- The US has spent over US$100 million fighting the drug trade in Peru. No decrease in the drug supply has been detected.
- The US Embassy, the Ford Motor Company assembly plant, the Sheraton Hotel, the offices of the Bank of America and Coca-Cola have all been attacked.
- Peru received a significant share of the annual US$147 million budget of the state department unit running drugs interdiction in Latin America.
- US aid to Peru in 1993 was US$129 million.
- US direct investment has decreased from US$2000 million in 1982 to US$500 million in 1990.

INTRODUCTION

Geography

With a total land area of 1,285,216 square kilometres, Peru is the third largest country in Latin America, and slightly larger than France, Germany and Poland combined. Peru shares borders with five countries: Bolivia to the east; Chile to the south; Brazil to the north-east and Colombia and Ecuador to the north.

The People

Peru has a population of 22.45 million (1992 estimate) of which 47.1 per cent are Quechua, 32.0 per cent are *mestizo*, 12.0 per cent are white, 5.4 per cent are Aymara, 1.7 per cent are other Amerindian and 1.0 per cent belong to other ethnic groups. The official language is Spanish, although Quechua is widely spoken by the 47.1 per cent that belong to this group. Indigenous religions are still highly active throughout the country, with a high incidence of syncretism between native and non-native religions.

The Conflict

The principal player in the conflict is the extreme left Maoist terrorist group Sendero Luminoso, or 'Shining Path'. Led by Abimael Guzman, Sendero began guerrilla activity in 1980. Initially, actions were concentrated in the Ayacuchean highlands, where Sendero enrolled the support of the Andean poor. It has had the greatest effect on the rural communities of Peru, specifically in the regions of Apurimac, Ayacucho, Cuzco and Puno. The vast majority of its recruits are *campesinos*, or peasant farmers.

Their active involvement was encouraged through a variety of means. Firstly, actual intimidation of the rural peasantry into joining Sendero ranks and secondly, Sendero manipulation of decades of resentment, alienation and impoverish-ment. By operating in areas that have traditionally been bypassed by mainstream society, thereby deprived of everyday basic services, investment and opportunities, Sendero has managed to channel societal anger into its cause.

A final reason for Sendero's longevity results from the state's response to terrorism, which has had dramatic effects on innocent civilians, further alienating them, and by its heavy economic measures or *paquetazos*, implemented to counter spiralling inflation and debt.

Initially carrying out small-scale actions, Sendero activity intensified to such an extent that the army was drafted to deal with internal security issues. Their active involvement in counter-insurgency during the 1980s further intensified the conflict. Until the recent capture of leading cadres, Sendero had the ability to make its presence very much felt, psychologically, economically and physically through actual attacks. Draconian measures and widespread human rights abuses caught the passive civilian in the cross-fire. Sendero's activity can be divided into a number of key stages;

- 1980–1986; Sendero's activity centres around the departments of Ayacucho and Huancavelica. The army is sent, and the population flees. Massive displacement begins.
- 1987–1989; Violence and terrorism spreads to towns. 1989 is the most intensive year of Sendero activity. Army counter-offensives inflict massive casualties on the civilian population.
- 1990–1992; Sendero activity concentrates in Selva Central and Lima.
- 1992–; Abimael Guzman, the inspirational leader of Sendero, and a large majority of Sendero's elite, are captured. Sendero activity decreases sharply, but does not disappear.

The Movimiento Revolucionario Tupac Amaru (MRTA) is another guerrilla movement that has intensified the conflict over the same period. Formed in 1983, the

MRTA was the result of the splitting of radical factions from mainstream left-wing political parties.[2] In contrast to Sendero, MRTA has presented a more benevolent image, through more effective campaigning and actions that include hijacking and distributing food deliveries to shanty towns and thereby gaining support from large sections of Peru's disaffected youth. Sendero and MRTA have not cooperated; but have instead repeatedly competed for control of key areas. In the words of Sendero leadership, the MRTA is the 'principal enemy of the revolution...that must be confronted because there cannot be the triumph of two revolutions.'[3] The MRTA has been decimated by government counter-insurgency actions, and plays little part in the contemporary events of the conflict.

In the latter half of the 1980s further warring factions entered the internal conflict, the most important being the drug cartels that operate in the Huallaga Valley. Spearheaded by the United States Drug Enforcement Administration (DEA), a new element of conflict has entered the arena: the fight against coca production and the drug cartels. This has largely failed, only leaving behind well-armed state security forces. Sendero, in return for protection, 'taxes' coca production, thus ensuring a resource base, making the conflict more complex. Under the Bush administration, the Drug Enforcement Administration (DEA) policy aimed to militarize those fighting the drug production.

Scope of the Study

This study examines the consequences of the conflict from the first year of Sendero activity, 1980, through to the present day. While it focuses on the actions of both Sendero and the MRTA, it is the actions of Sendero that have had by far the greatest effect, and these are emphasized accordingly. The study also examines links between Sendero and the drug cartels, and investigates the DEA's activities pertinent to the Peruvian conflict. Because of the insignificant involvement of other G7 countries, the study will focus solely on the nature and extent of this and other US involvement.

PERU

THE COSTS

Introduction

Peru is a country whose population, particularly that living in rural areas, has suffered from chronic poverty for many decades. In examining the effect of the conflict, it is important to remember that many development indicators were already at a low level. The purpose of this section is to demonstrate how those figures have been additionally affected by the conflict. Without question, the conflict has had a devastating effect.

Development

Health

International Fund for Agricultural Development (IFAD) figures show that only 17 per cent of the rural population had access to health services over the period 1980–87.[4] This figure is highly significant, given that conflict has had a disproportionate effect upon the rural population. At the national level, in contrast, 75 per cent had access to health services in 1980.[5]

Conflict has had a direct impact upon the incidence of disease. Vaccines and medicine stocks have been ruined by the countless *apagones* or power blackouts that have struck the major cities. The cholera epidemic of 1991, for example, worsened as a result of power lines being blown up which hindered water purification and placed additional strain on already low water standards and limited supply. Inaccessibility as a result of violence heightened the problem in, for example, the distribution of rehydration salts.

116

NGOs as targets

One international NGO, that wishes to remain anonymous for fear of reprisals, recounts the rising cost of the conflict upon the health components of its projects. Its project in the Selva Central area had to be moved when a number of local workers were killed and organization staff received threats from Sendero. Small aircraft are now used to fly the remaining health workers in and out. Not only are there economic implications, to the development organization itself, but the areas in question no longer have medical staff visiting them and have to rely completely upon local health workers.[6] While long-term negative ramifications were limited by the commitment and courage of local workers, other projects in Lima have had to be stopped for fear of Sendero infiltration and retaliation. The consequences are easily assessed: a population that stood to gain from development initiatives, now has nothing.

As a result of intimidation of health workers, the practice of immunization that had progressively increased in the period 1981 to 1988 dropped with the intensification of the conflict in 1989. The latest UN figures for immunization show that only 73 per cent of one-year olds were immunized in 1989–1991.[7] In Figure 5.1 is a breakdown of immunization against four major diseases.

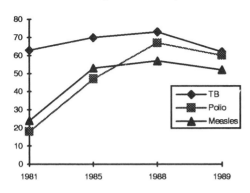

Source: UNICEF 1993, op cit

Figure 5.1: Immunization of one-year-olds (% of total)

Growing violence has meant that large areas are under emergency legislation and out of bounds to medical personnel. Sendero has targeted medical personnel which has resulted in a rising maternal mortality rate (MMR) in the most afflicted regions. In Apurimac, Ayacucho, Cuzco and Puno, both the infant mortality rate and MMR have increased.

The reality of the more isolated Sendero/army controlled emergency zones is bleak indeed. The department of Cajamarca has 20,000 people per doctor.[8] The same situation is applicable to the departments of Huancavelica and Apurimac, where there are 25,000 inhabitants per doctor.[9] These figures fall far short of World Health Organisation (WHO) recommendations of one doctor per 1250 population. Moreover, doctors have been driven out of certain sectors and health care is left to health workers who often lack medicine or funds. An area's reputation for being unsafe prevents adequate services from developing. Despite there having been no attacks in over two years, one Ayacuchean community had not been visited by a doctor in that same period.

The statistics for the population per doctor and distance to the nearest hospital fall into insignificance when a large portion of the Peruvian society cannot be included in such analysis. Some estimates believe that as a result of violence, poverty and isolation, 95 per cent of the rural population is dependent upon traditional herbal medicine.

UNICEF estimate that 78 per cent of the urban population has access to safe water, while only 10 per cent of the rural population enjoys such access. While the urban setting has improved considerably since 1980 (67 per cent), the conditions for the rural setting have deteriorated substantially from the original figure of 15 per cent.[10]

Sendero attacks against electricity pylons not only affect the industrial sector (see pages 125–7), but have also aggravated the poor levels of access to safe water. When a power line is destroyed, water supply is interrupted, purification plants closed and subsequent standards of water supply drop. Sendero attacks on power lines have been planned to cause maximum effect. For example, Sendero disrupted Lima's power supply when the Peruvian women's team were playing in the Olympic volleyball final of 1988.

'Of Peru's 22 million people, about 38 per cent are children under 15 years of age, and about 13 per cent are children under 5 years of age.[11] Of children under five, 49 per cent suffer from malnutrition, 9000 of which die annually.[12] (Figure 5.2) Like many developmental organizations, UNICEF identifies that 'terrorism and drug trafficking activities...have had a major impact on the country's socio-economic situation and are reaching critical levels'.[13]

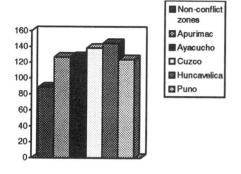

Source: Paredes and Sachs, op cit

Figure 5.2: Infant mortality rate, by region: deaths per 1000 children one year or younger (1986)

The five departments (regions) with the highest levels of IMR are those most affected by conflict: Apurimac, Ayacucho, Huancavelica, Cuzco and Puno. The above data correspond to Sendero strategy for the same period which was to concentrate on Ayacucho and Huancavelica. While the departments of Puno, Cuzco and Apurimac have traditionally had high levels of IMR, these rates have been aggravated by the second phase of Sendero strategy in the second half of the 1980s, of concentrating on the larger towns, many of which are located in these regions.

Education

While there has been a substantial decrease in national drop-out rates, it is virtually impossible to collate accurate enrolment statistics for the emergency zones which Gloria Helfer, ex-Minister for Education, terms the 'black boxes'.[14] Drop-out rates in the emergency zones may be as high as 100 per cent in cases where the actual educational establishment, namely the school itself, has been destroyed by Sendero. Since the conflict began, 70 schools have been destroyed and 71 teachers have disappeared.[15]

While the adult literacy rate in Peru has increased on a par with Latin America as a whole, there has been a drop in access to educational establishments and thus literacy. For the displaced, who largely lack documentation, there is little or no chance of registering their children at school. Nor can they legally work if they lack documentation. They thus cannot become part of formal society.

Sendero Luminoso cadres have been active in the universities for many years. Actions carried out here have not only been against individuals but also the very infrastructure of the university. Security forces have returned violence with violence and alarming rates of disappearances of both students and staff have been reported. While the drop in university lecturers can be partly attributed to government economic mismanagement and failure to sufficiently fund universities, they have increasingly become targets for both the armed forces and Sendero Luminoso. All the above actions combine to worsen the lot of the student to an extent that in 1987 only 10 per cent of its 44,000 students graduated.[16] Long-term ramifications are that Peru will lack skilled personnel when and if reconstruction begins.

Civil and Political Rights

Number of deaths

The conflict had claimed an estimated 26,000 to 30,000 lives by 1993. These figures

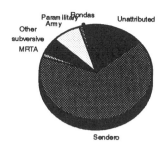

Source: Asociacion Pro-Derechos Humanos
(APRODEH), US State Department and Coordinadora
Nacional de Derechos Humanos (CNDDHH) figures
in *Latin American Weekly Report*, 1993 'Washington and
rights', 11 March 1993.

*Figure 5.3: Cross-section of casualties – Jan-Nov
1992*

include civilian, military and senderista
casualties.[17] In the period January–
November 1992, 988 deaths were recorded.
These figures are attributed to different
factions in Figure 5.3.

Number of terrorist attacks

Between 1985 and 1986, the number of
terrorist attacks more than doubled from
the previous years, from 695 to 1327. In
1987, there were 433 attacks recorded in
Lima.[18] The expansion of Sendero was such
that by the end of 1989 only one out of a
possible 24 departments escaped unscathed
from Sendero action. Terrorist activities in
Lima increased while actions in Ayacucho
dropped.[19] The first five months of 1991
marked one of the bloodiest periods of
Sendero and MRTA activity, with 660
attacks registered by the Peruvian senate.[20]

Following the capture of Guzman in
September 1992, there was a noticeable
decline in the number of Sendero attacks. In
the last quarter of 1992 there were 658
fatalities while in the first quarter of 1993
the figure had dropped to 413.[21] Enrique
Bernales, thought to have the most reliable
statistics on Sendero actions, confirmed the
drop in terrorist activity. The number of
terrorist raids dropped from 6.25 actions
daily to 4.69 in the same period. MRTA
action rapidly declined in the same period
with Sendero accounting for 85.4 per cent of

all actions. The attacks have been
concentrated in the Lima and Callao area
while those in areas such as Ayacucho have
declined.[22] In January of 1993, for the first
time in ten years, more Peruvians died of
common violence (such as road accidents,
domestic disputes etc) than through
political violence.[23]

Sendero attacks against both Peruvian
and international aid workers have made
any development work harder. Leading
development organizations convened in
Lima and had little other option than to
withdraw future support for projects in
conflict areas. Workers on US-funded coca
reduction programmes have been the
targets of a disproportionate amount of
Sendero attacks. Between 1983 and 1989, 27
eradication workers for the Upper
Huallaga Valley Coca Reduction Programme (CORAH) workers were killed,
while their progress against drugs over that
same period was negligible, accounting for
the eradication of a mere 1 per cent of the
total Huallaga Valley crop.

Number of political prisoners

Since President Fujimori introduced new
terrorist laws in May 1992, 432 terrorists
have been found guilty by military judges,
163 of whom are serving life sentences.[24]
Since Fujimori's auto-coup on 5 April 1992,
in which he suspended parliament, 4000
suspected terrorist have been detained by
the security forces.[25]

There have been several cases of
human rights abuses against political
prisoners. The most important incidences
were in 1986 and 1992. In June 1986, 300
senderista political prisoners were killed
after a mutiny in three Lima gaols.[26] In May
1992, during the transfer of female
senderista prisoners from Canto Grande, a
riot broke out which took four days to
quell. In the ensuing struggle to regain
control of the prison, 50 prisoners died.[27]

The Washington Office for Latin
America (WOLA) estimate that there are
currently 5000 political prisoners, often
held incommunicado and without access to
defence lawyers. They believe that at least
one-third of them are innocent, detained

Table 5.1: Disappearances and extrajudicial executions under Fujimori (elected 28 July, 1990)

Period	Total Documented	Later released	Later acknowledged in detention	Later found dead	Remained unaccounted for
28/7/90–31/7/91	372	79	4	17	272
1/8/91–31/7/92	298	37	1	13	247
1/8/92–30/5/93	76	16*	2	17	41
Total	746	132	7	47	560

*One of these victims escaped

Source: Amnesty International, 1993, op cit

under the Draconian 'preventative' measures imposed by Fujimori.[28]

Number of disappearances

Peru maintained its lead for the highest number of 'disappearances' in the world for the third consecutive year in 1990, according to a UN report of February 1990.[29] In 1992, there were 112 'proven cases', once again placing Peru as the country with most disappearances.[30]

Figure 5.4 shows the rate of disappearances during 1987–92 and Tables 5.1 and 5.2 show disappearances and executions inder Fujimori.

Table 5.2: Number of people documented as extrajudicially executed

Period	Number of people
28/7/91–31/7/91	88
1/8/91–31/7/92	105
1/8/92–30/4/93	35
Total	228

Source: Amnesty International, 1993,. op cit

Disappearances in Peru

On 18 July 1992, a group of 60 masked soldiers raided the male dormitories at La Cantuta forcing the students to lie face down. A soldier pulled out students from the group using a list he had brought. A similar raid was carried out in the female dormitories concluding with a final operation when Hugo Munoz was taken from the professor's residences. In all ten people were taken away.

The La Cantuta disappearances became national and international news again when, in April 1993, Henry Pease, a member of the interim governing committee, the Congreso Constituyente Democratico (CCD), revealed an apparent internal military document that stated that the students had been executed on the night of their abduction. The leaked document was signed by Leon Dormido or Sleeping Lion, a party that describes itself as a group of active-duty mid-level officers committed to human rights. Leon Dormido outlined the sequestration, listing four high-level security officers who were in charge of the operation, among whom was Vladimiro Montesinos, Head of the Servicio Intelligencia Nacional (SIN) and close advisor to Fujimori. The government vehemently denied any knowledge of the administration.[31]

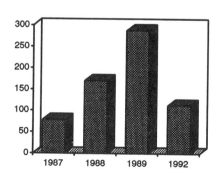

Source: United Nations Estimates from Andean Newsletter in Woy-Hazleton and Hazleton, 1990, op. cit.

Figure 5.4: Number of disappearances

Incidence of torture

The practice of torture is widespread in Peru, and is used by all warring factions.

In the 13 months leading up to April 1993, Amnesty International received information regarding at least 40 cases of torture and ill-treatment. Amnesty International believes that these cases do not represent the real figures for torture since many people fear reprisals, should they report attacks.[32]

Rape has been used as a psychological weapon of torture against women by the armed forces and is 'committed in the course of armed conflict, usually in order to punish'.[33] A report by Americas Watch documents 40 rapes by police and security personnel carrying out interrogation. These 40 rapes are only a fraction of the real number of rapes committed in Peru, since only an estimated 10 per cent are ever reported. Sendero recruits have also committed rape, despite Sendero ideology that men should not sexually molest women.[34]

Level of democracy

In a recent survey on levels of democracy, Peru ranked lowest in Latin America. This rating was established by leading academics, journalists and human rights professionals, evaluating the rating through a study of key indicators within four categories; the existence of free and fair elections; an open and accountable government; civil and political rights and a democratic society as a whole. (See Figure 5.5)

Several elected mayors of Villa El Salvador, a shanty town on the outskirts of Lima, have been killed by Sendero since 1980 including María Elena Moyano, who actively campaigned against Sendero and was highly involved with grassroots soup kitchen organizations.

While *campesinos* account for the majority of Sendero victims (76 per cent), the second major target is government officials. By August 1989, 92 public officials had been assassinated, leaving 80 districts and 4 provinces without municipal

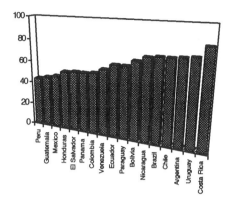

Source: *The New Statesman and Society*, 'Planetary Probe' in Bite the Ballot, 2,500 years of Democracy, Special Supplement, 29 April 1994

Figure 5.5: Latin American countries by democracy rating

authorities.[35] Since 1989, attacks on government officials has continued; the Mayor of Pachacamac, Paul Poblet, assassinated in May 1991, became the 139th mayor to be killed by Sendero since 1984.[36]

In some towns the democratic system has been repeatedly dismantled by Sendero. In the town of Aucayacu, for example, of the last five mayors, two were assassinated while the other three were given a 24-hour notice to leave their posts.[37] Huánaco has had the same history. Of six mayors, three were murdered and three resigned after receiving death threats.[38]

Extent of despotism

Since carrying out his 'auto-coup,' Fujimori has extended the power of his rule through numerous decree laws which are tantamount to acts of despotism. His initial action, carried out through Decree Law 25418, invalidated all laws and constitutional provisions that countered the objectives of the government's plans for national reconstruction.

Fujimori consolidated his power base through a string of decrees, among which were a range of laws that included: the suspension of all judicial and prosecutorial services; mass sacking of the judiciary and the establishment of 'faceless' judges; incommunicado 'preventive detentions' for 30 days; and for terrorism *apologia* was deemed to constitute treason and would be subject to prosecution by the military and a possible life sentence.[39] All the above actions are equivalent to acts of despotism. The apologia laws are the most significant for, under these laws, a doctor that treats injured *senderistas* is in danger of being imprisoned, as is a lawyer who defends them.

Tolerance of minorities

In 1990, the MRTA, was accused of targeting indigenous leaders and gays in the eastern jungle department of Ucayali as a part of its new strategy.[40]

The Ashaninka Amazonian tribe (numbering some 50,000 to 80,000) has come under direct fire from Sendero. They have been the target of Sendero recruitment and in the attack of 18 August 1993, Ashaninka *senderista* recruits were involved in the massacre of more than 60 of their own people.[41] The Ashaninka have become involved in Peru's war as coca growers have encroached upon their land. Some sources believe that Sendero are currently holding 10,000 Ashaninka captive. A 1993 report claimed that 5000 were held captive and that as much as 80 per cent of Ashaninka territory was under Sendero control.[42] Ashaninka involvement has been increased by the presence of both the army and Sendero, who vie for their allegiance.[43]

NGOs as targets

Sendero's objections to aid, be it national or international, stems from its belief that it leads to *asistencialismo*, or dependence. Their fight against *asistencialismo* is clearly demonstrated by the murder of two Polish Franciscan missionaries in August 1991, whom Sendero accused of controlling the masses by creating dependence.[44] The numerous murders and attacks on food programme leaders show the extent to which Sendero is prepared to combat *asistencialismo*.

Women have also come under attack from Sendero for their involvement in NGO activities and politics in Peru. Sendero ideology dismisses feminist belief as an international conspiracy. Issues such as contraception and equal pay for women for equal work are counter-revolutionary. Sendero has accused women of attempting to starve the Sendero forces of future members.[45] Ironically, 60 per cent of Sendero leaders and total membership is made up of women.[46]

Peru's 3000 NGOs involved in education, health, the arts and development have come under fire from Sendero, which accuses them of defending the existing order and collaborating with the government.[47] In Villa El Salvador, a large number of *comedores populares* or popular kitchens/soup kitchens have emerged. These centres are largely run by women in response to the growing poverty, and produce food at a nominal fee. Following the severe economic measures carried out by Fujimori in 1990, the number of soup kitchens in Villa El Salvador rose dramatically from 2800 to 7000. Nearly a third of Villa El Salvador's 300,000 population benefit from either *comedores populares* or milk programmes.[48] Sendero has justified its attacks on these soup kitchen organizers by arguing that they 'maintain an enormous, extremely impoverished mass of beggars, without a critical spirit, without will to fight, who think of nothing more than the next plate of food to be given.'[49]

The security forces have not only failed to protect individuals involved in such activities, but have sought to involve them in counter-insurgency actions, and have attempted to convert them into a militarized civil society. Such actions have further endangered such workers, as they are thus made more likely to be attacked by *senderistas* who wrongly accuse them of siding with the Government.[50]

Sendero has carried out numerous armed interventions against soup kitchens and their organizers including:

- assassinating ten female leaders in the period 1985–1993.
- forcing hundreds of women to

abandon their posts.
- dynamiting a food warehouse used by FEPOMUVES (Popular Federation of Women of Villa El Salvador), leaving 90 kitchens without food.[51]

In one settlement, Sendero made threats to kitchens and community-run chemists (*botiquines comunales*). Of 30 kitchens, only two were left functioning following these threats.[52] Not only is Sendero carrying out armed attacks, but it is infiltrating the kitchen organizations with the long-term aim of splitting the leadership and precipitating their collapse.[53]

The Economy

A combination of poor economic management by successive Peruvian administrations and the rising costs of conflict have had major negative impacts on Peru's GDP. While it is impossible to quantify the exact contribution of the war, it can be assumed the ramifications have been significant; social expenditure has been removed to support the military budget; food production in conflict areas has plummeted and the industrial sector has been plagued by attacks and power failure.

Actual damage caused by conflict is estimated at US$22 billion. Peru's export rate growth declined in the period 1980–85 by an annual average of 1.1 per cent and in 1986–89 by 1.7 per cent.[54] 'The direction of causality between economic crisis and violence is not one way. Violence and the uncertainty it generates have increased firms' costs, encouraged emigration and capital flight, and discouraged investment.'[55]

GDP

Between 1950 and 1975, real GDP grew at an annual average of 5.3 per cent, exceeding population growth in all but two of those years. In 1976–89, growth slowed down to only 1 per cent with a decrease in GDP per capita in more than half of those years.[56]

'At the end of the 1980s per capita GDP was lower than in 1975 and similar to the level recorded in 1961. For per capita GDP to recover its 1975 level by 2000, it would

have to grow at an annual growth rate for total GDP of 5.8 per cent, a rate achieved only in the most prosperous periods of the second half of the century. In any case, Peru has already lost a quarter of a century of economic growth.'[57]

Real GDP per capita showed a small increase since 1960 when it was US$2130. By 1990 it was US$2622.[58] This rise of US$532 over three decades is equivalent to an increase of 23 per cent and is not comparable to that of neighbouring Chile (64 per cent), Ecuador (110 per cent) and Bolivia (38 per cent).[59] Moreover, in the 1990s, real GDP per capita continued to plummet and in 1992 stood at US$2,014, below the figure for 1960.[60] Figure 5.6 shows the change in GDP per capita from 1983 to 1991.

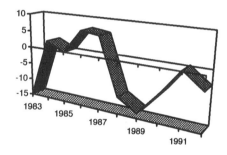

Source: Fidler, S[3]., 'Price has risen steeply in two years', in *The Financial Times*, Special Survey on Peru, 29 September 1993.

Figure 5.6: Real GDP per capita (% change)

External debt

Peru's foreign debt rose from US$13.94 billion in 1985 and was recently estimated to be US$22 billion.[61]

Figure 5.8 shows the dramatic nature of Peru's external debt. Standing at US$22 billion, the total external debt represented 483.6 per cent of exports of goods and services in 1991.

Trade

Prior to the conflict, Peru boasted an underfunded yet, by Latin American standards, extensive manufacturing sector. Conflict has led to greater underfunding,

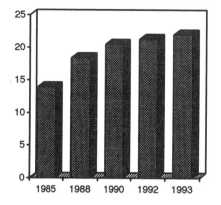

Source: Paredes and Sachs, op cit; EIU 4th quarter
1993, op cit

Figure 5.7: External debt – Peru

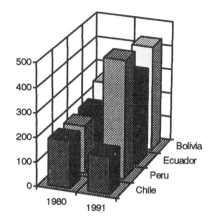

Source: World Bank, *World Development Report 1993*,
Oxford, 1993

*Figure 5.8: Total external debt as a % of goods and
services*

and loss of earnings and manufacturing effectiveness.

Although inextricably tied up with the conflict, cocaine remains Peru's strongest export. No proceeds enter the economic system and the industry informally employs 100,000 with an annual turnover estimated at US$1 billion. It has led to a narrowing of the tax base and subsequent government revenue.[62]

Imports

Growing import of foodstuffs demonstrates a growing food insecurity brought about by the rural population fleeing from the conflict zones to the cities in their tens of thousands. As illustrated in Figures 5.9 and 5.10, Peru's food import dependency has increased noticeably while that of Chile and Bolivia has dropped. In the period 1984–88 for example, it was reported that in the province of Aymaraes, 60 per cent of the population had left, resulting in a 42 per cent drop in land cultivation.[63]

Loss of earnings

One sector of government revenue that has been particularly badly hit since the conflict began is tourism. Potential tourists have stopped visiting Peru due to the increasing violence, although this is only very

occasionally directed at foreigners. The cholera epidemic of 1991 further deterred potential visitors. Some sources estimate that in the last five years the normal high of 120,000 tourists visiting Cuzco has dropped to perhaps a quarter of that figure.[64] In a town like Cuzco, where nearly 95 per cent of the population are in some way linked to tourism, the drop has been particularly detrimental. It has led to the closure of many hotels and tourist enterprises.[65] Tourism, a major revenue earner, accounted for US$402 million in 1989.[66]

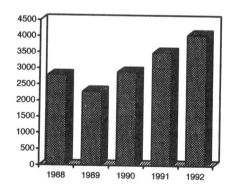

Source: EIU, 1993a, op cit

Figure 5.9: Imports, 1988–1992 (US$m)

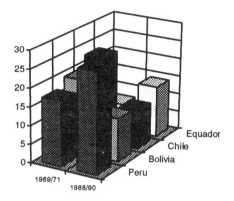

Source: United Nations, 1993, op cit
Note: 'Food import dependency ratio': The ratio of food imports to the food available for internal distribution: that is, the sum of food production, plus food imports, minus food exports.

Figure 5.10: Food import dependency ratio (%)

Military expenditure

Peru spent US$188 million on arms imports between 1987–91, accounting for 5.8 per cent of all imports in 1990.[67] This figure however, does not take into account the arms that Sendero imports through drug cartel funding. Arms suppliers are shown in Figure 5.11.

Infrastructure

Power supply

In the so called 'third stage' of actions by Sendero beginning in 1990, attacks began to be increasingly directed against the nation's economic infrastructure. A higher incidence of attacks against power stations, bridges, factories and farming enterprises was recorded.[68] Costs to infrastructure during the 1980s were placed at US$9.2 billion, the equivalent of more than half of the 1989 GDP.[69]

There has been severe electricity rationing following more than 1319 attacks on high-tension power towers.[70] In 1988 alone, 200 power lines were blown up by Sendero. The city of Lima loses US$6.6 million of revenue for every day without

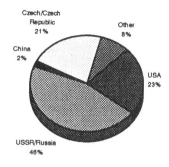

Source: SIPRI; World Trade in Conventional Weapons 1988–90

Figure 5.11: Suppliers of conventional weapons to Peru 1988–90 (US$m constant 1990 prices)

electricity. In addition to terrorist attacks, maintenance costs have constituted less than 1 per cent of assets, which has led to a rapid deterioration in standards.[71]

1991 was the worst year for attacks against power lines, with an estimated 1.5–2.0 per cent of GNP lost due to *apagones* (blackouts) and rationing.[72] In 1988, the National Association of Industries (SNI) estimated that power cuts had forced hundreds of companies and factories to close through loss of earnings.[73] At the Archbishop Loayza Hospital, emergency treatment for dehydration and intestinal problems due to power failures increased by 25 per cent in 1989.[74]

Examples of infrastructural damage

12 December 1988: Sendero attacked a milk plant near Concepción, dynamiting holding tanks, machinery, a laboratory and administrative buildings. Losses at the plant, which was capable of producing 5000 litres a day, were estimated at US$400,000.

In November 1988, Sendero attacked SAIS Cahuide (Huancayo), the nation's largest agricultural cooperative which covers 675,000 acres and employs 5000 families. Senderistas sacked, burnt, and dynamited, killing hundreds of sheep and alpaca and paralysing production of meat, cheese, milk and wool. Damage was estimated at US$3 million.[75]

In May 1990, Sendero attack the International Centre for the Study of the Potato. Research staff later left Peru permanently. This withdrawal shows the fear among the international community, a fear that is leading to growing reluctance to invest both resources and personnel in Peru.

In May 1990, Sendero destroyed Latin America's leading cattle semen bank at Lima's National Agrarian University.

As well as attacking agricultural instit-utions, Sendero has also attempted to stop planting. State figures estimated in 1989 that agricultural production would drop by 8.3 per cent, while poultry was expected to drop by 28 per cent, rice by 23 per cent and potatoes by 15 per cent.[77]

Transport

Peru's transport infrastructure consists of: 65,000 kilometres of road, but only 10 per cent are paved; 2500 kilometres of railways, largely inferior to the railways systems of neighbouring countries; and 35 airports, although only one (Lima) is large enough and sufficiently equipped to handle international flights.[78] There has been a growing deterioration of the roads, rail and air services. Reasons for such a deterioration are twofold. There has traditionally been a failure to invest in maintenance and increasingly the guerrilla war has damaged communication systems. Given the nature and objective of Sendero to cut off the cities, the communication network has been a prime target. Total Sendero control of some areas of Peru has also meant that communication imp-rovement could not be carried out, should funds be made available. In 1989 for example, Sendero managed to isolate fully the regional capital of Huanaco for several days, by blowing up five bridges.[79]

Property ownership

Land ownership has been affected in several ways. Firstly, through the displacement of a large population: 600,000 people have lost access not only to their land but also to production. Larger farmers have been forced to pay 'taxes' to the Sendero and in some cases abandon their land.[80]

Refugees

The number of internally displaced has been calculated at between 600,000 and 1 million. Displacement occurred in three main phases that correspond to Sendero strategies. Having abandoned the conflict areas, the displaced population face further dangers, because they have no place of fixed address, they lack any means of formal identification; 'the lack of identification papers turns the displaced into a type of 'dead' citizen–people who do not legally exist'.[81]

The displaced are the first targets of security forces who detain them for lack of documentation. Additional hazards to their future development are that displaced children cannot be registered at school. A final but equally important factor is that those displaced cannot become part of the formal system. Without documentation, they cannot find employment and face further impoverishment and possibly imprisonment. Of Peru's 22 million inhabitants, as many as 20 per cent do not have documents. This places them at high risk from the authorities.[82] Setting aside the human cost, those without documents cannot be included in the tax base, thus their incomes cannot be harnessed to national development.

Migration patterns show that of the displaced population, 60 per cent have settled in the shanties of Lima, 20 per cent in Huancayo and 10 per cent in Ica.[83] The remaining 10 per cent have settled in the city of Ayacucho, the flashpoint of the conflict in 1980. Some sources estimate that the population of Ayacucho has exploded from 30,000 to 200,000 since 1980.[84]

The costs of such displacement are numerous, both to the displaced people and the communities they have left behind. In the Ayacucho department itself, it is estimated that thousands of centuries-old communities have become ghost towns as they are abandoned.[85] For the displaced there is little chance of employment in cities like Lima where only 10 per cent of the displaced population are adequately employed, 25 per cent unemployed and the remainder under-employed.[86]

A 1993 report states that nearly half of the 600,000 displaced are willing to return but fear for their lives and need resettlement aid.[87] This is an important point to be highlighted. The state can shrug off the issue of displacement, citing the dominance of economic *pull* factors in determining urban drift. However, the fact that half of those displaced would like to return to the countryside demonstrates that much of the population are displaced because of the *push* of violence.

Conclusion

While always a country suffering from poverty, Peru's chances of improving the lives of its people have been decimated for the last decade, and probably for the decade to come, by the civil war. It remains an undeveloped country, with its infra-structure continually threatened and unable to support an industrial base and therefore unattractive to foreign invest-ment. Its health and education facilities are primitive and unable to cope with the hundreds of thousands of citizens displaced by the fighting. The civil rights of the people are further impinged upon by a government which has increasingly adopted a tyrannical stance against the terrorist movements; a stance, unfortun-ately, that has entangled thousands of innocent civilians.

THE UNITED STATES

THE COSTS

Introduction

Despite the collapse of the Soviet Union, the US continues to place great geopolitical significance upon Latin America as a region. US policy towards Peru and Latin America as a whole has, and continues to be, one that promotes 'stability'. Stability 'is presumed to be necessary for security, for reliable economic relations, and for predictable diplomacy.'[88]

The US has played an important role in Peru's internal affairs since the early days of the conflict. This intervention has primarily taken the form of economic aid and assistance, but has recently, in the post-Cold War era, undergone a period of redefinition. The conflict in Peru is now termed a 'low intensity conflict' (LIC). The definition of LICs is: 'those situations which threaten US national interests, values and free institutions. Such situations exist at levels below conventional war but above the routine, peaceful competition among states.'[89] Because of the increase in drug flows from South to North America, the US has determined a more military response, by arming those involved in the fight against drugs. This has led to the further arming and militarizing of the conflict.

Public Costs

The war on drugs and economic and military aid

In Peru, 'the rampant poverty of the Andean region... has spurred coca produc-tion and played into the hands of the revolutionary Sendero Luminoso, a faction that has formed alliances of convenience with the drug traffickers; a development that holds serious political consequences for both Lima and Washington.'[90] Peru, with 230,000 hectares of coca,[91] is estimated to produce two-thirds of the total coca production. It received a significant share of the annual US$147 million budget of the State Department unit running drugs interdiction in Latin America. In November 1993, the State Department announced a cut of US$47 million to this budget.[92]

Under the Reagan and Bush admin-istrations, policy toward Peru was spearheaded by a 'war on drugs'. This war involved the militarization of anti-narcotic operations, implemented through the training and arming of Peruvians by the DEA. The Bush administration set aside US$35 million to militarize the drug war in 1990 and the same amount in 1991.[93] The US has also established, in the town of Santa Lucia, a police base at a cost of US$3 million, with annual running costs of US$13 million[94] and has also donated arms and anti-narcotic aircraft such as helicopters and spotter planes. However, as with the crop assistance programme, these measures have all failed to have any marked impact on coca production.

In an era of waning military spending, the war on drugs has become an increasingly larger expense. The DEA was established in the 1960s by Nixon, and since then its budget has steadily increased. Under Reagan, the global DEA budget grew from US$705.3 million in 1981 to US$1.221 billion in 1985. The Bush administration set aside US$5 billion in his first term rising to US$9 billion in 1990.[95] The Clinton administration is thought to be reversing the DEA strategy under Bush.

The US has given Peru economic assistance in an attempt to implement alternative crop programmes. To date these have had limited success given the massive economic benefits derived from coca production. US operations in Peru have ranged from Operation Green Sea of 1979–80 to Operation Condor and Operation Snowcap. They all failed to have any long-term impact on cocaine levels. Under Bush, the Andean Initiative maintained an equally poor record of cocaine reduction.

US policy towards aid to Peru and human rights has varied immensely. US aid to Peru dropped in 1993 to US$129 million from the 1991 figure of US$173 million pending an improvement in human rights standards. Given such improvements, the US planned to upgrade to US$345 million.[96]

The US has also frozen a further US$105 million until human rights improve, but this policy does not affect other loans of US$91.2 million in food assistance, US$37 million for projects already in progress, US$35.2 million for research into future programmes and US$25 million earmarked for efforts to counter drug trafficking.[97]

International Monetary Fund (IMF) loans for US$1.4 billion have been postponed pending improvement in human rights but 'bridging loans' will be given by the US and Japan.[98]

Economic assistance has always been closely tied to the political and security interests of the US, and therefore often includes military assistance packages.[99] Figure 5.12 shows US military assistance to Peru, Bolivia, Chile and Ecuador. Of the four countries represented, Peru received the largest assistance package.

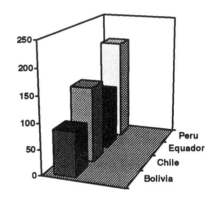

Source: Molineu 1990, op cit

Figure 5.12: Military assistance to Bolivia, Ecuador, Chile and Peru 1962–87 (US$m)

Private Costs

Reductions in investment

Attacks against the US and its commercial interests occurred as Sendero and the MRTA diversified their attacks from the rural setting to the capital. These attacks included attempts against the US embassy, the Ford Motor Company assembly plant, the Sheraton Hotel, the offices of the Bank of America and Coca-Cola, all in Lima.[100]

US investment in Peru steadily declined during the 1980s (Figure 5.13) as investment security was reduced by increasing violence. The ex-President Garcia's decision to reduce debt repayment worsened Peru's image in the US as a secure investment.

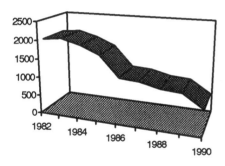

Source: Investment figures from the *Survey of Current Business*, supplied by the US Department of Commerce. Figures for 1982–84 inclusive from August 1986, Volume 66, Number 8, Tables 12–14. Data for 1985–87 inclusive from August 1988, Volume 66, Number 8, Tables 11–13. Data for 1988–90 inclusive from August 1991, Volume 71, Number 8, Tables 11.1–11.3

Figure 5.13: US direct investment, 1982–90 (million dollars)

With the capture of Guzman in 1992, and the progressive decline of Sendero activity, confidence is once again being restored and investment may increase. Other economic indicators suggest this. The day after Peruvian forces captured Guzman, leader of Sendero, the stock market rose by 10 per cent, the maximum permitted daily movement.[101]

THE BENEFITS

There are few benefits to the US of an ongoing civil war in Peru. While Sendero's involvement in the drugs trade has allowed the Pentagon to justify some objections to military budget cuts in general, this has not been significant.The conflict may have allowed the US a certain amount of extra influence within Peru, but this is difficult to quantify and is in any case probably negligible. Arms sales are similarly insignificant.

CONCLUSION

The principal effect of the conflict on the US has been centred around the entangled connections between Sendero Luminoso and the drugs cartels. Sendero 'protecting' the coca plantations has allowed the cartels to continue production for sale on the American market, while also costing the US government millions of dollars in DEA expenditure. Moreover, the funds the US has provided for alternative crop programmes have had little impact either on the conflict, or the flow of drugs into the US. There are few benefits to the US of the conflict continuing. Declining US investment in Peru (see Figure 5.13) and the quantity of US aid effectively negate any economic benefits from purchases of aid provisions for Peru from US companies, or profits from arms sales to the Peruvian government, which, in any case, have not been substantial.

IF THE CONFLICT HAD NOT OCCURRED

Introduction

By using Bolivia, Chile and Ecuador as case studies, this section carries out cross-sectional analysis to extrapolate the potential benefits Peru and the US may have accrued, had conflict not occurred. Bolivia, Chile and Ecuador share some principal characteristics with Peru. For example, all of the countries have had similar historical and political antecedents; and all were plagued by military regimes during the 1960s and 1970s, returning to democratic rule by the 1980s. Culturally, similarities are obvious through language and religion and, with the exception of Chile, have a rurally based indigenous population. Moreover, in recent decades, all four countries have experienced similar phenomena such as growing urbanization and increasing rural–urban migration. Economically, many interests are shared: Peru, Bolivia and Chile have large mining sectors that have been affected equally by international prices and policies.

Peru

GDP growth

Figure 5.14 illustrates the average annual GDP growth rate of the case-study countries. While all the countries, with the exception of Chile, have experienced a decline in GDP growth due to international recession, Peru recorded the most significant drop with a negative growth rate over the period 1980–1990.

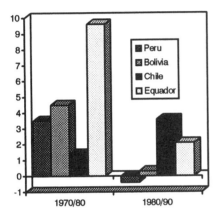

Source: World Bank, 1993, op cit

Figure 5.14: Average annual GDP growth (%)

In line with the negative GDP growth rate over 1980–90, per capita GDP has grown slowly in Peru, barely exceeding population growth. In contrast, the real GDP per capita in Chile and Ecuador has grown more significantly, although the growth rate in Bolivia has been similarly small. (See Figure 5.15).

Inflation

As illustrated in Figure 5.16, Peru underwent one of the most dramatic rises in inflation.

While the annual average over 1980–91 was 287.3 per cent, inflation peaked at 1775 per cent in 1988 and 2775 per cent in 1989.[102] In contrast, Chile and Ecuador have carried out more effective economic management, thereby controlling inflation and its negative ramifications.

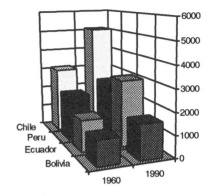

Source: World Bank, 1993, op cit
Note: % change based on author's calculations

Figure 5.15: Real GDP per capita (US$) 1960 and 1990

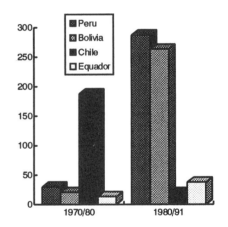

Source: World Bank, 1993, op cit

Figure 5.16: Average annual inflation rate (%)

External deficit

With the total costs of conflict estimated at US$22 billion, Peru's external deficit has grown most dramatically over the period 1980–91 (Figure 5.17). Bolivia and Chile in contrast, have managed to prevent their debt from ballooning.

While all of Latin America suffered during the 1980s, 'no main Latin American country fell further...than Peru.'[103] Peru's debt crisis and general economic decline was further heightened by the falling

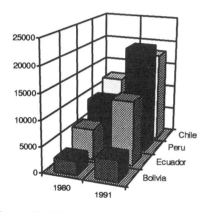

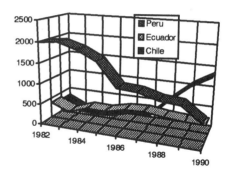

Source: World Bank, 1993, op cit

Figure 5.17: Total external debt (US$m)

Source: US Dept of Commerce, op cit

Figure 5.18: US direct investment in Peru, Ecuador and Chile, 1982–90 (US$m)

commodity export prices and high inflation. With a declining export base, debt repayment has been slow while additional debts have been incurred.

Infrastructure

Prior to conflict, Peru had a more extensive and developed communication infrastructure than that of neighbouring Bolivia but, as discussed earlier, actual attacks and failure to maintain this infrastructure meant that the quality of roads has declined significantly. In contrast, Bolivia invested substantially in the road system. In areas such as the Chapare in Bolivia, which experienced growing coca production in the 1980s, recent development initiatives and domestic rural investment policies have increased road networks and subsequent access to markets. By so doing, the Chapare area, previously excluded from mainstream society, has been harnessed to the national economy, boosting Bolivia's export base with non-traditional exports such as fruits.

The United States

US investment in South America varies in trend quite markedly from country to country (Figure 5.18). Nevertheless, as a whole since 1989 it has shown a modest increase (Figure 5.19). Peru has suffered a

steady and marked decline over the full length of the ten-year period. This would seem to represent a considerable loss of potential investment, undoubtedly kept away by the unstable political situation, but also discouraged by the damage inflicted on the country by the activities of Sendero.

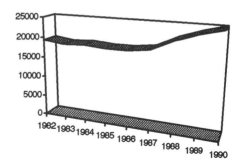

Source: US Dept of Commerce, op cit

Figure 5.19: US direct investment in South America, 1982–90 (US$m)

Conclusion

The conflict has had a marked influence on Peru's economic health compared to other countries in Latin America, or indeed over Latin America as a whole. The opportunities that exist in the rest of Latin America, in terms of a safe investment environment, while limited, simply do not exist in Peru. While other countries are diversifying and expanding their industrial bases, Peru remains stuck on the same course as ten years ago, with a large agrarian-based economy, unskilled labour and few investment opportunities. While US investment has not shown a marked increase in Latin America, at least not until 1989, it is certain that had the conflict not occurred, US investors would have found Peru a considerably more advanced investment environment, with its infrastructure still intact and would not have been discouraged by attacks on US commerical interests. Peru's resource potential would have thus been more fully realized.

REFERENCES

1 McCoy, J, 'Human rights trampled in Peru's 'emergency zones", in *Latinamerica Press*, 14 July 1988.

2 Woy-Hazleton, S & Hazleton W A, 'Sendero Luminoso and the Future of Peruvian Democracy', in *Third World Quarterly*, Volume 12, No 2 April 1990.

3 Ibid.

4 International Fund for Agricultural Development (IFAD), *The State of World Rural Poverty: An inquiry into its causes and consequences*, IT Publications, London, 1993. Table 3.

5 United Nations Children's Fund (UNICEF), *Country Programme Recommendation: Peru*, 20 February 1992.

6 This does not intend to insinuate that local health workers are incapable of carrying out medical duties. There may be instances however where a fully trained physician would have been more suitable but the conflict situation does not allow him/her to enter the region.

7 United Nations, *Human Development Report*, Oxford University Press, Oxford, 1993. Table 11.

8 *Encyclopedia Britannica*, 1993.

9 Paredes, C E, and Sachs, J D, (Eds) *Peru's Path to Recovery: A Plan for Economic Stabilization and Recovery*, The Brookings Institution, Washington, 1991.

10 UNICEF, 1992, op cit. Most recent figures expressed as a percentage of the total urban/rural population respectively.

11 Ibid.

12 Bowen, S, 'Peru Plea For Aid On Poverty', in *The Financial Times*, 22 June 1993.

13 UNICEF, 1992, op cit.

14 Marino, J, 'Peru: School Dropout Rate Increases', in *Latinamerica Press*, 18 April 1991.

15 The Peru Support Group, *Peru: The Dispossessed*, a special publication of the Peru Support Group, PSG, London, 1993.

16 *Latin American Weekly Report*, 'First Signs Of Turnaround In War', 29 April 1993.

17 Americas Watch, *Peru Under Fire: Human Rights Since The Return Of Democracy*, Vali-Ballon Press, New York, 1992.

18 McCoy, July 1988, op cit.

19 Woy-Hazleton, and Hazleton, 1990, op cit.

20 Chauvin, L, 'Peru's Human Rights Record Remains Dismal', in *Latinamerica Press*, July 18, 1991.

21 Statistics from 'Investigacion de la Defensa Nacional' (Iniden) in *Latin American Weekly Report*, 1993 and 'First Signs of Turnaround in War', 29 April 1993.

22 Bowen, S, 'Sickened by Violence', in *The Financial Times*, Special Survey on Peru, 29 September 1993.

23 Ibid.

24 *Latin American Weekly Report*, 'Sendero Offensive Nipped In The Bud', 1 July 1993.

25 Bowen,2 September 1993, op cit.

26 Ibid.

27 Cooper, M, 'The Country That Died Waits For A Miracle', in *New Statesman* and *Society*, 7 August 1992.

28 The Economist Intelligence Unit, Country Report:
Peru: 4th Quarter 1993.

29 *Latinamerica Press*, 26 July 1990.

30 United Nations Working Party on Disappeared Persons in *Latin American Weekly Report*, 11 March 1993.

31 This case study is a summary of: Americas Watch, 1993 *Anatomy Of A Cover-Up: The Disappearances At La Cantuta*, Human Rights Watch, Washington, September 1993. La Cantuta serves to illustrate the widespread powers of the Government of Peru

32 Amnesty International, *Peru: Human Rights Since The Suspension Of Constitutional Government*, published by the International Secretariat, London, May 1993.

33 Americas Watch, *Untold Terror: Violence Against Women In Peru's Armed Conflict*, Human Rights Watch, Washington, 1992.

34 Ibid.

35 Woy-Hazleton and Hazleton, 1990, op cit.

36 Chauvin, 1991, op cit.

37 Avignolo, M L, 'Peru: In Aucayacu, Maoist Sendero Luminoso Is The Only Real Authority', in *Latinamerica Press*, 9 November 1989.

38 Woy-Hazleton and Hazleton, 1990, op cit.

39 Decree Laws taken from Americas Watch,

Human Rights In Peru: One Year After Fujimori's Coup, Human Rights Watch, Washington, April 1992.

40 *Latinamerica Press*, 26 July 1990, op cit.
41 Bowen, S, 'Jungle Villages Drawn Into War', in *The Financial Times*, Special Survey on Peru, 29 September 1993.
42 The Peru Support Group, 1993, op cit.
43 Ibid.
44 Poole, D, and Renique, G, *Peru: A Time of Fear* Latin American Bureau, London. 1992.
45 Americas Watch, 1992, op cit.
46 The Economist Intelligence Unit, 1993 *Peru: Country Report*, 3rd Quarter 1993.
47 Ibid.
48 Americas Watch, 1992, op cit.
49 Ibid.
50 Ibid.
51 Ibid.
52 Ibid.
53 Ibid.
54 Paredes and Sachs, (eds) 1991, op cit.
55 Ibid.
56 Ibid.
57 Ibid.
58 United Nations, 1993, op cit.
59 Based upon my calculations from United Nations, 1993 Table 4. In the period 1960 to 1990, Chile's real GDP rose from $US 3,103 to 5,099 (+1,996/+37%), Ecuador from 1,461 to 3,074 (+1,613/+110%), Bolivia from 1,142 to 1,572 (+430/+37%).
60 Key facts from *The Financial Times*, Special Survey on Peru, 29 September 1993, page IX.
61 Ibid.
62 Paredes and Sachs, (eds) 1991, op cit.
63 Alcalde, J G, *Development, Decay and Social Conflict*, University Press of America, Maryland, 1991.
64 Bowen, S, 'A Paradise For Pioneering Spirits', in *The Financial Times*, Special Survey on Peru, 29 September 1993.
65 Ibid.
66 *Britannica World Data*, 1993.
67 United Nations, 1993, op cit.
68 McCoy, J, 'Peru: Guerrillas Launch Drive To Worsen Quality Of Life', in *Latinamerica Press*, 26 January 1989.
69 Paredes and Sachs, (Eds) 1991, op cit.
70 Kirk, R, 'Peru: Guerrillas Mark Their Tenth Anniversary', in *Latinamerica Press*, 17 May 1990.
71 Paredes and Sachs, (Eds) 1991, op cit.
72 Kuczynski, P P, 'Task For Foreign Funders', in *The Financial Times*, Special Survey on Peru, 29 September 1993.
73 McCoy, 1989, op cit.
74 Ibid.

75 iIbid.
76 Kirk, 1990, op cit.
77 McCoy, 1989, op cit.
78 Paredes, and Sachs, (eds) 1991, op cit.
79 Ibid.
80 McCoy 1989, op cit.
81 Oscar Schiappa, quoted in Portillo, Z, 1993 'Peruvian Violence Leads To Forced Migration', in *Latinamerica Press*, 6 May 1993.
82 *Latinamerica Press*, 1992 'Undocumented Peruvians Stateless In Homeland', September 10, 1992.
83 Portillo, 1993, op cit.
84 Veeken, H, 'Letter from Peru: a country torn apart by violence' in *The British Medical Journal*, Volume 306, 8 May 1993.
85 Portillo, 1993, op cit.
86 Ibid.
87 *Latin American Weekly Report*, 'First Signs Of Turnaround In War', 29 April 1993.
88 Molineu, H, *US Policy toward Latin America*, Westview Press Inc, San Francisco, 1990.
89 Fidler, S, 'US May End Backing For Anti-Drug Drive In Peru', in *The Financial Times*, 21 November 1993.
90 *The Economist*, 1993 'Peru's Financial Markets: About Face', December 11 1993.
91 Simpson, J, In *The Forests Of The Night*. Hutchinson, London, 1993.
92 Fidler, 1993, op cit.
93 Day, M, 'Peruvians Balk At U.S. Military Interference', in *Latinamerica Press*, May 10 1990.
94 Fidler, S, 'Review Report Awaited' in *The Financial Times*, Special Survey on Peru, 29 September 1993.
95 Ibid.
96 Kavell, J A, 'Peru: US Report Claims State Has No Strategy Against Sendero', March 27 1993. Source unknown from the database at the Latin American Information Centre, Manchester.
97 Source unknown, from the database at the Latin American Information Centre at Manchester, article from the Interpress Service, August 11, 1993.
98 Source unknown from the database at the Latin American Information Centre in Manchester. Reuter article dated 23 February 1993.
99 Molineu, 1990, op cit.
100 Poole and Renique, 1992, op cit.
101 *The Economist*, 1993 'Peru's financial markets: About Face', December 11 1993.
102 Paredes and Sachs, (eds) 1991, op cit.
103 Kuczynski, P P, 1993 'Task for foreign funders', in *The Financial Times*, Special Survey on Peru, 29 September 1993.

6

THE SUDAN CONFLICT
(1983–   )

Nicholas Shalita

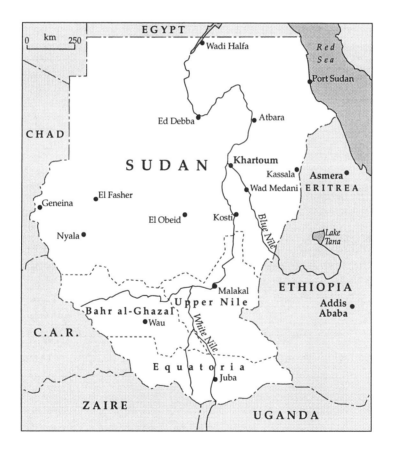

Area (000sq km)	*2506*
Population (000)	*25.9*
Human Development Index	*0.158*
Population density (per sq km)	*8*
Capital	*Khartoum*

KEY IMPACTS OF THE CONFLICT

ON SUDAN

- Five hundred thousand, mostly civilians, dead as a direct result of the war since 1983.
- Up to 1 million injured as a direct result of the war.
- Life expectancy at birth in southern Sudan is 36.
- The economy shrunk by 11 per cent in 1992.
- Inflation was 220 per cent in 1993.
- The Sudanese government spent $1.01 billion on arms in 1992.
- To pay for the war, the Sudanese government has been exporting food, in the middle of the worst famine in the world this century.
- All infrastructural development has been halted, and much of what has been completed has been destroyed.
- Lack of fuel has led to the destruction of thousands of hectares of woodland, which in turn has turned to desert.
- Six million people have been displaced as a result of the war.
- Twenty per cent of refugee children are malnourished.

ON NEIGHBOURING COUNTRIES

- Up to 150,000 refugees are currently occupying border areas of Kenya and Uganda.
- Seventy thousand head of cattle have been stolen from Kenyan farmers by armed Sudanese refugees.
- Ugandan support for the Sudan Peoples' Liberation Army (SPLA) has led to Sudan arming Ugandan terrorists.
- The Sudanese airforce has 'mistakenly' bombed Ugandan villages near the border.
- Egyptian support for the SPLA has led to Sudan aiding Islamic fundamentalist terrorists in Egypt, which has led to a 35 per cent decrease in the number of tourists visiting Egypt.

ON THE UNITED STATES

- Sudan is vulnerable to an Islamic fundamentalist takeover.
- US companies have lost over a billion dollars of investment in Sudan.
- US investment in, and trade with, Sudan has halved in five years.

INTRODUCTION

Geography

Sudan is the largest country in Africa with a total land area of 2,505,800 kilometres (237.6 million hectares), or about the size of Austria, Belgium, Denmark, France, Finland, Germany, Luxembourg, the Netherlands, Norway, Sweden, Switzerland and the UK, combined. Stretching for 2090 kilometres from north to south and 1770 kilometres from east to west over flat and featureless terrain, Sudan consists mainly of desert and semi-desert in the north, inhabited by nomadic pastoralists, and savannah and tropical rainforest in the south, inhabited by both pastoralists and cultivators.

The People

Historically, Sudan consists of two regions. Two-thirds of the population live in the north and are Muslims by religion and Arab in culture. The population of southern Sudan is principally traditional or Christian, and consists chiefly of the indigenous African groups: the Haemitics, Negroids and Nilotics. The two regions were kept separate, initially at the end of the 19th century, as a result of British/French rivalry. This split was cemented under British rule that began in 1898, ending with independence over 50 years later. This split resulted in the two regions developing different identities, different levels of development, and different concepts of nationhood.

The Conflict

It was this unequal development, with southern Sudan the neglected region experiencing economic marginalization and social injustice, that contributed to the unrest that erupted between the north and the south of Sudan in 1955. However, the first civil war did not begin properly until 1963, when southern exiles, backed by Ethiopia, Israel and Congolese rebels, formed a resistance movement. The resulting conflict continued unabated until the Peace Accord in 1973, signed between President Nimeiri of the north and the southern rebels. By this time 400,000, mostly civilian, lives had been lost.

Nimeiri's conversion to extreme Islamic fundamentalism, and the subsequent strict enforcement of Koranic law on the whole country, coupled with continuing economic inequalities and age-old antagonisms, led to growing discontent among the southern population during the years following 1973. When sections of the army based in the south broke away to form the SPLA (Sudan Peoples' Liberation Army) in 1983, civil war again broke out.

The conflict has continued unabated to the present day, and has been exacerbated by the fragmention of the SPLA into warring factions. The original faction is headed by Dr. John Garang de Mabior, and is known as SPLA-Main or SPLA-Torit. The largest splinter group is referred to as SPLA-United or SPLA-Nasir, and was formed in 1991 when Riek Machar broke away from Dr Garang. This group has also since split, when Lam Akol, the foreign-affairs spokesman and principal negotiator, was dismissed. Between 1991 and 1994, the SPLA-Main and SPLA-United have fought a bitter war which inflicted as much damage in parts of southern Sudan as had the war against the northern government.

The government in the north is now allied to Libya and dominated by a military junta under the leadership of Lieutenant General Omar Bashir, who overthrew the government of the Umma Party in 1989. Bashir is strongly supported by the Islamic fundamentalist National Islamic Front (NIF) headed by Dr Hassan al Turabi. It is has been suggested that it is Turabi who is the de facto leader of the current administration.[1]

Scope of the Study

This study will focus on the consequences of the conflict between the SPLA and the northern government since 1983, and the more recent conflict between the rival SPLA factions. In addition to examining Sudan, it will also investigate the neighbouring countries upon whom the impact of the conflict has been particularly marked. These countries are Uganda, Kenya and Egypt. The costs and benefits of the war to the United States, as the Western power with the most significant interests in the region, will also be examined. By comparing Sudan's economic performance with other similar countries in the region, it is possible to hypothesize about the benefits that might have accrued to Sudan and its Western trading partners, if the conflict had not occurred.

However, it should be noted that because of the chronic lack of any form of administration or bureaucratic infra-structure in the south, it has been difficult to obtain figures that relate specifically to this area.

SUDAN

THE COSTS

Introduction

Sudan is by any standard among the poorest nations on earth. Its human development index rank is 158 of 173 nations. The combined effects of the war, drought and national debt have cut GDP per capita to US$100, the second lowest in Africa, and 85 per cent of the population live in absolute poverty.[2] Additionally, Sudan has been badly affected by a series of droughts whose consequences have not only exacerbated, but have been exacerbated by, the conflict. It is therefore difficult in some instances to attribute particular consequences solely to the conflict.

Seventy-eight per cent of the population live in rural areas where they experience poverty and deprivation at its worst. The national life expectancy at birth is 50.8 years, though it is as low as 36 in most parts of the south. Inadequate health and other public services has meant that the infant mortality rate remains extremely high at 102 per 1000, and 191,000 children die before the age of five, as high as 165 per 1000 in some areas, the sixth highest in the world.

Development

Health

Health services in Sudan reflect a 'tale of two Sudans'. While the north enjoys a fair level of health services, with 70 per cent of the population having access to health care, the situation in the south is at best desperate.

The health infrastructure, rebuilt and re-equipped in the south in the peaceful years, with assistance from Britain, Norway, the Netherlands and Kuwait, has been largely destroyed. Of the 34 hospitals, 16 health centres, 176 dispensaries and 746 primary health care units operating in 1983, all but the Juba Teaching Hospital, el Sabah Children's hospital and the Wau regional hospital are either closed or in an extremely poor state.[3]

In the hospital in Mundri (estimated population 85,000) retreating government troops burnt all medical supplies, equipment, vehicles and buildings. In Maridi (estimated population 60,000), the hospital and most primary health care units were looted and equipment burnt by government troops. In both Mundri and Maridi, the destroyed hospitals were the only functioning institutions at the time (1992). It has been suggested that the government is destroying health facilities in the south, and transferring health personnel to the north as a deliberate act to weaken the SPLA's support base. Figure 6.1 shows the number of hospitals in selected regions in 1973, 1983 and 1988

The government currently allocates 0.3 per cent of GDP spending on health care, in contrast to its current 16 per cent of GDP spending on the military.[4] In other parts of Sudan, the government's meagre health budget has prevented the establishment of facilities which would more adequately meet the people's requirements.

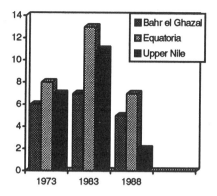

Source: Twose and Pogrund, op cit

Figure 6.1: Number of hospitals by selected regions

The ratios of doctors to population and maternal child health workers to mothers and children are very low.[5] Most qualified medical staff are disproportionately located in the urban areas of northern and central Sudan (Figure 6.2). While the ratio of doctors per 100,000 of population is estimated at 98 in Khartoum, it is only 0.7 in the Upper Nile and 0.8 in Bahr el Ghazal. Because of the civil war in the south, health workers have either been forced out of the region or have been transferred by the government, who fear they may join or be captured by the SPLA. As a result of this and the general lack of drugs and equipment, the great majority of inhabitants in the south do not have their

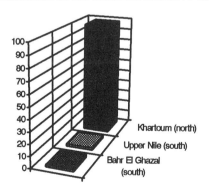

Source: UN, op cit

Figure 6.2: Number of doctors per 100,000 population by selected regions (1991)

primary health requirements fulfilled. Additionally, in other parts of southern Sudan, the shortage of doctors remains acute. Many Sudanese doctors have left the country for Saudi Arabia and other Middle Eastern countries where they do not live in fear of political persecution, and where salaries are up to 100 times higher. As a result, doctors are now being forcefully prevented from leaving the country.[6]

Professionals as targets

In 1990 Mohammed Nowar Aso, a dentist and former member of the doctors' union, and a father of eight, was picked up by military intelligence. Although the authorities claim he was subsequently released, he has not been seen since his arrest. It is thought he was picked up because he had protested at plans to convert a civilian hospital to military use. He has 'disappeared' and is believed to have been killed.[7]

With the possible exception of Juba Teaching Hospital and the southern hospitals at el Sabah, Wau, Malakal, Yambio and Yei, no other health facilities have qualified resident doctors. The hospitals in Yei, Yambio, Wau and Malakal regions, an area larger in size than the UK, and with a population of about 1–1.5 million people, have one doctor each and are lacking in almost all essential drugs and equipment.[8] Malaria, upper respiratory infections, trauma and injury, tuberculosis, typhoid, viral fevers and meningitis are now common in southern Sudan. As a result, life expectancy at birth is 36 years (among the lowest in any region in the world), compared with 51 years in the rest of Sudan. Infant and maternal mortality rates are far above the already high national rates of 102 per 1000 live births and 700 per 100,000 live births[9] respectively, and some of the most preventable diseases such as malaria and measles are the leading causes of death among children.

These health problems are aggravated by a lack of food. Tied to the shortages of food caused by famine and the war-incapacitated infrastructure, are chronic malnutrition problems in Mundri and Maridi, as in other parts of the south. The entire area, with a population of about 150,000–200,000, has only 25 water boreholes. Water has to be fetched from up to 15 kilometres away. The lack of water creates numerous hygiene and sanitation problems that in turn cause disease. A survey carried out in southern Sudan in 1989 found that one-third of children under the age of five were 'stunted' and/or 'wasted.'[10] This results in general weakness among children, who become prone to attacks of fever, diarrhoea, vomiting and other illnesses.

In other parts of Sudan not directly affected by the conflict, health services are inadequate to meet the rapidly expanding refugee population. Overcrowding in towns caused largely by immigrants from rural areas fleeing war and poverty and already destitute and malnourished, is common. People often succumb to infections or communicable disease in the densely packed squatter camps, where hygiene is poor and clean water and medical supplies are not available. In Port Sudan for example, few if any of the many illegal households have toilets. As a result, the slum is polluted with excreta.[11] These are the conditions which encourage cholera. Incidences of respiratory infections and diarrhoea are increasing, and are being exacerbated by malnutrition.

Education

Education is one of the areas in which it is difficult to ascertain the extent to which past policies, periodic droughts, or the war are responsible for Sudan's current plight. For example, a census taken in 1955 (before the conflict began), revealed that 95 per cent of Sudan's population had never attended school. The situation was rapidly redressed in the north of the country through a series of initiatives by the government and local communities. However, the outbreak of war in the south in 1955 prevented such progress, and the meagre educational facilities there were destroyed.

Progress was made, however, during the peaceful years of 1973–83. School enrolment had come closer to the national average at 45 per cent in Equatoria province, though it remained disappointingly low at 16 per cent and 6 per cent in the Upper Nile and Bahr-el-Ghazal provinces respectively.

However, following the outbreak of war in 1983, the situation deteriorated. The educational sector faces near complete collapse in the south. Today, very few, if any, of the rural schools which once catered for over 90 per cent of schoolchildren in the south are still operational. Of the schools remaining, fewer than 20 per cent have permanent buildings. Schools tend to attract the fighting parties, who use the buildings for temporary shelter, and have therefore become targets for destruction. For example, there were three secondary schools in Yei district in 1989. Of these: all were severely lacking in furniture and equipment; one had no furniture and equipment, another had neither furniture, equipment or buildings; and the third had to be closed for lack of food for students. In Bahr el Ghazal province, of the 130 primary schools, 65 were without buildings and only 18 per cent had buildings in a reasonably good condition. In Raga district, 74 per cent of schools had no buildings, and only four schools in the entire district had a toilet.

Student–staff ratios are extremely high in the south: as high as 94:1 in Aweil district.[12] Overcrowding in classrooms is commonplace, and many schools have no desks, blackboards, textbooks, laboratories or libraries. Very few schools have water and toilets and only two schools in the entire southern region have any electricity.[13]

Sudan's adult literacy rate is 27 per cent, much lower than most African countries.[14] This contrasts sharply with the situation in schools in northern Sudan and the Khartoum area where most schools are well equipped, have water, electricity and food, and pupil–staff ratios are in the region of 35:1.[15]

School life in Sudan

A young boy in southern Sudan raced up to a UN relief vehicle outside Bor and begged, not for food, but for a pencil for school. Most boys in school are naked; their families have no money for clothes. Girls are modestly clad. As quickly as schools open, they are flooded with students hungry to learn, despite extreme poverty, uncertainty about food and occasional aerial bombings. A typical scene in a school in rebel territory is 45 boys and a few girls sitting in the dirt under a tree listening to their teacher. There is a single book which the teacher uses, a blackboard propped up on three sticks, chalk and eraser; and for the children, pencil stubs and notebooks cut in half are all the school has for supplies.[16]

The illiteracy rate in the south is amongst the highest in the world: 90 per cent among women and 80 per cent among men. If the prospects for the development of Sudan lie in the education of the youth, then Sudan's prospects are bleak.

Civil and Political Rights

Observers' estimates of the numbers killed since 1983 vary. Such estimates are made more uncertain by the difficulty in attributing deaths to either the war or the famine. However, estimates of around 1 million dead as a result of both war and famine, with roughly half directly attributable to the war, are not unusual. To this figure should be added the incalculable number of injuries, at least another 1 million.

Numerous cases of human rights violations have been reported in all parts of Sudan throughout the period of conflict. The Western and southern parts of the country have, however, been most affected. Cases of human and civil rights violations by all parties in the conflict are numerous and horrific. The government and rival SPLA factions are implementing a policy of 'ethnic cleansing' in the south which has resulted in hundreds of thousands of deaths and the displacement of some 3

million others. Destruction and genocide by all parties is deliberate and calculated.

The government has followed a counter-insurgency policy of setting up and arming militia groups known as *muraheleen*, which have been allowed to raid and plunder the Nuba mountain villages thought to be sympathetic to the SPLA, with impunity. Numerous extrajudicial killings were reported in these raids. In July 1988, for example, 88 people were killed in a militia attack on the village of Dorein.

Detention is also common. Political detainees were reported by Amnesty International to number 250 in Khartoum alone in 1992. Large numbers of prisoners are also known to be kept in security headquarters and 'ghost houses' where torture is common. Prisoners are said to be beaten, whipped, shackled and suspended upside down from prison cell walls, beaten on their testicles and kidneys or electrocuted.[17]

Thousands of others are kept in 'peace villages' where they are denied basic rights and freedoms of movement, speech and association. The villages are controlled by the army and a government-controlled Islamic militia known as the Popular Defence Force (PDF), who have been responsible for thousands of extra-judicial executions, rapes and abductions.

In other cases, suspected opponents of the government are required to report daily to police stations where they are kept waiting all day with no food or water. Trade unionists, doctors and other civilian workers had their freedom restricted in this way in 1992 and 1993.[18]

Ethnic cleansing In Nuba

Allegations of 'ethnic cleansing' in Sudan's Nuba mountains have been levelled against the military government by Africa Rights and backed by Western diplomats. 'Many facts point to a systematic campaign aimed at the eradication of Nuba ethnicity', involving brutal attacks from government-controlled militia, leaving many dead and the population frightened into submission. The population are then forcefully relocated from their hilly fertile region in central Sudan and separated according to sex. The men are taken to labour camps for large commercial farms, and women and children to cities in the north where they become domestic servants, receive no pay, are denied the most basic human rights and are often physically and sexually abused.[19]

Most political parties have been banned in Sudan since the military coup in 1989 and any leaders arrested, or forced into hiding, or exile. Tirab Tindal Sultan, a member of the Umma Party, was arrested in January 1992 and held without charge until September. Members of the Democratic Unionist Party (DUP) were detained in 'ghost houses', including Mirghani Abdel Suleiman, a former government minister. Hassan Osman and two other suspected communists were arrested in April 1992 for distributing a banned newspaper and were still in prison at the end of the year. Scores of other activists, community leaders and others have been held for long periods of time without charge in prisons and 'ghost houses'.[20]

Attacks on civilians

In December 1992 army and PDF troops attacked al-Atmur al-Nagrah, a Nuba village in Ningele. The village priest Matti al-Nur, the deacon Bolis, along with village elders and 20 other members of the village were captured at prayer in the grass-roofed church, which was locked and set alight. All were killed. Kamal Tutu, also a member of the village, was tied and thrown on to the embers, suffering crippling burns. The entire village was then destroyed.[21]

Educated people and community leaders in the west and south of the country suspected of not being sympathetic towards the government have been detained without trial, tortured or have 'disappeared'. In rural areas in the south there are many reports of government troops and pro-government militia extrajudicially executing and torturing suspected and actual opponents. In Juba, hundreds of civilians and civil authorities 'disappeared' after the government restored control after the May 1992 SPLA incursions.[22]

The attacks on civilians, which had become part of the government's military tactics by 1991, were intensified in 1992 with the declaration of a *jihad* (holy war) by the government on the SPLA. The Western mountains between Lagowa and Dilling, home of the Kamda, Tuleishi, Katla and Tabaq sections of the Nuba were targeted, especially between November 1991 and June 1992.[23] In February 1992, PDF troops reportedly executed 25 villagers in the al-Faus area. In March and April over 40 civilians were executed in Jebe Tabaq. Further attacks were carried out in the western and southern hills in late 1992 and early 1993 around Tima, Heiban and Moro. Over 100 were killed in Tumbira in December and their homes set alight.[24]

Both the Torit and Nasir factions of the SPLA have also committed gross human rights violations. Many such killings have been ethnically motivated. The SPLA-Nasir faction is believed to be responsible for numerous brutal killings by strangulation, clubbing, burning and spearing. The SPLA-Torit faction has also victimized civilians regarded as sympathetic to the rival Nasir faction. Villages like Pathai, Pagau and Paiyoi have been burnt and the locals executed. In November 1992, 20 Acholi and Madi people were executed by the Torit faction, and a further 200 suspected deserters in December 1992.

The Economy

The conflict in Sudan has taken a heavy toll on the country's economy. Sudan is the 11th largest country in the world, ten times the size of the UK. It is resource rich, yet is among the world's 15 poorest nations.

After a decade of positive growth, the resumption of conflict in 1983 plummeted the economy into chronic decline. In 1991, it shrank by 8 per cent and a shocking 11 per cent in 1992 (Figure 6.3). GDP in 1991 was US$8.16 billion, falling to US$6.38 billion in 1992.[25] Real GDP per capita halved from 1980 (US$14) to 1990 (US$7).[26]

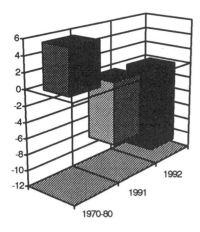

Source: UNDP, 1993 op cit; IISS, 1993, op cit

Figure 6.3: GDP growth (% change)

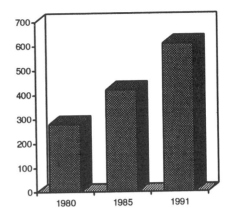

Source: EIU Reports, op cit

Figure 6.4: Total external debt per capita ($US)

Sudan's external debt has increased from US$13 billion in 1989 to US$16 billion in 1992; more than doubling the total external debt per capita in ten years from US$280 in 1980 to US$610 in 1991. International reserves fell from US$176 million in 1989 to US$3 million in 1992.[27]

As a result, the business community and foreign investors have expressed low confidence in the economy. With the exception of a paltry US$4 million in 1989, net foreign direct investment has been US$0 since 1970, with a net divestment of US$3 million since 1985.

It is difficult to attribute Sudan's economic problems to anything but the conflict. Almost the entire southern and western regions of the country are subject to periods of insecurity, so economic activity is continually disrupted. Destruction of infrastructure has worsened Sudan's already skeletal transport and communications network, making it difficult for traders and farmers to transport their produce to the market or the coast. It has also severely disrupted government support services such as agricultural services to farmers, locust control and drought preparedness, thereby further crippling the economy. The result is that 85 per cent of the Sudanese population live below the UN poverty line.[28]

The inflation rate remains high, with an estimated rise to 300 per cent in 1994 (Figure 6.5).[29] Government-controlled prices for essential commodities and massive civil service pay rises, designed to increase the government's support, only created further constraints and further exacerbated inflation.

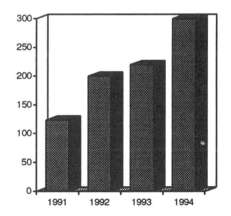

Source: EIU Reports, op cit; IISS, 1993, op cit

Figure 6.5: Inflation rate (%)

Military expenditure

Despite the economic crisis, the government has spent enormous amounts on arms. Government military expenditure has risen five-fold in ten years from US$234.5 million or just under 3 per cent of GDP in 1982 to US$1.01 billion or 16 per cent of GDP in 1992.[30] The 1992 spending compares with 0.3 per cent of GDP spent on the health sector and 4.8 per cent of GDP spend on education[31] (Figures 6.6 and 6.7).

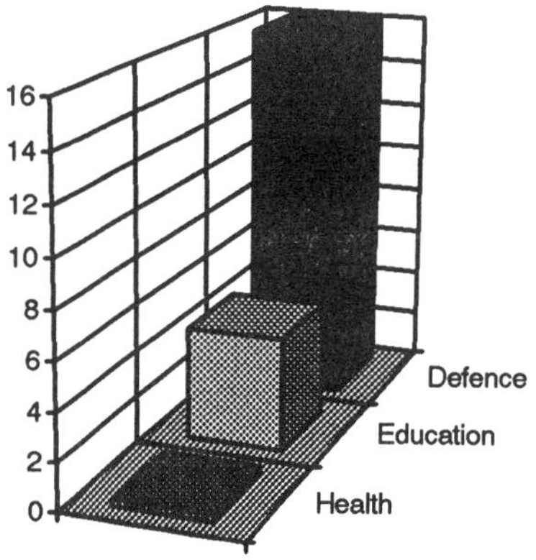

Moreover, while the country is wracked by famine and drought, the Khartoum government is selling grain to fund its arms purchases. In an article in *The Observer* in 1991, Jonathan Dimbleby revealed EC customs forms which showed Sudan had exported 97,000 tonnes of sorghum to the EC for animal feed in 1990.[32]

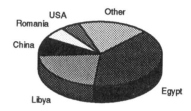

Source: UNDP Human Development Report, 1994.
Note: This includes arms supplied to both the Khartoum government and the SPLA

Figure 6.8: Principal arms exporters to Sudan (1980–90)

Source: UNDP, 1993, op cit

Figure 6.6: Government expenditure on selected items 1992 as a percentage of total government expenditure

Figure 6.8 illustrates principal arms exporters to Sudan up to 1990. This changed after 1990, with Iran and China becoming major suppliers.

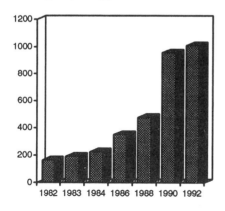

Source: IISS, 1993, op cit

Figure 6.7: Military expenditure (US$m)

Infrastructure

The cost of damage caused to the infrastructure as a direct result of the conflict is catastrophic. In most parts of southern Sudan, petrol and kerosene are scarce, and there is no electricity or any other source of energy except woodfuel. This partly explains the depletion of forests in the south of the country. Infrastructural development has been halted because of the war, resulting in the destruction or degradation of the developments that had taken place. The 320 kilometre Jonglei canal scheme, initiated in 1978 at enormous cost, had to be stopped and all the machinery, including the gigantic excavator, has since been destroyed or looted. Bridges are often destroyed in combat as offensive or defensive tactics, and most have never been repaired. In one case, the Sudanese government troops destroyed a 70-metre bridge over the Yei River. This has made it impossible to reach the Loui hospital, which is now reported to be in a very poor condition.

Among the other early SPLA targets

was the 1400 kilometre oil export pipeline between the Unity field and a new terminal which was to have been built in Port Sudan. The American petroleum company Chevron had invested US$1 billion. The subsequent destruction of the pipeline, and general insecurity in the south, has prevented any exploitation of the oil resources there, costing Sudan an estimated potential annual earning of US$136 million.[33]

The shortage of fuel has severely hampered economic activity, even in parts of Sudan unaffected by conflict. It is now extremely difficult and costly to transport goods or travel. The industrial sector has been badly affected, because of its dependency on hydroelectric power and petroleum for energy, both of which are either scarce or not available.

The Environment

The destruction of infrastructure as a result of the war, and the failure by the government to develop an extensive use of an energy source other than wood, has led to widespread deforestation. This in turn has led to soil erosion, and has accelerated the rate of desertification. The average family in north Darfur uses up to 200 trees or large shrubs every year, a loss too large to sustain.

The loss of woodlands is a major cause of the overall environmental decline. Many of the cultivated areas in Sudan are merely sand dunes covered with a thin layer of topsoil. Without the protection of forests which act as windbreaks and anchors for the soil, this thin layer of soil is blown away, turning the land into desert.

The use of scorched earth military techniques by all sides has destroyed vegetation and crops and exposed topsoil to wind and water erosion. Those fleeing the war often leave their land without any crops or vegetation for long periods of time, also exposing it to erosion.

Refugees

There are 4.5 million refugees in Sudan and 1.5–2 million refugees in neighbouring countries,[34] particularly in Uganda and Ethiopia and, to a lesser extent, Zaire, Kenya and further afield in Europe and north America. According to the US Committee on Refugees, there are no less than 1 million displaced persons in the three cities that comprise Sudan's capital, Khartoum, Khartoum North and Omdurman. The majority of these people are from the southern regions of Bahr el Ghazal, Upper Nile and Equatoria and have fled either the war or the famine, or both.[35]

Living standards in the refugee camps are appalling. The refugees live in bamboo, cardboard and plastic dwellings without water, electricity, toilets, schools or medical services. A survey conducted in these refugee settlements by UNICEF and other organizations revealed that one out of three children suffered from diarrhoea, and only 10 per cent of children had been inoculated against measles. Malnutrition among children was 20 per cent and infant mortality for children under five years was as high as 165 per 1000.[36]

Many refugees have been killed or maimed while fleeing across war zones or minefields. During migrations, there are many risks ranging from wild animals, theft of livestock and other property by hostile locals, rape of women and kidnap of children. Often children become separated from their parents in the course of the migration, or their parents are killed.

It is clear that all sides in the conflict are using displacement as a means to weaken their enemy's support bases. Government troops have been particularly successful in this by making it too insecure for many Dinka, Nuer and Nuban supporters of the SPLA to live normal lives in their villages. This has been done by either raiding the villages and forcing the villagers to flee, or by arming and facilitating *murahaleen* raids. The situation is aggravated by the rival SPLA factions each persecuting supporters of the other.

In the mid-1980s, there was a series of campaigns by the then government to 'cleanse' the capital Khartoum of the non-Muslim, predominantly black, African refugees. In the expulsions, thousands were forced out. The operation, known as *kasha*, planned to forcibly move about 500,000 of the refugees to a desert camp several kilometres away, where a UN official once remarked 'not even a locust can survive'.[37] There were reports of killings, rape and looting by the authorities in the operation.

After the fall of the Ethiopian President Mengistu in 1991, the new government of the Ethiopian People's Revolutionary Democratic Front (EPRDF) formed an alliance with the Sudanese government. They then unleashed a campaign of terror on the southern Sudanese refugees in south-Western Ethiopia. Camps at Gambella, Panyido, Didomo, Itang and Bilpam that collectively had 500,000 Sudanese from the war in southern Sudan were affected.[38] Well organized and coordinated, the attacks were carried out by Sudanese and Ethiopian troops. Fortunately, because the Sudanese refugees had already been made to feel uncomfortable and unsafe, many had left before the worst of the attacks had been carried out. The exercise was clearly aimed at the massacre and molestation of thousands of southern Sudanese refugees, in contravention of international law and the Geneva Convention.

Some refugees have resorted to raiding UN and NGO food and supply stores and food convoys. The situation was reported to be so bad by a UNHCR spokeswoman, that 'lorry drivers were too frightened to drive convoys to the [refugee] camps'.[39]

CONCLUSION

The people of Sudan have suffered the worst forms of social and economic deprivations and human rights abuse for all but ten of their 38 years of independence. The abuses have been perpetrated by all sides in the conflict to achieve their own political and military objectives. Recent government offensives in the south have resulted in further killings and displacement. The failure of the SPLA factions to resolve their problems will continue to be a source of further violence. Although it is impossible to give an exact figure of the value of destruction caused by the war, it is without a doubt an enormous cost that will remain a

colossal burden on the peoples' shoulders; particularly when one considers theUS$1 billion the Khartoum government spent in 1992 on the military and is expected to spend again in 1993.

NEIGHBOURING COUNTRIES

THE COSTS

Introduction

In this section, the effects of the conflict in Sudan on the three neighbouring countries most seriously affected, Kenya, Uganda and Egypt, will be examined. Additionally, the unique way in which each of these countries has been affected demonstrates clearly how neighbouring countries are often drawn into civil wars, either through concerns about their own security, or by the unwelcome influx of large numbers of refugees. The active role these countries have taken will be examined, and the perceived benefits of the conflict will be juxtaposed against the costs.

Kenya

Refugees

The great effect of the conflict in Sudan on Kenya is mostly the costs incurred by the Kenyan government and Kenyan NGOs in the accommodation of Sudanese refugees in Kenya. In October 1993, the UNHCR reported that there were some 33,500 Sudanese refugees in Kakuma, north-Western Kenya. Since the beginning of the dry-season offensive on the rebels, that number has significantly increased. In February and March 1994, 150,000 people were said to be fleeing government air and ground attacks and moving towards the Ugandan and Kenyan borders.

These refugees have, in the words of a Kenyan government official: 'outstretched the infrastructure and medical services'.[40] Kenya, which has been suffering from the freezing of balance of payments support from international financial institutions, has had to provide education, medicine, water, sanitation, food and security for the refugees, in addition to catering for the needs of its own population, at considerable cost.[41]

Security

The presence of armed refugees has also caused security problems. In 1993, a Kenyan government spokesman reported that the Sudanese and Somali refugees had 'seriously compromised the security of this country...'[42] Some Sudanese and Somali refugees are reported to be engaged in cattle raiding of the Turkana and Boran peoples of Kenya. The Kenyan government reported that in the months of March, April, May and June of 1992, 173 Kenyan civilians had been killed and 70,000 head of cattle had been stolen from Kenyans by armed refugees.[43] This, coupled with the growing levels of urban crime and prostitution being attributed to the refugees, has led to widespread resentment of them by the Kenyans. These problems come at a time when the country is economically weak and deeply divided ethnically.

Uganda

Security

Since the collapse of Mengistu's regime in Ethiopia, Uganda's president Yoweri Museveni has been the SPLA'S main ally in the region. Indeed the Sudanese government has on many occasions accused Uganda of providing Dr Garang with military support and a political platform.

In 1992, in an incident that caused considerable embarrassment to the Ugandan government, Uganda's Ambassador to the USA and two senior Egyptian army officers were arrested in the USA for allegedly attempting to export arms and helicopters to Uganda illegally. It has,

however, since emerged that the weapons were destined for southern Sudan and the SPLA. It is likely that a significant contribution to the cost was made by Egypt and Uganda.

The Khartoum government has reacted to Uganda's support of the SPLA by bringing together Ugandan refugees in Sudan and organizing and training them to cause instability in Uganda. A substantial quantity of arms and logistical assistance to the rebel Lord's Resistance Army (LRA) in Uganda has been granted by the Sudanese government in return for LRA's cooperation in dislodging the SPLA in northern Uganda.[44]

Aside from the insecurity caused by the LRA, the location of SPLA strongholds along the Ugandan border means that fighting tends to spill over into Uganda, causing loss of life and property. The Sudanese airforce has on several occasions 'mistakenly' bombed Ugandan villages along the border, including the town of Nimule.

The Ugandan government has provided moral and material support to the SPLA and thus fuelled the conflict, which has in turn created refugees and insecurity on its northern border. The deployment of military personnel and equipment in northern Uganda to combat the LRA, the refugees and displaced persons from the conflicts both in Uganda and Sudan, has been highly costly to the Ugandan government, and has contributed significantly to Uganda's military budget.

The Ugandan government's strategy of supporting the SPLA in order to secure short-term security along its much troubled northern border had been working in providing security to the war weary districts of Gulu and Kitgum. This policy has, however, recently backfired. The northern Sudanese forces have secured a strip of land along the border with Uganda which they have used to encourage Ugandan rebels led by Juma Oris, a minister in the Idi Amin regime, to carry out acts of terror in Uganda. In March and April 1994 insecurity returned to the region, undermining its capacity to make a complete recovery from previous wars, and threatening the long-term security of Uganda's border.

Egypt

Egypt has been entangled in Sudan's affairs since 1819, when, for a period, it controlled much of Sudan from Cairo, until Egypt itself was occupied by the British in 1878. However, Egypt and Sudan have enjoyed more cordial links. During the years when Nimeiri and Egypt's President Anwar Sadat were in power, the two countries developed very strong links, Nimeiri resolutely defending Sadat for making peace with Israel.

Security

The political events in Sudan have exacerbated the current political turmoil in Egypt. The Egyptian government has acknowledged that 'promotion of the Islamization of Sudan has repercussions for Egypt'.[45] Should the NIF become an important force in an Islamicized Sudan, Egypt is seriously concerned that its own indigenous fundamentalist movement may become energized, both politically and militarily. It is apparent also, from the growing influence of fundamentalism in Algeria, that this is a growing trend in the states of northern Africa.

Thus, Egypt, with the help of the US, has sought to influence Sudan's domestic politics. In 1991, they quietly supported anti-Bashir forces in the ruling National DUP, which is affiliated to the pro-Egyptian Khatmiyya sect. Egypt wanted to see the DUP leader, Ahmad al-Mirghani, assume a greater role in Sudanese politics. However, the monopoly of power held by the NIF has ensured this policy has reaped little reward.[46]

Moreover, Cairo has accused Khartoum of working with Iran in training terrorists to destabilize Egypt. The guerrillas are believed to enter Egypt from Sudan. Western tourists have been the main targets, the intention being to cripple the huge Egyptian tourist industry. Since 1992,

when a British nurse was killed in an attack by terrorists, there have been numerous other terrorist attacks. The effect has been a 35 per cent drop in tourist receipts.[47]

CONCLUSION

Egypt, Uganda and Kenya are all seriously concerned about the future security implications of the war in Sudan. In addition to the long-term consequences of the war, in terms of refugee flows and localized instability in border areas, there are the ominous long-term consequences of an unfavourable outcome. Should the Khartoum government prevail, these countries are in danger of finding their internal ethnic and political problems fomented by an aggressive neighbour.

THE UNITED STATES

THE COSTS

Introduction

US involvement in Sudan has tended to be concerned with achieving national and international objectives often unrelated to the civil war. Thus, while the fall of Mengistu in Ethiopia in 1990 significantly affected the geopolitical significance of the region which had always made superpower rivalry inevitable, and into which the US had poured $1.4 billion of military aid between 1977 and 1985, US policy was also affected by regional political and economic considerations. When the Khartoum government began forging increasingly strong links with Libya in 1985–86, the US began to cut back on its economic and military assistance to Sudan. This was further prompted by Sudan's inconsistent economic policies and the subsequent effect on its balance of payments (see Sudan economy section). Thus, with the exception of some human-itarian aid, the conflict fought between the successive governments in Khartoum and

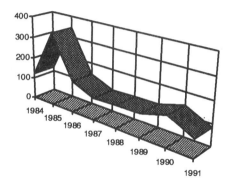

Source: OECD, Development Cooperation, 1993

Figure 6.9: Total US overseas development aid to Sudan (US$m)

the SPLA has had little effect on US economic and military aid flows. The most significant impact this war has had on US interests has been on US trade and investment.

The Economy

Humanitarian aid

Since 1989, aid has been restricted entirely to humanitarian assistance. Total US government humanitarian assistance to Sudan in 1993 alone was US$97.6 million.[48] This was channelled through several NGOs and UN agencies to provide relief to victims of war in Sudan and its neighbours. Figure 6.9 shows US aid from 1984 to 1991.

Trade

Sudan has found it increasingly difficult to import goods from the US. Almost all categories of agricultural exports from the US to Sudan, while small, recorded significant falls between 1988 and 1990, and further falls in 1991, the year in which the effect of the war on Sudan's economy was most apparent, and in 1992 (Figure 6.10). Sudan's payments deficit had peaked and the military expenditure of US$1.01 billion had become too heavy a burden to carry.

A similar fall was reported in the export of manufactures. The US's percentage share

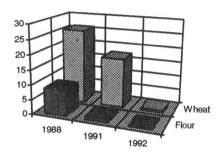

Source: US Dept of Agriculture

Figure 6.10: Principal US agricultural exports to Sudan (US$m)

of Sudan's imports fell from 10.4 per cent in 1987 to 8.9 per cent in 1988 and 4.2 per cent in 1989 (Figure 6.11).[49] In 1992, US exports to Sudan fell to about a quarter of the 1982 figure, from US$192.5 million to US$51.5 million.[50]

Investment

As a result of the poor business climate, US companies have sustained losses of income and investment. Infrastructure built by foreign companies has been a target of SPLA attacks. The 1410 kilometre oil export pipeline between the Unity fields and Port Sudan, for example, was targeted. The pipeline and terminal were built with a total investment of US$1 billion by Chevron,

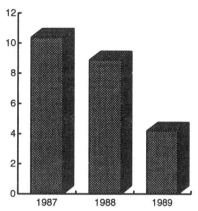

Source: EIU Reports, op cit

Figure 6.11: US share of total exports to Sudan

the US petroleum company, and have yet to produce a single barrel of oil. Other oil companies are beginning to leave Sudan. The French oil company, Total, left Sudan early in 1994 and its partners, Marathon and a Kuwait oil company, are said to be considering pulling out.[51]

As demonstrated in Figure 6.12, the net income from US companies based in Sudan has almost continually been in the negative.

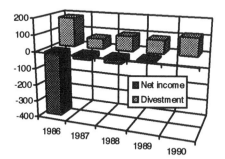

Source: USA Survey of Current Business

Figure 6.12: US net income and divestment from Sudan (US$m)

Long Term Strategic Costs

There are implications for US strategic interests if the NIF-backed government of the north should eventually defeat all factions of the SPLA. Since the resurgence of militant Islamic fundamentalism in the 1970s and the 1980s that saw the assassination of the pro-Western Egyptian President Anwar Sadat, the US has been anxious to maintain a neutral balance among the Arabic states in the Middle East and North Africa, and thereby protect their interests in the region.

Militant Islamic fundamentalism has been on the rise in the Middle East and North Africa in the past two decades. A series of international and local events ranging from the overthrow of the Shah of Iran, the Camp David peace accords and the Gulf War, to the violent suppression of Islamic political movements in Egypt and Algeria, have increased tensions in the region, and undermined the position of moderate forces. With the continuing

conflict in Sudan being made to appear increasingly like a religious war for the defence of Islam and a *jihad* against Christians and Western influence in the south, there is a danger that the conflict will make heroes of the NIF and PDF. Islamic fundamentalism in Sudan is already having an effect in the region. The emergence of ultra-orthodox Islamic groups, often militant, in the coastal towns along the Kenyan coast, in Uganda (where a militant Tabiq sect is active) and even more significantly in Tanzania, have caused division among the people. Islamic fundamentalism in these countries, which only began to emerge about five years ago, has drawn moral and material strength from the Islamic government and organizations in Sudan. Indeed the Islamic Party of Kenya is believed to have backers in Sudan.

Should this be allowed to grow unchecked, it may pose a serious threat to Western interests, both economic and strategic, in the region. For example, the massive investments in tourism and other industries made by Western firms in Kenya, Uganda and Tanzania could be affected if the forces of fundamentalism were to use violence as a means to gain recognition. The modest economic growth and development being achieved in Uganda and Kenya could be undermined. For this reason, the international community, particularly the US and the East African states, have an interest in containing Islamic fundamentalism in the Horn of Africa and East Africa.

THE BENEFITS

While there was a clear strategic benefit in the US supplying military and economic assistance to Sudan as a counter to the Marxist government in Ethiopia, there are few benefits to the US, or for that matter, to any Western countries in the civil war in Sudan continuing. While it could be argued the SPLA is aiding the US in containing fundamentalism, particularly given recent events in Algeria and Egypt, and despite meetings between Garang and high-ranking US officials,[52] the fact that the US is apparently not actively supporting the SPLA, suggests that, for the moment, the US sees no role for the southern rebels.

CONCLUSION

It is clear that, with no compensating economic, strategic or other benefits, the civil war in Sudan has had an effect on some sectors of the US economy. There have been falls in exports of agriculture and manufactures as well as returns on US investment in Sudan. The people and government of Sudan are too short of cash to continue importing US goods. Consumption patterns in Sudan continue to be severely distorted because of the high rate of inflation, thus affecting US investors and affiliated companies.

IF THE CONFLICT HAD NOT OCCURRED

Introduction

This section will compare Sudan's current economic plight with that of two similar countries in the region in order to demonstrate how Sudan might have benefited, had the conflict been resolved. The extent to which the West might have benefited from closer economic relations with Sudan will also be examined.

One can contrast Sudan's situation with that of Kenya, where there is a big and steadily growing US business interest. The Kenyan government recognizes the importance of US business and finance for the country's growth and development. It will also be useful to compare Sudan's macroeconomic indicators with those of Uganda, another underdeveloped African nation which has similar problems of debt, declining commodity prices, low income, a small domestic market, and infestations and droughts (though not as severe as Sudan's). In assessing the potential benefits

to Western countries, trade figures for Uganda and Kenya will be used to demonstrate how significantly Western–Sudanese trade might have risen over the past 11 years of conflict.

Sudan

Trade and investment between Sudan and the West have fallen significantly over the past decade (since the commencement of the conflict in 1983), while significant rises in trade with Kenya and Uganda, both poor countries like Sudan, have been recorded.

Like Sudan, Uganda has been through a series of painful civil wars, the last of which occurred between 1981 and 1986. During those years, Uganda experienced large falls in national income and a doubling of the balance of payments deficit.[53]

However, although Uganda's economic position remains weak, since 1986, when peace was restored, it has experienced encouraging economic trends. Real GDP growth has averaged about 6.5 per cent per annum since 1986, while Sudan has averaged –4.2 per cent per annum. While Uganda's current account balance declined in 1991–1992 to US$–184 million from US$–263 million in 1990 and US$–260 million in 1989, Sudan's current account deficit nearly trebled in the same period from US$–369 million to US$–958 million (Figure 6.13).

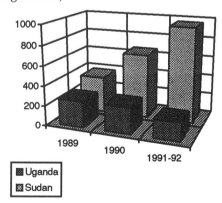

Source: EIU Reports, op cit

Figure 6.13: Comparative current account deficits, Sudan and Uganda (US$m)

151

Although Uganda's external debt increased slightly from US$1.95 billion in 1988 to US$2.8 billion in 1992, Sudan's increased by four billion from US$11.9 billion in 1988 to US$15.9 billion in 1992.

The rate of inflation in Uganda declined from 238.1 per cent in 1987 to 82.4 per cent in 1989. By the beginning of 1994, Uganda's inflation was below 10 per cent. In Sudan, however, the rate of inflation has continually been on the increase: from 64.7 per cent in 1988 to 300 per cent in 1994.[54] (See Figure 6.14)

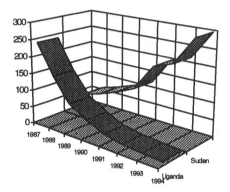

Source: EIU Reports, op cit

Figure 6.14: Inflation rates, Sudan and Uganda

Manufacturing output in Uganda has increased by 78 per cent since 1987, while it continues to decline in Sudan. The volume of exports from Uganda has increased steadily since 1986, although the value has declined because of falling world market prices. In Sudan, both the value and the volume of exports have greatly diminished over the past ten years of conflict.

All this has undermined confidence in the Sudanese economy. The war and accompanying insecurity, increasing international isolation and the rapidly declining economy have discouraged potential traders and investors from any engagement with Sudan. As a result, there has been a large amount of capital flight and divestment from Sudan. US companies alone have divested as much as US$581 million from Sudan between 1986 and

1991.[55] In Uganda on the other hand, investment levels have been rising steadily since 1989. A good political and economic climate, a growing middle class and an investment code designed to attract investors, have made Uganda a destination of investment for the US and Western Europe.

The West

In almost all cases Western exports to Kenya have significantly increased, doubling or trebling in some cases since 1982. Similar progress has been registered since the end of the civil war in Uganda. As the situation stands at the moment, the value and volume of exports from G7 countries to Sudan, has significantly declined since 1982.

In 1982, Sudan was among Africa's largest importers of goods and services from Western countries, particularly France, Italy, the US and the UK. Today, after a decade of conflict, it is among the smaller importers.

In 1992, US exports to Sudan fell to about a quarter of the 1982 figure, from US$192.5 million to US$51.5 million.[56] In that same period US exports to Kenya doubled from US$68 million in 1982 to US$123 million.[57] (Figure 6.15). US exports to Uganda also doubled in that period.

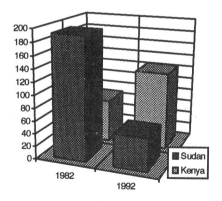

Source: UN, 1993, op cit

Figure 6.15: US exports to Sudan and Kenya (US$m)

French exports to Sudan fell by more than 50 per cent from US$133 million in 1982 to US$53 million in 1992. French exports to both Kenya and Uganda increased by 50 per cent during the same period.[58] UK exports to Sudan fell by about 60 per cent between 1982 and 1992 from US$237.5 million to US$92 million.[59]

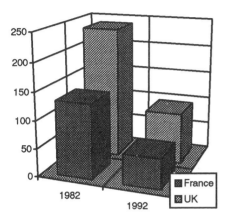

Source: UN, 1993, op cit

Figure 6.16: UK and France exports to Sudan (US$m)

The biggest fall in this figure was recorded during 1983–1985 (shortly after the commencement of the conflict), when the value of UK exports to Sudan fell by US$100 million in only two years.

Peace in Sudan would also make it possible for oil exploitation to recommence in the south. This would not only mean more income and overseas employment for Americans and higher capital remittances from companies like Chevron, but would also mean that the US would not have to rely so heavily on petroleum from the Middle East. This would be beneficial to the US for both economic and strategic reasons.

Finally, the absence of war in Sudan would have the effect of reducing the enormous amounts of aid that is spent by the US every year. The US has spent over US$100 million on disaster assistance in Sudan in the past two years.

Conclusion

Cash strapped, suspended from the IMF and the International Islamic Council, and increasingly isolated by the international community, Sudan's support for Iraq in the Gulf war, its continued committing of human rights atrocities, and the issuing of fatwas (death sentences) on opponents, and the forming of alliances with other international outcasts such as Iraq and Iran, all reinforce its reputation as a pariah state. Unsurprisingly, the value and volume of exports from every Western country to Sudan has significantly declined since 1982.

The effect this war and the accompanying isolation have had on Sudan, is clearly demonstrated by the comparative success of other countries in the region. In many cases, Western exports to Kenya have significantly increased, doubling or trebling in some cases since 1982. Uganda shows the debilitating effect of war on all important macroeconomic indicators, yet also shows quite dramatically how the absence of war impacts positively on these same indicators.

Had there been no conflict, Sudan would still have been troubled by problems of drought, debt and declining world market commodity prices which other developing African nations experience. However, it is also clear that in the absence of conflict, Sudan would also be in a considerably stronger position to address its economic problems and make greater strides in social development.

For the West, as demonstrated by the impressive growth in trade and investment with Uganda and Kenya, substantial business opportunities have been lost. This is clearly illustrated from the dramatic departure of Western capital since 1983. If no conflict had occurred, it would be reasonable to assume the not inconsiderable levels of Western economic interest in Sudan would have continued to rise.

REFERENCES

1 Wyllie, James; 'Sudan–Going for Broke' *Jane's Intelligence Review*, May 1994.
2 *New Internationalist* 'The Horn of Africa–The Facts', December 1992.
3 Twose N, Pogrund B, *War Wounds*, The Panos Institute, London 1993.
4 The Military Balance 1993–4, International Institute for Strategic Studies, London, 1993.
5 House, William 'Population, Poverty and Under-development in Southern Sudan' *The Journal of Modern African Studies*, 27 February, 1989.
6 *Sudan Update*, March 1994.
7 Amnesty International, *Sudan: The Ravages of War. Political Killing and Humanitarian Disaster*. September 1993..
8 Twose and Pogrund, 1993, op cit.
9 United Nations, *Human Development Report, 1993*, Oxford University Press, New York, 1993.
10 House, William J, 'Population, Poverty and Underdevelopment in Southern Sudan.' *The Journal of Modern African Studies*. 27, 2 1989.
11 Forman S, *Port Sudan Survey*. Save the Children Fund. 1992.
12 House, 1989, op cit.
13 Twose and Pogrund, 1993, op cit.
14 United Nations, 1993, op cit.
15 Ibid.
16 *Christian Science Monitor*, 26th January 1990
17 Amnesty International, 1993, op cit.
18 *Sudan: Patterns of Repression*, Amnesty International. February 1993.
19 Sudan Human Rights Voice, November 1992.
20 Ibid.
21 Amnesty International, 1993, op cit.
22 Ibid.
23 Amnesty International. February 1993, op cit.
24 Ibid.
25 IISS, 1993, op cit.
26 UNDP, 1993, op cit.
27 Ibid.
28 *New Internationalist*, 1992, op cit.
29 *EIU Country Report* 4th quarter 1993, The Economist Intelligence Unit, London, 1993.
30 IISS, 1993, op cit.
31 UNDP, 1993, op cit.
32 Quoted in Index on Censorship, October 1991.
33 Twose and Pogrund, 1993, op cit.
34 Mohammed S, *Environmental Degradation and Migration in Africa*. Institute for African Alternatives, London, 1992.
35 Burr M, *Khartoum's Displaced Persons: A Decade of Despair*. US Committee for Refugees, 1990.
36 Ibid.
37 Ibid.
38 'Southerners on the Run Again: Refugees Flee Ethiopia', *Sudan Democratic Gazette*. London 1991.
39 Ibid.
40 *The Guardian*, 20 Jan 1993
41 *Information* Bulletin, UNHCR, Nairobi. October 1993.
42 *The Guardian*, January 1994, op cit.
43 'East Africa: Swamped, Refugees Flood Kenya' *The Economist*, 6 June 1992.
44 *Sudan Update*, 15th April 1994.
45 *The Guardian*, 15th December 1993.
46 IISS, 1993, op cit.
47 'When Taming is Inflaming: Egypt's Fundamen-talists', *The Economist*, 19 December 1993.
48 'Sudan– Civil Strife/Displaced Persons' *USAID, Situation Report*, No 7 Washington DC 1993.
49 *EIU Country Profile 1991–92*, The Economist Intelligence Unit, London 1992.
50 United Nations, Commodity Trade Statistics, *Statistical Papers*, Vols XXXII, XXXV, XXXIX, XLI, XLII 1993.
51 'Total Pulls Out' *Sudan Update*, 15th March 1994.
52 Lefebvre, J A, 'US Arms Transfers to Sudan', *Armed Forces and Society*, Vol 17, No 2 Winter 1991.
53 *Business America*, 1989.
54 EIU Reports, 1993, op cit.
55 *USA Survey of Current Business*, 1991.
56 United Nations, Commodity Trade Statistics, op cit.
57 Ibid.
58 Ibid.
59 Ibid.

7

THE FORMER YUGOSLAVIA CONFLICT (1991–)

Angela Burke and Gordon Macdonald

Area (000sq km)	255.8
Population (000)	23.7
Human Development Index	na
Population density (per sq km)	93
Capital	na

KEY IMPACTS OF THE CONFLICT

ON BOSNIA-HERZEGOVINA

- Prior to the conflict, the infant mortality rate per 1000 live births for former Yugoslavia as a whole was 28.2. The WHO estimate that this has doubled in Bosnia-Herzegovina during the conflict.
- Of all pregnancies 25 per cent result in spontaneous abortions and premature births due to malnourishment of women.
- Approximately 200,000 people, the vast majority civilians, have been killed during the conflict.
- Human rights abuses have included the detention of civilian population, mass killings, torture of both civilians and captured military personnel, mass systematic rape, forced eviction from homes and villages, shelling of urban centres and obstruction of humanitarian relief.
- The most reliable estimate puts the number of Muslim women raped at 20,000.
- Nearly 1 million Muslims have been trapped in besieged towns, subject to shelling, sniper fire, hunger and disease.
- It is estimated that between 2 and 4 million landmines have been laid.
- The cost of restoring the railway network may exceed $150 million.

ON SERBIA

- There has been the delay (or suspension) of transition to a real and functioning liberal democratic system of government.
- The combined GDP of Serbia and Montenegro fell (in comparison to the previous year) by 8.4 per cent in 1990, 11 per cent in 1991, 27 per cent in 1992 and 35 per cent in 1993.
- The total cost to the economy of UN sanctions has come to some $20 billion.
- An estimate puts hyperinflation at 310 million per cent per month at the end of April 1994.
- Estimates of the number of refugees in Serbia average around 500,000.

ON CROATIA

- A minimum estimate of the number of casualties from this war is 7693 killed (of which 1200 were military personnel) 23,167 wounded (of which 6,786 were civilians) and 13,153 missing.
- Attending schools in Croatia are 14,500 displaced and 21,000 refugee children.
- Dubrovnik was attacked three times in the autumn of 1991. In the process it is estimated that US$2 billion of damage was incurred by the municipality which included the destruction of 75 per cent of industrial facilities, 40 per cent of shops, 60 per cent of hotels and 2500 family homes.
- Industrial production fell by 23.7 per cent in the first nine months of the Croatian/Serb war of 1991.
- Estimates put lost direct income from tourism at about US$1 billion and indirect earnings at US$5 billion.
- Real wages fell at least 66 per cent between 1989 and 1992.
- Up to 6500 kilometres of roads were made unusable, with 33 bridges destroyed and another 24 damaged.
- 30 per cent of the railway network is out of operation.
- In June 1993, there were 254,413 displaced persons within Croatia and 240,000 from Bosnia-Herzegovina.

ON THE EUROPEAN UNION

- Since the deployment of the UN Protection Force (UNPROFOR), 90 soldiers (including some from countries outside the EU) have been killed, and over 900 injured during operations in the former Yugoslavia.
- In March 1994, the number of troops serving with UNPROFOR was 31,425.
- The total UN costs for UNPROFOR, including operations in Bosnia-Herzegovina, Croatia and Macedonia, amounted to $250 million in 1992 and $1 billion in 1993.

- The number of refugees residing in EU countries reached 509,714 by May 1994
- The inability of the EU to project a united policy or implement an effective response to the conflicts in the former Yugoslavia has discredited the Union and arguably encouraged the continuation of the conflict.
- The conflict in former Yugoslavia has the potential to embroil neighbouring countries and raise ethnic tensions throughout the region.

INTRODUCTION

Geography

Yugoslavia consisted of six republics; Slovenia, Croatia, Bosnia-Herzegovina, Serbia, Macedonia and Montenegro; and two autonomous provinces, Vojvodina and Kosovo. Located in the Balkans on the Adriatic sea, Yugoslavia had borders with Italy, Austria, Hungary, Romania, Bulgaria, Greece and Albania.

The People

The former Yugoslavia was a community of South Slavs initially united in one kingdom in 1918. The reconstruction of Yugoslavia by Tito after the Second World War was accompanied by efforts to create a pan-Yugoslav identity. However, decentralization and greater autonomy among the republics (a result of the 1974 constitution), reinforced national identities within the republics. Serbo-Croat was the most widely spoken language throughout the republics, with the Serbs and Montenegrins using the Cyrillic script and Croats and Slovenes using the Latin script. In recent years both the Serbs and Croats have attempted to disentangle Serbo-Croat into separate languages and enforce the use of Cyrillic and Latin scripts in their territories. The three main religions are Orthodoxy (41 per cent), Catholicism (31 per cent) and Islam (12 per cent). Religion and nationality are closely linked; the majority of Serbs are

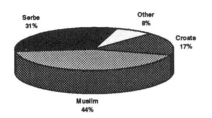

Source: EIU Country Profile: *Bosnia-Herzegovina* 1993–94

Figure 7.1: Ethnic composition – Bosnia-Herzegovina (1991)

Orthodox, while Croats and Slovenes are predominantly Catholic. The Muslim population is primarily based in Bosnia-Herzegovina (See Figure 7.1).

Yugoslavia also contained a large number of minorities, including Hungarian, Albanian, Romanian, Bulg-arian, Greek and Slovak. The 1974 constitution contained provisions for the protection of minority rights and prohibited the creation of ethnically pure states.

The conflict

The causes of the conflict in the former Yugoslavia can be located in the disintegration of Yugoslavia, a consequence of the crisis of legitimacy faced by the Federal authorities with the decay and collapse of communism, coinciding with severe economic problems and conflicting demands for and resistance to the democratization of Yugoslavia's political structure.

The area has a legacy of fratricidal violence, a consequence of the civil war (1941–45) between the Communist Partisans and Nationalist Chetniks, when an estimated 99,000–150,000 Yugoslavs were killed, the majority by fellow Yugoslavs.

The cohesion of Yugoslavia had been dependent on Tito's personal authority, the strict imposition of communist ideology and the precarious balancing of interests between the republics which had been formalized in the constitution. The death of Tito in 1980 and the fundamental questioning of communism during the late 1980s combined to destabilize Yugoslavia.

Throughout the 1980s there were increasing calls for political liberalization. The adoption of the concept of a multi-party system by the Federal League of Communists in January 1990 paved the way for the creation of opposition parties and democratic elections. The transition to democracy was subsumed in the emergence of ethnically based politics, with political parties relying heavily on nationalist sentiments for support. Ethnic politics were used as a means to secure political legitimacy, the result of which has undermined the survival of a multicultural society.

The results of democratic elections, held throughout Yugoslavia in 1990, reflected the ethnic composition of the republics. In Slovenia, elections were held in spring 1990. The 'Demos' coalition, with a nationalist manifesto, was returned to power with 55 per cent of the votes. In Croatia, the Croatian Democratic Union (HDZ), under the leadership of President Tudjman, received 42 per cent of the votes. Elections in Serbia provided President Milosevic with a mandate for his nationalist policies, as the Socialist Party of Serbia secured 77 per cent of seats in parliament with 48 per cent of the votes. The election results in Bosnia-Herzegovina, held in November 1990, reflected the ethnic composition of the Republic. The Party of Democratic Action (SDA) received 35 per cent of votes, the Serb democratic party, under the leadership of Dr Radovan Karadic secured 29 per cent, with the Croatian Democratic Union, led by Mate Boban, receiving 18 per cent of votes. A coalition government was formed with Alija Izetbegovic, leader of the mainly Muslim SDA, as President.

During 1990 the Federal authority in Yugoslavia ceased to function. Demands for political reform, particularly from Croatia and Slovenia, who pressed for a confederational arrangement between the republics, were met with staunch resistance from the Serb representatives within the government.

The Serb President, Milosevic, revived Serb nationalism as a means to secure loyalty to the political structures of Yugoslavia which had been discredited by the fall of communism. Milosevic argued for stronger central government within the former Yugoslavia, with his ultimate aim being the creation of a greater Serb state. Attempts to re-establish a more stringent central authority based in Belgrade were opposed by Croatia and Slovenia and provoked their declarations of independence on 25 June 1990.

Slovenia secured independence from Yugoslavia following a ten-day war with the Yugoslav Peoples Army, sparked by the unilateral declaration of independence on 25 June 1991. In Croatia, the large Serb minority responded to moves towards independence by establishing an autonomous Serb Republic of Krajina. With the declaration of independence, conflict erupted between the Serbs, who had unwillingly become a minority in a Croatian state, and the forces of the Croatian government, in their attempt to re-establish control of territory within their state borders. The Croatian Serbs received substantial financial and military support from Serbia in their war efforts.

With the creation of an independent Croatian state, President Tudjman gave no guarantees for the protection of minority rights. The nationalist policies of the HDZ exacerbated the fears of the Croatian Serbs. On assuming power, the HDZ rekindled memories of atrocities committed against the Serbs during the Second World War by reviving symbols prominently used by the Ustasa government throughout the occupation.

The pursuit of independent statehood by Slovenia and Croatia placed the Muslim-dominated Presidency of Bosnia-Herzegovina in a dilemma. Bosnia-Herzegovina was faced with the unenviable choice between remaining part of Yugoslavia and accepting Serb dominance or declaring independence, in the knowledge that such a declaration would be resisted by the Bosnian Serbs. Encouraged by the international community's promise of recognition, Bosnia's leaders, and a majority of the population, chose the latter. A referendum, held in March 1992, resulted in a large majority for independence, which was duly declared. The referendum was boycotted by the Bosnian Serbs who were not prepared to accept the creation of an independent Bosnia.

The cohesion of Bosnia-Herzegovina was fatally undermined by the opposition of the Serb Democratic Party and by the Croatian government, which saw Bosnian independence as an opportunity to expand Croatia's borders. The Serb Democratic Party, taking advantage of its access to abundant Yugoslav army supplies, established control over large swathes of territory in the east and north of the country. In January 1992, the pro-Bosnian leader of the main Bosnian Croatian political party had been replaced on orders from Zagreb, and Croats soon seized control of much of the west of Bosnia, declaring the state of 'Herceg-Bosna' in June of that year.

The mainly Muslim government of Bosnia-Herzegovina has insisted on the maintenance of a unitary and multi-ethnic state with its capital in Sarajevo. Although the Bosnian Croats had initially supported the Bosnian government against the onslaught of the Bosnian Serbs and Yugoslav Peoples Army, disagreements arose as to the structure of the new state. The Bosnian Croatian leadership supported a 'cantonized' arrangement, in which a Croatian autonomous region could develop close ties with, and later be incorporated in, Croatia. This disagreement laid the foundations for the subsequent Muslim/ Croatian conflict.

Bosnian Croats and Bosnian Serbs have worked in collusion with, and been supported by, Croatia and Serbia in their war efforts to establish ethnically pure regions within Bosnia-Herzegovina. Negotiations channelled through the international community have been focused on the creation of ethnic 'cantons' or regions, while ostensibly supporting the inviolability of Bosnia-Herzegovina's borders.

In Bosnia-Herzegovina the Bosnian Serbs have secured 70 per cent of the territory and fighting continues between the mainly Muslim government forces and the Bosnian Serbs. The conflict between Bosnian government and the Bosnian Croats has been tentatively resolved by a UN-brokered agreement for a ceasefire and the creation of a Bosnian-Croatian Federation.

In Croatia, the conflict between the minority Serb population and the Croatian government forces has been tentatively stabilized by the presence of UN forces in the areas of Croatia currently under the control of Croatian Serbs. With the Croatian government determined to reestablish control of all its territory and the Croatian Serbs adamant that they will not live in a Croatian state, the potential for further conflict remains high.

Scope of the Study

This study will examine the impact of the conflicts in both Bosnia-Herzegovina and Croatia. The costs and benefits of the conflicts to Serbia are also considered. In addition to these states, the impact of the conflicts on the US and the EU is explored. Finally, consideration is given to the potential benefits to these countries, had the conflict not occurred.

BOSNIA-HERZEGOVINA

THE COSTS

Introduction

Since declaring independence, Bosnia-Herzegovina has been the victim of the strategic agenda of its more powerful neighbours, Serbia and Croatia. With the EU apparently unable and unwilling to prevent it, its population have been forced to flee their homes in villages claimed by the Bosnian Serb and Bosnian Croat governments. Many have been tortured or killed. Others have lost their homes and livelihoods.

Development

Health

Prior to the conflict, extensive health care provision existed throughout former Yugoslavia. In Bosnia-Herzegovina by 1989 there were 636 people per doctor, 8218 beds in general hospitals, 4469 in specialist hospitals and 7000 in other medical institutions.[1] During the conflict not only have many these health care systems and facilities been destroyed, but also those functioning are overburdened by greatly increased numbers of emergency cases due to war casualties. At the same time, supplies of drugs, anaesthetics and other material inputs are in desperately short supply. Added to these problems are the frequent breakdowns of water and electricity supplies as a result of infra-structural damage.

Water-borne contagious diseases pose the biggest health threat in Bosnia-Herzegovina. Thus far, serious epidemics have been avoided, but how long this can continue in unhygienic conditions in urban areas is not clear. Indeed 700 cases of enteroculitis were registered in July 1993 and 80 cases of hepatitis A among children during the summer of 1993.[2]

Prior to the conflict, the infant mortality rate per 1000 live births for former Yugoslavia as a whole was 28.2. The WHO estimate that this has doubled in Bosnia-Herzegovina during the conflict. Furthermore, 25 per cent of all pregnancies result in spontaneous abortions and premature births due to malnourishment of women. Child malnourishment is also a problem and in some parts of the country 20 per cent of women and children suffer from anaemia.[3]

In addition to physical treatment there is also a desperate need for greater psychiatric resources. Current resources are already overstretched. Moreover, there is likely to be a greatly increased incidence of post-traumatic stress problems as people come to terms with their war experiences.[4]

Extensive psychological counselling will be required for women and girls who have been raped. Children who have seen friends and relatives killed, injured, tortured or raped will also need emotional support and counselling. A UN Children's Fund (UNICEF) survey of children in East Mostar found that there were high instances of strong psychological reactions, such as experiencing flashbacks, loss of sleep and stomach aches among the children living there. Of the children sampled, 85 per cent had fled their homes, 62 per cent had been separated from their parents or close family members and 19 per cent had had siblings killed in the conflict.[5]

Education

Before the war there was universal education for all children between 6 and 14.

The education system consisted of 2211 schools with 22,939 teachers and 538,475 pupils. In addition there were four universities located at Sarajevo, Mostar, Banja Luka and Tuzla and an Academy of Arts and Sciences in Sarajevo.[6]

Since the war began, the education system has been totally disrupted, either due to schools and other institutions being destroyed, or because they have been converted for use as shelters, military barracks or refugee centres. Schooling has continued in a haphazard manner in basements and flats. Often these schools are run by volunteer teachers, as many Serb and Croatian teachers have left the region. In East Mostar in 1992, only 50 per cent of children were attending school, and the majority of these were makeshift.[7] The University in Sarajevo remained nominally open, but in reality classes have ceased. Other universities were also forced to cease operating.

The pre-war school system in former Yugoslavia was highly integrated to include health checks, dental care, immunization, sports, music and vocational activities. The breakdown of the school system in Bosnia-Herzegovina has consequences beyond just a poorly educated generation of children. It may well also lead to a generation with poor physical and mental health, unable to engage in productive employment as adults.

Civil and Political Rights

Number of deaths

Extensive documentary evidence and personal testimonies support the reports that all the warring parties have committed serious abuses of human rights at various times throughout the conflict. However, there can be little doubt that the Muslim population has suffered the most serious violations. The Muslim and Croatian communities in northern Bosnia appear to have been the first targets of Serb atrocities. Human rights violations were also committed by the Croats against Muslims and Serbs and by forces loyal to the Bosnian government against Croats and Serbs. Human rights abuses have followed the tide of the military conflict and have included the detention of civilian population, mass killings, torture of both civilians and captured military personnel, mass systematic rape, forced eviction from homes and villages, shelling of urban centres and obstruction of humanitarian relief.

It is estimated that approximately 200,000 people have been killed during the conflict in former Yugoslavia. This represents almost 1 per cent of the pre-war population. A substantial number of those deaths have occurred in Bosnia-Herzegovina, of which it is estimated up to 15,000 were children. Another 35,000 have been wounded.[8]

Civilian targets

In January 1994 six children were killed in Sarajevo as they played in the snow. During the shelling of the market in Sarajevo on 5 February 1994 over 60 people were killed. However, these examples do not reveal the extent of indiscriminate shelling of civilian population centres. The scale of this outrage is better reflected in the report from radio amateurs that 1500 shells landed on civilian targets in Maglaj in one day in late February 1994. During this bombardment the health centre was reportedly hit and five medical personnel killed.[9] A report tells us that 1400 shells fell on Bihac city on 6 February 1994.[10]

Human rights abuses committed against Bosnian Muslim civilians have included summary executions, torture, rape, detention, hostage taking, and the destruction of Muslim villages and towns. Evidence suggests that, at best, Serbian forces con-done such actions and, at worst, are responsible for such atrocities.

There is also evidence of human rights abuses against Bosnian Serbs. In February 1993, mass graves containing the bodies of Serb combatants and civilians were discovered in the town of Kamenica. One grave contained between 18 and 23 bodies. According to one foreign journalist: 'One corpse was decapitated and the feet of

another were tied with wire', indicating that the victims were summarily executed and possibly tortured.[11]

Detention

During the early stages of the war, there were widespread instances of civilians being held in detention camps. These camps, reminiscent of Nazi concentration camps, were part of the so-called 'ethnic cleansing' process. Unlike their Second World War models, the camps were exposed at an early stage of the Bosnian war, due to the persistence of Western media reporters. Intense international political pressure caused a reduction, but not an elimination, of the camps and the extrajudicial detention of civilians.

Detention camps were run by all sides, but the Bosnian Serbs had by far the largest number of camps and detainees. The International Committee of the Red Cross (ICRC) registered 10,273 people being held in 41 places of detention between 7 July 1992 and 31 October 1992. Of these, 8,046 were held by the Bosnian Serbs at 14 sites, 988 by the Bosnian Croats at 16 sites and 1,239 by the Bosnian government at 11 sites.[12] The ICRC estimate that thousands more detainees existed whom the ICRC had been unable to visit, due to lack of notification or refusal of access by local authorities. It is also suspected that the Bosnian Serbs may have moved detainees prior to examination of camps by the ICRC. It is alleged by the Bosnian government that 260,000 prisoners have passed through Serb-controlled camps.[13]

Abuses by Serbian soldiers of prisoners of war in Omarska camp, Prijedor region

'Not one evening would pass where four to five youths between the ages of 18 and 25 weren't taken out and killed. There were also times when we had to lie down with our faces pressed against the courtyard floor and, if we were not lying close enough, ten men would jump on us. They also used a hose to spray us with ice-cold water. They made us stand on one foot and those who couldn't were pulled out and beaten.[15]

Conditions in detention camps were appalling, with routine overcrowding, poor supplies of food and water, and incidents of killings, beatings and torture. Some were detained in their own cellars, others in hotels, dormitories, warehouses, schools, sheds, farms, factories or even football stadiums in addition to prisons, military bases and police stations.[14]

Village killings

The situation in the village of Bosanski Petrovac between June and September 1992 is representative of widespread mass killings of Muslim civilians by Bosnian Serbs. In total about 50 individuals out of a population of 2,000–3,000 were killed.[16] It is alleged that 30 Bosnian Croatian civilians were massacred in the town of Uzdol by forces loyal to the mainly Muslim government. The Bosnian Croatian militia promised revenge, which was subsequently fulfilled on 23 October 1993, within earshot of UN observers, in the Muslim village of Stupni Do.[17] The UN detail the massacre at Stupni Do of an estimated 36 individuals out of a population of 235. UNPROFOR military personnel were prevented from entering the village whilst the massacre was conducted.

Torture

Victims of torture

'I was arrested in front of my children by HOS, the Croatian Defence Forces...They took me to a prison in Mostar.. After ten days of terrible torture, they took us to a camp in Dretelj'

'About 40 men were in my warehouse. They lined eight of us up and three of four of them beat us for an hour with rubber truncheons, fists and rifle butts.'[18]

There have been widespread reports of torture committed during the war in Bosnia-Herzegovina, by all sides in the conflict, against both civilians and military personnel. Incidents of torture against those in detention camps have included systematic beatings with rubber truncheons, fists, rifle butts and knives, deprivation of food

and water and incidents of mutilation.[19]

Torture has been particularly evident in places of detention run by all the warring parties, where there were beatings of civilians and prisoners of war. One example was the regular beatings of prisoners at the Bosnian Serb detention centres, to which many young men were taken from the village of Bosanski Petrovac. These beatings continued even after visits by the ICRC to the detention centres concerned.[20]

Torture methods

An example of the young Bosnian soldier tortured by his Serb captors, is given by the UNHCR. They state: 'The victim's left arm was chopped off by a machete, his right arm slashed with a knife, a right eye pierced by a nail and a bullet smashed into his skull.'[21]

Rape

The war in Bosnia-Herzegovina has been characterized by extensive incidences of rape organized in a systematic manner and often condoned by local officials. Muslim women have suffered most from this crime and the most reliable estimate puts the number of Muslim women raped at 20,000.[22] Other estimates reach as high as 50,000. Clearly such figures are difficult to verify, but there can be little doubt that many thousands of women and girls have been raped. Mr Tadeusz Mazowiecki (the UN Special Raporteur) has well summarized the situation. He said: 'It is less important here to specify the exact number of victims as to stress the massive and criminal character of [these events].'[23] For many the psychological trauma that accompanies rape will stay with them for a life time.

Eviction

Throughout the war, homes and property have been destroyed to force people to leave; those forced to flee are subsequently more vulnerable to attack by opposition forces.

All the above abuses have been used to terrorize civilian populations and force them into leaving their homes. Incidents have been reported of forced eviction by compulsory transfer of property ownership rights or destruction of houses. This has been particularly prevalent in northern Bosnia in areas controlled by Bosnian Serb forces. However, there have also been incidents of forced population transfer between Croatian and Muslim communities. In some places, houses have been blown up or landmines laid to prevent the return of displaced persons to their previous homes. Those evicted from their homes face the prospect of living for many years as displaced persons or refugees. Those left behind are likely to face continued discrimination in social and economic life.

Made homeless

'Since Serb houses were being set on fire every night, we hid in the forests. They found us there and took us to Bosanski Brod, to a warehouse in the Bulek settlement which had been turned into a prison. Six of us girls were immediately separated from the other, older women. [We] were picked out by whoever wanted us.'[24]

Indiscriminate shelling and snipers

Another characteristic of the war has been the blatant and indiscriminate shelling of the civilian population in many Muslim towns. The shelling of Sarajevo and other towns, such as East Mostar, Gorazde, Zepa, Srebrenica, Bihac and Maglaj, are well known. In Sarajevo 300,000 people were trapped and subject to shelling and sniper fire for two years. In East Mostar 50,000 people have been trapped and little UN aid was able to be delivered. Another 300,000 people are living in the Bihac area. In total nearly 1 million Muslims have been trapped in besieged towns, subject to shelling, sniper fire, hunger and disease.

The effect of shelling and sniper fire on Muslim towns has been paralysing. The whole economy of the town ceases to function. People are unable to go to their work and have to stay indoors to avoid becoming targets. The shortage of fuel and damage inflicted on water pipes results in frequent stoppage of supplies of running water. Those who venture outside for water or food risk being killed.

Landmines

It has been estimated that 50,000 landmines are laid every week in former Yugoslavia.[25] Overall it is estimated that between 2 and 4 million landmines have been laid during the conflict.

Obstruction of humanitarian relief

Humanitarian relief has frequently been prevented from reaching besieged Muslim towns and other areas, principally as a means to facilitate the military defeat of the forces occupying these areas. This tactic has been used to hinder the delivery of aid to all the prominent besieged Muslim towns. In the Muslim enclave of Maglaj (also Tesanj), the UN High Commission on Refugees (UNHCR) unsuccessfully tried to send a convoy five times in five weeks. It was the first to do so in nine months. A similar situation existed in Srebrenica and the impasse was only broken when General Brigmont, the then UNPROFOR commander in Bosnia-Herzegovina, personally travelled to the town.

The Economy

The pre-conflict economy of Bosnia-Herzegovina consisted primarily of extractive industry (minerals, timber and hydroelectric power) and some manufacturing (both heavy and light industry), including a large armaments sector. Already affected by falling real wages as a knock-on effect of the Croatian war (discussed in detail in the Croatia section below), the Bosnian economy has been utterly devastated by the conflict. In the first eight months of 1991, exports from Bosnia-Herzegovina totalled $1027 million and imports $793 million, a trade surplus of $234 million. Because of the destruction of government administration, no figures exist after this date to illustrate the extent of the collapse. However, the effect can be understood when overall figures for ex-

Yugoslavia are examined.

In the first eight months of 1991 (during the Croatian war), industrial production in former Yugoslavia dropped by 18 per cent overall. Extractive and heavy manufacturing industry suffered most. In former Yugoslavia as a whole, coal processing fell 45.3 per cent, iron ore mining by 41.8 per cent, manufacture of leather goods by 37 per cent, and machine building by 36.3 per cent, in the first nine months of 1991.

Internal and export markets throughout former Yugoslavia have seized up. Trade has been severely restricted due to the blocking of transport routes, shelling of factories and markets, the cutting of supplies of inputs and energy and sanctions on Serbia and Montenegro.

The continuation of the conflict, political turmoil and lack of foreign currency, have dramatic implications for Bosnia-Herzegovina's foreign trading capabilities. Even if a political settlement to the conflict were implemented, the reconstruction of the economy and re-emergence of a viable export market will be a long-term project.

Arms trade

The one area of the Bosnian economy which has been flourishing during the conflict is that of the arms trade. The international arms embargo has forced the Bosnian

government to be largely self-sufficient in arming its troops. Whilst some illegal imports have been delivered to the Bosnian authorities (see below), for the most part the Bosnian army has been equipped with small arms manufactured within Bosnia-Herzegovina. Those illegal supplies which are delivered to Bosnia most probably originate from other Muslim countries or former Warsaw Pact countries, and are usually transported via either Slovenia or Croatia. For example, four helicopters were purchased by the Bosnian government from Ukraine with the deal financed by an unknown Arab state.[26] Iran also has supplied weapons and machinery to Bosnia.[27]

For strategic reasons, the military industry in former Yugoslavia was diversified and located throughout the country, with a large segment located in Bosnia-Herzegovina. Whilst many of these factories have been damaged or looted, many remain active. Individual factories are controlled by the Bosnian government, the Bosnian Serbs or the Bosnian Croats. Table 7.1 estimates the current state of the military industry in Bosnia-Herzegovina.

Infrastructure

Overall access for railway and road transport has been greatly reduced. Many

Table 7.1: Military industry in Bosnia-Herzegovina

Location	Product	Controlled by	War damages
Gorazde	ammunition	Bosnian govt	damaged
Koran	tank engines	Bosnian Serb	undamaged
Mostar	aeroplane/helicopter engines	BosnianCroat	machinery looted
Konjic	ammunition	Bosnian govt	not damaged
Hadzici	weapons/vehicle	Bosnian Serb	machinery looted
Travnik	weapons servicing	Bosnian govt	damaged
Novi Travnik	ammunition/grenades	Bosnian govt	damaged
Vitez	explosives	Bosnian Croatian	damaged, but operational
Banja Luka	vehicle servicing	Bosnian Serb	undamaged
Hrasnica	vehicle engines	Bosnian Serb	damaged, but operational
Vogosca	ammunition/grenades	Bosnian Serb	damaged, but operational
Sarajevo	infra-red sights	Bosnian govt	damaged, but operational

Source: Andelic, N, Radio Sarajevo, 1994

road and rail bridges have been destroyed, cutting off whole communities from the outside world.

Railways

At least seven railway bridges have been destroyed, cutting off Sarajevo from Ploce on the Adriatic coast, Zagreb and Belgrade. Mostar is cut off from both Sarajevo and Ploce. A small section of line operates near Zenica. It is estimated that the cost of restoring the railway network may exceed $150 million.[28] The historic Sarajevo tram system has been unable to operate and was only able to function in a very limited capacity from March/April 1994.

Roads

Road transportation is an extremely difficult and dangerous task in many parts of Bosnia-Herzegovina. Roads are often mined in conflict areas, and these mines have to be defused before traffic can pass. There is also danger of ambush from the various fighting forces.[29] The difficulties of road transportation are highlighted by the recent experience of a UNHCR refugee convoy from Sarajevo to Zagreb over the New Year. The journey from Sarajevo to Zagreb would have taken 5 hours before the war, but took the convoy 83 hours and 30 minutes.

Water and electricity supplies

Clean water and consistent power supplies are crucial to the health of all the besieged towns in Bosnia-Herzegovina. In Sarajevo, there are frequent breakdowns in the supply of running water, due to damage incurred through shelling or cuts in the electricity supply (which powers the water pumps). In Sarajevo there are only three main pump stations that still function and 30 per cent of the city's pumps are out of action due to shelling, lack of power or lack of spare parts. Moreover, it is estimated that 60 per cent of water volume in the system leaks due to damaged pipes.

A fight for water

In Sarajevo, when electricity supplies were cut, the water stopped flowing and the population was forced to use local wells or travel to a central distribution point at the Sarajevo brewery. Up to 70,000 people gathered each day to collect 2 litres of water each, some having walked 10 kilometres, exposing themselves to risk of injury from shells or sniper fire, to get there. These 2 litres compare with an average personal water consumption of 80 litres per person prior to the conflict. Between 20 June and 20 July 1993 no fuel was allowed into the city and the brewery wells could not function. Sarajevans could only use the Jahorina spring, which could provide 0.5 litres per person per day.[30]

Refugees

It is difficult to obtain accurate figures on refugees and displaced people from the conflict in former Yugoslavia. Indeed, in eastern Bosnia-Herzegovina, the UN agencies no longer distinguish between the displaced, refugee and local populations.

In Bosnia-Herzegovina, there is massive population displacement as a result of the war. Whole communities have been forced to flee their homes. This was particularly severe in northern Bosnia, and is exemplified by the Muslim population from the village of Bronzani Masjdan which, after persistent nocturnal violence, fled, en masse, to Banja Luka.[31]

The size of the problem can be measured from UNHCR calculations. They calculate there are 2.7 million beneficiaries from their work in Bosnia-Herzegovina out of a pre-war population of 4.3 million.[32] UNICEF estimate that of the 1,546,000 children who lived in Bosnia-Herzegovina prior to the war, 930,000 (60 per cent) have been displaced or become refugees.[33]

As at 31 May 1992, UNHCR estimated a total of 752,500 refugees and displaced people originated from within Bosnia-Herzegovina, of whom 482,000 were located outside the territory. More recent estimates put the number of refugees from the former Yugoslavia within the EU at 509,714, and at 750,000 in all of Europe excluding former Yugoslavia (May, 1994). The composition of those displaced throughout the former Yugoslavia is shown in Figure 7.2.

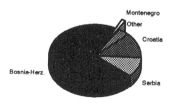

Source: UNHCR Information Notes on former Yugoslavia, May 1994

Figure 7.2: Refugees and displaced persons within former Yugoslavia

Such is the scale of the migration problem that it is unlikely that most of those displaced will be able to return to their previous homes in the medium to longterm. Moreover, the nature of the displacement that has occurred, due to the implementation of the 'ethnic cleansing' policy, has left a legacy of bitterness and hatred among former friends and neighbours. It may well prove difficult for those who do return to their previous homes to live peacefully with individuals who either participated in or permitted murder, rape, torture and detention of those returning, their family and/or friends.

Added to the already confused situation regarding displaced persons is the threat of more disruption if, and when, a political settlement of the war in Bosnia-Herzegovina is finally agreed. If the Bosnian Serb forces withdraw from territory which they hold at present, there will almost certainly be an exodus of remaining Serb civilians from these areas.

There are estimated to be approximately 240,000 refugees from Bosnia-Herzegovina in Croatia and over 450,000 in Serbia. Thousands of others have fled to

Montenegro, Macedonia, Slovenia, Austria, Germany, Hungary and Italy. As at 31 May 1992, UNHCR estimated a total of 752,500 refugees and displaced people originated from within Bosnia-Herze-govina, of which 482,500 were located outside the territory. More recent estimates put the number of refugees from ex-Yugoslavia within the EU at 509,714 and over 1 million in all of Europe.[34]

There is considerable doubt about the long-term viability of the Muslim enclaves in eastern Bosnia (Gorazde, Zepa and Srebrenica), cut off both physically and economically from other territory controlled by the mainly Muslim Bosnian government and dependent upon the goodwill of the surrounding Serb forces and civilians.[35] It is likely, given the opportunity of freedom to travel unhindered, that many of those trapped in these enclaves will seek to leave. In addition, there are still 30,000 Muslims in northern Bosnia living in areas under Bosnian Serb administrative and military control. There are also estimated to be 300,000 people trapped in the Muslim Bihac enclave adjoining the border with Croatia. Many in these areas may also seek to leave once freedom of movement is attained.

Conclusion

The war in Bosnia-Herzegovina exemplifies the tragic consequences of ethnic conflict. In seeking to promote its own perceived self-interest, to the detriment of the collective good, each ethnic group has incurred substantial costs. Failure by the warring parties to agree a settlement is likely to lead to increased pressure for the withdrawal of UN troops and the lifting of the arms embargo on the Bosnian government. Sadly it is the civilian population of Bosnia-Herzegovina who will suffer most in this scenario.

SERBIA AND MONTENEGRO

THE COSTS

Introduction

Despite Serbia's role as the chief perp-etrator of the conflict, it has suffered immensely as a result of the conflict. Not only has its pre-war economy essentially ceased to exist, its relatively advanced welfare state has all but disappeared as a result of the channelling of resources into the war effort, and the economic sanctions. The costs to Serbia and Montenegro of the conflict fall into four broad categories; economic, refugee accommodation, development and political.

Development

The health and education systems of both Serbia and Montenegro have been placed under severe pressure in seeking to accommodate refugees from the conflict.[36] This has been aggravated by the sanctions regime imposed in May 1991, which has restricted the import of basic medical and educational materials. This is in spite of the fact that medicines and pharmaceutical raw materials are specifically exempted from the sanctions regime on approval from the Sanctions Committee of the UN.

Health

The WHO have attributed the decline of this extensive health care system in Serbia and Montenegro to three factors. Firstly, there is the collapse of the second world trading system, due to the fall of Communism. Secondly, the war has prevented inter-Yugoslav trade. Finally, there is the blow of sanctions enforcement. As a result, whereas prior to the conflict Serbia and Montenegro spent 4.5 per cent of GNP on healthcare, now 15 per cent of GNP is being spent.[37] Despite this, overall health care expenditure in Serbia and Montenegro

has fallen.

The effect of the sanctions regime has been to curtail the import of drugs and raw materials into Serbia and Montenegro. Although these goods can be imported under the sanctions regime, approval must first be obtained from the Sanctions Committee. Even if such permission is obtained, little hard currency is available to be spent on such 'luxury items'. Foreign banks have proved unwilling to make funds available for the purchase of medicines and other health care inputs. Even if money were made available for such uses, there is no guarantee that it would be spent appropriately. Foreign suppliers of spare parts and medical inputs are also unwilling to be associated with the Serb regime and hence will not sell to them. Consequently, although Serbia has two pharmaceutical factories which were able to meet 80 to 90 per cent of the former Yugoslav market for drugs, there is a desperate shortage of basic drugs and routine vaccines.[38]

Education

The education system in Serbia has come under severe pressure as a result of UN sanctions. There is now a crucial lack of basic educational materials. Textbooks, pencils, chalk and notebooks are all in short supply. At the same time, there has been an influx of refugee children escaping from Bosnia and Croatia. It is estimated that there are 55,203 refugee children between the ages of 7 and 14 accommodated in Serb schools.[39] Both local and refugee parents cannot afford to purchase basic educational items at their high price on the black market. As school budgets have decreased, there is now only money available for paying staff salaries and some building maintenance.

Civil and Political Rights

Freedom of expression, restriction of information and government propaganda

The political system in Serbia is nominally

democratic.[40] One political cost of the conflict has been the delay (or suspension) of transition to a real and functioning liberal democratic system of government in Serbia. Judicial connivance in suppression of opposition groups, media subservience to the regime's wishes, persecution of ethnic minorities and participation of officials in semi-legal financial and trading activities are all commonplace under the current regime.

The Serb government has imposed strict controls on the media, severely restricting freedom of expression, composed of 'freedom to seek, receive and impart information and ideas of all kinds'.[41] On assuming power, Milosevic targeted *Politika* (Serbia's largest circulating independent newspaper) and Radio Television Belgrade, ordering a thorough purge of both organizations, including the dismissal of many independent reporters. In passing the Radio and Television Act, 31 July 1991, the government secured the legal basis for full control of the media.[42] Yutel, the federal Yugoslav television service which managed to maintain a degree of objectivity, was ultimately denied a licence to broadcast. In addition to such 'legal' controls of the media, there have also been incidences of harassment and direct attacks on those working in the media, along with sabotage of premises and equipment.[43]

Kosovo

The Albanian population in Kosovo has been subjected to discrimination and violation of civil and political rights by the Serb authorities. This has included arbitrary detention, torture and ill-treatment while in detention, eviction, harassment and dismissal from employment on the basis of ethnic affiliation. In 1993, 13,431 cases of Serbian police violence against Albanians were reported. Over 2000 Albanians were arrested, 1994 families searched, 1777 people subjected to physical torture and 849 people taken to police stations for 'informative talks'. There were also 604 reported cases of violence against political activists, 53 families violently evicted and 50 Albanians forcibly conscripted by the Serbian army.[44]

The Economy

For Serbia and Montenegro, the economic costs of the conflict are threefold. Firstly, there are the direct costs of wars in both Bosnia-Herzegovina and Croatia, in terms of armaments production and the replacement of military equipment destroyed, though it is difficult to obtain figures on this. Added to this are the costs of maintaining, supplying and paying a large army in the field.[45] There are also the costs of additional medical treatment for war casualties.[46] Secondly, there are the costs of lost trade due to the disintegration of former Yugoslav markets and the disruption or cessation of supplies of industrial inputs from traditional suppliers in other republics of former Yugoslavia. Thirdly, there are the costs of lost international trade and investment due to the imposition of UN sanctions. As mentioned earlier, the loss of trade due to the sanctions regime also has knock-on effects for health care and education facilities, which in turn is likely to have a longer-term impact on economic development.

Lost inter-republic trade

Considerable reductions in intra-Yugoslav trade and sharp falls in GDP preceded the conflict. Indeed, prior to the conflict, increased ethnic tension had included the imposition of new tariffs by Serbia on goods from Croatia and Slovenia. Added to these, the violent breakup of former Yugoslavia has caused the formal internal market almost completely to cease to operate. The reduction of trade between the republics has caused many enterprises to cut their output, due to lack of inputs or markets, and in some cases close.

The combined GDP of Serbia and Montenegro fell (in comparison to the previous year) by 8.4 per cent in 1990, 11 per cent in 1991, 27 per cent in 1992 and 35 per

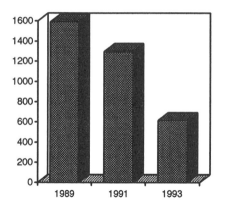

Source: EIU Reports, Country Profile: *Serbia-Montenegro 1993–94*

Figure 7.3: GDP – Serbia-Montenegro (YuD bn)

cent in 1993 (Figure 7.3).[47] Overall GDP for Serbia and Montenegro declined from YuD1592.8 billion in 1989 to YuD 1298.1 billion (at 1972 prices) in 1991.[48] It can therefore be estimated to have fallen to approximately YuD615.9 billion (at 1972 prices) by the end of 1993, an overall decline of over 60 per cent. Other estimates put Serbia's economy operating at 20 per cent capacity.[49]

Up to 600,000 individuals are now unemployed and a further 2,000,000 (60 per cent of the labour force) have been laid off on a temporary basis. Real wages in 1994 have dropped to a staggering US$6.46 per month and pensions worth US$1.29 monthly.[50]

It is likely that, even if a peace settlement is reached, it will take a long time to restore the internal market of former Yugoslavia as it existed prior to 1989. Indeed, some former Yugoslav republics, such as Slovenia and Croatia, may have little interest in the restoration of this lost market. Rather, Slovenia and Croatia are likely to seek to associate themselves with the single European market of the expanding EU.

UN sanctions

The imposition of UN sanctions on Serbia-Montenegro on 30 May 1991 had a devastating impact on the economy. It is claimed by the Serb authorities that the total cost of UN sanctions to the economy has come to some $20 billion.[51] The Serb regime has substantially financed the war by printing money. Hyperinflation has rocketed, reaching an estimated 1 million per cent in December 1993.[52] Another estimate puts hyperinflation at 310 million per cent per month at the end of April 1994.[53] Clearly such figures can only be the roughest of estimates, but they do reveal that normal financial transactions had become impossible.

Legal trade has become severely restricted due to the sanctions regime. A UNICEF report suggest that even trade which is allowed, such as medicines, under the provisions of the UN sanctions, has not been forthcoming due to shortages in foreign currency.[54]

As in many former centrally planned economies, there is a large informal sector which operates in conjunction with a formal sector made up of large state-owned industrial enterprises. Consequently, considerable sanctions busting has occurred and a sizeable 'black market' operation in illegally imported goods and foreign currency has developed.[55] There has almost certainly been official connivance, and quite possibly particip-ation, in this trade. It is also likely that any foreign currency available to the govern-ment is used for the purchase of high priority items of military importance, such as oil, rather than routine medicines

From 17 January 1994, a new stabiliz-ation programme was introduced by the federal Yugoslav authorities on the recommendation of a team of 70 local experts headed by Dragoslav Avramovic (a former employee of the World Bank), the Governor of the Yugoslav National Bank. This was necessary due to the effects of hyperinflation. The stabilization policy introduced in January 1994 is based on the introduction of a new gold dinar with circulation limited to 150 million. Each of the new dinars will be fixed at a value of DM1 (US$1.54). The Yugoslav authorities hope thus to eliminate hyperinflation and great claims have been made in this respect.[56] However, many economists seriously doubt the sustainability of this apparent recovery in the Yugoslav economy.[57] There is a real danger of hidden inflation expressing itself through shortages, as was common in the former second world under communism. Furthermore, the business community have taken out credits from the central authorities, but it is unlikely that they will be able to repay these debts as inflation is likely to outpace any return on investments made.[58]

However, despite the likelihood of a continuing decline in the Yugoslav economy, it is still well capable of sustaining the political and military priorities of the regime. As long as the Serb war economy is able to provide enough food to feed the army and population, the military equipment required and smuggled oil supplies to power the army, the war can continue to be fought.[59] The UN sanctions monitors, having no power to seize smuggled goods, are of limited value and mainly of use for information-gathering purposes. The willingness of the authorities in neighbouring countries to turn a blind eye to sanctions breaking, fuels the Serb war effort and crucially undermines the credibility of the UN. Ultimately it may prove impossible to effectively enforce the sanctions regime.

Disruption of trade

With the outbreak of war there has been damage to transport infrastructure (eg bridges destroyed), routine mining of transport routes, telecommunications systems made inoperable and numerous road blocks erected which are often controlled by irregular, drunk and poorly disciplined troops. All these have contributed to the almost total breakdown of the internal former Yugoslav market.

Yugoslav exports to the developing world have also suffered. The defence industry was a major export earner. It is estimated that former Yugoslavia exported military equipment to a value of $12 billion from 1981 and 1991.[60] The majority of these sales were to the former Soviet Union, but

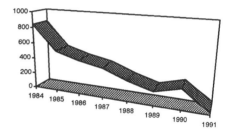

Source: US Arms Control and Defence Agency, (ACDA) World Military Expenditures and Arms Transfers, Washington DC, 1992

Figure 7.4: Arms exports – Yugoslavia (US$m)

some were also to developing countries. The contraction of former Yugoslavia in the international arms market has encouraged others (eg China) to step in and fill the gap.

Refugees

Estimates of the number of refugees in Serbia vary, but average around 500,000.[61] The majority of these refugees are of Bosnian Serb or Croatian Serb origin. There are also some Muslim and Croatian refugees in Serbia, in addition to 65,000 refugees in Montenegro of which about 40 per cent are of Muslim origin.[62]

There have been allegations that the Serb authorities have actively sought to hinder Serbs from Bosnia and Croatia from obtaining refugee status. The authorities have claimed that the areas controlled by Serb forces in Bosnia and Croatia are safe and that there is therefore no need for the population to leave. This seems to be an attempt by the Serb government to encourage Bosnian and Croatian Serbs to stay at home and fight with Serb forces. Furthermore, there are also reports of refugee men of military age being forcibly conscripted into Serb forces fighting in Bosnia.[63]

THE BENEFITS

Strategic Benefits

The principal benefit to Serbia of the

171

conflict in former Yugoslavia is that, at the time of writing, President Milosevic's desire for a greater Serbia has been all but realized. Serbia has helped to secure the Serb autonomous region in Croatia, Krajina. Indeed, the establishment of a UN protective force around Krajina has made it more likely that it will become a de facto Serb territorial gain.

In Bosnia-Herzegovina, the Bosnian Serbs, supported by Belgrade, have captured large swathes in the east and north of the country, extinguishing any notion of an independent Bosnia.

Furthermore, Milosevic's objectives have obtained popular support by him playing to the historical Serb sense of grievance that they have been discriminated against over centuries. In essence, at the current time, war seems to have awarded the aggressor.

Wider afield in the Balkans, the conflict has effectively silenced Albanian demands for independence in the region of Kosovo. With the threat of genocide and violence, the Albanian population are having to accept that the price of independence is very high.

One political benefit to the ruling clique is the delay (or suspension) of transition to a real and functioning liberal democratic system of government. The necessities of war have been used as an excuse by Milosevic and his clique to pervert democracy by manipulating the political system to oust opponents from positions of authority, and suppress political opposition by police repression. Milosevic has eradicated most criticism of the war so that even the political opposition must adopt a Serb nationalist stance. In doing so Milosevic has cemented his own political supremacy as the only person who can save Serbia from its enemies.

There have also been personal benefits to the Serb elite as a result of the conflict. The Serb government itself looted the gold stocks of the former Yugoslav central bank. Many officials have participated in both the formal and informal sectors of the economy to enrich themselves from semi-legal and illegal activities. Some of this personal wealth was being invested in property abroad during 1993 despite UN sanctions. Vast profits have also been made through smuggling to break UN sanctions

CONCLUSION

At the time of writing, Serbia can be seen to have benefited significantly from the conflict. Indeed, Milosevic's objectives of a greater Serbia have been realized. However, in achieving this, Serbia has paid a heavy price, politically and economically. It has become one of a handful of internationally recognized pariah states. Unfortunately the political legitimacy of the Serb regime is closely tied in to the pursuit of nationalist goals and it is, therefore, unlikely that the Serb regime will give up its nationalist ambitions. While it may be possible that a peace agreement can be reached in Bosnia-Herzegovina, this will not resolve the problems of minorities within Serbia itself. Nor would such a settlement eliminate tensions between Serbia and neighbouring states. The UN (and G7) would then be faced with the prospect of having to lift the sanctions regime against Serbia and Montenegro without having effectively resolved the crisis. A future outbreak of renewed hostilities would thus be a real possibility.

CROATIA

THE COSTS

Introduction

The 1991 Croatian/Serb war was triggered by Croatian secession from former Yugoslavia on 25 June 1991. Although nationalist Serbs had previously, on 1 April 1991, declared an autonomous Serb republic of Krajina it was the declaration of Croatian independence which provided the excuse the Serbs needed: they claimed they feared discrimination by the Croatian authorities. Croatia has played a dual role in the conflict in former Yugoslavia. This role has been both that of a combatant in the

Croatian/Serb war of 1991/92 and that of an active supporter of one side in the war in Bosnia-Herzegovina which started in mid-1992. While this section focuses both on the earlier conflict between Croatian government forces and an assortment of Serb forces comprising local Serbs living in Croatia and units of the Yugoslav National Army (JNA), and the war in Bosnia-Herzegovina, the majority of the consequences of these conflicts stem from the former. This analysis treats Croatia as both a target country and an active neighbour.

The role of Croatia in the war in Bosnia-Herzegovina has been that of supporter of the Bosnian Croatian army. Although officially not involved in this war, the Croatian government has been the chief supplier of weapons and other supplies to the Bosnian Croatian forces. Furthermore, there are allegations that elements of the Croatian army have on occasions fought in Bosnia-Herzegovina.

Development

Health

As in Bosnia-Herzegovina and Serbia, a major strain has been placed on the health facilities in conflict areas, due to high numbers of military and civilian war casualties and the destruction of hospitals and shortages of equipment.

Most primary health needs of the population in Croatia have been met due to the combined efforts of the Croatian government, UN agencies, bilateral assistance and NGOs. There have, however, been some gaps in routine immunization programmes due to the curtailment of supplies of vaccinations from factories situated in Serbia. There are also reports of malnourishment among children and unhygienic, overcrowded conditions in refugee camps. These pose the risk of mass deaths among the malnourished due to epidemics of treatable diseases.[64]

Education

The education system has come under pressure in coping with children displaced from both within Croatia and from Bosnia-Herzegovina. It is estimated that 14,500 displaced and 21,000 refugee children attend schools in Croatia.[65] Additionally, it is estimated that 120 schools were destroyed during the Croatian/Serb conflict of 1991.[66] Schools are commonly overcrowded with the need either to share resources and/or to run extra lessons. In conflict areas, schools have been ethnically divided, with the danger of cementing ignorance and ethnic tension for the next generation.

Civil and Political Rights

UN Protected Areas (UNPAs) have been established in western Slavonia, eastern Slavonia and Krajina. Yet, UNPAs are predominantly areas in which Croatian Serbs have de facto control and policies of 'ethnic cleansing' against Croats have been carried out by Serbs in these areas. Atrocities include executions, 'disappearances', harassment and intimidation, and the destruction of property including homes and churches.[67]

A minimum estimate of the number of casualties in this war is 7693 people killed (of which 1200 were military personnel), 23,167 wounded (of which 6786 were civilians) and 13,153 missing.[68] However, the real casualty count is likely to be higher.

Croatian civilians have been victims of atrocities committed by Serb forces. A mass grave discovered outside Vukovar, for example, contained the bodies of hundreds of Croatian men, women and children murdered by Serb soldiers.

As Croatian soldiers retreated from Vukovar on 15 and 16 November 1991, it is alleged that they dragged Serb civilians from their cellars and massacred them. In Gospic, between 16 and 18 October, 1991, 24 Serb civilians were slaughtered by Croatian troops. Another 500 have disappeared.[69]

Loss of homes

Thousands of Croats, who have been forced to flee from their homes by the advancing Serb troops, face little prospect of ever reclaiming their property. Entire villages have been evacuated, and Serb civilians have been moved in.

Shelling of urban areas

Indiscriminate shelling of civilians has been a hallmark of Serb military strategy throughout the conflict in former Yugoslavia. This tactic was first adopted during the 1991 war in Croatia. The most ruthless besieging of population centres occurred in eastern Croatia (eg Vukovar and Osijek), but for Western television audiences it was the shelling of the historic town of Dubrovnik which was most striking. This beautiful and ancient port city had been a medieval trading centre and popular Western tourist resort. Its architectural monuments date from the 15th and 16th centuries. Its reputation as a cultural centre (due to its many paintings, sculptures, applied art and documents) attracted many foreign tourists prior to the conflict. Consequently it was easier for the Western public to identify with the agony of the city and her suffering population. After the bombardment, this popular tourist destination (with hotels, bars, cafes, museums, libraries, hospitals and schools) was transformed. Dubrovnik was attacked three times in the autumn of 1991. In the process it is estimated that US$2 billion of damage was incurred, which included the destruction of 75 per cent of industrial facilities, 40 per cent of shops, 60 per cent of hotels and 2,500 family homes.[70]

Finally, it is estimated that there may be up to 2 million explosive devices in civilian areas within Croatia.[71] Many of these are extremely difficult to detect, and can lie active for decades.

The Economy

Croatia was one of the most economically developed republics of former Yugoslavia and has experienced serious economic decline as a result of conflict. This is due to war damage to industrial infrastructure, the conflict-related decline in domestic and foreign trade and the high cost of the war

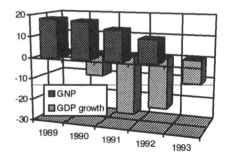

Source: EIU, Country Report: *Croatia*, 1993–94

Figure 7.5: GNP ($USbn) and GDP growth (%) – Croatia

effort. Figure 7.5 shows economic decline in Croatia since 1989.[72]

Most noticeable is the massive decline of approximately 50 per cent in Croatian GNP, since 1989. Although the GNP decline started prior to the conflict, it has accelerated from 1991. One estimate suggests that industrial production fell by 23.7 per cent in the first nine months of the Croatian/Serb war of 1991.[73] In the same period, real investment fell by 33 per cent and retail trade by 10 per cent.[74] Croatia was severely affected by macroeconomic instability throughout 1991 and 1992. The Croatian dinar fell from an average in 1992 of 257 to the US dollar to 3053 at the end of June 1993.[75] Real wages fell at least 66 per cent between 1989 and 1992.[76] Hyperinflation has been present both prior to and throughout the conflict, with retail prices increasing 610 per cent in 1990, 123 per cent in 1991, 664 per cent in 1992 and 1,207 per cent between January and March 1993 (Figure 7.6).[77] Those in employment fell sharply in 1991–92 with unemployment reaching a peak of 284,000 in 1991.[78]

Industry

Industry has suffered most as a result of the war. Croatia's shipbuilding industry has been unable to complete a number of orders due to shortages of raw materials. Indust-

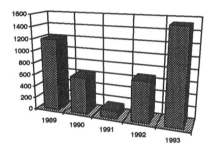

Source: EIU, Country Profile: *Croatia*, 1993–94

Figure 7.6: Inflation – Croatia

rial enterprises destroyed by the Serb assault include a radio and television factory in Slunj, a dairy and some textile factories in Duga Resa (near Karlovac), mineral water complexes in Lipik and Jamnica, and textile and car component factories in the Vukovar area. In other instances, the ethnic division of the country has restricted industrial activity, as exemplified by the sugar factory near Osijek which is under Croatian control, whilst the fields which supplied the sugar beet are under Serb control. Power failures have also affected industrial activity and many factories in non-conflict areas have been unable to function at their full capacity as a result.[79]

These problems are exacerbated by government manipulation of and interference in the financial sector. Tax laws are regularly altered and prudent banking practice is flouted to obtain foreign currency to finance the continuation of the conflict. In addition, currencies are frequently devalued and, as a short-term measure to control hyperinflation, even replaced.

Agriculture

Agriculture made up 10 per cent of Croatia's GDP prior to the conflict. The loss of farmland in eastern Croatia (Slavonia) has reduced the output of raw materials used in the textile industry.[80] Additionally, sniper fire and large-scale use of landmines severely restricted the opportunities for farmers in conflict areas to work their land.

The presence of these unexploded devices will ensure that farming is a dangerous business in some areas for years to come.

Tourism

Official figures of direct earnings from tourism prior to the conflict were US$2 billion per year. Indirect earnings from tourism, prior to the conflict, are estimated at US$5 billion.[81] Other estimates put lost direct income from tourism at about US$1 billion and indirect earnings at US$5 billion.[82] It is estimated that direct earnings from tourism were US$300 million in 1991, US$550 million in 1992 and nearly US$800 million in 1993 (Figure 7.7).[83]

Added to losses from falls in the numbers of tourists visiting Croatia has been widespread damage and destruction of tourist infrastructure. Many hotels in prime tourist destinations have been shelled, burnt or vandalized. This is particularly so of the area around Dubrovnik and in the Plitvice Lakes national park.[84] All these will have to be repaired before Croatia's tourist industry will be able to return to preconflict levels. Environmental damage may affect eco-tourism in the long-term.

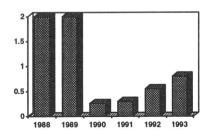

Source: EIU Reports, op cit; IUCN 1991

Figure 7.7: Tourism receipts (US$bn) – Croatia

Foreign trade and investment

Falls in industrial output reduced Croatia's capacity to earn foreign exchange through export of manufactured goods. With less hard currency available there was a sharp fall in foreign trade in 1991. Imports decreased from US$5.2 billion in 1990 to

US$3.8 billion in 1991.[85] Foreign direct investment (FDI) has also dried up and in the first six months of 1993 was only US$94.6 million, of which 43.3 per cent was of German origin.[86] The Croatian economy experienced a sharp fall in foreign trade in 1991 as a result of the war.

Infrastructure

Damage incurred to infrastructure as a result of the 1991 war has been severe and is estimated to be at 20 per cent overall.[87] This includes 12 per cent of the housing stock, including 27,000 houses and 210,000 flats.[88] There is now a need to replace these and also to build extra accommodation for refugees from Bosnia-Herzegovina. Cultural monuments were targeted in an attempt to eliminate the national identity of displaced populations. Of the 801 cultural monuments destroyed or damaged, 468 were churches and 42 convents.[89]

Both the railway system and road network were heavily damaged.[90] Up to 6500 kilometres of roads were made unusable with 33 bridges destroyed and another 24 damaged. This included the Maslenica bridge, which linked southern Dalmatia with the rest of Croatia. Although replaced by a pontoon bridge, road traffic is still diverted to, and restricted by, the capacity of a ferry service located further north. The motorway from Zagreb to Belgrade has become impassable, with a massive knock-on economic cost for industry and transit traffic. It is estimated that 30 per cent of the railway network is out of operation including 18 railway bridges and 66 railway stations.[91] Zadar, Dubrovnik and Osijek airports were heavily damaged due to shelling, as have been the port of Sibenik and a number of smaller ports.[92]

Other damage to infrastructure has included the shutting of electrical power plants, destruction of hospitals and health centres, closure of and damage to educational institutions, attacks on and vandalism of tourist hotels, the destruction of the Peruca dam and the shutdown of the oil pipeline to Central Europe. Overall, it is estimated (by the Croatian government) that the total cost of damage to infrastructure incurred as a result of the 1991 war reaches US$23 billion.[93]

The Environment

In the course of the war, both environmental and cultural damage has occurred. These have been mainly concentrated in the conflict areas and have included both the wanton destruction of plant and animal life in national parks and shelling of historic urban centres.

Documented evidence shows that damage has been inflicted upon Plitvice Lakes national park which is located in Croatia and classified a World Heritage Site. Due to military and paramilitary activity in the region, park staff were evicted from the park. Both Croatian government forces and elements of the Yugoslav National Army moved into the park with about 30–50 tanks present. In the course of the military occupation trees were felled and it is also alleged that bears have been shot for sport.[94] In addition, 2500 hectares of forest were burnt down in Krka national park.[95]

Other parks and bird sanctuaries have been caught up in military exchanges involving heavy artillery. The 500-year-old Arboretum in Trsteno, near Dubrovnik, was burnt down after being targeted by incendiary shells from tanks and artillery.[96] The bombing of the Sisak oil refinery and a waste water reservoir released over 100 tonnes of oil and waste water into the Sava river.[97]

Refugees

After the Croatian/Serb war of 1991, 30 per cent of the territory of Croatia was under Serb control, as a result of which a large number of Croats have been displaced. In June 1993, there were still 254,413 displaced persons within Croatia as a result of this war.[98] Many of these people have had their homes destroyed (often deliberately) and are unable to return to their home areas. Croatia has also been one of the major recipients of refugees fleeing the conflict in Bosnia-Herzegovina. It is estimated that approximately 240,000 refugees from Bosnia-Herzegovina have fled to Croatia.[99] These people, together with the displaced from the earlier Croatian/Serb war, place a heavy burden upon Croatian government expenditure. Altogether, refugees and displaced people make up one-sixth of the Croatian population.[100]

From 13 July 1992, the Croatian government has refused to register any more refugees. This means that more recent arrivals are not entitled to aid from the Croatian government, and must rely on NGOs or seek illegal work. Moreover, there has been lost income due to the displacement of people from their home areas and traditional (mainly agricultural) employment.

THE BENEFITS

Strategic Considerations

Although independence was claimed before the war erupted, the principal benefit to Croatia of the conflict in former Yugoslavia has been the creation of the opporuntity to establish Croatian independence.

Political benefits

The adoption of an aggressive nationalism by the Croatian authorities was used as a means to secure the political legitimacy of the republican authorities at the expense of the multi-ethnic Federal regime.

Strategic benefits

The conflict in Bosnia-Herzegovina has also acted as a diversion of Serb aggression away from Croatia itself. The Serb/ Croatian war of 1991 has been frozen rather than resolved. The war in Bosnia-Herzegovina has occupied the full resources of the Serb strategists, giving them little time to reignite the war in Croatia. This has provided the Croatian

government with a 'breathing space' to rebuild the military sector. The incorporation within Croatia of Bosnian Croatian areas within Bosnia-Herzegovina would also provide an added territorial buffer against Serb aggression.

Presented with the opportunity to expand Croatian territory into Bosnia with the Serbian invasion of Bosnia-Herzegovina, a major war objective of the Croatian government has been the creation of a 'greater Croatia' to include Croats living in Bosnia-Herzegovina. As such, the Croatian government has encouraged and supported the Bosnian Croatian political and military leadership in their drive for an autonomous Bosnian Croatian region (which could be later incorporated into Croatia). Indeed, in May 1991, the Croatian and Serbia presidents went as far as to agree a division of Bosnia-Herzegovina between their two states.

The Economy

Croatia was one of the most economically developed republics within former Yugoslavia. Croatia's secession from former Yugoslavia has enabled the Croatian economy to break its previous links with more economically underdeveloped republics and to begin to reorientate towards trade with the expanding EU and other growing central European economies. The precedent for this course of action was set by Slovenia, which had most to gain by seceding from former Yugoslavia.

The reorientation of trade and improvements in the economies of both Slovenia and Croatia in 1993 have resulted in increases in German and Italian exports to these countries. In addition loans have been made to Slovenia and Croatia by the World Bank and the EBRD. To date US$100 million has been lent to Croatia to repair war damaged power lines, transport equipment and air navigation systems. There are also plans for a US$50 million loan to aid in a highway reconstruction project.[101] Although small when compared to the task at hand, they mark a start down the path of economic recovery.

CONCLUSION

For Croatia, the conflict has entailed substantial costs both in terms of direct war damage and indirect spillover costs from the war in Bosnia-Herzegovina. These have included loss of human life, the ethnic division of the country, loss of 30 per cent of the pre-war republic's territory, the costs of accommodating half a million refugees and displaced persons, destruction of environmental and cultural sites, damage to transport and power infrastructure, declines in agricultural, industrial and macroeconomic instability. Croatia has paid a high price for its independence and its support of the Bosnian Croats.

THE EUROPEAN UNION

THE COSTS

Introduction

The conflict in the former Yugoslavia was initially considered to be a European problem; negotiations for a political settlement were conducted through European Union (EU) mechanisms. Member states of the EU have exerted considerable diplomatic pressure to resolve the conflict and have also provided considerable support to UNPROFOR.

The costs of the conflict in the former Yugoslavia to the EU are both direct and indirect in nature and can be divided into two distinct categories. Firstly, there are economic and other intervention costs which are incurred at both a supranational and national level. This category can be subdivided into public sector costs and private sector costs. Secondly, there are strategic costs which are mostly incurred at the supranational level. These include the direct effects of political turmoil in the former Yugoslavia on the EU, the precedents set by the conflict there for settling ethnic disputes both in the Balkans and elsewhere, and the wider geopolitical implications for the progress of European integration and the formation of common defence, security and economic policy.

Human Costs

UNPROFOR has been repeatedly subjected to direct attack while escorting aid convoys. Since the deployment of UNPROFOR, 90 soldiers have been killed, and over 900 injured during operations in the former Yugoslavia.[102] Eleven UNHCR staff or staff associated with UNHCR's operations have also been killed in war-related incidents.[103] France has lost 20 personnel during the conflict in the former Yugoslavia and over 300 French soldiers have been injured.[104] There have been 7 casualties among UK military personnel on UN peacekeeping duties, 1 civilian Overseas Development Agency (ODA) driver, 1 NGO relief worker and a number of British mercenaries.

Economic Costs

Humanitarian intervention

The EU has taken a leading role in providing assistance to humanitarian operations in the former Yugoslavia. This has taken the form of: direct aid through the European Commission Humanitarian Office (ECHO) and EC Task Force (ECTF); assisting in projects in co-ordination with the Croatian govern-ment; financial aid to NGO operations in the former Yugoslavia; and direct contrib-utions to the UNHCR. The EU, as of 13 December 1993, had contributed ECU700 million ($588 million) in humanitarian aid for those adversely affected by the conflict in the former Yugoslavia.[105]

In October 1993, the European Commission approved $85 million, as part of a package of ECU89 million drawn on the reserve for emergency humanitarian aid.[106] This was used to maintain existing EU initiatives, support new appeals for aid projects and prioritize the distribution of essential items such as food, medicines, sanitation, clothes and shelter. The ECTF established operations in Zagreb in 1992 to provide assistance, including direct food aid to the refugees and displaced persons residing in Croatia. At the end of 1993, the ECTF was distributing 5200 tonnes of food products a month, in a programme supported by numerous NGOs financed by the Community. Financial assistance was also provided for the refugee reception structures set up by the Croatian government.[107]

In December 1993, the European Commission decided to allocate a further ECU86 million (US$100 million) in aid to assist the estimated 4.2 million people at risk as a result of the conflict.[108] This aid was prioritized throughout the winter months to cover costs of direct food aid, fuel and clothes and was distributed according to the severity of need in each of the former republics (Figure 7.8).

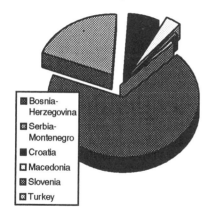

Source: European Commission, `New humanitarian aid for victims of conflict in the former Yugoslavia: Winter programme', IP/93/1118, 13 December 1993

Figure 7.8: Geographic distribution of aid (%)

In addition to the ECU700 million (US$588 million) contributed by the EC until the end of 1993, a further ECU48.3 million ($41 million) was approved by the European Council to finance aid convoy requirements in Bosnia-Herzegovina (until 31 March 1994).[109] The Commission has also approved a donation of ECU275 million ($231 million) to the mobile hospital in Banja Luka, which was initially opened with a grant of ECU2 million ($1.7 million) from the ECHO in July 1993.[110]

The EU has also contributed financial assistance, military personnel and equipment to the UNPROFOR. The total UN costs for UNPROFOR, including operations in Bosnia-Herzegovina, Croatia and Macedonia, amounted to $250 million in 1992 and $1 billion in 1993.[111] EU countries collectively account for 33 per cent of UNPROFOR costs according to UN assessments.[112] The EU has contributed $158 million towards the UNHCR programme to provide assistance to those affected by the conflict.[113]

In March 1994, the number of troops serving with UNPROFOR was 31,425, of which 15,733 were stationed in Bosnia.

Table 7.2: EU troop commitments to UNPROFOR, March 1994

Country	Number
France	6803
UK	3109
Denmark	1290
Spain	1189
Netherlands	1055

Source: *Jane's Defence Weekly*, 'Paratroopers bolster Russian units in Bosnia', Volume 21, No 14, 9 April 1994.

Germany has no troops serving in the former Yugoslavia, but has donated equipment including 140 anti-personnel carriers.

Country case study: UK

The total UK humanitarian aid to former Yugoslavia had reached over £173 million ($259.5 million) by 31 March 1994. The ODA has instituted a large direct aid operation in former Yugoslavia. The financial cost of this operation as at 31 March 1994 had totalled £94 million ($141 million). Over £79 million ($118.5 million) has been donated through EU aid.[114] The ODA operation has constituted primarily food convoys and medical aid. By September 1993, there had been over 900 convoys, which had delivered over 72,000 tonnes of supplies. It has included 58 British trucks, land rovers, civilian drivers and support staff.[115] In addition, approximately £600,000 ($900,000) has been donated to the US Air Force airdrop operation.

The total financial cost to the UK government of humanitarian aid and participation in international action relating to the war in former Yugoslavia is estimated to be £292.36 million ($438.54 million).[116]

Trade and Investment

The EU is a major trading partner with Croatia, accounting for 41.7 per cent of all imports in 1992 and increasingly taking a greater share of the market as trading patterns are reoriented. Total imports to Croatia decreased from $5,188 million in 1990 to $3,828 million in 1991; the EU accounts for a high proportion of Croatia's investments, and such losses adversely affect European businesses.[117] Many of the foreign companies operating in Croatia have been there since pre independence and are confronted with an economic environment characterized by the dangers of renewed conflict, high taxes, confusing and shifting legislation and acute shortage of cash and credit among customers.[118]

Comparison of economic data from the former Yugoslavia is hindered by the transition from centralized trade statistics for the whole of Yugoslavia, to the collation of separate economic information by each of the former republics. However, the disintegration of Yugoslavia and subsequent outbreak of conflicts has had a devastating effect on the economies of the former republics, with an unavoidable negative impact on foreign trade and investment. Unstable financial markets, hyperinflation and the disruption of the republics, have severely hindered trade. The EU accounted for 39.2 per cent of Yugoslav imports in 1988 and 38 per cent of exports, representing a considerable proportion of the country's foreign trade.[119] Yugoslavia's main imports were machinery, petroleum and petroleum products, chemicals, iron and steel, and transport equipment.[120]

Overall exports from EU countries to the former Yugoslavia fell during 1990–92. Latest available import and export figures show a clear disparity between the trading activities of the former republics, reflecting, in part, the impact of the conflicts in Bosnia-Herzegovina and Croatia on trade (Figures 7.9 and 7.10). The reorientation of trade and improvements in the economies of Slovenia and Croatia, however, have resulted in Germany and Italy actually increasing their exports to these countries in 1993. Imports from Germany increased in the first nine months of 1993 up 38 per cent to $759 million, while imports from Italy in the same period increased 11 per cent to $651 million.[121] These increases are, however, offset by the loss of trade with former Yugoslavia. Mihael Akermann of Drager

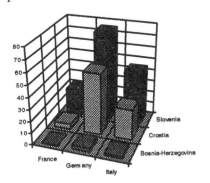

Source: EIU Country Reports: *Bosnia, Croatia and Slovenia*, 4th quarter 1993

Figure 7.9: Principal EU imports from Bosnia-Herzegovina, Croatia and Slovenia (1992) (US$ '000, monthly averages)

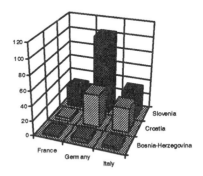

Source: EIU Country Reports: *Bosnia, Croatia and Slovenia*, 4th quarter 1993

Figure 7.10: Principal EU exports to Bosnia-Herzegovina, Croatia and Slovenia (1992) (US$ '000, monthly averages)

Croatia, a German medical equipment manufacturer, reported, 'There are no profits, only losses' and concluded 'Business levels are staying low or getting worse because the economic situation is getting worse'.[122]

The UN sanctions imposed on Serbia-Montenegro have effectively curtailed foreign trade. No reliable figures have been available since the imposition of sanctions in 1992, either for food and medicines which are not restricted or for illegal trade activities. The rapidly depreciating Yugoslav dinar and five digit inflation renders foreign trade statistics virtually meaningless. A Business International report, produced in 1992, predicted that 'Companies can thus anticipate a virtual collapse of foreign trade with Serbia-Montenegro and widespread loss of any import purchasing power, through the life span of the sanctions and well into any post-sanction period'.[123] The rapid deterioration of the Serb economy, the demise of foreign exchange holdings early in 1993 and uncontrollable inflation, has meant that imports, whether permissible under the sanctions controls or not, could no longer be afforded.[124] The trend of foreign trade with Yugoslavia is shown in Figure 7.11.

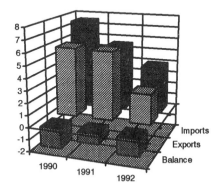

Source: EIU, Country Reports: Bosnia-Hercegovina, Croatia, Macedonia, Serbia-Montenegro, Slovenia, 4th quarter 1993.

Figure 7.11: Trend of foreign trade, Yugoslavia (US$00m)

Private investment

The liberalization of the Yugoslav economy led to an upsurge in foreign investments between 1987 and 1988, with a total investment of $285 million.[125] Despite the negative factors facing potential investors, including Yugoslavia's poor economic performance, high inflation and restrictions on hard currency, Western investors were clearly interested in the potential of the Yugoslav market. Between 1985 and 1988, 117 joint ventures between foreign and Yugoslav companies were established. Investments from French business accounted for the major share of such investments at $143.3 million, of which $120 million was placed in one large tourism project. Over the same period Italian firms invested $31.9 million.[126] Investments were largely concentrated in the tourist industry and in the production of ferrous and non-ferrous metals, chemicals and transport. Joint venture projects were mainly focused in the more economically advanced areas such as Slovenia, Croatia, Serbia and Vojvodina.

Country case study: UK

Trade between former Yugoslavia and the UK has been severely affected by the conflict. An overall downward trend is noticeable in both exports from the UK to former Yugoslavia and imports into the UK from former Yugoslavia in the years 1990–1992. Only in 1993 did UK exports to former Yugoslavia increase on the previous year. Trade with Bosnia-Herzegovina has been particularly low in comparison to other former Yugoslav republics (except Serbia/Montenegro) and this reveals the extent to which the war there has disrupted Bosnian trade.

Business International reports that while thousands of foreign firms launched business interests in Yugoslavia at the end of the 1980s, 'The outbreak of Serb-Croatian violence subsequently frightened away many investors; only a portion of contracted foreign investment actually entered the country, mainly in the form of know how and equipment'.[127] For example, in Croatia in 1992, foreign investments amounted to just $16 million.[128] This rose to $94.6 million in the first half of 1993, with Germany accounting for $41.1 million or 43.3 per cent of total foreign investment for this period.[129] The UK situation is discussed below and shown in Figure 7.12.

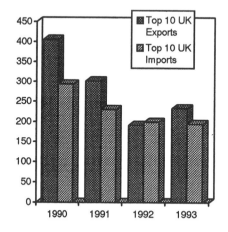

Source: (UK) Department of Trade and Industry database

Figure 7.12: UK trade with former-Yugoslavia (excluding Serbia and Montenegro) (US$m)

However, investments in Croatia, although indicating a slow recovery, are subject to tremendous uncertainty. In January 1994, *Business Eastern Europe* (a publication which targets investors with interests in eastern Europe), classified Croatia as an area of 'instability' with 'increased risks'. In March, Croatia was reclassified on the 'Political risk monitor' as an area of consolidation, with a 'falling risk' for foreign investments.[130] The overriding feature of the Croatian economy remains that of continued unpredictability. There is no guarantee that a political settlement will be reached with the Serbs in Croatia and increasing concern that if a peace settlement is agreed, pent-up grievances over pay and wages may result in widespread strikes, causing further disruption to the economy.[131]

The current lack of foreign investment is likely to hinder severely the economic recovery of the former republics, the repercussions of which may be further political unrest and destabilization. Moreover, with the economies of Serbia-Montenegro, Macedonia and Bosnia-Herzegovina in a state of collapse and the transition to market economies in Croatia and Slovenia severely disrupted, Europe has lost a potentially lucrative market.

Refugees

EU member states have been severely affected by the flow of refugees from the former Yugoslavia. In response to the huge numbers of people fleeing the conflict areas, many countries have imposed visa restrictions for Bosnian nationals, delayed consideration of asylum applications or granted temporary protection status outside the 1951 UN Convention relating to the status of refugees.

In some countries admission is increasingly dependent on whether the refugee has a relative who can cover costs, thus removing the financial burden from the state. The number of refugees residing in EU countries had reached 509,714 by May 1994.[132]

Germany has received the largest number of refugees from the former Yugoslavia, due in part to its relative geographic proximity to the conflict and its (initially) more lenient immigration laws. There are an estimated 400,000 refugees and displaced persons from the former Yugoslavia living in Germany.[133] The government provides full support for some 200,000 of these, in the form of housing, food, medical care and clothing; the annual cost of this support is DM3.100 million (US$1.9 billion) per year. Another 150,000 people are with host families and receive medical expenses from state funds, at an annual cost of DM200 million (US$125.9 million). This brings the total cost for refugee provision to DM3,300 million (US$2 billion) a year.[134]

In addition to the considerable financial costs incurred by the refugee crisis, the German government has also been faced with increasing social unrest and racial tensions in response to the rising number of asylum seekers, coinciding with a decline into recession, increasing unemployment and the growing poverty of marginal groups. The refugee population, which includes a large number of people from eastern Europe, along with those fleeing the former Yugoslavia, has been targeted as the focus of this unrest. This unrest has manifested itself in violent attacks on individuals, arson on refugee accommodation, and increasing xenophobia channelled through far-right political movements.[135]

Strategic Costs

Strategic costs to the EU as a consequence of the conflict in the former Yugoslavia include the threat to the EU integration process, the immediate and long-term security threats caused by war in Europe, and the dangers inherent in the violation of fundamental principles on which international peace and security are dependent.

Discrediting the EU

The inability of the EU to project a united policy or implement an effective response to the conflicts in the former Yugoslavia has discredited the Union and arguably encouraged the continuation of the conflict.

Firstly, the dilemma as to whether to recognize the independence of the federal republics of Slovenia and Croatia threatened to split the Union. In December 1991, Germany's announcement that it would recognize Slovenia and Croatia unconditionally, confronted the Union with a major challenge at a time when the creation of a united foreign policy was in its formative stages. The German decision 'Made a mockery of the consensual foreign policy which the EC was striving to build on its way towards economic and political integration'.[136] Serious political embarrassment and the possible disintegration of a common approach to foreign policy and security issues, was avoided by a combination of German diplomatic

pressure, concessions, compromises and the pragmatic realization that the stability of the EU took precedence over the issues raised by the disintegration of the former Yugoslavia. Slovenia and Croatia were accordingly recognized as independent states by the EU on 15 January 1992. However, very little thought seems to have been given to the implications this would have for Bosnia or for Bosnia's status within Yugoslavia.

Secondly, serious differences have emerged over the issue of direct military intervention since the outbreak of the conflict. This was particularly apparent with the use of UN/NATO airstrikes against Serb forces besieging Sarajevo in February 1994. The UK strongly opposed direct military involvement, on the grounds that it would jeopardize the neutrality of the UN forces, directly threaten the safety of UK personnel in UNPROFOR, hinder humanitarian aid operations and mean a long-term and costly commitment in a brutal conflict. Greece strongly opposed any use of force against the Serbs, while France, Germany, Belgium and Holland expressed support for strong military action.

Perpetual vacillation regarding the possible use of military force, coinciding with the lack of repercussions for breaking negotiated agreements, convinced warring parties that they could pursue their war aims with impunity. This has had an unquestionable influence, both on those involved in the conflict and on the credibility of the EU.

Finally, in defiance of the other members of the Union, Greece has unilaterally imposed a trade blockade on Macedonia. Diplomatic efforts to persuade Greece to allow Macedonian goods through the port of Thessalonika (the traditional access route for Macedonian goods), have met with stark refusal, resulting in the Union taking legal action. In an unprecedented move, Greece was brought before the European Court of Justice, where fellow members asked for an injunction on the embargo which has been described as a 'serious contravention of European Law'.[137]

The decision to take legal action against Greece (particularly embarrassing as it coincided with Greece holding the Presidency of the Union), represents an 'awkward and open rift in the 12-nation Union'.[138]

European security

A major strategic cost of the conflict in former Yugoslavia is its potential to embroil neighbouring countries and raise ethnic tensions throughout the region. The rise of nationalism and increasing discrimination against ethnic minorities threatens the fragile stability both within, and between countries. Romania, Bulgaria, Hungary, Albania, Macedonia, Greece and Turkey all contain the potential for protracted ethnic conflicts.

The destabilizing effect of the conflict spreading to neighbouring countries has been recognized as a dangerous potential, and a strong line has been taken on preventative measures designed to contain the conflict. This has included the presence of UN forces in Macedonia to monitor the border with Serbia, intense diplomatic activities in Turkey, and a firm line against Albanian unification with their fellow nationals in Kosovo and Macedonia.

Serb paramilitary groups in the province of Vojvodina have conducted a policy of terrorizing minority groups, including forcible eviction from their homes and villages.[139] Hungarians, Croats and Slovaks have been subjected to intimidation, discrimination and violence. The increasing ethnic tension in the province contains the possibility of a direct conflict between the Serb authorities and the Hungarian minority. This could escalate to include a wider confrontation between the Hungarian government and Serbia. Furthermore, a strong response from the Hungarian government could fuel fears in Romania of Hungarian expansionism and increase traditional suspicions and animosities between Romania's Hungarian minority and native population. This in turn could stimulate closer cooperation between Serbia and Romania, with both at loggerheads with Hungary.

The Bulgarian government is wary of its Muslim minority becoming radicalized as a result of increased Islamic consciousness in the Balkans. There is also a serious danger of the conflict spreading to Kosovo. The almost complete repression of Kosovo's ethnic Albanian population may provoke incidents of social unrest. Although Serbia has little to gain from provoking a direct conflict in the province, any subsequent action by the Serb military or police to suppress dissent by the Albanian majority could result in the intervention of troops from Albania itself, thus posing the risk of a direct conflict between Albania and Serbia. As such, Kosovo has been described as the most pressing problem for the region because it is the closest to conflict'.[140]

There is also the fear that an ethnic Albanian rebellion in Kosovo might spill over to include Muslim minorities in western Macedonia. Furthermore, the unification of Albanian minorities in Kosovo and western Macedonia is the stated policy of the Albanian government. The potential for conflict here is widely recognized, hence the efforts by the international community to maintain stability in Macedonia by the presence of UNPROFOR and the declarations against any attempt by Albania to unify Albanian populations across the country.

There is also a continuing dispute between Greece and Albania over the treatment of the Greek Orthodox minority in southern Albania. The recent arrest of 30 ethnic Greeks by the Albanian authorities has further heightened tensions.[141] The Greek government is also alarmed by the presence of 300,000 to 400,000 illegal Albanian immigrants in Greece.[142] The Albanian government is concerned at Greek threats to expel these immigrants. Demands by the ethnic Greek minority in Albania for self-determination are also an area of contention.

The re-establishment by Greece of ties with their fellow Orthodox Christians in Serbia is a severe embarrassment to the EU, and contains the potential for Greece supporting Serbia through a military confrontation with NATO. This scenario could raise the spectre of Greece becoming involved in direct conflict with NATO and jeopardizing the very survival of EU alliance.

The religious element of the conflict in the former Yugoslavia also has potentially very serious repercussions. The Islamic Conference Organization has shown an increasing interest in the plight of the Bosnian Muslims, with accusations that the anti-Muslim sentiments of the Western powers are responsible for the lack of repercussions on the Serb perpetrators. Iran has expressed concern at the failure of Western powers to prevent ethnic cleansing in Bosnia and has called on the UN to lift the arms embargo on the Bosnian Muslims.[143] In May 1994, 400 Iranian revolutionary guardsmen were sent to Bosnia to organize Muslim terrorist forces in the former Yugoslavia, under the direction of intelligence officials at Iran's Zagreb embassy. The CIA have expressed fears that Iran intends to use terrorist cells in Bosnia for subversion, not only against Serbia, but also against western Europe; as a Pentagon official remarked, 'Tehran sees this as a way to get at the soft underbelly of Europe'.[144] Iran has also sent large quantities of arms to the Bosnian Muslims, in defiance of the arms embargo. This has included rifles, machine guns, mortars, millions of rounds of ammunition and equipment which will enable the Bosnian Muslims to produce their own small arms.[145]

Although Russia has been careful to avoid confrontation with the US and EU, evidence of their sympathies for the Serbs has been demonstrated by their opposition to military attacks against the Serbs. American speculation over the possible lifting of the arms embargo on the Bosnian Muslims provoked a strong warning from Russia's Foreign Minister; 'Don't do anything unilaterally', he warned Washington, 'if you want to avoid a Balkan war.'[146] Furthermore, extreme nationalists have expressed open support for the Serbs, as Zhironosky's visit to Bosnia in 1994

testifies. The rise of nationalist sentiments in the former Soviet Union and increasing radicalization of Islamic states in South-Eastern Europe remains a distinct possibility and one which contains the potential for open conflict based on religious allegiance. 'Europe is dividing again along the line of the Great Schism, the most persistently unstable border on the continent'.[147]

The conflict in the former Yugoslavia has seriously discredited the UN and the EU. Endless resolutions, which have been violated with impunity, have merely reinforced the notion that the international community is unable, or unwilling, to enforce its decisions.

The crisis in Yugoslavia has sharply focused attention on the weaknesses of international institutions which are dependent on consent in order to be effective. For example, recent votes in the US House of Representatives in support of lifting the arms embargo to the Bosnian Muslims, when the US holds a permanent seat on the Security Council, leaves the UN in a precarious position. Although it is perhaps unlikely that President Clinton would sanction the unilateral lifting of the arms embargo, the fact that UN decisions are being undermined both by the warring factions and democratic institutions in the US can only have negative implications for the role of the UN in the future. If UN threats of repercussions on aggressors and war criminals are no longer considered credible, the potential for conflict resolution is also undermined, as there will ultimately be no deterrents to aggression on an international scale. By failing to curtail a brutal war in Europe, prevent ethnic cleansing on a vast scale or even establish a credible war crimes tribunal to punish the perpetrators, the principles of democracy, inviolability of state borders, non-use of force and respect for fundamental human rights have been blatantly violated, with seemingly scant repercussions.

THE BENEFITS

EU countries have gained little from the continuation of the war in the former Yugoslavia. The sanctions imposed on the Federal Republic of Yugoslavia have suspended foreign trade outlets, the Bosnian economy has all but collapsed; and the UN arms embargo excludes governments and companies from the lucrative profits to be made from any legal trade in armaments. There are essentially no economic, financial, or political benefits to the EU from the war in former Yugoslavia.

Some individuals and companies have benefited, however, by encouraging black market deals in arms and drugs and money laundering. Individuals and companies based in the EU have been implicated in violation of the arms embargo to the former Yugoslavia.

Croatia has engaged in a major arms-buying operation around the world. Paul Beaver, in a study on Croatia's defence expenditure in 1992, reported 'We estimate that they spent something between two hundred and three hundred and fifty million dollars in trying to re-equip their armed forces, from fighter aircraft, through tanks and artillery'.[148] Although many of the weapons originated in former Warsaw Pact countries, Croatia has also obtained weapons from EU countries. These include: Heckler and Koch MP-5 rifles, 'Armburst' anti-tank weapons systems from Messerschmidt-Boelkow Blohm (produced in Germany, though licensed in Singapore); mines and ammunition.[149]

Heckler and Koch, a German-based subsidiary of the UK armaments manufacturer Royal Ordnance, has been implicated in illegally selling arms to the countries of the former Yugoslavia. These allegations were denied by a spokesperson for the company, who claimed to have no knowledge of how Heckler and Koch weapons reached the former Yugoslavia, later claiming that the weapons had been produced by Enfield production, a British former licence holder for Heckler and Koch.[150]

In the effort to enforce the arms embargo to the former Yugoslavia, Munich police uncovered around 40 cases of illegal arms deals in 1991. Violations continue to be widespread and have included:

* A DM20 million (US$12.5 million) deal involving the Czech Republic and Poland and two German investment consultants
* The sale of thousands of rifles to Czechoslovakia, Poland and Hungary by Rainer Eppelmann, many of which found their way to Slovenia and were later sold to Croatia[151]
* Attempts by agents of the neo-Nazi Croatian Party of Rights to transport weapons directly from arms manufacturers in Germany, Austria, Italy and Spain
* Admissions by Karl Heinz Schulz, that he has 'Fulfilled concrete arms requests for the Croatian warring parties through the intermediary service of the German Intelligence Service at Pullach' BND[152]
* An attempt by Bosnian Serbs to purchase laser-guided British missiles worth approximately one million pounds on the black market in London.[153]

CONCLUSION

The conflicts in the former Yugoslavia have had serious consequences for the EU, posing a major challenge to the concept and plausibility of a united foreign policy, indicating the inadequacy of European mechanisms for conflict prevention, threatening vital security and economic interests and resulting in substantial financial outlay for humanitarian aid.

The EU, by its failure to agree on a common policy with which to challenge blatant aggression, has permitted the fundamental principles on which European security is dependent to be undermined. The long-term consequences may prove severe and are unlikely to leave the EU unaffected.

The precedent has been set by a) the success of the Serbs in creating 'ethnically pure' areas (Greater Serbia) b) UN/EC support for a negotiated settlement based on ethnic division, for nationalist governments elsewhere to deal with the 'problem' of their minority groups, not by implementing a system of minority rights, but through repression, expulsion or execution of those considered to be from the 'wrong' ethnic origin. The implications of this go far beyond the boundaries of the former Yugoslavia. 'The ethnic state leaves no room for people with different ethnic identities, and ethnic cleansing can turn ethnic identity into a matter of life or death. If it prevails, it is the end of our civilization as we know it'.[154]

THE UNITED STATES

THE COSTS

Introduction

The US's strategic interests and economic relations with Yugoslavia since Tito's break with what was to become the eastern bloc in 1948 were founded on the importance of Yugoslavia as a non-aligned country, strategically placed between the East and West. In the period of the Cold War, America had a direct interest in maintaining Yugoslavia as a neutral and independent country which acted as a buffer to potential Soviet expansion into Europe. While the majority of Yugoslavia's trade was with COMECOM countries, with the Soviet Union the largest single trader, nearly all of Yugoslavia's external debt was with the West.

With the collapse of communism, the strategic interests of the US in a neutral and independent Yugoslavia were dispelled. Moreover, the opening up of economic markets in the East offered alternative opportunities for American investment and trade, reducing the importance of Yugoslavia, whose exports to the US had accounted for less than 5 per cent of foreign trade.

The outbreak of conflict in the former Yugoslavia provoked little initial response in the US, which considered the crisis largely a European problem to be resolved through the EU. US policy, though somewhat ambiguous, has consistently supported a negotiated settlement; advocated a tough stance on sanctions imposed on Serbia and Montenegro; and been adamant that there will be no deployment of American troops in the war zones without an agreed 'peace-plan' to be enforced.

Despite America's apparent limited strategic and economic interests in a post-Cold War Yugoslavia, the costs to the US of the continuation of the conflict are substantial.

Economic Costs

Humanitarian intervention

The UN Security Council Resolution 743 (21/2/1992) established the UN Protection Force to undertake peacekeeping operations in the former Yugoslavia. Initially, this force consisted of 8332 troops from 31 member countries. The assessment of US contributions towards UNPROFOR operations amounts to 31.7 per cent of total costs in 1992 and 1993.[155]

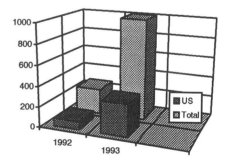

Source: UN Dept, British Office of Foreign and Commonwealth Affairs.

Figure 7.13: US contribution to total UN costs (US$m)

US personnel in former Yugoslavia

As mentioned above, no US troops have been sent to the war zone. The US initially assigned 300 troops to Macedonia, sending an additional 180 troops in April 1994 to reinforce the UN peacekeeping contingent monitoring the border with Serbia.[156] To date, there have been no casualties among US personnel serving in the former Yugoslavia.

Aid

In addition to contributions through the UN, the US has coordinated relief flights to Bosnia-Herzegovina. The Sarajevo airlift began on 3 July 1992 and has involved 2502 missions by the US (as of 12 January, 1994) at an average cost of US$1 million per month, which the State Department estimated would increase as the number of US flights increased in January 1994.[157]

Airdrops

The US has also undertaken 1440 missions in airdrops to Bosnia-Herzegovina since they began on 28 February 1993. The total cost of US relief flights averages US$2.25 million per month (again due to increase as of January 1994).[158]

The total cost of assistance which the US government has provided in grants to NGOs and UN agencies in food, rehabilitation and refugee assistance, field consultants and transportation is illustrated below. Total cost over the period 1991-94 to the US was US$504 million.[159] (Figure 7.14)

Trade and Private Investment

The US accounted for less than 5 per cent of Yugoslavia's foreign trade at the outbreak of the conflict. Imports from the US consisted mainly of wheat, leather, synthetic and artificial fibres, coal and machinery.[160]

The economic sanctions imposed on Serbia and Montenegro by the UN has effectively reduced the flow of goods into and out of Serbia and Montenegro by approximately 75 per cent.[161] The contin-

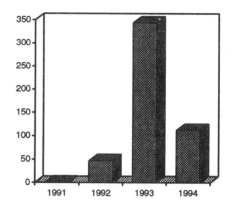

Source: US State Department database, 1994

Figure 7.14: Total cost of US assistance (US$m)

uing war in Bosnia-Herzegovina has severely affected economic activity and foreign investment has virtually ceased. The US has maintained some trading activities with Croatia and Slovenia.

The US supported the extension of economic sanctions to Croatia in response to the Bosnian Croatian blockade of Mostar and atrocities against the Muslim populations, and in the event that demands for the estimated 5000 Croatian troops in Bosnia to be withdrawn were not fulfilled.

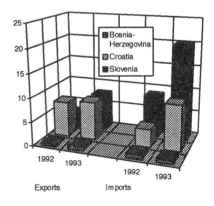

Source: EIU, Country Reports: Bosnia-Herzegovina, Croatia, Macedonia, Serbia-Montenegro, Slovenia, 4th quarter 1993,

Figure 7.15: Trade with Bosnia-Herzegovina, Croatia and Slovenia (US$000, monthly averages)

188

The threat of sanctions against Croatia was curtailed by the lack of consensus among the international community and subsequently by the agreement between the Bosnia government and Bosnia Croats to implement a ceasefire.

The costs to the US in terms of lost trade and investment resulting from the conflict in the former Yugoslavia have not been severe, due to the level of trading activity between the two countries prior to the outbreak of the wars. The agreements secured by the Clinton administration at the General Agreement on Tariffs and Trade (GATT) and the North American Free Trade Association (NAFTA) negotiations in early 1993, combined with the liberalization of economies in eastern Europe reduces the significance of lost trade due to the conflict in the former Yugoslavia.

Debt

In the mid-1980s Yugoslavia was seventh in the league table of great debtor countries, with a debt of US$20 billion in 1984.[163] The strategic advantage of supporting Yugoslavia through their economic crisis prompted President Reagan to declare 'For our part, we will lend our assistance, in cooperation with other Western governments, international financial institutions and commercial banks'.[164]

Refugees

The US government has offered to accept an estimated 11,000 people in need of temporary resettlement from the former Yugoslavia. The actual number of people who resettled in the US between October 1992 and March 1994 was 1625, of which 534 were ex-detainees, 696 were their dependants and 395 people were from other vulnerable groups.'[165] The Office of Refugee Resettlement of Health and Human Services has estimated that between 5000–6000 refugees from the former Yugoslavia will be accepted by the US in the financial year 1993–94. Refugees are eligible for both financial and medical assistance, which is provided by the state in which refugees take up residence.

Levels of financial assistance vary between US$72 and US$452 per month depending on state policy.[166] Although this represents a subsistence level of support for the individuals concerned, the cost of maintaining those who resettle in the US amounts to millions of dollars.

Strategic Costs

The conflict in the former Yugoslavia has raised intense debate about what constitutes vital US security interests and strategic consideration.[167] The inability to reach a consensus on these key issues and the complexity of the situation in the former Yugoslavia itself has been reflected in America's ambiguous response to the conflict.

American policy reflects the view that the conflict in the former Yugoslavia is not perceived to be of direct strategic significance to the US. America has been adamant that no US troops will be stationed in the conflict zones. While the US has undertaken intense diplomatic activities, encouraged negotiated settlements and made substantial financial contributions to humanitarian operations, the use of direct military intervention has not, as yet, been a serious option.

Clinton seized on the issue of Bosnia during his election campaign, criticizing President Bush and promising a tougher American stance. This emphasis on the conflict in Bosnia made Clinton's subsequent failure to influence the warring parties to curtail the violence, all the more devastating. 'Clinton properly criticized the policy of his predecessor but then failed in his effort to improve on it, leaving the situation unchanged except for the appearance of American weakness and inability to lead.'[168] Clinton's personal credibility and that of America as a world leader are both at stake, as Europe is confronted with atrocities of genocidal proportions which the international community has so far failed to constrain.

However, as with the member states of the EU, the US undoubtedly recognizes the potential for the conflicts in ex-Yugoslavia to directly impinge on its strategic and security interests in both the Middle East and Europe, if it were to spread. In December 1992, President Bush warned Serbia not to provoke a conflict in Kosovo and indicated that the US would be prepared to use military force.[169] Albania's stated policy is to achieve peaceful unification with the Albanian populations in Kosovo and western Macedonia. In response the US has warned all three Albanian populations that it does not support Albanian unification, and that the principle of inviolability of borders remains in force for Serbia and Macedonia, just as it does for Croatia and Bosnia.[170] This is a principle adopted both in recognition of the fact that the secession of Kosovo would result in war between the Serbs and Albanians and in appreciation of the dangerous potential such a precedent would entail.

THE BENEFITS

With the exception of some minor arms sales contracts for private companies, there are no benefits to the US of the war between the states of Yugoslavia continuing. Strategically, it serves only to cause divisions among its allies in the West (discussed in the EU section), and no economic benefits of any substance accrue.

CONCLUSION

With the transformation of eastern Europe into stable, peaceful democracies far from complete, America can ill afford to ignore the destabilization of the Balkans. The international community has descended into political turmoil in its attempts to find a solution to the conflicts in the former Yugoslavia. The inability to reach a consensual policy reflecting the different interests which the US, EC, Russia and Turkey have in the region bodes badly not only for the resolution of this conflict, but for resolution of the many current and imminent conflicts around the globe.[171]

IF THE CONFLICT HAD NOT OCCURRED

Introduction

The purpose of this section is to show how the countries of the former Yugoslavia might have developed if the conflict had not occurred. In so doing, it aims to explore the extent to which the US and the member states of the EU could have benefited economically if the conflict had been avoided.

Former Yugoslavia

Former Yugoslavia ranked at the top of the middle income bracket in lists of developing countries. As such it can be compared favourably with other European countries such as Eire, Spain and Portugal. It had a well-developed heavy manu-facturing sector (based mainly in Croatia and Slovenia), was self-sufficient in military-related industries and had a large agricultural sector (Serbia). The war has destroyed some of this industrial sector, broken up supply lines and made agricultural land unusable. The former Yugoslavia has entered severe economic decline, which is due in a major part to the conflict.

Bosnia-Herzegovina

Bosnia-Herzegovina has only very recently become a separate economic entity; it is therefore impossible to compare its economic performance with that of another country. However it is possible to explore the kinds of benefits it would have been able to take advantage of, if the war had not occurred.

EU membership

The issue of European integration is the crucial factor of any macro level cost/benefit analysis of the conflict in former Yugoslavia. The end of the Cold War and the dual transition of formerly communist centrally planned economies to the free market and democracy have unleashed a tide of ethnic expression and economic decline throughout the former second world. They have also opened up the possibility of these countries being allowed to join the 'rich man's club' of the EU. This opportunity brings with it a promise of future economic prosperity after an initial period of severe adjustment. Those countries which most energetically reform their economies are likely to be the first to be allowed to enter the new European economic region. It is the promise of this prize that the former Yugoslav republics have sacrificed in their pursuit of raw nationalism.

There can be little doubt that without the conflict the economy of Bosnia-Herzegovina would be stronger and better placed for economic growth after the adjustment process. As the overall European economy recovers and comes out of recession, Bosnia-Herzegovina would have been able to expand its export sectors. Growing intra-Yugoslav trade would have been to the long-term benefit of all participants in the conflict.

Croatia

In examining the benefits that might have accrued to Croatia, we can draw some comparisons with Slovenia, the northernmost state of the former Yugoslavia, and the one state to have so far escaped serious unrest. While both Slovenia and Croatia are heavily industrialized, Slovenia is more so, and is more wealthy generally than Croatia, its traditional trading links with Germany being at least partly responsible for this. Additionally, both countries have suffered economically as a result of the war, with Croatia being the most affected. A comparison of official data on industrial output in Slovenia and Croatia during 1992/93 shows that whereas Slovenia was operating on average at 70 per cent of its 1989 output Croatia was operating at only 50 per cent of its 1989 output. Whereas gross industrial production in Croatia fell by 29 per cent in 1991 and 15 per cent in 1992 for Slovenia it

fell by only 12 per cent in 1991 and 13 per cent in 1992.[172] These factors should be borne in mind when considering the following analysis.

As mentioned, Slovenia has been least affected by the political and economic reorientation of the Yugoslav economy. Slovenias economic potential has actually increased with independence. In 1991, direct foreign investment in Slovenia amounted to US\$65 million, rising to US\$100 million in 1992. There were 638 companies in Slovenia wholly owned by foreigners in 1993 and an additional 1332 joint ventures between foreign and Slovene partners.[173]

Because Croatia has suffered considerable war damage, not only to its factories but also to its infrastructure, foreign investors find little prospect of safe investment, with the kinds of minimum requirements such as a functioning transport network lacking. Slovenia, on the other hand, has suffered no such war damage and in fact is predicted to be an area of increasing investment in the next few years. The most significant problems foreign investors face are the relatively minor issues of familiarization with the technicalities of Slovene privatization. Incentives for such investment include the enormous future potential of markets, with cheap production, resources and low costs also a consideration.

The Slovenian government have been very successful at reducing inflation, which was running at about 5 per cent by January 1993. In contrast Croatian inflation was approximately 30 per cent in January 1993, inflamed by the massive purchases required to maintain the war effort.[174]

Slovenia is the one former Yugoslavia state largely unaffected by the conflict and is, without question, in considerably better economic shape than Croatia. While both countries have felt the effect of the war, Croatia has been one of the worst affected, and will thus remain in the economic doldrums while it stays entangled in the conflict. In contrast, Slovenia is already being viewed as a site of considerable economic potential.

Serbia

For Serbia, the major benefit of the conflict not having occurred is that Serbia would not have been isolated, both politically and economically, from most of the rest of world. The UN sanctions regime would not have been imposed. Serbia would still have been able to find buyers for its manufactured exports (principally arms). Instead it is estimated that Serb trade has fallen by 75 per cent as a result of the sanctions regime.

The Serb economy is primarily an agricultural-based economy. Economic isolation and UN sanctions exclude Serbia from fully benefiting from the recent GATT agreement which will liberalize trade in agricultural products. The GATT agreement provides an opportunity for certain East European countries to exploit the freer access to industrial country markets, gaining valuable export earnings which can in turn be invested in new 'high tech' industries aiding the economic development of the country. Serbia, with its geographical proximity to the EU, its trained, healthy and educated labour force, its extensive agricultural sector and its concern to develop the industrial sector was well placed to take full benefit of these changes in the international economy.

The European Union

The conflict in the former Yugoslavia has resulted in the loss of substantial potential benefits in trade and investment for the EU and the US. This can be seen by comparing the development of trade and investment opportunities by Western companies within the former Yugoslavia and other Central and Eastern European Countries. The pre-conflict economy of the former Yugoslavia is comparable with the pre-transition economies of Poland, Hungary, Romania and Bulgaria. Each of these countries had state-controlled industrial sectors and peasant-based agricultural production. Although the economy of the former Yugoslavia had both substantial state and private sectors, it pursued the same state-directed industrialization strategy as other socialist countries in eastern Europe.

All countries in the region have experienced economic decline due to the contraction of the state sector and transition to market economies. Nevertheless, many opportunities exist for Western companies to trade with and invest in East European enterprises. Meanwhile, investment opportunities in the former Yugoslavia have been severely constrained by the conflict.

Trade

The breakup of the socialist-managed trade system and the discrediting of communism, resulted in a reorientation of Central and East European trade from the Council for Mutual Economic Assistance (CMEA) towards the West. As a result, these countries are now heavily dependent on trade with the EU and the US. This has given central and eastern European goods access to Western markets and has opened up new markets in the region for European and US exports.

The principal economic benefit, had the conflict not occurred, for the EU and US would have been access to the former Yugoslav market. The conflict has raised both military and political barriers to the free flow of trade and caused the disintegration of this market. In addition, the breakdown of links between the former Yugoslav regional economies has placed economic obstacles (for example new tariffs), which constrain the passage of international trade.

Investment

FDI in the former Yugoslavia is confronted with similar obstacles to those facing international trade. Substantial insecurity of investments deters most capital flows. The extent to which foreign investors have been deterred from former Yugoslavia is revealed by FDI in neighbouring countries. Recent foreign investment in Poland has been in the pharmaceutical industry, automobile manufacturing, air travel, oil and gas exploration, computer software and soft drinks. British Gas, for example, has won new exploration rights with an initial investment of US$25 million, with the potential for large profits if successful.

Similarly, in Bulgaria there has been foreign investment in the petrochemical industry, mining and automobile manufacture. Rover Group are transferring production of their Maestro cars from Britain to Bulgaria, with the aim of producing 10,000 cars per year for export throughout east/central Europe. In Romania investment has been in the automobile industry, telecommunications, petrochemical industry and fast food chains. It is expected that the first McDonald's restaurant will open in Bucharest in 1995 and as a result of a US$100 million investment will soon spread to other cities.

In stark contrast there has been scant foreign investment in former Yugoslavia, with the exception of Slovenia, which has been less directly affected by the conflict. Whilst the conflict continues, the potential for business expansion and extraction of minerals is severely restricted. Furthermore, when the conflict finally ceases, a costly reconstruction of war-damaged industries and infrastructure will be necessary.

EU membership

The EU has signed association agreements with the majority of East/Central European countries. Moreover, Hungary and Poland have both applied for EU membership, with the expectation that this will come to fruition around the year 2000. The extension of the European single market to include post-socialist countries in East and Central Europe, promises to be beneficial for all the members. Already the reduction of tariff barriers by associates is benefiting West European industry as these markets become more freely accessible. Indeed, trade statistics show that generally east/central European imports from western Europe exceed exports to Western Europe. This applies also to the former Yugoslavia, but to a lesser degree than neighbouring countries.

Conclusion

All the states of former Yugoslavia have lost years of economic development as a result of the conflicts. Moreover, at a time when the rest of Europe is drawing together economically into huge common markets, the Balkan states are missing economic opportunities that would contribute significantly to their economic growth and well-being in the future. Similarly, the US and the EU have been denied lucrative opportunities for investment and trade, which have been traditionally strong. The major concerns of Western governments must now be the danger of political instability and ethnic conflict spreading throughout the region.

REFERENCES

1 Economist Intelligence Unit, Country Profile: *Bosnia-Herzegovina*, London, 1993-94.
2 UNICEF, *Water and Sanitation Programme, Sarajevo: One Year Report*, October 1993.
3 Ibid.
4 Whilst the demand for psychiatric treatment and psychological counselling is set to increase the war has caused the postponement of the construction of a new psychiatric hospital in Tuzla. See ICRC, *Information Kit on Bosnia-Herzegovina*, Geneva, September 1993.
5 UNICEF, Report from a UNICEF Pilot Study in Mostar: 'Children's Exposure to Violence and Trauma-Reactions', 1993

6 Economist Intelligence Unit, Country Profile: *Bosnia*, London, 1993–94.
7 UNICEF, 1993, op cit.
8 UNICEF, *Situation of Women and Children and UNICEF Activities in Former Yugoslavia: An Overview*, March 1993.
9 UNHCR, *Information Notes on Yugoslavia* No 1/94, January 1994.
10 Ibid.
11 Helsinki Watch, *War Crimes in Bosnia-Herzegovina* Volume II, (Human Rights Watch) 1993.
12 Amnesty International, *Bosnia-Herzegovina: Gross Abuses of Human Rights*, October 1992.
13 Bosnia File, UN Information Office,

London. The accuracy of this figure is questionable as it includes those living in refugee camps in Serbia. This figure should be considered as an example of the disinformation which has been used by all sides in their war propaganda.

14 Amnesty International, October 1992, op cit.
15 Helsinki Watch, *War Crimes in Bosnia-Herzegovina, Volume II*, (Human Rights Watch) USA, 1993.
16 Amnesty International, *Bosnia-Herzegovina: Rana u dusi - A Wound to the Soul*, January 1993.
17 Economist Intelligence Unit, *Bosnia-Herzegovina: Country Report*, 4th Quarter 1993.
18 Helsinki Watch, 1993, op cit.
19 Ibid.
20 Amnesty International, January 1993, op cit.
21 UNHCR, January 1994, op cit.
22 European Commission, Report to EC Foreign Ministers: EC Investigative Mission into the Treatment of Muslim Women in the former Yugoslavia, 1993.
23 UN Economic and Social Council, *Situation of Human Rights in the Territory of the Former Yugoslavia*, 4 March 1993.
24 Helsinki Watch, 1993, op cit.
25 The Refugee Council, *Mines: Anti-personnel Landmines and Refugees*, Refugee Council Factfile, No 11, November 1993.
26 Information received from N Andelic of Radio Sarajevo, 1994.
27 Adams J, 'Iran guns tilt balance for Bosnia Muslims', *The Sunday Times*, 3rd July 1994.
28 UNHCR, January 1994, op cit.
29 Evidence of this is provided by the hold up and shooting of three British aid workers as they drove to their hotel. The three were held up by renegade elements of the Bosnian army and one of the aid workers, Paul Goodhall, was shot dead.
30 UNICEF, October 1993, op cit.
31 UNHCR, March 1994, op cit.
32 Ibid.
33 UNICEF, March 1993, op cit.
34 *The Guardian*, 24 May 1994.
35 The dependence of these enclaves on Bosnian Serb goodwill has been demonstrated many times by Bosnian Serb civilians and military personnel blocking UN convoys from proceeding to and entering these towns. There is also the ongoing threat of military action by Bosnian Serb forces against these towns.
36 The 500,000 refugees in Serbia make up approximately 6 per cent of its population.
37 World Health Organisation, *Humanitarian Aid for ex-Yugoslavia*, WHO Area Office Belgrade, 12th October 1993.
38 Ibid.
39 UNICEF, March 1993, op cit.
40 As in many former Communist countries in the Second World and Third World democracy, as advocated by Western 'experts', has become the flavour of the month. The problem is that there is no guarantee that these paper democracies will provide reasonable civil rights to their citizens or any real participation in power to the political opponents of the regime.

41 'War Crimes in Bosnia-Hercegovina', *Helsinki Watch*, (Human Rights Watch, USA) 1992.
42 Ibid.
43 Ibid.
44 'Kosova Communication', Bulletin of the Ministry of Information of the Republic of Kosova, No 153, 10 January 1994
45 Also the cost of paying a domestic police force estimated at 100,000 individuals .
46 All these direct costs of conducting the war fall primarily on Serbia.
47 Economist Intelligence Unit, *Country Profile: Serbia-Montenegro*, London, 1993–94.
48 Ibid.
49 *The Economist*, 1st July 1994.
50 Tanjug News Agency, Belgrade quoted in the BBC World Service, 'Weekly Economic Reports', Summary of World Broadcasts, 27 January 1994.
51 Tanjug News Agency, Belgrade: quoted in BBC World Service, 'Weekly Economic Reports', Summary of World Broadcasts, 3 June 1993.
52 BBC World Service, 'Weekly Economic Reports', Summary of World Broadcasts, 27 January 1994.
53 'Serbia's Economy: Gurgles in the Pipeline', *The Economist*, 7 May 1994.
54 WHO, October 1993, op cit.
55 'UN Failing to Halt Sanction-Busting Trade with Serbia', *The Daily Telegraph*, 12 May 1994.
56 The claims reported in the Western press have been made by Dragoslav Avramovic. See 'Serbs have faith in their new saviour', *The Financial Times*, 9 May 1994 and 'Serbia's Economy: Gurgles in the Pipeline' *The Economist*, 7 May 1994.
57 Ibid. See for example the comments by Ivan Vujacic of Belgrade University.
58 'Serbs have faith in their new saviour', *The Financial Times*, 9th May 1994.
59 It is estimated by the Yugoslav authorities that 1.7 million people live off the land in the Federal Republic of Yugoslavia. See the 'International Weekly': quoted in BBC World Service, 'Weekly Economic Reports', Summary of World Broadcasts, 1 July 1993.
60 Beaver P, 'Yugo-Arms: Enough to Export', *War and Reconstruction in Yugoslavia*, Yugofax: Helsinki Citizens' Assembly.
61 For example a figure of 480,000 is given by the Refugee Council at September 1993 where as a figure of 530,000 is given by the UN Special Rapporteur on Human Rights at 17 November 1993. See Refugee Council, 'Former Yugoslavia: Refugees from Bosnia, Croatia & Serbia', Factsheet 7, September 1993. and Mazowiecki, T, Situation of Human Rights in the Territory of Former Yugoslavia, ECOSOC, 5th Report, 17 November 1993.
62 Refugee Council, 'Former Yugoslavia: Refugees from Bosnia, Croatia & Serbia', Factsheet 7, September 1993.
63 Mazowiecki, 1994, op cit.
64 UNICEF, *Situation of Children and Women and UNICEF Activities in Former Yugoslavia: An Overview*, March 1993.
65 Ibid.
66 UNICEF, *Education Report*, June 1993.

67 Economic and Social Council, 'Situation of Human Rights in the Territory of the former Yugoslavia', Commission on Human Rights, 49th session, E/CN4/1993/50

68 Pitter l and Beiser V, 'Reforms Under Siege', *Business Central Europe*, September 1993

69 *Marxism Today*, London, March, 1993

70 Ibid; Article by Pero Poljanic, Lord Mayor of Dubrovnik. NB: these figures may not be very reliable and should be treated with caution.

71 UNICEF, March 1993, op cit.

72 Other factors are also partly responsible for Croatian economic decline. These include the breakdown of the Communist managed trade system, structural adjustment as part of transition to a market economy, economic recession in the West and a decline in the strategic importance of former Yugoslavia.

73 Gabrisch H, et al, *Depression and Inflation: Threats to Political and Social Stability*, Vienna Institute of Comparative Economic Studies, 1992.

74 Economist Intelligence Unit, Country Profile: *Croatia*, 1993–94.

75 Ibid.

76 Ibid.

77 Gabrisch H, *Under the Impact of Western Recession: The economic situation of the post-socialist countries in the first quarter of 1993 and the outlook for 1993/94*, Vienna Institute of Comparative Economic Studies, June 1993, No 197b, Table 5.

78 Economist Intelligence Unit, Country Profile: *Croatia*, 1993–94.

79 Information on War Damages received from N Andelic of Radio Sarajevo, 1994

80 Economist Intelligence Unit, Country Profile: *Croatia*, 1993–94.

81 Ibid.

82 Report on The Yugoslav Conflict: A Summary of reported impacts on the natural values of Croatia and Slovenia, November 1991, p 4, received from The World Conservation Union (IUCN). Also information on war damages received from N. Andelic of Radio Sarajevo, 1994

83 Economist Intelligence Unit, Country Profile: *Croatia*, 1993–94.

84 Information received from The World Conservation Union (IUCN).

85 Rounded to the nearest US$100 million. Actual figures are US$5.188 million and US$3.828 million.

86 'Reforms Under Siege', *Business Central Europe*, September 1993.

87 Economist Intelligence Unit Country Profile: *Croatia*, 1993–94.

88 Economist Intelligence Unit Country Profile: *Slovenia, Croatia, Macedonia and Bosnia-Herzegovina*, 1993–94.

89 Zitovcic, D, *Information Sheet*, Croatian Embassy London.

90 Ibid.

91 Ibid.

92 Information on war damages received from N Andelic of Radio Sarajevo, 1994

93 Ibid. The reliability of this figure may be questioned as the primary purpose of those calculating this figure was to support the claim by the Croatian Government for US$20.727 billion in reconstruction aid from the international community.

94 Information received from the World Conservation Union (IUCN), *The Yugoslav Conflict: A Summary of reported impacts on the natural values of Croatia and Slovenia*, November 1991.

95 Information received from The World Conservation Union (ICUN), *Important Bird Areas in Croatia: Impacts of the War*, December 1991.

96 Ibid; *The Yugoslav Conflict*, September 1991.

97 Ibid; *Important Bird Areas in Croatia*, December 1991.

98 See 'Let Bosnia Live', leaflet published by the Irish-Bosnia Solidarity Group, Dublin.

99 Refugee Council, 'Former Yugoslavia: Refugees from Bosnia, Croatia & Serbia', Factsheet 7, September 1993.

100 Ibid.

101 Information received from the Banking South department of the European Bank for Reconstruction and Development

102 *Jane's Defence Weekly*, 'Gen de Lapresle: Guarding a Fragile Peace', Volume 21, No 23, 11 June 1994.

103 Ibid; 'Security incidents, 3 September 1992 – 28 February 1994'.

104 *The Times*, 18 May 94

105 European Commission, 'Humanitarian aid for victims of the conflict in the former Yugoslavia`, IP/93/904, 25 October 1993.

106 Ibid.

107 Ibid.

108 European Commission, 'New humanitarian aid for victims of conflict in the former Yugoslavia: Winter programme', IP/93/1118, 13 December 1993.

109 European Council decision, 'Supplementing the joint action on support for the convoying of humanitarian aid in Bosnia-Herzegovina', 93/729/CFSP, 20 December 1993.

110 European Commission, 'Humanitarian aid for the former Yugoslavia: Extension of aid action for the mobile hospital in Banja Luka', IP/94/101.

111 Information taken from 'UN Status of Contribution Report'(as of 31/12/94), supplied by the Foreign and Commonwealth Office, London.

112 This percentage exclude the assessed contributions to UNPROFOR by Greece and Portugal for which figures were unavailable.

113 Figures available as of April 1994. UNHCR Office of the Special Envoy of the Former Yugoslavia, `Information Notes on the former Yugoslavia', No 4/94, April 1994.

114 April 1994 Press Briefing from the Overseas Development Administration (ODA).

115 Often the drivers and support staff are ex-military personnel, who are likely to be better qualified for operating in a war zone than other civilians with no military experience.

116 This figure consists of humanitarian aid (£173 million), UNPROFOR contributions in 1992/93 and 1993/94 (£21.8 million + £45.34 million), sanctions monitoring (£1 million), European Union monitors (£7.15 million), the International

Conference on Former Yugoslavia (£435,000) and the 50% of excess Ministry of Defence (MOD) costs which are not reclaimable in 1992/93 and 1993/94 (£26.35 million + £17.29 million).

117 Economist Intelligence Unit, Country Report, *Croatia*, 1st Quarter 1994.

118 *Business Central Europe*, 'Reforms Under Siege', September 1993.

119 Artisien, P, 'Back from the Brink?, Yugoslavia to 1993', EIU. Special Report, no 2004, September 1989.

120 Economist Intelligence Unit, Country Report: *Bosnia-Herzegovina, Croatia, Macedonia, Serbia-Montenegro, Slovenia*, 4th Quarter 1993.

121 Ibid.

122 Ibid.

123 Business International, 'Doing Business with Eastern Europe, Slovenia, Croatia, Serbia-Montenegro (formerly Yugoslavia)', *Global Business Information Advice*, No 144, USA, 1993

124 Economist Intelligence Unit, Country Report: *Croatia* 4th Quarter 1993.

125 Artisien, September 1989, op cit.

126 Ibid.

127 Business International, No 136, 3.1, op cit.

128 EIU, 'Country Profile', 1993–4.

129 Economist Group, 'Reforms Under Siege', Business Central Europe, September 1993.

130 Economist Intelligence Unit, *Business Eastern Europe*, Volume XXIII, No 12, 21 March 1994.

131 Economist Intelligence Unit, *Business Eastern Europe*, Volume XXIII, No 1, 3 January 1994.

132 Figures available as of May 1994. *The Guardian*, 'Desperately seeking refuge', 24 May 1994

133 Embassy of the Federal Republic of Germany, Press Release, 'German aid for the victims in former Yugoslavia', 20 August 1993, (Annex 2: 'Fluchlinge und Vertriebene aus dem ehemaligen Jugoslawien')

134 Ibid.

135 Bade, K J, 'Immigration and Social Peace in United Germany', in *'Daedalus' Journal of American Academy of Arts and Sciences*, Volume 123, No 1, winter 1994

136 Glenny, M, *The Fall of Yugoslavia* Penguin, Harmondsworth, 1993.

137 European Wireless File, 'European Union Acts against Greece', USIS Information File, EFS415 (14/4/94).

138 Ibid.

139 'War Crimes in Bosnia-Hercegovina', *Helsinki Watch*, (Human Rights Watch, USA) 1992.

140 Glenny, 1993, op cit.

141 Smith, H, 'Athens inflamed by arrests in Albania', *The Guardian*, 27 May 1994.

142 Ibid.

143 *Military News*, Volume 94, No 16, 6 May 1994.

144 'Iranian guards recruit Bosnia terror force', *Evening Standard*, 3 June 1994.

145 'Iran guns tilt balance for Bosnia Muslims', *The Sunday Times*, 3 July 1994.

146 Glenny, 1993, op cit.

147 Ibid.

148 Beaver, P, Media Transcript Service,

Transcript Reference No 2213, Channel Four Television 7pm News, 25 January 1993.

149 Stamkosk, G, *Military data on the former Yugoslavia*, 1994

150 Van Beveran, T, 'Arms Trade, Uncontrolled Substances: the export of death', *War Report*, No 17, January 1993.

151 Rainer Eppelmann was the first defence minister of the interim government of the German Democratic Republic.

152 According to a German TV report, Karl Heinz Schulz made this statement to the Managing Director of the Institute for Peace and Politics in Weilheim.

153 'Yard foils Serb attempt to buy laser missiles', *The Sunday Times*, 20 February 1994.

154 Soros, G, 'What's at stake in Bosnia', *Helsinki Citizens' Association, Quarterly*, No 8, Autumn 1993.

155 Information supplied by Foreign and Commonwealth Office (UN Department). Figures taken from UN status of contribution reports, as at 31/12/93. President Clinton has made a commitment to fulfil America's financial obligations to the UN. The US is currently $1.1 billion in arrears to the UN peacekeeping budget. Friedman, 'Pentagon is 'playing double game' on blue beret budget', *The Guardian*, 28 May 1994

156 *Jane's Defence Weekly* 30 April 1994.

157 United States, State Department 'Update on Relief to Former Yugoslavia', USIS Wireless File 18 January 1994.

158 Ibid.

159 Ibid.

160 Yugoslav Survey – A record of facts and information' *Quarterly* 1, Vol XXIX 1988 (Jugoslovenska Stvarnost, Yugoslavia) 1988.

161 White House fact sheet, 'Serbia/Montenegro sanctions enforcement', USIS Wireless File, 29 March 1993

162 *The Economist*, 12 February 1994.

163 Pavlowitch, S K *Yugoslavia, the unlikely survivor* (Hurst, London) 1988.

164 Yugoslav Survey, 1988, op cit.

165 UNHCR Office of the Special Envoy for former Yugoslavia, 'Information notes on the former Yugoslavia', No 4/94 February 1994.

166 Automated State AFDC Plan, 'Need standards and payment amounts', Office of Refugee Resettlement of Health and Human Services (United States Government), May 1994

167 Congressional Research Service, Report for Congress, 'Congress and the conflict in Yugoslavia in 1992', 16 February 1993.

168 Wolfowitz, P D, 'Clinton's first year', *Foreign Affairs*, Volume 73, No 1, January/February 1994.

169 Congressional Research Service, Report for Congress, 'Yugoslavia's successor states', 12 February 1993.

170 Glenny, 1993, op cit.

171 Ibid.

172 Gabrisch 1993, op cit.

173 *Business International*, No 149, 3.4

174 Ibid.

8

WHAT IS TO BE DONE?

POLICY INITIATIVES FOR THE INTERNATIONAL COMMUNITY

The message of the seven conflict studies presented in this book is unequivocal. The impact of conflict on human lives, economic development and the environment is devastating. While there will always be those who benefit from conflict, the studies demonstrate that these gains are short-term and partial, and are outweighed by the wider, long-term costs of war. Quite apart from the costs to those directly involved in conflict, the costs to the Western industrial nations are substantial.

The proliferation of conflicts, and especially of intra-state conflicts in recent times, plainly demands a clear and effective response from the international community. This requires the international community to place a higher priority on conflict prevention and resolution. It is part of the purpose of this book to demonstrate the case for international action on early conflict resolution. By identifying the costs of conflict to the international community, the book attempts to show that the case is not simply a moral one. There is a powerful economic and strategic case for better conflict management as well.

It is imperative that the international community develops a coherent policy framework for early conflict management and prevention . The failure of the United Nations to respond to conflicts until they become disaster areas obviously limits the options then available. The result is frequently a need for extensive military and humanitarian intervention, which individual member states are then reluctant to endorse. By taking the right preventive measures the international community could reduce the need for such large scale interventions and save the development agencies from exhausting their budgets and energies on disaster relief.

The implementation of the policy initiatives outlined in this chapter would contribute to the international community's ability to forestall conflicts and facilitate their early resolution if they do break out. The proposals focus on existing mechanisms, principally the UN, where the role of the powerful industrialized nations is crucial.

The policy proposals illustrate some of the options available to the international community; they are not intended to be exhaustive.

ESTABLISHING CLEAR PRINCIPLES FOR INTERNATIONAL ACTION

Before the international community can take more effective action on conflict, it needs clearer criteria to determine when and how such action should be taken. The UN's current rather ad hoc responses to conflict are unsatisfactory. Why has the international community not developed more consistent and effective policies for preventing and managing conflict ? The main reason appears to be a perception that the conflicts of the 1990s do not significantly concern the interests of most states. As this book suggests, it is a view which overlooks the real costs of failing to manage them.

Thus the international community responds to some conflicts, such as Iraq and Bosnia, but largely neglects others, such as East Timor. A more consistent approach is needed. A useful first step would be to clarify what kinds of situations justify UN action.

The precedents set by the UN Security Council since the end of the Cold War, and the wide international support for those precedents, suggests that there is growing recognition of a de facto right of the international community to take action to prevent, or respond to three kinds of situations: threats to international security; threats to legitimate state authority; or large-scale human suffering and loss of life.

Having defined those situations in which the UN should take action, the international community needs to establish guidelines for such action. The following criteria could help guide international responses to conflicts

- international action should be taken under *legitimate authority* (either the UN Security Council or regional organizations). In the case of military intervention the Security Council should be considered the only legitimate authority
- *democratic* and *open* decision making
- international action should be

proportionate both to the scale of the conflict and to the potential consequences of the action
- any international action should have a *reasonable chance of success*
- states or organizations undertaking international action should be *accountable* to the body authorizing the action
- *early action to prevent and limit conflicts* is required, rather than responding only when large-scale violence has broken out.

Once the decision is made that the UN should intervene, the response should be guided by clear international goals. They should include minimizing and alleviating human suffering, preventing escalation of conflict, early conflict resolution and enforcing international law.

RESPONDING TO THE SPARKS OF CONFLICT

Effective early warning systems are needed to inform the UN's decision-making bodies of potential flash points. This is fundamental to effective conflict prevention. At present, although there are mechanisms within the UN for collecting the information needed, the organization rarely makes use of them as a basis for preventive action at an early stage.

An Office of Preventive Diplomacy, established within the UN, could help address this problem. It would have the tasks of monitoring volatile situations, collating and analysing information and making policy recommendations to the Security Council and the Secretary General. An Office of Preventive Diplomacy could provide a clear picture of potential conflict situations as they develop, drawing attention to any threats to international peace and security. Such a system could provide the Security Council with the regular analysis and policy options necessary for taking effective action.

The international community needs more sophisticated ways of applying pressure on the parties to a conflict. It also needs to implement them earlier as the conflict develops. Fact-finding missions, mediation and preventive diplomacy could be expanded as a means of reducing tension and helping resolve conflicts in their early stages. Such missions provide a forum for low-profile, neutral UN involvement in conflict flash points, and they are also an effective way of gathering information.

If low-profile mediation fails to resolve a conflict, a higher-level UN mission by a senior representative of the Secretary-General can help. For example, the visits of European ambassadors to Kashmir went some way towards internationalizing the conflict and adding to the pressure on India to negotiate a solution.

Where the negotiations have reached stalemate, and specific UN recommendations for voluntary resolution of a dispute are ineffective, further pressure is needed. A range of pressures is possible, from sanctions to military action.

APPLYING ECONOMIC SANCTIONS

Economic sanctions have long been used by the UN as a form of pressure on intransigent governments and warring parties. The history of sanctions, however, shows that they have frequently been ineffective, hitting the poorest in society without touching those in power, as has been the case in Iraq.

Sanctions therefore need to be targeted in more sophisticated ways and imposed at an early stage of the conflict. Methods of applying greater pressure on governments and armed forces, while minimizing the impact on civilian populations, need to be found. Such methods might include targeting the transfer of particular goods, technologies and finance which are crucial to those in power. Greater attention should also be paid to how sanctions could be enforced. For example, UN monitors could be deployed along the borders of countries neighbouring those states which are the targets of sanctions.

DEPLOYING UN TROOPS

The United Nations is increasingly confronted with situations in which mediation, political pressure and economic sanctions are ineffective in resolving conflicts, once the conflict goes beyond a certain point. The persistence of the Bosnian Serbs against these measures and their continual defiance of the UN indicates the limitations of persuasive methods once a conflict has escalated.

Clearly there are situations in which a more direct military response by the international community is appropriate. There are also situations in which the military could help defuse conflicts at an early stage. There is therefore an urgent need to adopt a more systematic approach to UN military involvement in conflict resolution and prevention. There are several options for military intervention available to the UN.

Preventive Deployment

In situations of potential conflict, preventive deployment of UN troops could act as a deterrent to the outbreak of violence. The deployment of UNPROFOR troops in Macedonia to monitor the border with Albania and Serbia, authorized by the Security Council in December 1992, was the first deployment of its kind. It has so far proved successful. Preventive deployment could be highly cost-effective, dispensing with the need to intervene with larger peace-keeping or peace enforcement forces and to mount expensive humanitarian relief operations later. Relatively small, lightly-armed forces would be seen as a precedent for more forceful action, increasing their deterrence value.

Peace-keeping Action

UN forces could be deployed where violence has not yet broken out, in order to build confidence, reduce tensions and resolve low-level disputes. Peace-keeping forces deployed once a settlement has been agreed can monitor cease-fire agreements and prevent the renewal of conflict. In Mozambique the UN has deployed a 7000–strong force, including military and police, to maintain peace during the post-conflict rebuilding of civil society.[1]

The deployment of peace-keeping forces is dependent on the consent of the parties to a conflict. This limits their effectiveness, and it may also be curtailed by their inability to use force in response to a crisis. The UN should therefore determine the circumstances in which it is appropriate to deploy an international force within a sovereign state without that state's consent. It should also consider the circumstances in which an international force can operate beyond a traditional peace-keeping mandate.

For example, UN peace-keeping forces could be mandated to use force to respond to cross-border aggression. Had the Security Council authorized the deployment of a force in Kuwait in 1990, mandated to respond to any act of cross-border aggression, the Iraqi invasion might have been deterred.

Humanitarian Aid

In response to the deliberately induced humanitarian disasters in northern Iraq after the Gulf War and during the war in Bosnia-Herzegovina, armed forces have been used to support the delivery of humanitarian aid to civilian populations. Armed forces can also play a more direct role, forcing aid convoys through a war zone and protecting aid distribution and delivery points.

Shifting Military Balances

Where there is a clear aggressor, limited force might be used to shift local military balances to deter further violence. Many have argued that, had the UN been willing to use air strikes and limited ground forces to defend places like Vukovar and Dubrovnik early in the conflict in the former Yugoslavia, Serbian aggression could have been deterred and much subsequent bloodshed avoided.

Safe Havens

Safe havens were initially created after the Gulf War to protect the Kurds in northern Iraq. International enforcement of these havens has largely succeeded in deterring attacks against civilians, in contrast to the continued targeting of the Shia population in southern Iraq. Safe havens have also been established in Bosnia-Herzegovina, with varying success.

The bombardment of Goradze in April 1994, when 65,000 refugees were besieged, reinforces the need for adequate ground forces and close air support to defend safe havens from attack. Establishing and continuing to defend safe havens requires a high level of commitment from the international community.

UN Trust Territories

The international community could impose peace in a country afflicted by civil war by establishing a UN Trust Territory. Having declared a country a Trust Territory, military force would need to be used to enforce a cease-fire, demobilize local troops and de-militarize the country. Such operations require a large and long-term military presence. As such, the concept has limited viability, but it should not be precluded as an option.

CURTAILING THE ARMS TRADE

Without the prolific supply of military equipment the impact and scale of conflicts would be greatly reduced throughout the world. It is ironic that the five permanent members (P5) of the Security Council, which has ultimate responsibility for peacekeeping, are also the most prolific suppliers of arms. In 1993 the P5 countries accounted for 95% of all arms exports to the third world.[2]

The 1990 Gulf War exemplifies the dangers of exporting arms to volatile regimes. Military equipment supplied by the West was used against allied forces.

Indonesia also receives arms from Western countries, notably the US and UK, and it uses them to defend its occupation of East Timor and repress the population.

Adopting a Code of Conduct

The international community could adopt three specific measures to curb the international arms trade. A code would lay down binding criteria to regulate arms exports. Limited progress has been made, with the permanent members of the Security Council, the European Union and the Council for Security and Co-operation in Europe agreeing broad arms export criteria.

At present there is no common interpretation of such criteria, which results in uncoordinated and divergent policies on exports. For example, although the US agreed to the P5's criteria governing arms exports to the Middle East, between 1990 and 1993, it agreed arms transfer deals to this region worth US$39.4 billion. In Europe, the UK has exported Hawk jets to Indonesia, whereas Italy and Portugal have self-imposed arms embargoes.

Introducing Greater Transparency

So long as supplier arrangements are shrouded in secrecy it will be difficult to establish any control over the arms trade.

In this respect, the UN Register of Conventional Arms is a valuable step forward. Established in 1991, the Register covers seven categories of weaponry. These are the weapons reckoned most likely to be used in large-scale offensive military operations. However, the Register has no means of enforcing all countries to submit returns, and information on the Middle East and sub-Saharan Africa is incomplete. As such, the Register may fail to increase transparency in the regions that need it most.

The Register also neglects one of the most important weapon categories, small arms. Of the 31 wars being fought in 1994, all were being fought predominantly with small arms. Including these weapons in the

Register will be vital to strengthening control over the trade in small arms.

Reducing the use of landmines

Anti-personnel land mines kill indiscriminately and remain active for decades. In Mozambique landmines have killed between 10,000 and 15,000 people. In Bosnia an estimated two to four million landmines have been laid. The international community should follow the lead taken by the US, France and Germany and establish an export ban on anti-personnel mines. There is an opportunity to advance such an initiative at the review conference in 1995 of the Inhumane Weapons Convention. The conference could oblige signatories to ban the production and export of anti-personnel mines altogether.

UPHOLDING HUMAN RIGHTS

Conflict is the primary cause of the violation of fundamental human rights, such as the right to life. But human rights violations can often be the very source of tension which escalates into violent conflict, as in Kashmir or Sudan. It follows that efforts by the international community to uphold human rights are central to conflict prevention.

The current provisions in the UN system for enforcing human rights are limited. However, more effective monitoring of human rights, and action against states which violate them, are both feasible. In recent years there has been a dramatic increase in ethnically-based conflict, and the need to address minority rights is obvious.

By addressing human rights violations at an early stage, inter-ethnic rivalries and tensions could be checked before they become violent. In situations where the potential for violence is evident, low profile, neutral mediation by the UN, together with advice on how to accommodate minority rights, could help scale down tension and allow disputes to be settled by political arrangement rather than force of arms. The international community should also consider the circumstances in which a right to self-determination can legitimately be supported.

When governments violate human rights the international community should make clear that future political contacts and economic aid will be conditional on the violations ceasing. The US government, for example, expressed disapproval of alleged human rights abuses in Kashmir by cutting $24 million from a $1.4 billion aid package to India. The Organisation of Islamic States has also threatened economic sanctions against India because of its policies on Kashmir.

UN institutions like the World Bank and IMF could also apply pressure on governments which violate human rights. Aid and soft loans could be made conditional on the recipient country's respect for human rights. In more serious cases the UN Security Council should consider properly targeted sanctions against human rights abusers. The implementation of such policies towards the former Yugoslavia prior to the conflict would probably have alleviated ethnic tensions. Had the West made it clear to the Serbian-dominated federal government in the late 1980s that future political and economic ties would depend on respect for minority rights, the prospects for a confederal Yugoslav state could well have been improved.

Likewise, international recognition of Slovenia, Croatia and Bosnia-Herzegovina as independent states should have been made conditional on satisfactory minority rights provisions in those states. A declaration to uphold minority rights, monitored by the UN, would surely have reduced the potential for conflict within Croatia.

CONCLUSION

If the devastating impact of modern conflict is to be contained and reduced, the international community urgently needs to adopt more consistent and effective ways of dealing with conflict. There is international support for redressing the current inadequacies of the UN's response to conflict, but member states have not given the UN the political, economic and military backing it needs.

A secure financial base for UN operations requires greater willingness to fund them by the international community. Although governments baulk at this, effective international peacekeeping represents a pragmatic cost-effective option compared to what is spent on current UN military operations, let alone world military expenditure. The total annual UN peacekeeping budget is in the order of US$3.6 million. Annual global military expenditure is roughly $1 trillion.[3] International peacekeeping also represents a real investment, where the payback is the avoidance of the kind of costs documented in this book.

Above all, the international community needs the political will to address the proposals outlined in this chapter and improve the world's ability to manage conflict. This book shows how wars damage the West because of the interdependence of the modern world, yet that very interdependence gives the West leverage to prevent those wars. If moral reasons do not give rise to the political will needed, then national self-interest should. From lost investment opportunities in Africa, and the entanglements of the drugs and civil wars in Peru, to nuclear brinkmanship in Kashmir, the international community does not lack reasons to be decisive.

REFERENCES

1 Britain, V 'A state remade to the United Nations' design', *The Guardian*, 6 August 1994
2 Grimmett, R F 'Conventional Arms Transfers to the Third World, 1986–93', CRS Report for Congress, 29 July 1994
3 D'Orville, H and Najman , D, 'A New System to Finance the United Nations' *Security Dialogue*, Vol 25 No 2, June 1994; *Jane's Defence Weekly*, 5 February 1994

INDEX